NOTHING
BUT AN UNFINISHED SONG

Bobby Sands, the Irish Hunger Striker
Who Ignited a Generation

DENIS O'HEARN

NATION
BOOKS

NOTHING BUT AN UNFINISHED SONG
BOBBY SANDS, THE IRISH HUNGER STRIKER WHO IGNITED A GENERATION

Copyright © 2006 by Denis O'Hearn

AVALON
(publishing group ?vol portid e)

Published by
Nation Books
An Imprint of Avalon Publishing Group
245 West 17th St., 11th Floor
New York, NY 10011

Nation Books is a co-publishing venture of the Nation Institute and
Avalon Publishing Group Incorporated.

Library of Congress Cataloging-in-Publication Data is available.

ISBN: 1-56025-842-X
ISBN 13: 978-1-56025-842-1

Book design by Maria Elias

Distributed by Publishers Group West

For those who die too young.
For my nephew, James Padraic O'Hearn.

May your heart always be joyful,
May your song always be sung.

Contents

In the twilight of my last morning
I
will see my friends and you,
and I'll go
to my grave
regretting nothing but an unfinished song . . .

Nazim Hikmet,
Bursa Prison, Turkey, 11 November 1933

Prelude

The screws brought Bobby Sands back to his cell in H-Block 3 at a quarter to nine. They took him from the administrative area, in the crossbar of the "H," down the long gray corridor to his cell at the bottom of the wing. As he passed by rows of solid steel doors on either side of the corridor some of the other prisoners called out to him.

"Right, Bobby?"

"Cad é an scéal, Roibeard?" ("What's the news, Robert?")

Sands finally reached his cell. The prisoners around him waited anxiously to find out what was happening. They had been waiting ever since the screws took Bobby away at a quarter past six. They expected him to return with the good news of a victorious end to the hunger strike that was now over two months old. At the very least, they expected some indication that they were closer to a successful resolution of their four-year struggle to win recognition as political prisoners. They knew that one of the hunger strikers, Sean McKenna, was near death but there had been talk of last-minute British concessions to end the protest before a death ignited Irish society.

"Teapot" was in a cell beside Sands. What he heard next was "a bolt from the fucking blue." What their friend and commanding officer told them made their hearts sink to rock bottom.

Sands spoke out the door in Irish to Bik MacFarlane, his second in command. He was bitter, deeply angry; he felt betrayed. There was more of Calvary than Bethlehem in his voice. It felt more like a week to Easter than a week until Christmas.

"Tá an stailc críochnaithe" ("The hunger strike is over"), he told Bik.

"Cad é a tharla?" ("What happened?")

"Fuair muid faic." ("We got nothing.")

Sands withdrew momentarily from the door. He could not settle. Well, he could never settle but now his mind was racing even more than usual. He strode quickly to the back corner of his cell and lay down on his filthy sponge mattress by the heating pipe to talk to Teapot, who had his ear to the crack in the shit-smeared wall at the other side.

"Another fucking hunger strike . . . crazy . . . die . . . crazy," were the jumbled words that Teapot could make out from Sands's low voice. It was enough to tell him what Bobby had already set his mind to do.

Then, unable to sit still for even a few seconds, Sands rose and paced back to the cell door to speak to Bik.

"Bhuel, Bik, beidh stailc eile ann." ("Well, Bik, there'll be another hunger strike.")

"Tá an ceart agat." ("You're right.")

And that was it. In the minds of the prisoners around Sands, the men who effectively made up the leadership of all the Irish Republican prisoners in the H-Blocks, the die was cast. They immediately began to plan another hunger strike, speaking through their cell doors in Irish. They talked over how it would go, but whatever way they played it the plot ended the same way. Bobby Sands would certainly die.

Friday, December 19, 1980

Sands met twice with the commanding officers (OCs) of the other H-Blocks that housed protesting IRA prisoners. The screws brought them in to see him in the "big cell" at the bottom of the wing. He could not just repeat "we got nothing" to them, as that would wreck the morale of the whole prison. He had to give them some measure of hope. He told the OCs bluntly that the agreement they got after the hunger strike ended was not what they wanted, that it was full of holes. But maybe, he said, they could step through those holes to achieve some form of political status. At least, *maybe*, they could get their own clothes to wear and then continue struggling for more rights.

Seanna Walsh, OC of H5 and one of Bobby's oldest friends, did not believe the positive spin he was hearing. He knew Sands too well and he could see right through him. He could tell from Sands's demeanor that there was really little hope of getting anything concrete from the agreement that Margaret Thatcher's government had offered them the night before. Not even their own clothes, much less their other demands, like the right to free association and freedom from prison work.

They had been protesting for four years to achieve this goal, ever since young Kieran Nugent refused to wear a prison uniform after he was convicted of hijacking a car for the IRA in 1976. Sands had only to look around him to see how far the protest had come, for bad and for good. Now, more then three hundred prisoners had joined the protest. Not only were they living naked in their eight-by-ten foot cells, as they had been from the beginning of their protest, with only a blanket and a small towel to keep them warm and hide their nakedness. Not only were they locked up twenty-four hours a day, without even a book to read, a radio to listen to, nor pen and paper with which to write. They were not even allowed to leave their cells for exercise or meals or even to go to the toilet and have a wash. Now, they were literally living in their own shit—heaps of it, along with rotted food and maggots, lay in the corners of each cell. The cell walls were plastered in it. Some of the lads hadn't seen their families or loved ones for years. Never mind their families, some of them had not even seen each other. Some of their closest friends were just disembodied voices that came out of a crack in one cell door and back in through a crack in their own cell door. By now, they knew more of the intimate lives of these disembodied voices than they did of their own family members.

Despite these unimaginable conditions, they had never been crushed. Deprived of radios and reading materials, they invented their own forms of entertainment: bingo, quizzes, and, best of all, the "book at bedtime" where they told each other stories out the door. Kept from formal education, they organized their own classes, with teachers shouting out the lessons through the cell doors. Many men who never finished secondary school were now fluent in Irish and experts in history and political theory. Paper and pens were banned, yet they had developed a communications infrastructure that kept them in constant contact with each other and with their comrades outside of prison. Under Bobby Sands's direction, they were running a virtual propaganda industry, churning out hundreds of letters about their protest to movie stars, journalists, and politicians around the world. Tobacco was banned, so they found ways to smuggle it into the jail and then to manufacture cigarettes and to distribute them from cell to cell so that each prisoner could enjoy a smoke in the evening.

After all they had endured and all they had achieved, Sands told the other OCs, they would not quit now, short of gaining recognition as political prisoners. He said he would talk to the prison governor and offer to end the prison protest if the prisoners were allowed to wear their own clothes. He expected that the appeal would fall on deaf ears.

Sands's prediction came true within hours. Bobby met with the governor, who took his offer to his political bosses and then came back and told him that all he could offer was "prison-issue civilian-type clothes" during non-working hours. After a few days to build up their strength after their long protest, they would have to start doing prison work. And they would have to wear the prison uniform when they were working. After all, the government still considered them to be criminals.

"*Your* civilian clothing is nothing but a uniform," Sands bitterly told Governor Hilditch. "Not only will we *not* be ending the protest but we will escalate it and take other actions."

"What actions?" asked the governor.

Sands knew that he was taken aback by the blunt refusal of his offer of civilian-type clothing.

"You'll find out," was Bobby's reply.

Back in his cell at three o'clock, Sands asked his cellmate Malachy for a pen and some paper. Malachy carefully slid his thumb and forefinger into his anus and slipped out a huge wad wrapped in plastic wrap. He carefully unwrapped the package, took out a refill for a ballpoint pen and some cigarette papers, and handed them over. Sands hunched down on his bit of filthy foam mattress and wrote a letter to his old friend Gerry Adams, the man he called *comrade mor* ("big comrade"). He told him what had transpired over the past twenty-four hours and gave him the "disturbing" news that they would soon be starting another hunger strike.

Two hours later, at five o'clock, Sands told the other prisoners around him about the meetings he had held earlier in the day and about his encounters with the prison Governor. Again, they debated their options. With cooler heads than the previous night, Sands, Bik MacFarlane, Richard O'Rawe, Jake Jackson, and Pat Mullan discussed how they could carry the protest forward. Was there another way, short of another hunger strike? Bobby already knew the answer in his heart, but they all wanted to find some way out. The debate went on and on. People suggested some alternatives but they kept coming back to the same thing.

Finally, Pat Mullan stopped the discussion in its tracks.

"*Níl ach freagair amháin . . . ar ais ar stailc arís.*" ("There's only one solution . . . back on hunger strike.")

It was the end of debate. They all knew it.

Bobby had the last word. We can only begin to imagine the despair he felt when he told them,"I'm gonna wake up tomorrow morning and I'm not gonna like the first thought that hits my head."

From that moment, says Richard O'Rawe, Bobby Sands became less effervescent and more solemn . . . slightly more distant. Outside, he maintained his bubbly disposition, still optimistic, as was his character. But they could see through the surface to a difference on the inside.

"You just knew that there was a sadness in Bob."

• • •

When the first hunger strike ended a week before Christmas 1980, Bobby Sands was barely known outside of the prisons in Northern Ireland and a few neighborhoods in his native Belfast. He had spent nearly a third of his twenty-six years of life in jail. After first landing in jail at seventeen, he spent a mere six months in freedom. He never spent a Christmas outside of jail after the age of sixteen.

Yet, within a few short months of these events, Bobby Sands was one of the best-known names around the world.

He was elected to the British Parliament. He died after sixty-six days on hunger strike and was followed by nine of his comrades. They named streets and buildings after him in countries throughout the world. Nelson Mandela led young South African prisoners on Robben Island on hunger strike after his example. Legislatures in all of the six inhabited continents passed resolutions in his honor. His smiling face, a fuzzy photographic image taken in and smuggled out of jail five years before, became a political and cultural icon worldwide. It was rivalled only by the likes of Alberto Korda's portrait of Che Guevara or the youthful photo of Nelson Mandela who, like Bobby Sands, was also aging anonymously behind prison walls.

Yet, unlike Guevara or Mandela, Bobby Sands is still an enigma to all but a few people who knew him and who were active with him, politically and militarily, both inside and outside of prison. This account is an attempt to tell *who* Bobby Sands was and how he related to and was shaped by his time and place. Maybe then we can begin to understand why and how not just he but others like him could knowingly embark on and stay on such a deliberate, slow, painful, and ultimately fatal form of protest.

Those of us who have never set ourselves to such a course of action may never really begin to comprehend how men and women could do it. Even Margaret Thatcher, the hunger strikers' main adversary, said years later that, "It was possible to admire the courage of Sands and the other hunger strikers who died" even though she still maintained that Bobby Sands was a criminal because, in her famous (or infamous, depending on your perspective) phrase: "A crime is a crime. It is not political. It is a crime."

The words of Fidel Castro, spoken at the time of the Irish hunger strikes, are more sympathetic to Bobby Sands and to the other hunger strikers. Whether one finds the comparison with Christ compelling or repugnant, his words may come closest to explaining the enormity of what they did:

> *Tyrants shake in the presence of men who have such strength as to die for their ideals through sixty days of hunger strike! Next to this example, what were the three days of Christ on Calvary as a symbol of human sacrifice down the centuries?*

> Fidel Castro, "A todos hombres y mujeres que lucharon por la independencia de Irlanda," statement to the sixty-eighth Conferencia de la Union Interparliamentaria, September 18, 1981

Chapter One

Growing Up in Utopia

R osaleen Sands held her baby on her knee, nursing him. They were in the living room in their home at Abbots Cross and the radio was playing in the background. The song was a Perry Como hit from a couple of years before called "Because." The words of the song obviously affected Rosaleen very deeply, because she remembered it all many years later. She was full of hope for the young child, but she also remembered the difficulties she and generations before her had endured. The Second World War was not long over. And although things were relatively quiet now, conflicts broke out periodically between the Irish Republican Army and Northern Ireland's Protestant state.

Rosaleen looked down at the newborn child and spoke to him.

"Bobby, if there's ever a war, you and I will go down to the South where you won't be conscripted. And if the Troubles ever flare up here, and the IRA gets going, we'll go to the South."[1]

Rosaleen had plenty of reasons to worry. Northern Ireland—its six counties were carved in 1920 out of the northeast corner of the island of Ireland by the British—comprised the largest piece of that corner that contained an assured majority of three Protestants for every two Catholics. Protestants ran the state, ultimately giving their loyalty to the Queen of England. Most Catholics and a few Protestants refused to recognize it, instead aspiring to a united Ireland. In 1922, its first prime minister, James Craig, called the local government at Stormont, east of Belfast, "a Protestant parliament for a Protestant people." The current

Prime Minister Basil Brooke once told people not to employ Catholics, boasting, "I have not a Roman Catholic about my own place."[2]

Protestants ran the police forces, both the regular Royal Ulster Constabulary (RUC) and the state-sponsored paramilitary "B-Specials." Rosaleen remembered the B-Specials invading her neighborhood when she was a child. And now, in 1954, the industries that had assured jobs for working-class Protestants were rapidly falling apart. Places like the Harland and Wolff shipyard, whose proud Protestant workers built the *Titanic* in 1912, were shedding workers by the hundreds. What an explosive mix! A dominant population that was losing its economic advantages but which still had its police and plenty of guns, and a marginalized population with a history of rebellion.

Perhaps the most immediate social threat in Ireland's harsh climate, however, was the region's housing. After decades of neglect, three out of every ten houses were uninhabitable.[3] A higher proportion of Catholics lived in Belfast's overcrowded slums: the lower Falls, Ardoyne or Rosaleen Sands's childhood district of the Markets. Their labyrinths of narrow streets were lined by rows of two-story brick houses with outside toilets. The children slept several to a bed, head-by-toe, like sardines packed in a tin.

So when Rosaleen Kelly married John Sands on March 28, 1951 and they moved into a nearly new private house in a countryside village at 6 Abbots Cross, five miles north of Belfast, they thought they had a better future to look forward to. Both had come from Belfast working-class backgrounds. Rosaleen's father, Robert, worked as a groom in the Catholic Markets district. John's father, Joseph, was a "spiritgrocer," a fancy name for a bartender. Yet John's mother, Elizabeth Forsythe, was a Reformed Presbyterian, a particularly conservative brand of Protestantism that harkened back to Puritanism. John lived among Protestants until after he moved out from his parents' home and got work in McWatters's (later Inglis's) bakery in the Markets district where Rosaleen Kelly lived and worked as a weaver.

Abbots Cross was one of five experimental "garden villages" that were nestled in a scenic valley between Ben Madigan (now called Cave Hill) and Carnmoney Hill. Just south of Abbots Cross, the Glas-na-Bradan River flowed from between the two hills down to the Belfast Lough. The immediate surroundings were a far cry from the repetitive brick-terraced streets back in Belfast. Country roads were dotted with rural farmhouses. Within a stone's throw of the Sands's new house was "The Abbey," the magnificent country house of Sir Charles Lanyon, the architect who built most of the great buildings of nineteenth-century Belfast. The Sands family would eventually have a close association with two of them: the Crumlin Road Jail and Courthouse.

The Sands house was the second in a neat terraced street of twenty-four white houses, built in an open plan, with no fences or walls to divide the front gardens. The estate was neatly planned, incorporating features of the existing Irish landscape and built around a brand-new shopping center. Its utopian plan was so precise that the number of houses numbered exactly one hundred.[4]

But not everything was well within this utopia. Despite its stylish modernism, Abbots Cross was deeply sectarian. Directly behind the Sands's hedged back garden was a large, modern Presbyterian church. Directly across the street from the clean, white shopping center were a Congregational church and a brand-new Protestant elementary school. There was a Church of Ireland, Free Presbyterian, Methodist, Baptist, and Plymouth Brethren churches. There was a *community* for everyone . . . except Catholics.

The discomfort of Abbots Cross for a woman like Rosaleen Sands, brought up among anti-Catholic police actions in the 1920s and 1930s, was heightened by the numbers of policemen and state-sponsored paramilitaries (the B-Specials) living in the estate.

So Rosaleen Sands lived a fiction in Abbots Cross. She never let on that she was a Catholic. Sands, a good Ulster-Scots name, blended well among her neighbors: the Meekes, the Bairds, and the Craigs. Everyone took Rosaleen to be a Protestant because she was so quiet and did not bother with the neighbors.[5]

On March 9, 1954, two years after they moved to Abbots Cross, Rosaleen gave birth to their first child, a boy who they named Robert Gerard. She prayed that Bobby would never get caught up in the violence that she had known as a child. But it was not long before the IRA "got going" again, opening a bombing campaign along the Irish border in 1956. Sectarian tensions rose between Protestant and Catholic, or Unionist and Nationalist. The Sands family were unaffected as long as they could live quietly without discussing religion with their neighbors. They succeeded for several years, during which Marcella was born in April 1955 and then Bernadette in November 1958.

Eventually, however, the woman next door found out Rosaleen's religion.

She began taunting her when John was away at work. She hammered on the walls incessantly during the day. When Rosaleen took her washing out to hang it on the line, the neighbor put similar clothes on her line. If Rosaleen cleaned her windows the neighbor did, too. Rosaleen could *feel* her sneering across at her. Things got so bad that she took the children out for long walks during the day to avoid the neighbor. Eventually Rosaleen became ill. Her doctor took John aside and told him if he wanted his wife to regain her health, either take the neighbors to court or give up the house.

"So," recalled Bernadette years later, "my parents being so quiet and not wanting to bother anybody, they gave up the house."

• • •

For six months when Bobby was seven, the Sands family lived with relatives. In December 1961, they finally got a house in the new estate beside Abbots Cross. In the 1950s, the northern Irish government had begun building big public housing estates for some of the thousands of working-class families who urgently needed somewhere decent to live. The first estate, called Rathcoole after the Irish *rath cúil,* meaning "ring-fort of the secluded place," was built in phases, working its way up the foot of Carnmoney Hill. By 1961, Rathcoole comprised three square miles of public housing for fourteen thousand people.

Rathcoole was planned as a model estate for the "respectable working class,"[6] with jobs in nearby industrial projects. It was to be another utopia. But unlike Abbots Cross, a third of its new residents were Catholics. Among them was the Sands family, in a spacious house at 68 Doonbeg Drive, at the foot of Carnmoney Hill.

Bobby was surrounded by huge open green spaces. He and his sisters could go out their front door and climb up the Carnmoney mountain on trails that wound through dense gorse and nettles. They visited adventurous places on the mountain including the remains of ancient Celtic forts and monuments. It was thick with birds, which Bobby learned to identify.

Kids from the surrounding streets joined them. They would build a hut while Bobby built a fire. He took out his mother's pots and some food and they toasted bread or potatoes, imagining they were camping out. When Rosaleen caught them, says Bernadette, she would "half kill" them.[7]

Bobby was always doing something. He faced regular fights with the neighborhood kids with a degree of stoicism, bordering on stubbornness. If he got hit, he hit back. If he was badly beaten, he walked around the corner before he cried. He often turned his stubbornness on his mother. If Rosaleen sent him outside to play as punishment, he refused to come back when she called.

Yet he was very protective of his sisters. If anyone hit them he jumped to their defence. He was smaller than the other kids but he stood up for his sisters, no matter what the consequences.[8]

Bobby's education began at Stella Maris primary school, a mixed gender Catholic school close to his house that also served the surrounding districts of Glengormley, Bawnmore, and Greencastle. Later, he attended Stella Maris secondary school, next door to the primary school. He was never a very serious student, instead concentrating on organized sport. According to schoolmate Dessie Black, he was intelligent but lazy in school.

"All we wanted to do was just play football. More time was spent round picking football teams for matches and that than doing schoolwork and that."[9]

Outside of school, Bobby played soccer with a religiously mixed group of local boys, always including his best mate Tommy O'Neill. Together, they joined the youth team of Stella Maris, the local amateur soccer club. Stella Maris was a remarkable institution for the north of Ireland, where religious sectarianism was rampant. Although the team trained in the gym of Bobby's school, it attracted Protestant boys from surrounding areas. Terry Nicholl, a Mormon, joined Stella Maris because he had just one interest, soccer, and would have played for anybody.[10] Willie Caldwell and Geordie Hussey, two more Protestant "football fanatics," also joined. Nobody asked if you were Catholic or Protestant. If you were a half-decent soccer player, you were on the team.

Dennis Sweeney never liked Bobby Sands much. He thought he was an insecure person who tried to cover it up by showing off, sometimes even using violence on the soccer field. "Certainly not a leader by any means, more a person who was led," he thought.

But others describe Bobby Sands as an amiable teammate. Their recollections also reflect a trait that others would notice in his later life: extreme enthusiasm, sometimes expressed in behavior that went "over the top."

Geordie Hussey says Sands was "a bit of a grafter" who did his best at his position of left half. He didn't score many goals but he could be counted on to get the ball and he was a good tackler. What he lacked in natural ability, he made up in enthusiasm.

His enthusiasm extended into other sports. Bobby loved swimming but cross-country running was his real sporting passion. He won cross-country medals[11] and his love of running came through later in his prison writings. In *The Loneliness of a Long-Distance Cripple*, he compares his strength as a teenager winning a cross-country race to his deteriorating physical state in prison. In the story, Sands describes a long-distance race in the cold Irish winter that "bites deep into the lungs and reddens the nose and cheeks." He is excited by the race but surprisingly aware, even sad, at how the incursion of the runners scars the countryside. He is at once part of the environment and against it.

> *"Bang." The thrush fled and I sprang forward. The marshy ground churned and sucked and squelched as hundreds of foreign spiked feet mutilated and scarred its face. Across an open field we charged in a bunch. My mind was racing as I tried to weigh up the situation and opposition as the lay of the land was seen then gone in a matter of a few strides.*

Sands struggled to overcome the challenges both of the environment and the other runners until, finally, "I broke the finishing line, breathing like a racehorse in deep vast gulps." Although it was only a schoolboy race, "Victory was mine and I felt like an Olympic champion."

• • •

As Sands grew into his teens, his circle of friends widened. He went to the Alpha picture house or to dances at the local church hall. There was roller-skating in the religiously mixed Floral Hall in Bellevue near the Belfast Zoo. Weekend dances there were mainly Protestant but mixed. On Sundays a more Catholic but still mixed group attended dances in the Star of the Sea hall in Rathcoole or St. Etna's hall in Glengormley. Bobby's friends at the time remember him as a "happy-go-lucky" boy who loved dancing and the socializing that went with it.

Things were beginning to change, however, in the society around him. Systematic sectarianism was emerging. By 1966, Rathcoole was sitting on a powder keg. Many Protestants worried about losing their marginal advantages as traditional sources of employment dried up in the shipyards and elsewhere. Either they or someone they knew had lost a job. They responded by excluding Catholics. Protestants clung onto cultural advantages that assured them that they, and not Catholics, could fly certain flags, walk certain streets, and call on the support of the police and B-Specials. But a liberal unionist prime minister named Terence O'Neill (Protestant, despite his Irish name) began talking about reforms that looked a bit too much like civil rights to many Protestants. O'Neill did such provocative things as visiting a Catholic school and inviting the southern Irish Taoiseach (prime minister) to visit Belfast. While O'Neill's image as a reformer scared many Protestants, it raised Catholic expectations that discrimination would finally be addressed.

Simultaneously, 1966 was a highly emotive year for Protestants because it was the fiftieth anniversary of the Battle of the Somme. Although Catholics also died there, some Protestants held them responsible for treason against Britain because the mostly Catholic Irish Republicans launched an independence struggle while their forefathers were fighting and dying for Queen and country. Loyal Protestants were, therefore, on high alert for public manifestations of Republicanism. This was a problem, since 1966 was also the fiftieth anniversary of the Easter Rising in Dublin, the most significant event in the history of Irish Republicanism. Protestant paranoia increased after the IRA blew up the huge statue of Admiral Nelson that stood on an imposing pillar in the middle of Dublin for many years.

You did not have to go far from the Sands's front door to find the center of Protestant intolerance. Ian Paisley, whose power base was in the area around Rathcoole, freely mixed his religion with his politics. He was the head of his own church, the Free Presbyterians, and he received an honorary "doctorate" from the fundamentalist Christian and racist Bob Jones University in the United States. During 1966, while Paisley preached against treason and popery, [12] the re-formed Ulster Volunteer Force[13] launched a series of attacks on Catholic homes, schools, and shops. Late at night on May 7, the UVF killed an old Protestant woman who they mistook for a Catholic. On May 27, a UVF unit went to the Catholic lower Falls area and shot dead the first Catholic they could find. A few weeks later, some UVF men went for a late-night drink and shot dead a Catholic as he left the bar.[14]

About this time, Sands later told a friend, he noticed some of his Protestant friends starting to withdraw from his social circles. The parents of a Protestant friend from the Stella Maris football club told him not to bring Bobby around to the house. Sands wondered why some of his mates no longer treated him as a friend. He was still naïve about the virulence of sectarianism, and he had only a distant memory of how his mother was treated at Abbots Cross. Over the next few years these divisions would intensify, until things erupted after the rise of a Catholic civil rights movement in 1969. For Bobby Sands, this would be an education in sectarianism.

Chapter Two

Violence and Anger

S ociety was splitting apart. For Catholics in mixed areas, the most immediate worry was the emergence of violent racist gangs. Rathcoole's were among the worst. Years later, Bobby Sands wrote that his "life began to change" after 1968.[1] Civil rights marchers took to the streets and he watched as the television news showed the police attacking them. Sands was particularly impressed in early 1969, when a group of students from Queens University in Belfast set off on a civil rights march to Derry. Along the way they were repeatedly ambushed and the police blocked them from entering towns. The RUC were often observed chatting amiably with the attackers. As the students reached Burntollet Bridge outside of Derry, several hundred B-Special paramilitaries viciously attacked them. "My sympathy and feelings really became aroused after watching the scenes at Burntollet," he wrote. "That imprinted itself on my mind like a scar, and for the first time I took a real interest in what was going on . . . I became angry."

Bobby's anger grew throughout 1969 as the conflict heightened. In April, the police banned a civil rights march in the Bogside area of Derry. During the rioting that followed, a group of RUC men burst into a house and beat the Catholic owner to death. In August, a huge crowd of Protestants attacked Unity flats in Belfast. When local Catholics resisted, the RUC went on a violent rampage, beating one man unconscious and batoning another to death.[2] Three people had now died from the recent outbreak of "the troubles." All were Catholics. All had been beaten in the head by police batons.

By August, the trouble spiralled. In Derry, some older Republicans set up a defense committee to confront the trouble that always accompanied an annual Loyalist march around the city's old walls. They set up barricades at the entrances to the Bogside and when the marchers threw pennies at them the Bogsiders threw stones back. When the police attempted to invade the Bogside, Catholic missiles drove them back. Soon, they were firing petrol bombs and CS gas at each other. After two days of intense fighting, the British government sent in its army for the first time since the end of the IRA's 1950s campaign. Catholics like Bobby Sands watched the "Battle of the Bogside" on their TVs at home, encouraged by the feeling that they were recognized internationally as being "in the right."

Back in Belfast, the police patrolled the Catholic lower Falls district in armored cars mounted with .30-inch Browning machine guns. Catholics used stones and petrol bombs against the big machine guns while groups of Protestants and B-Specials took advantage of the melee and attacked Catholic houses. The RUC drove around Catholic streets, firing randomly. When they were done, nine-year-old Patrick Rooney lay dead in his bed with his brains scattered against the wall. In north Belfast, police shot dead one man as he sat in his front room and another as he walked along the road. Ten others were injured, eight of them by police bullets. All were Catholics.

To Catholics, many of whom initially welcomed them to their streets as protectors, the British army made a bad situation worse. They stood by while Protestant crowds burned out hundreds of Catholic homes. The violence went down in the memory of an increasingly angry and militant Catholic community as "the pogrom."

These events had a significant impact on Bobby Sands. Not only did he begin to link the police with violence against Catholics, he also began to view the British army as the enemy. Catholics generally began to feel that they must defend themselves. Yet they had no weapons and even the IRA had failed to stand up to their attackers. A famous wall slogan went up: "IRA=I Ran Away." By Christmas, a group of militants broke from the IRA and formed the Provisional IRA Army Council and an associated political party, Provisional Sinn Féin (the old movement became known as the Official IRA and Official Sinn Féin).[3] The Provisionals promised to protect the Catholic community, and eventually organized an all-out offensive against British occupation.[4]

This was the recipe for a powerfully popular movement. To angry young Catholics like Bobby Sands and even to a few Protestant Nationalists, the Provisional IRA became the defender of the community, the organization that would do what the Official IRA had failed to do.

But young Catholics were not the only angry ones. Protestants also watched the civil rights marches on television and many of them began to identify Catholics as "the enemy." Relations in areas like Rathcoole quickly deteriorated. Catholics were not welcome at the Friday night dances in the Rathcoole Youth Club. They stopped going to the movies at the Alpha picture house. The only dances that were open to Bobby and his friends were at Catholic halls like Star of the Sea. Sometimes, they had to run to school in the morning, dodging bottles and stones.

Then the center of Bobby's universe, the Stella Maris soccer team, fell apart. Protestant team members began to question whether they wanted to play with Catholics anymore. Terry Nicholl's thoughts were "going away from Catholics." He left the team for the summer in 1969 and never went back.[5] Only three Protestants came back the next autumn.

New, more sinister "teams" roamed Rathcoole. Teenage Protestants in "tartan gangs" wore a uniform of jeans and tartan scarves. Terry Nicholl, who later joined the UVF "to defend Ulster," joined a tartan gang because he felt the police and the British army were not doing anything to put down the rebellious Catholics.

"We were just fighting back, we never started it," he said. "They started it and our point of view is that if the army hadn't come in we would have finished it."

The tartan gangs beat up Catholics and trashed Catholic houses, businesses, and halls. Before long, it was no longer safe to attend soccer practice sessions at the Stella Maris school. The club disbanded and its members moved to the Star of the Sea soccer club just outside of Rathcoole.

Young men like Nicholl, who had Catholic friends just months before, found a more fulfilling identity as Protestants. Years later, some of them would be surprised at the bitterness they held against children outside of their identity. A sociologist from the area found "sectarianism from one end of the adult social spectrum to the other" within Protestant Rathcoole.[6]

To make things worse, the housing authorities encouraged an influx of new Protestant migrants from inner-city areas who fuelled the bigotry of the tartan gangs. Older residents began to complain that the housing authorities were using Rathcoole as a "sink" for "problem families."[7]

Bobby Sands had always had Protestant friends. All of a sudden, he hung out only with Catholics.

The intimidation worsened in 1970 when the Rathcoole tartans began calling themselves "the Kai," which was usually translated as "Kill all Irish." The Kai expressed their hatred in their fighting songs.[8]

> *We come from the 'coole and we hate the micks,*
> *We beat their bollix in with our sticks,*
> *We'll fight the Fenians 'til we die,*
> *We are the Rathcoole Kai-ai.*

Up to two hundred active "members" of the Kai patrolled Rathcoole at night, intimidating Catholics. They claimed territory by forming nightly patrols, congregating around shops, pubs, and the bookies, beating up intruders and even making violent incursions into surrounding neighborhoods.

● ● ●

Bobby Sands no longer owned his neighborhood streets. This was a problem as he traveled further for work and pleasure. He finished secondary school in 1969 at the age of fifteen and enrolled in Newtownabbey Technical College. He began working as an apprentice bus builder for Alexander's Coach Works in North Belfast in March 1970. Starting work was frightening but he earned eighteen pounds a week[9] and began to look forward to the social world that having a bit of money opened up.

"Dances and girls, clothes, and a few shillings to spend opened up a whole new world to me. I suppose at that time I would have worked all week as money seemed to matter more than anything else."[10]

Bobby dressed in the latest styles: jeans and jean jacket, always clean and pressed, and trendy checked shirts. He grew his hair fashionably long.

Mary McGinn and her circle of girlfriends thought "he was lovely." And he was "charming," even "caring," "respectful," and "gentle," terms that are rare for your average "hard man" from Belfast. It is worth adding, however, that his male friends use different words to portray him as "one of the lads" who was more than willing to join in the rougher sides of community life.

Bobby's interest in music took off. Socializing around music and drink solidified his Nationalist identity. With other boys from areas surrounding Rathcoole, he formed a gang called the "Muckerboys." They never hung out around the shops and street corners, staking out territory. The idea of the Muckerboys was mainly to distinguish themselves from Catholics who came to dances from other areas.

While money opened up new freedoms, socializing raised new dangers. Every time Sands went past the shops where the Kai hung out he risked getting a beating. Bobby and Tommy O'Neill learned safe routes home at night. If they were caught, it meant a fight. Luckily, they were both good runners, so whenever they saw a threatening group of lads they usually beat them in a chase to the closest safe house. Many times they arrived breathless at Mary McGinn's front door, slamming it behind to block their pursuers.

One night, when he was nearly home, the RUC stopped Bobby and sent him on another route because there was "trouble up ahead." His new route led up the alley behind his house and straight into a group of youngsters. They asked him for a light and when he stopped one of them stabbed him with a small knife. Bobby ran and just managed to jump across the wall into the back garden of his house. Typically, he hid his injuries from his mother, giving his bloody clothes to his sisters to wash and then going straight out again to a nearby friend who patched him up.

Sometimes the Kai broke up the mixed dances at the Star of the Sea hall, where Catholics sat on one side and Protestants on the other. Almost by arrangement at about 9:30, a wild fight started with, says one former Kai member, "Bottles, hatchets, every fucking thing."[11]

Perhaps the worst experience, however, was Bobby's job. The coachworks presented a new kind of sectarianism, hatred in the workplace, which he could neither avoid nor resist. Now he saw that sectarianism extended into all aspects of northern Irish life. Bernard Fox worked in Alexander's alongside Sands in 1971. He watched Bobby's fellow workers dish out constant abuse simply because he was Catholic. What Fox remembered most was that Sands was very meek in face of the intimidation; he never stood up for himself. Of course, he was hugely outnumbered and totally unprotected in the factory. Nonetheless, Fox was surprised when he met Bobby years later because the man he had thought to be meek or even cowardly turned out to be quite confident.[12]

Sands stayed in Alexander's for two years, enduring the intimidation as he learned a trade. One morning he arrived at the factory and some of his workmates were cleaning guns. One of them turned to Bobby.

"Do you see these here? Well, if you don't go, you'll get this."

Then he found a note in his lunch box telling him to get out. Another time, he found a note in his locker that said to get out if he valued his life. Yet he stuck it out until the boss called him in one day and told that the firm was restructuring and that there would be staff cuts. He was laid off the following day.[13] It was the only real job Bobby Sands would ever hold.

• • •

Rosaleen's worst nightmares were all coming true. Toward the summer of 1971 Bobby moved in with her mother in a flat above the Ballyhackamore Credit Union, a big three-story redbrick house two miles up the road from their original home in the Markets. In Ballyhackamore, a comfortable leafy middle-class neighborhood, Sands made one last effort at living a "normal" life by joining the Willowfield Temperance Harriers, a cross-country team that was located in the adjoining district.

If you wanted to find a truly Protestant sporting institution you could hardly do better. The doctor who organized the Harriers in 1898 put "temperance" in the name to denote that his runners were clean, unlike other racers who injected alcohol into their bloodstream before races.[14] The club's headquarters were in Hyndford Street (the birthplace of the singer Van Morrison), a particularly Unionist area of East Belfast just yards away from the Castlereagh police station (later, Bobby would know the place intimately). In another irony, Sunday training was on the grounds of Stormont, the "Protestant parliament for a Protestant people." Most Catholics never went near it. Yet the strongest memories that Willowfield club members have of Bobby is running around the grounds of Stormont, talking as they trained.

Sands stayed in the club for six to eight months over the summer of 1971, a period when the sectarian violence in Rathcoole was especially bad. He came out of nowhere but fit in quickly with some of the younger runners like Paul Scott, a Protestant from nearby Dundonald, and Larry Fox, a young Catholic from Ballyhackamore. It was a bit like the Stella Maris soccer club. If you could run, religion simply did not matter. Paul Scott never even realized Sands was Catholic until Bobby came late to training one Sunday morning because he had to go to mass. To the other runners, he was "just a guy," "very easygoing," "friendly and open." He was a "useful" runner who made the team but never won a race or even finished in the top places. Still, he regularly finished in the first twenty in a race of eighty to one hundred runners.

One weekend during the summer, the club members went on an outing in the Mourne Mountains, south of Belfast. The trip was for older runners only, and Bobby was not invited. But Bobby was not one to be stopped by rules and he just showed up when they were gathering to leave.

"I'm going," he said, and nobody was ready to stop him.

The group trained in the mountains and swam in a mountain lake. One guy brought a guitar and they sang songs. They listened to the radio and sang along. Diana Ross was just on the charts with "Nathan Jones." Bobby sang his favorite song, "Band of Gold" by Freda Payne.

• • •

In August, Sands suddenly left the Harriers. Rumors went around the club that his grandmother was burnt out of her house by Loyalists. Indeed, August 1971 was a watershed in the history of Northern Ireland. Whole neighborhoods went on the move, turning religiously mixed areas to segregated ones practically overnight.

While Bobby Sands was living in Ballyhackamore, a poorly managed semi-truce between the British army and the IRA broke down. After the IRA shot dead the first British soldier in the conflict in February, Prime Minister Chichester-Clark, who had replaced the "liberal" Terence O'Neill, went on TV to proclaim that "Northern Ireland is at war with the Irish Republican Army Provisionals."[15]

The war escalated. The IRA responded to a series of state killings of unarmed Catholics, now mostly by the British army,[16] with an escalation of its own war. Between March and August, the IRA exploded two bombs a day on average, including twenty in one day in July. It killed four British soldiers and wounded twenty-nine, while the British army killed three Catholic civilians and one IRA volunteer.[17]

Then, early in the morning of August 9, the army swooped on 450 people, practically all Catholics, and put them into internment camps. Most of the IRA leadership escaped. The anger of the Catholic population—practically every family either had or knew someone who was interned—was intense and violence surged. In August, the IRA exploded more than one hundred bombs. In the months leading up to internment, the IRA had killed four British soldiers and no police; in the four months after internment they killed thirty British soldiers and eleven police.[18]

The violence had direct consequences on Bobby Sands. Among those interned were some of his cousins from the Markets. Two days after the swoops, the IRA took over his father's place of work, Inglis's Bakery, and held it for several hours against three hundred British troops. After a "fierce firefight," the British army recaptured the bakery, killing an innocent bystander in the process. The British army claimed that the dead man was a sniper, a story that all the newspapers carried without question.[19] The locals knew better, and their seething anger was intensified by their impotence against a powerful media.

Sands took a salutary lesson from the false stories surrounding the battle at his father's place of work. He learned that there were two realities involved in a conflict: the real story and the media account. Although the truth would always have a deep impact on a few people who were directly involved, the media-inspired public "truth" formed the broad perceptions of the people at large. Hiram W. Johnson, the senator for California, had already said it in the U.S. Senate in 1917, "The first casualty when war comes is truth."

But people are also casualties. The August population movement cemented segregation between the two groups that the British media still likes to call the "warring tribes."[20] Protestants moved one way while Catholics moved in the opposite direction. One casualty of the population movement was Bobby Sands, who left Ballyhackamore to return to Rathcoole. There, the social changes around him would profoundly impact the rest of his life.

Chapter Three

Into the IRA

We are the Rathcoole boys, we make a lot of noise,
We chase the Fenians down the road,
We carry .45s, to take some Fenian's life,
We are the Rathcoole K-A-I!

—*Local sectarian song*

Rathcoole was imploding when Bobby Sands returned. The Kai now ran a concerted campaign to rid the estate of Catholics. So-called Vigilante Defense Associations were formed to "guard [our] homes against the Roman Catholics."[1] They patrolled the streets at night, armed with crowbars and guns. They made many Protestants feel safer. They terrified Catholics.

The police and British army appeared content to stay out of the way of the vigilantes and even gave them their support. "A lot of what they do is illegal, of course . . . , " said a British army officer, "but since they took over . . . tension is down and the people inside feel they can sleep through the night safely."[2] An RUC officer approved of the vigilantes because they had stopped rioting and "organizing themselves like this seems a far more responsible way of reacting to the troubles." The Rathcoole vigilantes also received support from their political representatives. The MP for the area, John McQuade of Ian Paisley's Democratic Unionist Party, said that, "I am behind my vigilantes who night after night look after streets in my constituency."[3] Even Prime Minister Brian Faulkner talked about regularizing them by working out a vigilante code of conduct.

The vigilantes claimed that they were protecting Rathcoole from the IRA.[4] Yet there was no IRA unit in Rathcoole, only two or three local men who were volunteers in "E Company," the IRA unit based in nearby Bawnmore. There had never even been any IRA attacks in the area.

Toward the end of 1971, the vigilantes launched a bold new tactic. They would target a Catholic family, breaking their windows or daubing slogans on their houses to shatter their nerves. If that didn't force them out, they would threaten a teenage member of the family or even give them a beating. Sometimes a young Kai would give a child a live bullet. Other times they would post threatening anonymous letters to the family.

In early 1972, residents began to notice vigilante "estate agents," women who took young couples around, pointing out Catholic houses for them to make their choice. The houses were then cleared for them. In another time, in another place, such tactics would be called "ethnic cleansing."

"Respectable" Catholic residents, frustrated by the apparent indifference of the authorities, began to discuss the need for their own Citizen's Defense Committee.[5] Young people like Bobby Sands had other thoughts. For him, the natural reaction to intimidation was to look to the IRA. Sands began to feel that he should get involved because "it was starting to hit home now."[6]

The nearest IRA unit, "E Company," took in Bawnmore, Glengormley, and Greencastle. It was part of the Third Battalion of the IRA, which covered all of North Belfast. Joseph Cunningham, officer in command (OC), lived in the street just behind the Sands house. He was a docker in his early twenties, known to his neighbors as a "quiet man."[7] His wife evidently knew little of his IRA activities.

If you lived in a Nationalist/Catholic ghetto and your father and your uncles and brothers were IRA volunteers, you joined, too. But if you were an isolated Nationalist among Protestants, like Bobby Sands, you thought harder about joining. You made inquiries about how to join and who was involved in the area. Your parents' reaction to the idea of joining the IRA might range from unsupportive to downright hostile. But if conditions were oppressive enough and if your reaction was to resist rather than to hide or leave, you would eventually approach someone about joining. Bobby Sands had already tried leaving. Hiding was not in his nature. That left just one alternative.

Sands began working nights as a barman at the Glen Inn, a pub in nearby Glengormley. Working alongside him was an older, more experienced barman called Gerry Noade, who lived across the green from the Sands family. Bobby began dating Gerry's daughter Geraldine. He took her to dances, where she introduced him to Tomboy Loudon from her old neighborhood around Unity Flats, the bleak collection of high-rise apartment buildings in inner-city north Belfast. The three saw each other from time to time at dances and sometimes over a drink at the Tavern Bar. They did not know it yet, but Sands and Loudon would repeatedly come together, almost as if by fate, and Tomboy would be one of Bobby's closest lifelong friends and comrades.

Several of the bar staff and patrons in the Glen Inn were in the IRA. Bobby learned through them that D— was setting up an auxiliary unit of young IRA men.[8] Auxiliary units were not allowed to do shootings, bombings, or even robberies. They played a supporting role, moving weapons, acting as lookouts, carrying messages, or gathering intelligence.

D— had seen Bobby with Geraldine at dances and he knew him as a barman. The most remarkable thing he noticed was how *un*remarkable Bobby was. He was a decent bartender, sometimes a bit of a show-off, flipping bottles and such. D— *did* notice, however, that Bobby had more confidence than most young men of his age.

One night toward the end of 1971, D— was sitting alone in the Glen Inn. Sands walked over to him with his confident swagger. He sat down and asked it straight out.

"Are you connected to the IRA? I want to join."

"Yes," D— replied, he was in the IRA. But he counseled Bobby to think carefully before joining. Things in Rathcoole were very bad. The Kai were dangerous and Catholics there were very isolated. The IRA could not protect a volunteer in such a place.

Nothing D— said could dissuade Bobby. He insisted that he wanted to join. D— said he would get back to him.

D— soon put Sands to the test. He needed to move a gun from Rathcoole to Glengormley. The volunteer who was supposed to do it had not shown. As D— left Rathcoole after the volunteer failed to show up he passed a soccer pitch near the Sands house. There was a match on and he recognized Bobby on one of the teams.

D— called Sands over and asked if he would do something for him. Without even a question, Bobby came off the field, changed clothes, and took the gun.

Sands soon recruited some of his mates into a small auxiliary unit of about six or seven volunteers. Bobby was their section leader. They were isolated, so they worked with other volunteers from surrounding areas.

In early 1972, the IRA saw its first serious action in Rathcoole. On January 13, a UDR sergeant drove his van out of a building site on the edge of Rathcoole. A stolen blue Ford Cortina pulled up beside him and one of the men inside fired two .45 bullets through the window into his head. The *East Antrim Times* called the killing the "first East Antrim terrorist murder."[9] Local Loyalists responded by painting intimidating slogans on the homes of people whom even the RUC called "law-abiding Roman Catholics."

Neither Bobby nor his local unit was involved, yet the operation heightened their belief that armed resistance could succeed. Yet war was still a bit of a game to them. There was still a naïveté about what they were up to.

That all ended in February of 1972, just after Bloody Sunday in Derry, when British paratroopers opened fire on civil rights marchers, killing fourteen of them. In response to the killings, the Northern Irish Civil Rights Association (NICRA) called for a day of widespread civil disobedience. Thousands of workers and students went on strike. They marched and blocked roads.[10]

That evening, Joe Cunningham and two IRA volunteers were in a stolen blue Ford Cortina at the side of the road running directly in front of the Sands house. Someone phoned the police about a "suspicious car." When two police cars went to investigate, the three IRA men got out.

The RUC said that they opened fire. The police returned fire and hit one of them. They took Cunningham to the hospital,[11] where he died from his wounds.

The two volunteers who got away said that Cunningham's Thompson machine gun jammed, so they immediately fled before firing any shots. The police fired, wounding Cunningham. They watched in horror as the RUC men approached the wounded man. One of them leaned down and shot him point blank in the head.

Cunningham's death had an enormous impact on Bobby Sands. For the first time, it hit home that this was serious business. Over the following days the atmosphere in Rathcoole was very tense. Along with Catholic men from the district, Bobby tried to protect Cunningham's family from reprisals until they got safely out of the estate. Cunningham was buried on Monday. They moved his wife and two children out of their apartment on Tuesday. The Rathcoole Defense Association moved in a Protestant family on Wednesday.[12]

Protestants were now swelling into Rathcoole. Vigilantes roamed the streets and the "Sons of Kai," a Loyalist flute band, paraded around the district adding fuel to the erupting situation.

The Kai began making nightly raids on Catholic houses, painting crosses on their doors and windows. The following night, rioters trashed every house with an "X" on it. They would knock on doors and shout at the "Fenian bastards" inside to get out before they broke the windows and doors. They pushed one man's ice cream van down the steps from the road into his front garden, wrecking it and leaving ice cream lollies scattered all around. Fences and rubbish bins . . . anything they could throw went in through the windows of the houses with crosses.

The Kai struck out at anything Catholic. One night they decided to burn down the Catholic chapel. They broke down the doors and piled the pews in the middle of the chapel and drenched them in gasoline. When the fire fizzled out, they took all the holy statues and broke off their heads.[13]

All in all, says one former Kai member, "it was really just a rake for us."

The "rake," however, was all on one side. As the gangs roamed with their paint pots and their bins and bricks, Bobby Sands sat up all night to watch the house.

Local Unionist politicians and the police tried to hush up the violence and intimidation in Rathcoole but reports started reaching the public at large. The local newspaper carried an item about forty Catholic families who received letters telling them to leave their homes or face the consequences. Their windows were smashed and their cars were damaged. Some had already left.

The RUC defended the Rathcoole Loyalists by playing down the threats to local Catholics.

"A lot of what is going on is sheer vandalism and has no sectarian significance," responded Chief Inspector William Kyle to the press report. "We suspect that a lot of these threats are the work of young hooligans and that there is nothing else to them."

Then he added, "While some cases are genuine, it seems that other people who moved were merely claiming that they had been intimidated as an excuse."[14]

Inspector Kyle was helping spread the rumor that local Catholics were inflicting violence on themselves so that the Housing Executive would speed up the process of moving them to another neighborhood. He interpreted this as typical Catholic fraud against the state rather than a cry for help by local people who would go to any lengths to get out of Rathcoole.

By late April, the violence made the big newspapers. A story in the *Irish News* reported that a hundred Catholic families had left Rathcoole during the previous nine months. A local Catholic shopkeeper said that the intimidation was not just random thuggery but was highly organized by the men that their local MP called "my vigilantes."[15] Every time a Catholic moved, their home was immediately taken over by Protestant squatters who later became lawful tenants.

The police still claimed that Catholics were exaggerating the problem.[16] Their public statements encouraged the vigilantes to intensify their intimidation. One day they sealed off Rathcoole, placing vehicles across the roads leading out of the estate. The flute bands and the Loyalist paramilitaries marched up and down Doonbeg Drive in full uniform, past the Sands house. The Sands family were sure that they would lose the house this time. Rosaleen wanted to get out but Bobby refused to budge. It was not right to be put out of your own house, he said. Besides, they would never get past the roadblocks at the top of Doonbeg Drive. They kept the lights out that night and sat quietly, waiting for something to happen. Bobby sat on the stairs facing the front door, carving knife in hand. Marcella sat beside him with the pepper. She would throw it in the face of any Loyalists who tried to come into the house, while Bobby stuck them with the knife.[17] This time they were lucky: no one came.

Bobby's few remaining Protestant friends on Star of the Sea could do little to help. Geordie Hussey said it would just be a waste of his time. To his surprise and embarrassment, Bobby Sands never said anything to get back at his Protestant teammates.

They did not know, however, that Bobby was already resisting. They never suspected that he was in the IRA or that his commitment to the organization grew with every family that was evicted and every police statement that tried to cover up the problem. His thinking was still instinctual, not highly political. Apart from basic arms training and moving weapons, he joined an IRA squad that marshaled the main Easter parade on the Falls Road in West Belfast. This was a source of great pride, and gave a tremendous boost to his sense of solidarity and identity.

• • •

A week later, Bobby's commitment was tested by an event that shocked both sides who were still left in the Star of the Sea soccer club. Willie Caldwell, a Protestant on the team, knew Charlie McCrystal, Samuel Hughes, and John McErlean as childhood friends in Bawnmore, where he'd grown up. Bobby knew them, too. Mary McGinn, Marcella's best friend, had a crush on John McErlean. Lately, Bobby had met them during IRA training lectures. But Willie Caldwell never suspected that these friends were in the IRA.

At two o'clock on Friday afternoon, April 7, the three were hard at work inside a lock-up garage, one of a row of ten on the quiet street of Bawnmore Grove. They had been busy assembling a time bomb consisting of thirty pounds of gelignite, a detonator, pocket watch, and batteries. It was their first big operation for the IRA so they took extra care. McCrystal got in the car and waited while Hughes and McErlean, ever so carefully, made the final connections to complete the circuit that would activate the bomb.

They were not careful enough.

A gigantic explosion reduced five of the garages to rubble and shattered the windows of nearby houses. A young boy's arm was broken from the impact of the blast. Charlie McCrystal's head, lying inside the twisted wreckage of the car in which he had been sitting, was the first gruesome sight the ambulance men saw when they arrived on the scene a few minutes after the explosion. Parts of the three bodies were scattered for fifty yards around the car. Locals identified McCrystal and Hughes. There was not enough left of McErlean for anyone to say who he was. Ambulance men, police, and British soldiers collected what they could of the bodies while they called in the heavy lifting equipment to clear away the rubble.

The funeral for the three IRA volunteers took place the following Tuesday at the Star of the Sea Church. There were no military trappings or IRA sympathy notices in the newspapers. But the five hundred mourners who packed the chapel and the hundred or so men who stood outside knew the status of the three boys who were blown up by their own bomb. Bobby stood among his comrades outside the chapel as the pallbearers brought the three coffins out into the bright sunlight, followed by twenty children carrying wreaths with green, white, and orange ribbons. The RUC and members of the British Parachute Regiment stood by and watched as the coffins were borne to a nearby graveyard.[18] From then on, Bobby Sands had no illusions about the seriousness of what he was involved in.

His commitment to the IRA was reinforced as the gangs roamed nightly past his house, shouting "taigs out." A woman around the corner was now an "estate agent." One day in June, Bernadette Sands saw the women standing outside of their house with a young couple, pointing over. A week later a rubbish bin came through the living room window. Then some stones. A couple of shots were fired at the house.

"They didn't even come to the door, they hadn't just got the guts to come to the door," recalled Tommy O'Neill. "Just threw bottles through the window, stones through the window."[19]

A Protestant neighbor came by to sympathize with the family. She told them it was terrible what was happening to them. But she could do nothing about it.

Rosaleen Sands went to the Housing Executive the next morning. They told her to go to Twinbrook where many other intimidated Catholics were moving. Twinbrook was all the way across Belfast to the south, at least ten miles away. When Rosaleen arrived at the Housing Executive office in Twinbrook, the girl there told her just to take whatever free house they could find.

"Put your curtains up, move some furniture in, and come back and tell us the number of the house."

They looked around and found a house at 11 Laburnum Way, facing a big expanse of green fields. They put up their curtains and moved some furniture. They were now residents of Twinbrook.

One by one, Bobby's friends left as well. The O'Neill's were forced to move to Ardoyne. "Benzie" Boyd and his family moved to Twinbrook. Geraldine Noade, Bobby's girlfriend, went with her family to Unity Flats. The McGinns went to Twinbrook. The Catneys moved to the lower Falls in West Belfast.

By 1973, only a handful of Catholic families remained in Rathcoole. Many older residents in Rathcoole regret what happened.[20] When the vigilantes drove the Catholics out, they say, the rot started because "scumbags" replaced them. Moreover, they sent good Catholics into bad lives. A taxi driver from Rathcoole says that the day they put a bin through his family's window, they "drove Bobby into the hands of the IRA."[21]

Other Protestant friends agree. A Protestant who ran with him in the Willowfield Harriers remembers Sands more in sadness than anger.

"Look, he got such a raw deal, you know, being beaten up and what happened to the family and that certainly contributed to the development."

Chapter Four

A Change of Scene

L ike so many working-class Belfast families, John and Rosaleen Sands were caught up in a whirlpool that carried them from one place to another despite their best efforts to lead normal and productive lives. They had done everything right. Or so they had thought. John had a good job. They were quiet neighbors who bothered no one. Yet accidents of birth and marriage conspired against them so that this was not enough. A quiet life was neither their destiny nor that of their children.

Physically, Twinbrook resembled Rathcoole. The same British architects designed all of these new estates. Twinbrook was greener, nestled in a valley of soft, sloping hills rather than the harsher and craggy Carnmoney. But the social environment was totally different. Although the local Catholic church was just a temporary hut instead of the grand cutstone chapel they were used to, the Sands family could walk there openly. Bobby could walk around the estate at night, slowly, if he wished.

Twinbrook was Northern Ireland's last big hopeful housing project. In 1965, when they began construction on 170 acres southwest of Belfast, the authorities still believed Catholics and Protestants could live together in harmony.[1] With an optimism that would later seem like a sick joke, the planners called the new estate *Twinbrook*, denoting two streams of Protestants and Catholics merging into a single peaceful river of life. To continue the pastoral theme, they named the streets after exotic trees: Juniper, Almond, Cherry, Laburnum, and Aspen.

By the time the first houses went up, it was already too late to harbor any serious hopes of a non sectarian haven. The earth-moving equipment arrived on the site just as the civil rights marches and police violence began to escalate in 1969. Prime Minister Chichester-Clark officially opened the first houses in February 1971, barely a week after the IRA killed the first British soldier and he had declared war on the IRA. The residents set up a Twinbrook Tenants Association (TTA) and tried to keep the membership restricted to the "right class of people." For the moment, their fear of squatters exceeded their religious divisions.

Then, suddenly, everything changed. The population movements that brought the Sands family from Rathcoole also brought hundreds of other Catholic families who sought a relatively safe haven. Living conditions were not good in Twinbrook. There was hardly any community infrastructure. Two wooden huts in the center of the estate served the recreation needs of the entire community. One was a social club run by the TTA, the other, a youth club. There was no pub, no pharmacy, no doctors, no dentist. There was not even a post office. A block of shops in the middle of the estate provided basic needs, from the VG foodstore at one end to Fusco's chippie at the other. The schools were mobile huts. A wooden hut served as the church. Buses were infrequent and the black taxis that carried people to and from the city center did not reach as far as Twinbrook.

Like the Sands family, new refugees just found an empty house and moved in. Some got rent-books, others were squatters. The Sands family was lucky. Their house was finished. Many refugees found themselves in unfinished houses without windows, doors, electricity, or water. The streets were mud tracks, without curbs. There were no front gardens and people had to walk across planks to their front doors. They went to the toilet in a bucket and emptied it at night across the fields.

The refugees created a community by helping each other. Since Rosaleen Sands had electricity and water, she and the girls took flasks of tea and hot water to less fortunate families. Bernadette remembers helping a family of ten that lived in a one-bedroomed unfinished shell of an apartment.[2]

Such solidarity, however, was not universal. Refugees were stigmatized by older residents who were afraid that they would bring the "troubles" with them. Like a scene from the *Grapes of Wrath,* some residents placed barricades across the road into the estate to stop lorries, packed high with furniture, from getting into the area.

Bitterness grew between the residents. The squatters gained confidence; Protestants moved out en masse.[3] Soon after the Sands family moved to Twinbrook, a Unionist politician visited the area and advised the remaining Protestant tenants to leave. Most of them did.

● ● ●

One social cleavage gives way to another. As the balance of power in Twinbrook shifted from the older tenants to the refugees, divisions surfaced among the newcomers. The main division was a feud between the Provisional IRA and the Official IRA, who were known as "sticks" because of their practice of sticking their commemorative paper Easter lily[4] badges to their coats rather than pinning them like the Provos. Although the organizations had political differences, the real source of the feuding was territorial. Small incidents, like raids by the British army to capture weapons or volunteers, provoked rumors that fed bad feelings. Sometimes, volunteers from one organization kidnapped members of the other; in the worst cases, gunmen from one group shot someone from the other. Once an Official shot dead Provisional volunteer Charlie Hughes on March 8, 1971, there was always the potential for more feuding.

This feud played out all over Belfast that summer of 1972. In Twinbrook, it was muted because young men from both groups had to mix due to their isolation. In the evenings, they waited together for a bus to take them several miles down the road to a pub. They came back together on the last bus at 10:00 o'clock.

Since the Officials were so strong in Twinbrook, most residents who supported the Provisional IRA kept quiet about it. A few experienced volunteers lived quietly in Twinbrook and operated militarily in their old neighborhoods. They left it up to younger refugees to organize the IRA in the new estate.

The first time C— met Sands was in his own house in the Juniper area of Twinbrook. C—'s parents were away and he was in the living room, meeting half a dozen teenage volunteers who made up the local "unit" of the Provisional IRA. Actually, it was more aspiration than reality for them to call themselves a unit. None of them had ever been officially sworn in as IRA volunteers. They were all very young. C— and T—, the most active among them, were eighteen and sixteen years old, respectively. Jim Kerr, the gentle giant who taught some of them how to drive, was just sixteen.

The singular force that drew these young people into the IRA and then kept them there was anger and resentment. The men in Twinbrook hung out in front of the VG store or Fusco's chip shop, talking and having a smoke. There was little else to do in the isolated, underdeveloped estate. Several times a week, British army foot patrols came and made them spread-eagle against the wall of the shops, old men as well as young, sometimes for an hour or more. Jimmy Rafferty, who became friendly with Bobby Sands, watched them spread-eagle older men like his father against the wall and he got very angry at the indignity of it all.

One time, the British army had a group of boys and men up against the wall. They were getting worse treatment than usual; one Brit kept sticking his baton against the back of Rafferty's neck.

"I'd love to get stuck into this cunt," he said to Bobby, under his breath.

"Don't be stupid," Bobby whispered back. "You'd only get yourself hurt. *There's a better way.* "

Another time, Rafferty and some others were up against the wall for over an hour. When they were finally released, he went to see Bobby, seething with anger. Bobby was watching TV.

"Did you get seeing *Zulu* last night?" he asked Rafferty, referring to the classic film starring Stanley Baker, Michael Caine, and a raft of unknown African actors and extras.

"Aye, I did," replied Rafferty.

But he didn't want to talk about the film; he wanted to vent his anger about being spread-eagled against the wall.

"I'm wrecked, Sandsy," he told Bobby. "These here Brits had me up against the wall for over an hour. One of these days I'm going to get laid into them bastards."

Bobby just gave him a disdainful look and referred back to the previous night's movie where the British army, outnumbered but with superior firepower wiped out thousands of Zulus in hand-to-hand combat.

"Look, Raff, are you gonna be Stanley Baker or are you gonna carry a spear?!"

Bobby had already made his choice after years of confrontations in Rathcoole in which he was always on the weakest side. Now, in Twinbrook, the British army had guns instead of knives and a whole state to protect them. No British soldier would ever be punished for putting a paddy in the hospital with a crack from a rifle butt to the head. Therefore, Bobby figured you had to hold your temper and fight the British army on your own terms, not on theirs. This meant active involvement in the IRA.

A comrade in Bobby's unit puts their attitude at the time in clear terms: "We weren't revolutionaries *yet*. Repression bred *resistance*, not revolution."

The young IRA men had enthusiasm bred of resistance but they did not have much confidence in their officer in command. He was a bit older and, as an ex-British soldier, had *some* military experience. Bobby's opinion of him was pretty low.

"He was up the left, straight up he was," he said.[5]

So, when John Rooney brought Sands to C—'s house and introduced him it was something of an event. Bobby had barely been in the IRA for half a year in Rathcoole but in Twinbrook, he was practically a seasoned veteran. C— watched him that night and right away he thought that their new comrade had strong leadership material.

Sands wasted no time becoming active in the unit. He called a meeting where an officer came up from the (First) Battalion staff a mile away in Andersonstown and swore in the young volunteers. The unit gradually became more organized.

Its main role was logistical support for the Battalion. An urban guerrilla army has four material needs, of which it seems it can never get enough: personnel, arms, money, and transport. Twinbrook supplied cars and money. In their own revolutionary terms, they "liberated" them, although the media and most of the general public would simply say that they stole them. Little planning went into these acts of "liberation." Instead, they depended on the "game" operator who was willing to go out and get cars and money. Bobby "was game for anything."

"He was like a restless person," says one of Bobby's IRA comrades. "He never had enough to do and would try anything. He was always the first to say, 'I'll do that!' He had to have a hand in everything."

Other comrades use words like "rash" and "fearless" to describe Bobby Sands. At the same time, one of his comrades remembers sizing up the boys in the unit. In spite of his reckless attitude, Bobby was the one who he knew was "in it for the long term." Something about him was just that bit more serious, more committed than the others.

Bobby was constantly getting cars. Jim Kerr was a mechanic at a garage in Belfast and through his job he got keys that gave them access to practically any Ford on the road. The Travellers Rest, a sprawling country pub in the nearby village of Milltown, always had cars parked while their owners lingered over a few pints. Another sure bet was the Stewarts supermarket in nearby Dunmurry. A couple of volunteers would pick a Ford, drive it back to Twinbrook, and park it until it was needed. Bobby Sands was usually one of the squad that went to get them. C—'s abiding memory from the time is standing in front of Fusco's with some of his mates when a gray Ford came screeching into the estate. It pulled up in front of them and the driver rolled down his window. It was Bobby, grinning from ear to ear.

Bobby's restless energy blurred the line between his personal and political lives. The unit obtained a flat for IRA business but Bobby moved in after he had some disagreements with his parents, who did not approve of his involvement in the IRA. His police files say that he "refused to live with his parents."[6]

The flat at 1F Jasmine End was on the top floor at the end of a new three-story beige-brick building that contained four blocks of flats. Each block had its own front and back door at either end of a central hallway. The flats were hardly luxurious. But Bobby had running water, heat, and a place to socialize with his mates.

Life was now pretty hard. Sands couldn't claim the dole because he didn't want to get into the social structure and have all his details on record. The IRA provided a modest weekly wage of about five pounds, just enough to get by. Sometimes Bobby depended on people in the community for meals or a bed for the night. Although he was going through a David Bowie phase in his musical tastes, pretending to be the Jean Genie from Bowie's popular song, Bobby went around in a terrible state, in sandals with his socks sticking out of the front end. At one point the other members of his IRA unit passed the hat around and collected enough money to buy him a pair of Doc Martens boots.

Often, Bobby went with T— to get their weekly subsistence money and they would take the bus to Keenan's Bar in the city center because T— was too young to drink legally and that was one of the few places that let him in. It was also just around the corner from Woolworth's, where Geraldine worked, so Bobby could visit her there or go on up to Unity Flats, where she lived with her parents.

It was on his way from visiting Geraldine one day that Sands and Tomboy Loudon, who lived in the Flats, first realized that they were both involved in the IRA. The feud with the Official IRA was at a bad stage and Tomboy was running around the landings with a gun because there were rumors that they were coming to shoot someone. He ran straight into Bobby, who knew from the gun that Tomboy was involved. When Tomboy explained the trouble, Bobby's response told Tomboy that he was involved, too. Tomboy showed him where to get a taxi.

After that they became very close friends. When Bobby visited Geraldine, the pair often wound up hanging out with Tomboy, as well. But Geraldine never mixed much with Bobby's Twinbrook comrades. Some of them felt that she was a bit resentful of them for taking Bobby away from her. For his part, Bobby tried to juggle his two lives but he couldn't.

"He lived the army," says a comrade. "The IRA always came first."

Another man in the Twinbrook unit, M—, was the opposite. Whenever they went to get him for something, his wife always answered the door.

"What do *youse boys* want?"

"Tell M— to get down to the flat, we need him."

But he seldom came. The boys made remarks about how M—'s wife controlled him. He was a part-time soldier and that would never have satisfied Bobby. Geraldine could never win. Looking back, Bobby's comrades have great sympathy for her.

Bobby tried to make his new flat a home. He took a garbage bin, filled it with the contents of a store-bought home brew kit, and placed a mesh window curtain over it. He had great expectations of an endless supply of cheap drink for socializing in the flat. But soon the whole thing was swimming in fruit flies and he had to throw it out.

His other chemical experiments were more exceptional. The unit did not have any commercial explosives, so T— and Bobby used the flat to mix an explosive from benzene. The mix stank so much that T— wondered how Bobby could live there.

• • •

As the unit became more active, the potential for conflict with the Official IRA increased. The Officials kidnapped T— a couple of times. Once, he expected to be "nutted" but he was reprieved when Bobby rounded up a couple of volunteers and kidnapped a local commander of the Official IRA, saying that he would hold him until T— was released. If any harm came to T—, he said, his hostage could expect the same. T— was released.

It would not be his last ugly run-in with the Official IRA. Yet the Officials had their attractions. Bobby's comrades were disorganized and lacked real political direction. They suffered from a chronic shortage of usable arms and Sands sometimes traveled to his old unit to borrow guns. On the political side, Sinn Féin hardly existed in Twinbrook. The shortcomings were so stark, Sands later told the police, that he considered defecting to the Official IRA.[7]

Yet joining the Officials was not really a credible option. Official Sinn Féin had difficulty developing any serious political program that would appeal to northern Irish Nationalists as an alternative to war. Their Marxism included some attractive class politics, but their policy of cease-fire with the British army and police provided no answers to Nationalists who faced harassment on a daily basis. Their military wing was redundant. Had he joined them, Sands would have wound up fighting his old friends rather than the British army. Their muscle flexing in areas like Twinbrook or the Markets had no apparent purpose other than to achieve local power and social control.

So Bobby stayed with his local Provisional IRA unit. He was enthusiastic enough to think that they could "build it up." First, however, there were internal problems to resolve involving the unit's OC, who was caught stealing funds and was to be expelled from the IRA.

T— remembers walking with Bobby across the large green field in front of Laburnum Way one day in August. He had a Webley revolver and Sands had two rifles slung across his back. They went to the OC's house, arrested him, and took him to the flat opposite Bobby's. They questioned him there for some hours. When C— arrived at the flat during the interrogation he got the shock of his life. John Rooney, always a joker, approached him in the living room while a couple of others held the OC in the next room.

"You're not going to like this," Rooney told C—, "but you're going to have to take this fella across the fields and shoot him."

C— nearly shit himself until he realized he was the target of Belfast's particularly black form of humor. The OC was not shot, just dismissed from the IRA. T— replaced him as commanding officer.

After the OC's dismissal, the guns that remained could not be fired. A Walther P38 had a missing firing pin and the trigger mechanism didn't work. Their .45 Webley revolver had a broken spring and a broken hammer. These weapons were only good for scaring people. Between the lack of weapons and military training, Sands was hardly involved in any significant military attacks on the British army or the RUC,[8] despite one of his most widely quoted writings, where he claimed that, "my life now centred around sleepless nights and stand-bys. Dodging the Brits and calming the nerves to go out on operations."[9]

He *attempted* military activities, however. Bobby and T— tried to make blast bombs with the benzene mix that they made in the flat. One day, they stuck a fuse into a homemade bomb and placed it on the side of a local hill to test it. They lit the fuse and ran away. The result was more Laurel and Hardy than Lawrence of Arabia. They waited several minutes for the blast but nothing happened. Finally, they decided that it was a dud and as they approached, it went off just in time to save them from serious injury.

Bobby constantly made plans to attack the British army. As you entered his apartment block from the back, the brick wall was patterned in a lattice, so that there were holes between the bricks. One day, as they passed the wall on their way out of the apartment, Jimmy Rafferty remarked to Bobby about the wall.

"See the way they left them bricks? That's a scandal, them builders should come back and put the rest of the bricks in and fill in them holes."

"It's supposed to be that way, Raff," Bobby replied. While Rafferty felt a blush rising from his chest up to his face, Bobby continued. "Anyway, we could use it to our advantage. The Brits always leave the estate up at the top of the road. We could put a rifle through one of them holes and blatter away at them as they're climbing into the back of the Saracen. They'd never see us, and if they did they could fire away at us all day and they'd never hit us."

Like his other plans, it never happened.

Bobby was more successful at fund-raising than military operations. On August 4, he robbed 220 pounds, a substantial amount of money, from an insurance salesman who lived in his apartment block.[10] Two days later, he and another man went into the VG Foodstore behind his flat with their defective pistols. When they pulled their guns out from the waist-band of their jeans, the woman at the till stood there in shock. He had to ask her a second time before she reached into the till, took out all the notes, and handed them to Sands, who stuffed them into his pocket. When he got home, he counted 210 pounds in notes.

Bobby's sheer fearlessness made him popular with the other volunteers. He organized more actions the following month. On the weekend of September 9, he and his comrades went to the Travelers Rest pub and took a dark blue Ford Cortina. They drove a mile down the road to a Jet service station where they got a mere twenty pounds from the two cash drawers. The next night they took the Cortina to the Kingsway gas station in Dunmurry, a mile away. This time they got about 70 pounds. It was the first occasion that Bobby Sands found himself in print, although not by name, when an article in the *Irish News* described the robbery.[11]

• • •

Geraldine stayed in the flat at the end of the summer, but not for long because things began to heat up and the flat became a dangerous place.

Bobby continued to hope that his local unit would "build itself up" to a point where it could launch military attacks on the British army. Yet such activities were difficult in Twinbrook. Among the terraced houses that formed a sort of Casbah in the old lower Falls district, you could fly in the front door of one house, out the back and across the brick wall, down the entry, over another wall, and into a safe house before the British army or the police knew you were gone. But Twinbrook was open spaces. There were spies and informers. And there were many ways for the army to watch the area.

One British army surveillance operation operated from a van with green lettering on the side: "Four Square Laundry." The van went from house to house in Twinbrook, collecting laundry for cleaning at cut-rate prices. Nobody ever thought to question why the laundry service was so cheap or why its friendly driver sat and chatted with the local women for so long. Nobody seemed to consider that the laundry was a British army undercover operation. As the van toured Twinbrook, two men in a secret compartment above the front seat took photos and made notes about the movements of people in the area. The driver and the laundry woman chatted up the customers. Then, they took the clothes away for forensic tests. They checked the shirt sizes against the known occupants of houses, to see if anyone was staying in a house who shouldn't be there. Then they returned them clean and fresh . . . and chatted some more.

Bobby was an obvious target of surveillance. It was enough to be young, male, and Catholic. But he also associated with other IRA suspects. By September, the authorities were well aware that he was involved in the spate of robberies in the area. The British army interrogated him at least once in a nearby house they had requisitioned.

The interrogation room in the basement of the old house on Black's

Road was terrifying. It was painted black, walls and floor, except for two white feet painted on the middle of the floor. That was where Bobby had to stand while two soldiers stood behind him with batons and three sat at a table in front; except you couldn't see them because of the bright light. The three asked questions and they dropped bits of information that let him know that they knew certain things that would be hard to find out. According to Bobby, the soldiers used their truncheons liberally. He suffered a terrible beating in the house and he came out of it badly shaken.

"Anybody would be rattled," said a comrade who was once there. "Bobby was fearless but he was human . . . he would have been rattled by that place."

By the start of October, Bobby was living on borrowed time. Things began to get very hot in Twinbrook after the IRA discovered the truth about the Four Square Laundry and decided to move against them.

At 11:15 on the morning of October 2, the Four Square Laundry van was delivering and picking up laundry around the corner from Bobby's flat. "Jane," the laundry woman who was really a member of the Women's Royal Army Corps, was inside a house collecting laundry when a blue Ford Cortina pulled up beside the van. A man got out and fired several bursts of automatic fire into it. The driver was killed instantly. The IRA claimed that two men in the secret compartment above the driver were also killed, although the British authorities denied it. A little girl who saw the whole thing from her parlor window, however, says she remembers the dead soldiers to this day. "Jane" was in a state of shock. The local women brought her in and gave her brandy and a nerve tablet and tried to console her.[12]

Bobby Sands had nothing to do with the attack. Another, more experienced IRA unit from the lower Falls carried out the operation. It was far too delicate an affair to leave to local youngsters. Nonetheless, the ambush stirred things up, which may explain why Sands and his unit went outside of Twinbrook for his next money-raising venture. On the day after the ambush, he went into the Belfast city center and took a blue Ford Cortina. He met three others back in Twinbrook and they drove to Gilkinson's, a gas station with a small grocery a couple of miles away. The road ran high up onto the side of a mountain, a semi-rural and heavily Loyalist area. They drove past the shop and then made a U-turn. When they got back to the shop, they drove into the forecourt and stopped next to the gas pumps.

Sands got out first and the two other passengers jumped out behind. He was carrying the defective Walther P38. One of his two companions had the Webley .45 and the other was unarmed.

Inside, the shopkeeper was serving a small girl. Sands stood behind her and the others fell in behind him, forming a line. Once the little girl was served, Bobby asked for two Mars bars. When the shopkeeper went to get them, the other two men went behind the counter. One of them produced his .45 and told her to give him the till. The woman panicked. She started to "squeal the place down" and made a grab for one of the men behind the counter. She tried to get past him but she tripped and fell. The two ran out of the shop and got into the car but Bobby was still in the shop when he saw her getting up.

As Sands left, the shop owner was coming toward him. Bobby pulled his gun and pointed it, waving it at him in a motion that warned him to stay back. He got to the car and the four men sped back home, empty-handed.

Perhaps the unit was desperate for money, for Bobby's next job was downright crazy.

On Tuesday, October 10 at about noon, the local rent collector was collecting in Bobby's building. She had more than three hundred pounds from the day's takings. As she left the building, she heard a male voice saying, "Come here, Miss."

The woman looked over her right shoulder and she saw a "tall slim youth" standing in front of rear door. Bobby Sands was wearing a green jacket with black fur collar. On his head he wore a bush hat and had a woolen mask over his face. She did not see the other man who was with him, carrying a toy dart gun. The rent woman thought Sands was going to go for her so she "just ran" out the door and up the road.

Two days later, on October 12, Bobby's luck ran out. The woman who lived in the bottom flat had given him permission to keep guns there, but she apparently panicked after the attack on the Four Square Laundry. She told the authorities about the guns and disappeared. Sands heard later that she "sold her soul for three hundred pounds and shot to England leaving the Brits in the house to wait."

Bobby was not in his flat at 5:33 in the morning when Lieutenant Donald Edmund McLaren of the Nineteenth Field Regiment, Royal Artillery, led a dawn raid on the woman's apartment. McLaren knew exactly where to look and what he was looking for. He found four pistols wrapped in polythene under the sink unit: a German .22 revolver, a Belgian-made .32 revolver, a Webley .45 revolver, and a Walther P38 automatic. They were all incapable of being fired conventionally and they had not been fired for some time.[13] His men found a bundle of tin foil and a yellow cardboard box in a recess behind the front door. The two packages held seventy-three rounds of ammunition: thirty-six British-made rounds for a .38 Smith & Wesson revolver and thirty-seven rounds of German and U.S.-made 9X19 parabellum.

Meanwhile, Lance Bombardier Anthony Halstead was upstairs leading a search party in Bobby's apartment. Along with his associate Gunner Spence he searched the bathroom. Spence watched Halstead search under the bathtub. Eventually, he produced a coffee tin and, according to their later testimony, when they looked inside they found four rounds of Swedish-made .38 ammo and three pieces of plastic tubing, one of which was stuffed with horse-shoe nails.

Bobby Sands was now on the run.

Chapter Five

A Trip to the South

O ctober 16, 1972 was a Monday. At about half past five in the evening, Bobby Sands met a man who instructed him to go to Dundalk, just across the border, to meet someone in front of the Imperial Hotel in the middle of the town. Since it was on the border and was well known as a base for IRA activities, people called the town "El Paso." Sands was to get arms and to bring them back up to Belfast for distribution to other IRA units.

The next morning, he drove south with another man and two women in a borrowed gray Ford Anglia. They headed toward Lisburn just south of Twinbrook, where they would join the main Belfast-Dublin motorway. They were observed. Just after nine o'clock Sergeant Finlay, who was on duty at the RUC Station at Lisburn, was told to go outside the station to watch the traffic coming from the direction of Seymour Street. If he saw a gray Ford with registration number CIA 524, he should stop it and apprehend the occupants. Finlay soon saw the car approaching in the stream of traffic. When it drew near, he stepped out and stopped it.

"Hello, Mister Sands," Finlay addressed Bobby.

Sergeant Finlay ordered the four out of the car and brought them into the station. He handed them over to Detective Inspector Hylands and drove the car into the station yard.

Bobby Sands had lasted just five days "on the run."

The police processed Sands and held him in the RUC station for questioning. After dinner, he had his first recorded interview. Detective Sergeant Gill questioned him while Detective Constable Walsh took notes. Their accounts are very straightforward and contain few clues about how they questioned Bobby. We cannot rule out rough treatment, as some years later Sands wrote that,

> *I was caught the first time in October 1972 in Lisburn and genuinely on the run. I was then eighteen and very naïve. Got bad time in barracks and I did sign a statement which was basic (i.e. not bad).*

And,

> *Have been interrogated in Castlereagh, Crumlin Road, detention center, Black Road, Musgrave billet, Dunmurry Bks, Lisburn Rd and Fort Monagh. The latter being the only one where I wasn't assaulted.*[1]

Gill first saw Sands at 7:45 P.M., ten and a half hours after the police detained him. He went through the usual procedures of cautioning Bobby that he was not obliged to say anything unless he wished to do so and that anything he said would be taken down in writing and may be given in evidence. Gill then informed him that they were investigating a number of armed robberies in the Lisburn and Dunmurry areas.

At some point that evening, says Gill, Sands requested to speak to him on his own and Detective Walsh left the room. Gill asked Sands if he had ever been involved in an armed robbery of a gas station at Stewartstown Road in Dunmurry, the Jet Station from the ninth of September. Bobby allegedly replied, "I was, I thought you were bluffing me."

Gill then asked him who was with him and Bobby replied, "I don't know his name, he came up the road."

Gill asked Sands if he was a member of the Provisional IRA.

"Yes," he replied.

Gill asked him what rank and Bobby replied, "O.C."

At this point, wrote Gill, he called Detective Walsh back and informed him what had transpired. Bobby smiled and said, "I held out well, didn't I? I thought you were bluffing me."

It was 8:15 P.M. If the detectives reported accurately, he had been under interrogation for about a half an hour.

Whatever transpired during that relatively short period when Sands was alone with Gill, by the time Walsh was called back into the interrogation room he was ready to confess to more than the Jet Station hold-up.

The interview, says Gill, was then "conducted on a question-and-answer basis" with Detective Walsh making notes. According to Walsh, Gill was trying to get Sands to admit other activities and to find out more about the IRA in Twinbrook. Bobby was more interested in explaining what he was doing in the car on the way to Dundalk. He clearly wanted to absolve the driver and the man who loaned them the car.

Years later, Bobby told a fellow volunteer from Twinbrook a story about the interrogation that never appeared in the official police accounts. He said that after he admitted to the detective that he was on a trip to procure weapons, he asked him, "What would have happened if you caught me *after* I got the guns?"

"Well, if you had of picked up the stuff and brought it back, we'd have shot you dead," the Special Branchman supposedly replied. "We wouldn't have stopped the car, we would have just shot you."

Bobby said that this was the most chilling moment of the interviews.

Although he admitted that he was a member of the IRA, Bobby refused to implicate anyone else in his activities. For example, when the police asked, "Is [T—] and [M—] IRA?" Sands answered, "They are nothing." Then, "John Rooney?" Bobby again answered, "He's nothing."

Sands admitted a few "knocked cars," possession of some faulty weapons, and the attempted robbery of the rent woman. But he denied involvement in an attack on a helicopter, a gun and blast bomb attack on the British army, and the attack on the Four Square Laundry van.

Detective Walsh remained in the room and questioned Sands further. Walsh's description of the next few minutes is nearly comical.

"After caution [Sands] said that he had done some jobs and if we told him what jobs he had done he would say whether or not he had done them."

Walsh mentioned his attempt to hold up the rent collector. Bobby replied that he had been involved.

Then Bobby made out a statement, the first of four that he would make in the Lisburn station. They all followed a set procedure, except that he made the first statement in his own handwriting while the others were dictated to his interrogators.

Walsh took out a sheet of paper and wrote the following:

Statement from Robert Gerard Sands. D.O.B. 9.3.54. Unemployed Coach Builder [11 Laburnum Way] 1F Jasmine End. Twinbrook taken by D/Cont Walsh in R.U.C. Lisburn on Thursday 17th October 1972

I have been told by D/Cont Walsh that I am not obliged to say anything unless I wish to do so and I understand that anything I say will be taken down in writing and may be given in evidence. I clearly understand this caution and wish to make a statement.

Walsh made a mistake on the address, giving it as 11 Laburnum Way (Bobby's parents' address). But that was stroked out and corrected to the address of Bobby's flat (the correction is initialled "R/S"). Sands then signed the caution and wrote the following statement,

Tuesday last 10th/10/72 I ROBERT Sands was waiting in the end flat Jasmine End twin brook with another volunteer wearing mask and cap's armed with toy revolver [whe] we attempted to hold her up. I wish to say that I do not know the name or rank of [th] my mate when I refer to her I mean the rent women the weapon was a diania repeater The [old] only words spoken was when I siad [sic] come here miss. My rank O/C.

[signed] Robert Sands.

Sometime later, Detective Walsh wrote a second statement at Bobby's dictation. This statement detailed the failed robbery at Gilkinson's gas station.[2] A third statement admitted taking a car that was never used before the British army recovered it a few nights later.[3] Finally, at 9:30 P.M. Bobby dictated and signed a fourth statement admitting robberies of the VG Foodstore, the Jet Gas Station on the Stewartstown Road, and the Kingsway Gas Station in Dunmurry.[4] It was probably not yet ten o'clock. In less than three hours, Bobby had signed away his freedom by admitting to a series of offences. Crucially, he never implicated anyone else, stating that, "I must tell you that as a member of the Provisional IRA I accept full responsibility for planning and carrying out these raids."

Had he implicated others, Sands would have been ostracized in prison. A shadow would have come over his future in the Republican Movement and perhaps Bobby Sands would now be living an anonymous life.

The next morning, Wednesday, Sands was charged with stealing 220.86 pounds from his neighbor, an insurance man, after "putting him in fear." Ironically, it was a charge that Bobby appears to have never admitted, either in writing or verbally. The police took him to the Petty Sessions Court in Dunmurry, near Twinbrook where he was formally charged. He refused to be represented by a lawyer and he refused to recognize the court.

The next day, for the first time, Bobby Sands's name appeared in the newspapers along with the account of his activities. Since the charge was relatively minor, it was buried toward the bottom of an article that listed more than twenty men who were charged on the same day for various offences.

"Robert Gerard Sands (18), an unemployed coachbuilder who claims to be a member of the Provisional IRA, was remanded in custody for a week charged with armed robbery by stealing £220 in cash from James Boyd, of Jasmine End, Killeaton, on August 4 last."

The judge sent Bobby to await trial in Long Kesh prison, just on the other side of Lisburn from Twinbrook. With the exception of a few short months, he would live within prison walls for the rest of his life.

Chapter Six

Prison

Long Kesh had eight compounds that the prisoners called "cages" because they were collections of Nissen huts surrounded by wire. They put Bobby Sands into Cage Eight with other men who were awaiting trial. The other cages housed uncharged internees, as they had done since September 1971 when the hastily built prison camp was opened. It was like something from a 1940s black-and-white movie, complete with barbed wire compounds, corrugated iron huts, watchtowers, and soldiers with Alsatian dogs patrolling the perimeter. Each cage had four Nissen huts and a wooden shower building. The first hut was the canteen, where the prison warders brought meals on wooden carts three times a day. The next was partitioned. The prisoners called it the "half hut" because they lived in the front half and used the back half for recreation. The other two were strictly dormitories. Next to the showers was a water tower.

The cages were built along the old runways of a former RAF air base, a long flat area among farmlands that took its name from the Irish *ceis fada*, the "long meadow." The ground was uneven and constantly full of puddles that the men had to avoid while walking or running around the yard. Wire fences topped by razor wire surrounded each cage and the prisoners got out, or the warders in, through "air-locked" double gates.

The Nissen huts were big, drafty, leaky buildings with tin roofs that turned them into ovens on summer days and cavernous refrigerators on cold days. Water seeped in around the windows and dripped through the roof. Winds blew through the cracks in the wooden walls at each end. The prisoners slept in bunks lined along either side of the hut.

Bobby soon got into the routine. Like most prisoners he became a news-hound, gathering round the radio on the hour to catch the latest news, especially "war news." If the news reported a successful IRA operation, a big cheer went up. Between newscasts, the major activity was walking around the perimeter fence, always in an anti-clockwise direction. Twice a week, two teams from each cage went to the heavily guarded soccer pitch at the edge of the camp. This was Bobby's favorite time.

Every Wednesday morning at 10:30 they took Sands to a special court set up at the prison, where the prosecution asked that he be remanded in prison for a further week because their inquiries were "not yet complete." Bobby, without a lawyer to represent him, always refused his right of cross-examination and said nothing.

A young volunteer, Seanna "Sid" Walsh, immediately struck up a friendship with Bobby. He was just a year younger than Bobby and his mother had just moved to Twinbrook, so they had something in common. Walsh came from an area near the Short Strand, a Republican stronghold that was full of IRA men and where joining the IRA was natural. Yet he was better educated than most, having gone to a Catholic grammar school where, among other things, he learned the Irish language. In June 1972, he attended a large meeting where some legendary IRA men made speeches that stirred his desires to join the IRA. In July he applied to join. He had to lie about his age: he was just sixteen and the minimum age of a volunteer was eighteen. By November he was a volunteer. By December he was in jail, arrested after an armed robbery for the IRA.

• • •

Things changed in the New Year. The previous May, IRA prisoners in Crumlin Road Jail had demanded to be recognized as political prisoners. They wanted to wear their own clothes, refrain from prison work, and be separated from the "ordinary criminals." Billy McKee, their leader, and five others went on a hunger strike to get their demands. Another six refused food a fortnight later and then another group each week after that. McKee was vomiting blood when British secretary of state for Northern Ireland Willie Whitelaw announced that he would give the prisoners "special category status" and move them to Long Kesh. In the middle of the night of January 7, 1973, all of the convicted prisoners were moved from the Crumlin Road Jail to Long Kesh in a big British army convoy. In exchange, Bobby and his comrades who were awaiting trial went to the Crumlin Road Jail.

"The Crum" began life in 1843-1845 as the "New House of Correction," a heavy cut-stone structure with a central administrative hall, or "circle," and three radiating wings of cellblocks: A-, B-, and C-. Each cellblock had three landings, the "ones" on the ground floor, the "twos" in the middle, and the "threes" on top. A distinctive tower was at the center of the jail, to draw fresh air into the wings. But the cells were more freezing than "fresh." The insides of their thick stone walls were plastered and painted cream, the cold, hard floors painted red. A barred window high up the back wall gave little light to the prisoners inside. A cast-iron heating pipe along the back wall of the cell gave little heat, especially on the cold January days when Bobby Sands landed in one.

Bobby shared a cell on the bottom landing of "A" wing with a prisoner from Ardoyne, near where his father grew up. Nearby were some prisoners from his old battalion area of Andersonstown. He hung around with them as well as his old friend Tomboy Loudon, who had been caught doing a robbery, and his new friend Sid Walsh.

Some of the prisoners called Sands "Rod Stewart" because he still wore his hair shaggy. Others called him "Sas," a joke about being caught so soon after the three SAS soldiers were shot around the corner from his flat. Sometimes he was "Sandsy" but mostly he was just "Bob."

The Crum was a bit of a madhouse. Most of the prisoners, like Bobby, were barely politicized. They hardly knew what they were there for apart from fighting back against the Loyalists, the police, or the British army. Their camaraderie expressed itself in youthful horseplay like water fights. The IRA staff encouraged the roughhousing to detract attention from escape attempts.

Danny Devenney arrived in the Crum soon after Sands. His first experience there was typical. He arrived to the usual fingerprinting, photos, and administrative formalities. Then he just wanted to get settled in his cell, put his few belongings away, get his bearings. Before he got started, a mate came up and told him he could do that later, to come and watch *Top of the Pops,* a high point of the television week. His mate led him into a medium-sized room with a big table, chairs, and about a hundred men watching the TV and talking. The noise was deafening and it was a scene of complete mayhem. One man was dancing on the table.

"Who the fuck's that eedgit?" Devenney asked his mate.

"That's our OC."

All hundred and fifty prisoners on the wing had free association with each other during the day. Bobby took his meals in the canteen on his landing and his exercise in the prison yard, two hours a day of soccer, walking and talking. At night he watched TV with the other lads. Three times a week he got a visit, one with his family but mostly with Geraldine.

One of these visits brought news that would make big changes in Bobby's life. Geraldine was pregnant. They decided to get married.

Bobby's impending marriage was the subject of some discussion on the wing. He was determined to do it and most of the other prisoners encouraged him.

"Aye, go ahead, fair play to you," was Tomboy's reaction. He knew them both and he figured they loved each other. It was obviously the thing to do.

Sid Walsh was more negative.

"See what we're at? We're running about killing people and constantly putting our life on the line. It's not right that we should ever ask any person to commit themselves to us in a relationship. We should just sort of stand back from all that."

Another prisoner cut in on Walsh with the majority view, "Catch yourself on. War. Peace. Whatever's happening, life carries on anyway and you just gotta go with it."

Sands ignored Walsh's protests and proceeded with his plans for the wedding, making a formal request to the prison governor.

Meanwhile, two weeks after he was transferred to the Crum, Bobby was taken to his regular weekly remand hearing at 11:00 in the morning. Only this time Detective Crawford met him there and preferred a further sixteen charges against him, from the VG robbery to possession of the weapons that the British army found during their raid on Jasmine End. Then Detective Walsh preferred charges eighteen to twenty-five, the attempted robbery of Gilkinson's, and two of the car thefts.

"Nothing to say," replied Bobby.

The prosecution asked the judge to remand Sands until February, when the court would hear depositions by the detectives, witnesses, and owners of the stolen cars.

On the morning of February 1, Sands sat through the depositions at the Petty Sessions Court in Dunmurry. The court heard about his interrogations in Lisburn. They were presented with transcripts of his signed statements.

In the end, Bobby's two charge sheets contained twenty-five charges. In a rather sloppy mistake, they got the name wrong and called him "John Gerard Sands" on charge seventeen, membership of the IRA.[1]

The judge informed Sands of his right to give evidence on his own behalf or to call witnesses. Did he wish to say anything in answer to the charges?

"No," replied Bobby.

Did he want to give evidence on his own behalf or call witnesses? "No."[2]

As an IRA volunteer, he was refusing to recognize the Queen's Court and its jurisdiction over part of the island of Ireland. His trial date was set for March 5.

But first he had another legal appearance. The prison governor set his wedding date with Geraldine for March 3, just before the trial began. Bobby asked his childhood friend Tommy O'Neill to be best man. Geraldine's sister Eileen was bridesmaid. When O'Neill pulled out at the last minute, Bobby contacted Diarmuid Fox, another friend from Rathcoole, to take his place.

The day of the wedding arrived. True to form, Bobby dressed up in a fancy new suit. It was modish, with wide lapels and a tartan pocket. Fox didn't own a suit so he had to borrow one from his brother. The guests met outside the jail before the ceremony: the seven-months pregnant bride Geraldine in a white wedding dress, the best man in his borrowed suit, the bridesmaid, and both sets of parents. A prison officer took them through the main gate, along a wide corridor, and up a stairwell to the prison chapel. Meanwhile, two warders led Sands from A-wing down another stairwell to the chapel where the priest was waiting. The ceremony was as normal as could be expected. The best man dropped the ring, vows were exchanged, and the witnesses signed the certificate, on which Bobby identified his occupation as "coach builder's apprentice." Then, a prison officer led the wedding party to the governor's office for tea and biscuits.

It was not easy to go back to his cell after the ceremony. Bobby's fellow prisoners had a party for him, with Mars bars and crisps and lemonade. They brought out the guitars and had a singsong. Predictably, Bobby sang his favorite Rod Stewart song, "Mandolin Wind."

Two days later, he was back in court. His family was there, including Geraldine. A jury of twelve was sworn in and Sands refused to recognize the judge, who entered a plea of not guilty on his behalf. Then the witnesses gave their evidence over two days without challenge or cross-examination.

Bobby's nineteenth birthday was the last day of the trial. He told Tomboy that he reckoned he was going down. He expected a sentence of five to seven years. But the British army witnesses took the stand and when they finished Judge William Johnson was unhappy. They had given irrelevant evidence that could prejudice the case.

Johnson asked if he wanted a retrial and Bobby agreed. What seemed like quite a nice birthday present later turned out to be a big mistake. If he had engaged a lawyer, he might have gotten off because of the soldiers' testimony. Instead, the judge simply struck out charges eleven and twelve—taking a Ford Cortina and driving it without insurance—and ordered a retrial for the following Tuesday on the remaining charges.

The second trial went more smoothly. At the end of the second day, the foreman of the jury announced that they found Sands guilty on twelve counts: four robberies and attempted robberies, four counts of carrying firearms, one count of possessing firearms, two counts of taking and using a motor car, and IRA membership.

As a juvenile, the Ministry of Home Affairs had to ascertain whether Bobby was suitable for Borstal Training. The prison governor said that Sands was "rather a self-confident type. Subject is charged with a serious offence—too serious to consider Borstal Training: not recommended."

Judge Higgins sentenced Sands to five years for the thefts and arms charges and a concurrent three-year sentence for IRA membership. When he passed sentence, Higgins had some remarks for him.

"I think that it is a tragedy for this community, for your family, and for yourself that you should have entered on this course of conduct."[3]

• • •

Sands was sent to Cage Eight in Long Kesh, which housed sentenced prisoners from both of the feuding Provisional and Official factions of the IRA. There, Bobby joined Tomboy Loudon and Seanna Walsh. Across the soccer pitches from Cage Eight, some new cages numbered ten and eleven were fully occupied by Provisionals.

There was constant tension between the Provisional and Official prisoners. The worst "aggro" was on the soccer pitch, where they sided off against each other for their weekly matches. Bobby played forward, which meant that he was always on the wrong end of rough tackles. He also got light-hearted abuse from his comrades for playing soccer ("the foreign game") instead of Gaelic football.

"You're a fucking soccer dog," the Gaelic football men would taunt him.

Ever restless, Bobby sought other activities. He decided to learn the guitar and began pestering Rab McCullough, the cage's best player, for lessons. McCullough finally gave in and taught him three basic chords. Off he went to spend hours strumming away at the chords, much to the chagrin of his hut mates.

Bobby soon had more to think about. On May 8, Geraldine gave birth to a boy who they named Gerard. As a sentenced prisoner, he now had only one visit a week instead of three. He looked forward to his visits with Geraldine because he got to see his new son, with whom he could never bond until he eventually got his release.

Gerard's birth impacted Geraldine's thinking in a different way from Bobby. She began to regret that she could not have a proper family life and she began to make plans for Bobby's release. One day, Diarmuid Fox, Bobby's best man, accompanied Geraldine and Gerard on a visit to Bobby and then Fox accompanied them to Twinbrook to visit Gerard's grandparents. On the way, Geraldine spoke up.

"I've had enough of the fight for Irish freedom," she told Fox. She said she was expecting Bobby to settle down on his release.

Back in Cage Eight, Bobby practiced his guitar while other prisoners made handicrafts or played cards. But Denis Donaldson was not interested in any of these things. He spent his time reading. Donaldson had given classes and lectures in the Crumlin Road to give the prisoners a sense of why they were fighting. The men heard about other struggles around the world: Tupamaros, the PLO, the Red Army Faction. They began wondering who these other people were, why they were fighting, and whether there was any connection with their own fight. They tried to make sense of world events and their own part in them. Soon they were reading Che Guevara and the Colombian guerrilla priest Camilo Torres.

The younger ones, like Bobby and Seanna Walsh, started asking the older prisoners about the struggle but what they were saying didn't resonate. It was too conservative and Catholic, too limited in its restricted Irish outlook. Some even supported the U.S. government against the Vietnamese, apartheid in South Africa, or colonialism in Mozambique.

Another incentive to learn was the Officials, who claimed that they were Marxists while the Provos were green fascists. Sands and Donaldson and some others asked themselves, "What are these guys on about? *Am* I a green fascist?"

Such political differences and name-calling had not been so important on the outside. But now, Bobby Sands and Seanna Walsh were among a group of younger prisoners who began to read political books. As they became politically aware, differences with other prisoners from other organizations began to matter. In jail, they felt like they needed to defend themselves intellectually as well as physically. Soon, other prisoners saw them reading and debating on political themes and more of them joined in. As they grew in knowledge they developed confidence. While Billy McKee and the older Republicans kept talking about the old ways, they were reading and talking about the *Communist Manifesto,* Trotsky, *Animal Farm,* Franz Fanon . . . everything. Then they learned that the older Republicans frowned on their readings, and that "made it even *more* interesting."

The hard end of political debate among the testosterone-pumped prisoners was still physical horseplay, which inevitably escalated into outright conflict. At the beginning of summer, the cage teams were playing their weekly soccer match when an Official prisoner brought Bobby down with an especially hard tackle. A fight started. Billy McKee went straight to the governor and demanded, again, that the Provisional prisoners be moved for their own safety. Finally, the governor agreed to move the men to some of the six new cages at the top of camp.

• • •

The authorities called Cages Sixteen to Twenty-One "phase six" of Her Majesty's Prison, The Maze. They had better huts, with brick ends that kept out the draughts and tarred roofs that blocked the rain. They had eight-foot high partitions inside, forming a hallway up the center of the hut with small rooms, or cubicles, to each side so that the men had a bit of privacy. The huts had little porches over the doors, which made it easier for the men to climb up on the roofs and look across the camp and to the outside world beyond.

In July, Bobby and Tomboy Loudon moved into a cubicle together in Cage Seventeen, next to Gerard Rooney from the Short Strand, and John

Kennan from County Fermanagh. Denis Donaldson and some of the other young radicals from the Short Strand were also in Cage Seventeen but Seanna Walsh for some reason got split from his friends when he was put into Cage Eighteen.

The Provo prisoners could organize themselves more easily in the new cages. Under the traditional leadership of Billy McKee, this meant organizing things on a militaristic basis. There were nightly parades where the staff read out important communications and conducted official business. On Sunday afternoons the prisoners fell into formation and observed two minutes silence for all those who died in the liberation struggle during the previous week. Then, the commanding officers gave out orders for the coming week and delegated work in the cage. Anyone who "broke the law" as McKee put it, had to get up an hour early and brush the yard. McKee feared the laziness that he observed in other prisoners. Everyone had to be out of bed by nine o'clock in the morning, no breakfast in bed. Lights went out at eleven o'clock every night. McKee knew that the discipline was a bit strict, but he felt it was necessary because they were a military force.[4]

The most oppressive structure was the division of cage life between "cleared" and "suspended" prisoners. Most suspended prisoners because they had broken under interrogation. Others had "undermined the authority of the IRA," which sometimes meant that they complained about the rigid aspects of cage life. Sands was cleared; although he had signed statements, his refusal to name others meant that he could play a full part in the social life of IRA volunteers within the jail. A suspended volunteer was a pariah. He could not participate in certain army activities or military lectures. He could not carry flags, hold office, or vote in elections. He was often shunned and looked down on by the others. There was even a caste system in operation, where the staff avoided dirty or menial jobs, and the worst jobs, like cleaning the toilets, were performed only by suspended volunteers.

The conservative leaders also discouraged open political discussion. The elders in Cage Eighteen held book burnings of Marxist books and pornographic magazines. They held courts of inquiry and encouraged prisoners to spy on each other. Things got so bad that Seanna Walsh requested to be transferred after he was asked to spy on a comrade who got into a row with camp staff. He was relieved when they sent him back to his old friends in Cage Seventeen.

Gerard Rooney, known simply as "Roon," was OC in Cage Seventeen. A staunch Republican and a natural leader, he looked a bit wild with his long blonde hair and shaggy beard. But he was full of street sense and had an authoritative air that commanded respect.

Roon had been a central character in one the most momentous court cases of northern Irish history. Charged with armed hijacking of a bus, the night before his trial began, two young men called at the house of the bus driver who was to give evidence against Roon. When the driver came to the door, one of them shot him dead. It stopped him from testifying but the jury still found Rooney guilty. The case became notorious in 1973 when Lord Diplock called it that "dreadful case" that convinced him that witnesses should not be compelled to testify in Northern Irish courts. His recommendations were accepted and from 1973 thousands of men and women were convicted in "Diplock courts" by a single judge without a jury. From that point, say scores of human rights activists, lawyers, academics, and journalists, normal police investigative work was replaced by interrogation, where teams of police detectives aimed to get a suspect to confess "at any cost," including mistreatment and even torture.[5]

Sands and Loudon gravitated directly to Roon when they got to Cage Seventeen. They looked up to him as a sort of mentor and Roon clearly enjoyed their loyalty. Most afternoons saw the three walking around the cage together, discussing politics, sport, or music. Being in Roon's confidence also put Sands and Loudon among a closely-knit group of prisoners from the Short Strand. For two young and impressionable men like Bobby and Tomboy, entry into such exclusive company was a cherished honor.

Life in the hut was organized around food. Between breakfast and dinner were classes and military instruction. Between dinner and tea, the prisoners trained and worked at handicrafts. From tea until lock-up at 9:00 P.M. they walked around the yard, watched TV, read, or wrote letters. Bobby read a lot and strummed on his guitar.

Each man got one "food parcel" per week from his family. Since prison food was pretty basic, parcels were important. They joined together in *cliques* ("food clicks"), and shared their parcels so that they would last the whole week. Sands and Loudon formed a click with Roon and Kennan in the next cubicle. Kennan's weekend parcel was the most important: every food click had to include a countryman because they got massive cardboard boxes full of home-cooked country goodies. Bobby looked forward to Mrs. Kennan's homemade "apple sodas."

The four men knocked down the wall between their cubicles and made one big cubicle. Bobby and Tomboy took two chairs, cut off their legs, and nailed them to the top of the partition. They called it the "cockpit." They sat there eating and watching their favorite programs on the TV at the bottom of the hut: *Top of the Pops* on Mondays, *Match of the Day* on Saturdays, wildlife documentaries any night.

Food clicks combined into larger groups to make handicrafts and share chores. Bobby's group of mostly Short Strand men called themselves a co-op. They produced leather belts and wallets, with "Long Kesh" and Gaelic designs. They worked away with music playing in the background, talking and getting into arguments. Seanna Walsh specialized in tooling the leather. Bobby dyed the designs after they were tooled. Then, the prisoners sent out the finished products and their supporters sold them to raise money for prisoners' families.

It would be hard to overestimate the importance that the solidarity and radical thinking among the prisoners from the Short Strand, under Roon's leadership, had on Bobby's intellectual development. He had already begun reading political books in Cage Eight, but Roon encouraged such intellectual development from the top.

Roon was a bit of an iconoclast as far as the prevailing rigidity of the IRA structures were concerned, a sort of an insulator between his radicals and the conservative camp leaders. This was most evident with regard to freedom to explore Marxist approaches to revolution. One of his first acts as OC was to appoint Denis Donaldson as education officer and to encourage him to build a more structured and radical program of lectures and debates.

Sands and Seanna Walsh soon immersed themselves in political study. As friends outside supplied books, they built up a revolutionary library including Carlos Marighela (*For the Liberation of Brazil*), Regis Debray (*Revolution in the Revolution*), Robert Taber (*The War of the Flea*), Franz Fanon (*The Wretched of the Earth* and *Black Mask White Skin*), and Che Guevara (*Passages of the Cuban Revolutionary War*). They read of guerrilla struggles in Colombia, Guine Bissau, Cabo Verde, and Mozambique. They read about revolutionary jail experiences in George Jackson's *Soledad Brother*. And they had classic works of Marxism like *Das Kapital* and *Quotations from Chairman Mao*. Bobby's favorite was Che Guevara.

As Bobby radicalized he became less religious and stopped going to mass. Seanna Walsh was a strict atheist. Walsh figured Bobby still believed in something but that he stopped going to mass because of the right-wing ideologies of most of the priests.

Organized education went beyond politics to the Irish language. Billy McKee appointed his closest friend, Prionsius MacAirt, to travel around the cages and keep an eye on organization and morale. A committed Irish speaker, as MacAirt went around, he taught Irish in classes of five to seven students. MacAirt taught the students classical Irish, using the old script rather than the Roman alphabet. The Irish language really took off when two Irish speakers from the south arrived in the cage and began teaching classes.

Typically, Bobby and Tomboy Loudon were among the first to learn Irish. When Seanna Walsh arrived back in Cage Seventeen he, too, joined the classes. They all quickly began to accumulate the *fainnes* (rings) that signified Irish proficiency. Encouraged by his success, Bobby began to see education as one of the more rewarding activities available to a prisoner. When debates were introduced to supplement political lectures, Bobby really took to them, despite his lack of experience in public speaking. Some time later, he would write of mindless activities like playing cards that, "alongside reading or writing, studying the Gaelic language or doing handicrafts it doesn't compare."[6]

But it was an effort to convince many prisoners of this. Most of them still saw themselves as mere guerrilla fighters whose main job was to get out of prison and back into the armed struggle. They were always trying to escape. They were reluctant to get involved in education because it was a diversion away from the "real struggle."

Danny Lennon, for one, had no time for education or lectures.

"Ah, fuckin' lectures, I'm not doing lectures," he would say to Sands and Walsh.

• • •

Bobby's energy carried over into cultural activities. He kept pestering Rab McCullough for guitar lessons. Tomboy was learning the mandolin, so they often practiced together. Then Bobby's brother John sent him in a guitar and he painted a colorful phoenix, the symbol of the Provisional IRA, on the back of it.[7] He spent hours in the evening strumming away, trying to learn more chords and songs, until somebody inevitably shouted, "Fuck sake, give it a rest!"

It wasn't just Bobby's guitar practice that annoyed people. There was only one record player between thirty-two men in the hut and he and Cleeky Clarke monopolized it. Sands got a copy of David Bowie's album, *Aladdin Sane,* and he drove the hut *in*sane playing it over and over again.

Thankfully, Bobby eventually got better on the guitar. His brother John started sending him books of songs and he learned dozens off by heart. The cage collection included several Clannad LPs and Bobby learned their Irish-language songs. He also learned songs from Christy Moore's album, *Prosperous.*

Soon, Bobby was in the middle of hut celebrations. If there was drink, nobody minded much how good he was at his instrument. Each hut made their own *poteen* (Irish moonshine) from fruit and smuggled yeast. They made a still by attaching the water pipes from the toilet onto the water boiler for tea. The "master distiller" mixed his ingredients, put weights on top of the boiler and sealed the lid with bread to keep in the steam. The worm went through a water trough for cooling, the condensed liquid coming out the other end. With great care, the distiller regulated the heat and then stood by with a plastic spoon to taste the first drops. He tested it for purity by dipping a cigarette paper into it, lighting it, and watching the color of the flame. Then a few lucky men got to put it into coffee jars, making sure to get their fill along the way.

The still was only one of the culinary inventions the men developed. Someone discovered that the big ceramic water heater in the showers was hot enough to cook on, so they made hot plates. Another discovered that he could remove an electric wire from the heater, stick it into an electric socket, and toast bread.

• • •

Eventually, Roon appointed Sands to his first position: cage sports officer. He kept team rosters and schedules and distributed the equipment to the teams. His new position put him at the center of at least one escape attempt.

Whenever a game was on, two screws[8] and a physical training instructor came to the soccer pitch, the screws to guard the soccer players and the instructor to help the men in the adjoining "gym." The escape began when one of the players walked up behind one of the screws, in full view of the watchtowers, and stuck a homemade automatic pistol in his back, saying, "I've got a gun, move around here toward the gym."

Meanwhile, the men in the gym had taken the physical training instructor and tied him up while one man put on his clothes. When they got the screw inside, one of the prisoners put on his clothes and then he went out and got the other screw into the gym in the same way as they tricked the first. When the second screw questioned whether their automatic pistol was real and began to make a move, the man with the gun cocked it and a round flew out of the chamber. It was a replica, made in the machine shop, but a convincing one that would cock if not shoot. The prisoners finished changing clothes and walked off the pitch, dressed as two screws and a physical training instructor with keys to all gates leading from pitch.

As the "screws" walked away, it was Bobby's job to supervise the soccer match and to make sure that everything kept on as normal. Everything went fine until the escapers got to the main gate, when a screw from another cage recognized them. Next thing, dozens of screws arrived at the soccer pitch where the teams were still playing. They took the men back to the cage for a head count. The prisoners messed about to confuse the screws as much as possible, in hopes that the three had escaped and that they could extend the time before the search for them began. Finally, the screws identified everyone but the missing three, who were already on their way to the punishment cells.

Chapter Seven

Things Get Hot

R elations between the prisoners and the authorities were bad and getting worse throughout 1974. To the (overwhelmingly Protestant) prison authorities, the prisoners were murderers and thugs who had attacked their community and their way of life. "Everybody heard plenty about the so-called ill-treatment of prisoners," complained a prison warder, "but we were having to cope at close-quarters with people who have killed and maimed men, women and children . . . Yet when we carried out searches or told them to turn out their pockets after a visit from a relative, in fact just do our job efficiently to make sure they were not planning a breakout, then there were often fisticuffs, or worse, all round and a major outcry from politicians and the public about us."[1]

To the prisoners, the screws represented an unjust state with which they were at war. The prisoners did not recognize their authority. They felt that it was their duty to resist. In short, Long Kesh contained two irreparably opposing groups whose conflicts were sometimes containable but irreconcilable. Conflicts inevitably escalated as the prisoners created new ways of resisting and the authorities found new forms of suppression.

In early 1974, a conflict emerged over the issue of compassionate parole. Prisoners from Northern Ireland got a few hours to attend a funeral when an immediate family member died. Prisoners from the south, however, got no parole. In March, a prisoner from Dublin heard that his father died and requested compassionate parole. The prison authorities refused. In response, the prisoners organized a hunger strike.

Five men started the protest on March 9. A week later, five others, including Gerry Rooney, joined the strike. Roon delegated Sands and Loudon to take his food to the gate after each meal to show that he hadn't eaten.[2] After about three weeks the authorities granted liberalized parole.

Relations worsened throughout the summer. The prisoners complained that rations were shortchanged and that food often arrived late and cold. They complained because their sheets were changed just once every two weeks. And the issue of visits continually galled them because the screws hovered over them, watching and listening as they visited their wives and children.

Visiting conditions worsened after one prisoner escaped by impersonating another who had been given temporary parole to get married. Although he was recaptured within days, prison Governor Edward Truesdale decided to prevent direct contact between prisoners and their visitors, thereby raising the level of animosity.[3]

The prisoners protested. On July 26, the prisoners threw seven hundred lunches over the fences and in one cage they burnt their bedding, beds, and mattresses.[4] At the start of September they began refusing prison food altogether. When it arrived, they chucked it over the fence, claiming that otherwise the prison staff would re-serve it to them the next day.[5] The prisoners did not worry as long as they had their food parcels and the prison shop, where they could buy packaged food. So the prison authorities stopped their parcels and closed the shop. Thereafter, the prisoners ate just the three slices of white bread and milk that arrived in the cage each morning.

To protest the shortage of clean laundry, they hung their dirty sheets and pillowcases on the barbed wire fences around the cages. They blamed the trouble on prison Governor Truesdale who, they said, just wanted to run a concentration camp.[6] The IRA issued a statement calling Truesdale a "dictator" who was at war against the prisoners and warned that if the problems were not solved that they would strike at "ALL THOSE who work in Long Kesh."[7]

Word went around the prisoners that they would burn the camp if the authorities did not make concessions. Roon advised the men in Cage Seventeen to send out their treasured possessions. Bobby sent out copybooks full of notes and his guitar to his brother Sean. Denis Donaldson sent out the cage library to his brother in Portlaoise jail in the south of Ireland.[8]

The prisoners made other contingency plans. They improved communications between cages by training squads in semaphore. A man standing on top of a Nissen hut could see across the whole camp. Two men in each cage learned semaphore; one wrote down messages while the other waved the flags and took messages from the other cages. As usual, Bobby and Tomboy were the first to volunteer.[9]

On September 23, as tempers ran high, warders caught two IRA prisoners attempting to escape.[10] In the aftermath, the British army took over the cages and carried out a thorough search.[11] The following day, the prisoners warned publicly that if the British army came back into any of the cages, "we will burn this camp to the ground leaving not one stone on top of another."[12]

After interventions by clergy and human rights groups, the tensions appeared to be defused. Truesdale said he would improve the food and provide more clean bedding. In response, the prisoners accepted the food and took the sheets down from the wire.[13]

But tensions remained and things finally boiled over a week later. Evidently, the problem started over two packages of pancakes.[14] Every evening around 6:00 P.M. the screws sent snacks such as sandwiches around the cages. That evening in Cage Thirteen, the prisoner in charge of the canteen found that they had only ninety pancakes for ninety-two men. When he went out to request more pancakes, the screw said the prisoners had stolen them and then hurled a tirade of abuse at the man. Eyewitnesses claim he was drunk.

A row ensued, which eventually turned bitter. The prisoners' commanding officer eventually used his only real weapon: he told the prison staff that they would not be allowed in the cage under any circumstances and that the prisoners would not talk to them or cooperate with them in any way.

"My two men will be in there at six o'clock tonight and you'll do nothing to them," the head prison officer responded.

When the warders came in, they were met by some of the toughest prisoners in the cage. Dozens more guards rushed in and a melee began.

In no time the assistant governor arrived at Cage Thirteen and called out the names of the commanding officer and his adjutant, saying that he intended to remove them to the punishment block.

"Go and fuck yourself," was the reply.

So the assistant governor threatened to send in the British army to take the two men from the cage by force.

"Fuck you and the British army both," said the commanding officer.

Word of the dispute quickly went round the camp. Bobby and Tomboy took their flags onto the roof of their hut to stand by for messages. They were the closest to Cage Thirteen, where the trouble originated, so they acted as liaison between there and the commanding officer of the prison, Davey Morley, next door in Cage Sixteen.

From the roof, Sands received the instruction from Morley: keep watch and send a warning if the British army approaches Cage Thirteen. Messages went back and forth furiously. One prisoner said that the semaphore flags were going like windmills.

Soon, Bobby and Tomboy saw the tops of helmets bobbing up and down behind the dog kennels. Troops were marching to a blind spot beside Cage Thirteen, preparing to go in. Sands flagged to Cage Thirteen that they were on their way while Tomboy told Morley in Cage Sixteen.

Morley asked the prison authorities if he could visit Cage Thirteen. They refused his request. So Morley shouted the order.

"Okay, burn the camp at nine o'clock."[15]

Bobby went back to his flags and began sending the signal to all of the cages.

"Burn the camp."

• • •

Denis Donaldson and Seanna Walsh were sitting in front of the TV in the Gaeltacht hut at a few minutes to nine. It was Monday night and they had been waiting all week for a program on UTV, *Year of the Wildebeest*, about the migration of wildebeest in the Serengeti. They were waiting for the documentary to start, pancakes on their knees, when a fellow prisoner ran in, shouting, "They're burning the fucking place."

He lifted the TV off of its stand and threw it to the floor, breaking it into pieces. Sands and Loudon came down off the roof. They went into their cubicle to rip up magazines and break furniture. Anything that would burn went into middle of hut. Then they threw gasoline all around and set the hut on fire. The huts were soon ablaze. They had removed all the furniture from the canteen to use it as a gym, so there was not a stick in it to burn. They just knocked the walls down on each end. There was no way to burn the brick washhouse so they broke up the toilets and sinks.

In Cage Six, on the internees' end of the camp, Gerry Adams was watching the huts burn. Through the smoke and flames he heard Kris Kristofferson singing "Me and Bobby Magee," one of Bobby's favorite songs. As the fire took hold of the record player, Kristofferson's gruff voice got slower and more distorted until it finally stopped altogether.

Back in Cage Seventeen, Roon gave the order to smash open the gate and burn the watchtowers. Seanna Walsh was in a group that pulled the British troops out of the watchtowers and then set them on fire. They took the butane gas bottles that the sentries used for heat and threw them into the middle of the fire. They barely jumped down from the towers before they came tumbling down as the bottles exploded.

Meanwhile, Sands and Loudon went to burn the long portakabins where visits took place. On the way back they pulled up wooden posts from the wire fences to use as weapons. By now, their huts were burnt and melted heaps. The corrugated tin sheets from their roofs lay crumpled and caved in.

The men broke through the chain-link fences onto the soccer pitches in the middle of the camp. Bobby went to the small gym next to the soccer pitch with a can of fuel to set it on fire. Diarmuid Fox, now imprisoned, came over and they exchanged a few quick words. Fox told him how Geraldine had said that she expected Bobby to leave the IRA on his release. Bobby had different intentions that "were not solely family oriented." He made it clear that he would be going back into the struggle when he got out. Even from their short conversation, Fox thought that Bobby was "surprisingly articulate," like he had been reading and developing himself. He left as Bobby finished setting fire to the hut. It would be the last time they ever saw each other.

By midnight, everything was burned that could be burned. The prisoners gathered on the soccer pitch. It was a clear, cool autumn night. They had taken the tins out of the prison shop before they burned it. They built fires and threw in the tins until they expanded with the heat. Then, they pierced them with knives and ate the cooked food.

The atmosphere was electric, despite the British army helicopters flying ominously overhead. The prisoners wandered freely, visiting friends whom they had not seen for ages. Some wore blankets over their heads like Mexican panchos. One man had taken a doctor's cloak and stethoscope from the hospital and he was going around impersonating a doctor.

Bobby met his old friend Jimmy Rafferty from Twinbrook and they had a long talk. Raff was back in prison, interned without trial for the second

time. They talked about the members of Bobby's old IRA unit. Raff saw two
of them from time to time because they had also been interned. Four others
had fled to Australia very quickly, perhaps in suspicious circumstances. Jim
Kerr had been killed by Loyalists. A couple of the women had fallen away.
There were just a couple of fellows left. The unit was practically devastated.

Talk turned to the future. Raff didn't say much; as an internee with no
release date the future was a bit of a black box. Bobby said he would go
straight back on active service as soon as he got out.

"But see this time, we have to be smarter about this," he said. "We also
have to get involved in the community. See this whole thing about Twinbrook being a stickie stronghold, that's all wrong. That's all a fallacy that
we have to destroy when we get out."

Rafferty was intrigued by this new, more political turn in Bobby's
thinking. His old friend was rapidly maturing in prison.

"That's all well and good," he replied. "But . . . what's a fallacy?"

Bobby explained the meaning of "fallacy" and the old friends parted.

The atmosphere quickly turned sour when the helicopters started dropping canisters on the prisoners below. The gas was evil stuff, much stronger
than CS gas. It burned the skin terribly. The gassing stopped and the men
eventually recovered and got back to socializing. There was still danger in
the air. Everyone knew the British army would eventually come in . . . heavy.

The army came at dawn, from all directions, firing hundreds of gas
canisters and rubber bullets. They rammed through the fences with their
Saracens and they flooded in on foot. A pitched hand-to-hand battle
began all over the soccer pitches. The prisoners fought with poles, bricks,
and whatever else they could improvize. Both sides took hostages
although neither had anywhere to put them. Both sides gained and lost
ground. But the result was a foregone conclusion.

Tomboy Loudon got hit with a gas canister on the back of his leg and
it swelled up so that he could hardly walk. Sands was bludgeoned by
batons. Seanna Walsh got split up from Bobby and was hit in the face
with a rubber bullet and knocked out. After three hours, the British army
finally began to wear down the prisoners.

Then, as one prisoner tells it, "the enemy donned strange looking
masks like something out of *Dr. Who.*" The helicopters came overhead
and dropped more gas. It was "totally effective." Prisoners doubled up in
pain and tried to throw up but they couldn't. It made Gerry Adams feel
like he was drowning.[16] Others thought they were on fire.

The British army closed in, firing rubber bullets. According to the prisoners, they beat them and then they made them run a gauntlet of baton-wielding soldiers. It was so bad that even the Loyalist prisoners shouted at the army to stop. The ground was littered with small gas cylinders marked "CR Gas" and "MoD."[17]

Then the British army herded them back into their cages and lined them up against the wire. Tomboy and Bobby watched in horror as British commandos forced the prisoners in Cage Sixteen to run piggyback through gauntlets of batons.

Then a soldier came over to them.

"Right. You two, clean those toilets."

They looked over at the brick washhouse where he was pointing. There were toilets, all right, but they were all smashed to bits along with the sinks. There was nothing to clean. Nonetheless, the soldier ordered them to grab a nearby rubbish bin and to take it over to an outside water tap and fill it. There was a hole in the bin and the water came flying out. The soldier made them each take a side of the bin and carry it round and round in circles, beating them as they went.

"Move, move . . . ," he shouted.

"Fuck away off," Bobby replied and then he fell. Tomboy tried to help him up but the Brit whacked them again.

"Move, move." He was at them again.

Just then a British officer drove up in a Jeep.

"Stop!" he commanded and he asked the soldier for his number.

Sands and Loudon turned and looked at each other.

"Thank fuck!" they said, in unison.

Then, all of a sudden, the British soldiers were away. The screws came back with carts loaded with milk and sandwiches. The men were totally exhausted and sore, yet their spirits were high. Over in Cage Thirteen, where the trouble started, a prisoner from Belfast looked at the sandwiches and shouted at the screws, "There better be ninety-two of these— or there's going to be fucking trouble here."

• • •

The cage was a smouldering ruin. Only the canteen and the washhouse were left standing. Seanna Walsh was in the Royal Victoria hospital. Others had been gassed, beaten, bitten by army dogs. Yet they felt a sense of victory that made their bruises and hurts worthwhile. In one cage, the prison warders laughed at the state of the prisoners until they all rose, produced a football, and began defiantly playing "forty-two aside" soccer.

The words of one prisoner captures the mood,

> *We were beaten but not broken; and since the object of the exer-*
> *cise was to break us, it failed. We claimed the victory; and in ret-*
> *rospect, I believe we won. The atmosphere among the prisoners*
> *before, during and after the fire was electric. We had compelled*
> *our enemy to use chemical warfare . . .*[18]

The burning of Long Kesh would be a key episode in Bobby Sands's life. He learned lessons about conflict. The material weapons were practically all on one side—from Saracens and rubber bullets all the way to helicopters and gas. Yet the prisoners had solidarity and common purpose. The more the enemy beat them physically, the more it lost morally. Throughout the months leading up to the burning, the prisoners learned to use their powerlessness as a weapon. The less they had—symbolically in terms of rights like freedom of movement, or materially in terms of food and bedding—the more they were able to mobilize a sense of righteous indignation both within themselves and from potentially sympathetic communities outside of the prison.

The months leading up to the fire had an unmistakable pattern of escalation. The prisoners created new forms of protest over an injustice. The authorities reacted with new kinds of repression, clearly hoping to contain rebellion through force. The prisoners reacted to every move by raising the stakes a little bit higher. They turned injustices back on the authorities by engaging in *self*-deprivation. The utter confusion and lack of control this imposed on the authorities and the sense of injustice it created within the wider society outside of prison, was perhaps the prisoners' greatest weapon. Their ultimate weapon: they destroyed their very surroundings, refusing to accept imprisonment physically *and* symbolically. In so doing they "compelled the enemy to use chemical warfare" and then to leave them in their devastation, giving the outside world no choice but to be horrified.

Bobby Sands learned a personal lesson from the confrontation: he could endure seemingly limitless physical and emotional degradations and even turn them to advantage. Was it possible, in certain circumstances, that the more one lost, the freer one became? His favorite Kris Kristofferson song began to have new meaning. *Freedom's just another word for nothing left to lose.* He had been beaten to a pulp, yet he achieved a greater exhilaration than he had ever felt in his life. Bobby was learning to transcend his immature youthful bravado into something much more powerful and sustainable.

Yet, he still had a relatively low level of political awareness. He did not have a deep understanding about *why* he and his comrades could endure these deprivations, apart from a gut-level "us" and "them" understanding of the necessity of opposing his oppressors. Nor were the prisoners fully aware of how they could effectively use the media in their struggle. They released press statements but they were still largely protesting and talking among themselves. Where would they go from here? How could they take their struggle to a higher stage?

The burning of Long Kesh was an important episode in the Irish Republican prison struggle. Yet it also forced the British government to find new ways of suppressing such rebellions. Their decisions would change the whole nature of the conflict between themselves and Irish Republicans, particularly in the prisons. To respond to the challenge, Bobby Sands and his comrades in the now smouldering ruin that was Cage Seventeen would soon have to undergo a process of political development beyond anything they had so far imagined.

Chapter Eight

Learning to Rebel

A fter the burning, the prisoners expected to be moved to another jail. The prison authorities kept them where they were. Given the state of the cage, the first order of business was to gather anything useable. Bricks, corrugated sheets, bits of wood, and wire all went together in a heap that the prisoners called "the pile." Some slept on the floor of the canteen. Others used stuff in "the pile" to make a shantytown of small huts, table height with a tin roof and sheets of clear plastic at either end to gather the sun and make them warm. A few men could sleep in each hut. A visiting priest compared their conditions to the slum dwellers of São Paulo. To make matters worse, it was wet and stormy the first night and many of their makeshift huts blew down.[1]

There were no toilet facilities so the prisoners pissed against the perimeter wire. If they needed a shit, they lifted a manhole cover where the huts used to be and squatted over it. They lived this way for weeks.

For a couple of days they lived on bread and milk and then the British army supplied porridge in the morning and stew for dinner. The screws brought British army mattresses and a couple of blankets for each prisoner. Roon sent out a call for supporters and community groups to send clothes. Slowly, the prisoners used their initiative to improve their primitive living conditions. Kevin Carson, the handyman, organized squads to clean off the bricks from the pile so that they could make a dry wall around the manhole for a privy. The British army pulled down the water tank so Carson worked up a stand where a fire could be built under it to heat water for baths.

Carson's inventiveness knew no bounds. At one point he got some rolls of polyurethane sheeting and two Ping-Pong tables and made a swimming pool. It was just a couple of feet deep, but to the prisoners it was a luxury. A sense of freedom prevailed. Men grew beards and spent their days rummaging for souvenirs, rigging up showers, building shelters, and telling tall tales about the "battle of the football pitch." At night they organized concerts around open campfires under the stars.[2]

Despite the high morale, this was not a sustainable lifestyle, especially for older or wounded prisoners. So the prisoners' leaders requested and got some small portakabins for these "hard cases" to sleep in away from the elements.

Boxes and bags of clothing soon began arriving from support groups and charitable organizations. The prison authorities held back the clothes until members of the clergy threatened to call in the Red Cross. One support group complained to the press when they heard that the men had not received their shipment of four thousand pounds worth of clothing.[3]

When they finally got the clothes, Roon gave Bobby and Tomboy the task of sorting them out. Bobby searched desperately for a pair of Doc Martens boots. In one shipment, they found some bush hats. They grabbed them immediately and wore them constantly. It became their symbol.

The prison authorities began to rebuild Cages Nine to Twelve to house the men in the burnt out cages but as the cold weather moved in and the bad publicity mounted, they moved the prisoners temporarily from Cage Seventeen into a hastily rebuilt Cage Twenty-Two. There, they doubled up with the men who were already there at more than seventy men to a hut.

Some compensation for the cramped conditions came when the men started getting visits again with their families and loved ones. Geraldine brought Gerard for her first visit on the same bus with Tomboy Loudon's parents. Sands and Loudon were called out together to see them. Rumors of seriously injured prisoners abounded after the burning and the visitors were relieved to see their loved ones unharmed.

About the only memorable thing about Cage Twenty-Two was an escape attempt. The prisoners decided to dig a tunnel. Conditions were ripe for it. Not only was the whole prison camp in confusion and the yard of Cage Twenty-Two terribly crowded, there was still building going on in Cages Nine to Twelve. As the men in Cage Twenty-Two tried to tunnel, another group in Cage Five succeeded in digging a 134-foot tunnel. Thirty-three men crawled through it and ran for the nearby motorway one early morning in November. British soldiers spotted them and shot one of them dead, Hugh Coney.[4] The rest were captured within hours.

The men in Cage Five were on the perimeter of the camp and did not have far to tunnel. Cage Twenty-Two, on the other hand, was in the middle of the camp. Yet the men figured that there must be a main sewer somewhere, connecting all of the cages in the prison camp. All they had to do was tunnel outward to find it.

Their tunnel's entrance was under the bed of a disabled prisoner who had been shot when he was captured. Whenever the screws came in to search the hut he lay there, unable to move "for medical reasons."

The huts' roofs were made of two sheets of corrugated roofing, with a four- to five-inch gap between the inner and outer layers. The roofing sheets had a big overlap, so the prisoners took out a few of the inner sheets and used them for shoring up the tunnels. The hut had six fluorescent lights so they took one into the tunnel and rearranged the others so that the screws never noticed. They used the fan from the hut's blow heaters to ventilate the tunnel. Water seeped quickly into the tunnel so Carson made an ingenious pump out of some downspouts, a metal mop handle, and some plastic sheeting. Everything could be set up, or taken down and put back into its original condition, within a half an hour.

For weeks they tunneled. Sands took turns down the hole. Seanna Walsh was too tall, so he sewed bags for the soil out of blankets and mattress covers. When they ran out of blankets, they tied up the sleeves of old shirts and filled them up with soil. They put the bags of soil between the external and internal sheets of corrugated tin. The inner tin sheets sagged so much that the men could not believe that the screws never spotted it. Then one day a prison officer came into the cage.

"Get your things together, you're moving to a new cage."

The men were in no mood to move. They reluctantly headed for their new home. On the way out someone put a big sign up over the hatch with an arrow pointing down to the floor. It read, TUNNEL.[5]

• • •

Cage Eleven was their new home. The Nissen huts were of the older, draftier variety. The most momentous change, however, was the arrival of two new prisoners who would have a tremendous impact on Bobby's life.

Gerry Adams had been interned since July 1972 in Cage Six of Long

Kesh, where he lived with his friend and comrade Brendan "the Dark" Hughes. They were never charged or convicted of anything but were nonetheless considered by the British to be top leaders of the Belfast IRA.[6] After eight months, Hughes escaped in the back of a garbage truck. Adams was not so lucky. In July 1974, he was caught for the second time trying to escape. Soon after the burning, the screws came and took him away to court. Ironically, escape from uncharged internment was his first legal conviction. Adams was given eighteen months imprisonment and transferred to the sentenced cages just in time to join the men in their move to Cage Eleven.

Meanwhile, Brendan Hughes had also got into trouble. Within days of escaping, he was back in Belfast working for the IRA. He dyed his hair, put on a suit, and established an identity as a traveling toy salesman. Hughes lived outside of the "war zones" of Belfast but traveled into them with his briefcase—not to sell toys but to organize IRA attacks. He got away with it for a year but in May 1974 the British army finally caught him and he went to Cage Eleven to serve his time alongside his old comrade Gerry Adams . . . and Bobby Sands.

Adams and Hughes settled together with other veteran prisoners in the middle hut of Cage Eleven, known thereafter as the "generals' hut" because of its high-ranking residents. The next hut over was the Gaeltacht hut where Bobby shared a cubicle with Tomboy Loudon. Prisoners in the other huts called them the "leprechaun men." Adams soon got to know Sands through political lectures and debates in the cage.[7]

The level of Irish in the Gaeltacht hut improved rapidly. No one was allowed to watch TV until nighttime. Only Irish was spoken before then. There were intensive Irish classes and prisoners from other huts came to learn Irish. The two main Gaelic teachers were Donal Billings and Cyril MacCurtain, two southern Irishmen. Sometimes classes were given by Daithi Power, a rather remarkable man who was illiterate in English yet taught himself Irish to a high degree of fluency.

Bobby had already achieved a level of competency in Irish well beyond Tomboy's. He began writing short pieces in Irish. In early 1975, soon after they moved to Cage Eleven, Sands and Loudon prepared for their gold *fainne* (ring), an award that indicates fluency in the Irish language. When they got to the half-hut before their test, MacCurtain was already there, chatting in Irish to Power. They brought Bobby and Tomboy into the conversation and everyone talked casually about politics, TV, and general events. After awhile, Bobby began wondering when the test would begin. Finally, just as they were about to complain, MacCurtain and Power interrupted the conversation to inform both of them that they had earned their *fainnes*. They never realized they had been taking a test!

• • •

The portakabins that housed infirm prisoners after the burning were turned into "study huts." When there were no classes, Bobby was often there strumming on his guitar. Nightly music sessions in the huts were common and Bobby now sang more songs in Irish. The men made a mock-up of one of these sessions so that they could photograph it for outside propaganda. In the photo, a dozen prisoners are sitting around a table set with coffee jars full of "poteen" (the jars were actually full of water; the real poteen was not yet ready). The men have cups of "moonshine" in their hands and clearly enjoying the "party." Bobby is in the middle of the back, with his hat and guitar and a big grin, leading the singsong.

The assessment of Bobby's voice depends on whom you ask. Physical descriptions of his voice range from "deep" to "gravelly" or even "raspy." He is most often compared to Bob Dylan, although his earlier friends associate him with Rod Stewart. Whatever the assessment of his singing abilities, Bobby clearly loved to sing and he had a remarkable facility for remembering lyrics.

When he was not playing music, Bobby swapped records with Cleeky Clarke or Danny Lennon, the other musical men in the cage. Favorite records now were by Wings, the Eagles, Bob Dylan, and Neil Young. Bobby and Cleeky shared a fondness for Loudon Wainwright III.

Joe Barnes came to the cage in early 1976 and his first memories of Bobby Sands are his singing. Barnes noticed that Bobby threw himself into everything he did with remarkable energy. One Christmas concert the curtains opened and Bobby was singing "Maggie May." Bobby threw himself into the song so completely that Barnes thought he was show-boating until he realized that it was just that Bobby invested so much energy into his singing.[8]

This unusual level of energy kept Sands going in prison. Unlike others, he was seldom visited by the "big D," as some prisoners called periods of depression. Jake Jackson remembers him as, "a happy guy, it was obvious to see he was quite content . . . he didn't do bird, he done time well."

While Bobby's musical and sporting interests continued in Cage Eleven, so did his sense of style. The most famous image of Bobby—the one which appeared on posters in Ireland and throughout the world during the hunger strike of 1981—was cropped from a group photograph with Tomboy Loudon, Gerard Rooney, and Denis Donaldson. In the photograph, Sands and Loudon are noticeably better groomed than the others. Clean-shaven Bobby, with his long amber hair, wears a trendy red V-neck jumper. In another set of photos, Roon wears a bush hat, cut-off jeans, and a sloppy black cardigan, unbuttoned at the bottom with his belly hanging out. Walsh is shirtless, with cut-off jean shorts and sunglasses. Donaldson is in shorts and a t-shirt. Yet Bobby is wearing a neat black knit shirt and pressed jeans.

• • •

Cage Eleven was made up of all sorts of people. As Gerry Adams described it, some were "quite innocent and uninvolved"; others were "innocent but had been politically active"; some just wanted to get their time in by doing handicrafts and maybe came along to the odd political debate; and, finally, there were some "political animals."[9] By now, Bobby was solidly among the "political animals."

He was already familiar with radical ideas, like the communal models of guerrilla organization and mutual solidarity that Che and Fidel had developed in the Sierra Maestra in Cuba. But radical as he was in his readings and discussions, he never seriously questioned the conservative IRA leadership in the prison. He generally accepted the militaristic top-down discipline that prevailed and was unable to confront the contradictions between the dictatorial, militaristic style of leadership that Davey Morley encouraged and the revolutionary thinking that he was confronting in his readings and educational discussions.

Bobby and his mates had not yet worked out the apparent contradictions between their interest in the radical internationalist politics of Che Guevara and the other very Nationalist and Catholic identity that centered on the Irish language. Joe Barnes, one of the more politically astute men in the cage at the time, ranked the Gaeltacht men "pretty much along with the political dinosaurs."

There were also personality issues. Gerard Rooney, Bobby's role model, was close to the prison leadership, especially after he was promoted from cage OC to camp quartermaster in 1974. Roon, in turn, sponsored and protected Sands and Loudon. He appointed them to important positions, like organizing his quartermaster's supplies. Under Roon, Bobby was not *just* a volunteer but a trusted favorite who was picked to do important tasks and who performed them enthusiastically and unquestioningly.

He was also still young and inexperienced. He and Tomboy had just turned twenty in 1974 and Seanna Walsh was even younger. The parades, the training, the orders were all very impressive to young volunteers. Without alternative role models—charismatic leaders who challenged the conservative ethos—young volunteers like Bobby could hardly translate their readings into revolutionary practice. They needed their own "Che," to challenge them and encourage them in more radical directions. As circumstances would have it, the arrival of Gerry Adams and Brendan Hughes brought just such an influence to the young radicals. In so doing, they would change the direction of the whole Republican Movement.

● ● ●

Adams's and Hughes's arrival in Cage Eleven started a pot boiling that had been simmering for some time. The latent dispute between younger volunteers and the more conservative and Catholic veterans coincided with a parallel dispute within the IRA about Britain's intentions in Ireland. 1974 had been a bad year in Ireland and England, not just in terms of IRA bombs and other violence but also with the collapse of an attempted power-sharing government in Northern Ireland. At the end of 1974, after a group of Protestant clergymen opened a series of talks with the IRA, contacts between the British government and the IRA led to a truce. What began as a limited Christmas cease-fire was extended throughout most of 1975. British Secretary of State Merlyn Rees promised the IRA that if it extended its cease-fire, he would phase out internment, quit detaining young Catholics, replace British troops with police and introduce other reforms. Ultimately, he hoped, a permanent reduction of IRA violence would enable him to establish local government and allow the RUC to take over functions from the British army.

Every British "concession" had two sides. They would end internment but also remove political prisoner status and treat IRA prisoners like "ordinary criminals." They provided "incident centers" for Sinn Féin that gave the party a legitimate political presence at British government expense, but these centers also gave British intelligence an invaluable resource to watch the comings and goings of Republican activists. Rees was clear in his own mind that the reforms would only "normalize" Northern Ireland, without endangering its constitutional position within the United Kingdom. Ultimately, he aimed to defeat the IRA. In his own words, Rees figured that, "the longer the cease-fire lasted, the more difficult it would be for them to start a campaign from scratch."[10] The IRA leadership insisted that the British were beginning to withdraw from Ireland.

This assertion was nothing new. The IRA leadership had been claiming that victory was "imminent" since late 1973, when the *Republican News* ran an article entitled "British Army Starts Withdrawal."[11] In May 1974, the paper ran a front-page story claiming that the British Minister of Defense Roy Mason had admitted that his troops had "lost the war," and cited the last day of 1974 as the planned "English withdrawal date."[12] Now, the IRA leadership claimed that British withdrawal was an integral part of the truce process.

Many younger prisoners believed them. They had been in jail for years and were now being told by their leaders that they would soon be released because the British were withdrawing.

"We wanted to see this in terms of a British withdrawal, so we did," admits Seanna Walsh.

Bobby's continuing belief in the leadership is displayed in a scribble that he wrote on the inside cover of an Irish book that he was reading: "Roibeard Ó Seachnasaigh, Cas 11, Ceis fada, Blian 75, Blian Saoirse" (Bobby Sands, Cage Eleven, Long Kesh, 1975, Year of Freedom).[13]

Adams and Hughes argued the opposite: the British were not withdrawing, the war was not yet over, and the struggle had to be rebuilt with politically educated rank-and-file volunteers. They spoke of a "long war," with implications for all aspects of the struggle. Most importantly, the struggle had to become more politicized; it had to offer something to the communities at its center if they were to support it over the long haul. They opposed the IRA's strategy outside of jail. They viewed the struggle as an anti-colonial war of liberation and saw the IRA's retaliatory campaign against Protestants as a diversion that played straight into the hands of the British state. Inside prison, they opposed the undemocratic, authoritarian, non-transparent, overly militaristic, and anti-Marxist leadership of Davey Morley and his camp staff.

Adams and Hughes had considerable personal charisma. Adams was tall and skinny, with a very quick mind and an ability to analyze and persuade. But he was thoughtful and careful, considered all of the angles, and rarely made a decisive move until he knew he could win. Hughes, on the other hand, was legendary as a man of action. Like Adams, he was extremely personable, with a ready wit and an almost immediate ability to relate to his comrades. Unlike Adams, he had a quick temper and spoke his mind with ruthless honesty. Their charisma made the pair a threat to the prevailing IRA leadership both inside and outside of prison.

Hughes chafed at Morley's oppressive discipline, which he described as "a British army-type of militarism."[14] Adams, less dramatically, viewed the problem as "little bits of schism of factionalism" that were inevitable when you had a couple of hundred men of all ages put together, whether in a monastery or a prison camp or a commune. Nonetheless, he immediately recognized big differences in Cage Eleven from the lifestyle he had as an internee. Although the younger men from Cage Eleven describe their time there as a bit of a wild party, Adams thought it was "almost monastic." The internees never really settled down much. But the sentenced prisoners had fixed terms to serve, up to twenty years or even life, so they settled into a routine. They studied and made handicrafts. The lights went off at a respectable time. People sat about reading and writing letters. The television was kept at a respectable volume.

Adams could see good and bad aspects of this discipline. The openness to education, reading, and learning was good. Life could be a lot less hectic for him than it had been in the internment cages. But the daily parades and drills, frowning on prisoners who read Marx, or pressuring them to attend mass were negative aspects of control that were imposed on the younger men by older prisoners who had been socialized into prison struggles in the 1940s and the 1950s.

While he sympathized with the desires of his new comrades in Cage Eleven to create a liberalized regime and a radical ethos, Adams says he had no intention of leading them in that enterprise.

"My very firm intention when I went to the sentenced end was to do my time and to learn Irish . . . I got a sentence of three years and then I got another sentence, so I didn't want to be involved in any of this at all."

Yet he was "inveigled" into a leadership position by the men in Cage Eleven, who wanted him to help them sort out their differences with the militaristic camp staff. Adams began to liberalize the militaristic ethos and to secularize what he calls the "broad Catholic ethos" of the existing prison regime, largely by intensifying the radical education program in the cage. Despite his initial reluctance, Adams admits that "education helped me to do my time."

Adams was cautious. He constantly beat into the others, including Hughes, to stay within the Movement's lines because he knew that Cage Eleven was barely tolerated by the camp staff. Hughes, on the other hand, could not contain his open disdain for Morley and once told him straight to his face that he could build a far better group of volunteers with self-discipline and comradeship than Morley's brand of enforced discipline.[15]

The militaristic leadership tried to control dissent by creating a culture of mistrust. Hughes describes a "frightening" regime where men literally hid in lockers listening for signs of dissent. Hughes and Adams joked about a secret "Morley pill" that the commanding officer dropped into a prisoner's tea to turn him into a snitch.

Morley's people, however, insisted that Adams and Hughes simply failed to accept discipline. They had been top leaders outside of jail but now they could not stand being under the discipline of the camp staff.[16]

The thoughtful and careful Adams began to educate the younger radicals in Cage Eleven, encouraging them to question the prevailing leadership and their strategies. He took their discussions and debates as the basis of a series of articles he wrote under the name "Brownie," which he smuggled out for publication in the movement's Belfast newspaper, *Republican News*. These articles challenged the existing leadership in subtle ways, chipping away at them through reasoned argument and clever analogy.

Brendan Hughes was not so subtle in his opposition.

"It was clear where I stood, quite clear where I stood," he recalls. "Gerry was shrewder in his opposition . . . Me being who I was I was more verbally antagonistic toward them all."

While the men in Cage Eleven immediately accepted Adams as their OC, they were far from unified about the need for change either in the prison leadership or in the overall leadership and strategy of the IRA. For Bobby, continued support for Davey Morley was a matter of army discipline. He was an IRA volunteer who had been trained to follow orders without question.

Hughes's open defiance of the leadership led to his first direct encounter with Bobby Sands. Hughes had been criticizing the IRA leadership in front of other prisoners for their sectarian bombing campaign against Protestants, which he said played into the hands of the British government's campaign to portray the Irish struggle as tribal warfare between two equally repugnant groups of natives.

One day, Roon brought Bobby and another prisoner into the Dark's hut to arrest him. They escorted Hughes to the study hut, where Roon accused him of dissenting against the authority of the IRA leadership and gave him a severe reprimand. Roon ordered Hughes to stop his opposition to the leadership or he would be court-martialed.

Hughes went back to his hut, seething with anger. He packed up his gear and prepared to leave Cage Eleven to join the Irish National Liberation Army (INLA) prisoners in another cage.[17] Adams persuaded him to stay.

In hindsight, Hughes admits that the position of the arresting party that detained him was not as clear-cut as he thought at the time. Once he got to know Bobby and began talking to him, he realized he and Roon were already coming round to his way of thinking. But they were disciplined IRA volunteers. Bobby's heart was not in the arrest, yet he did it as a matter of IRA discipline.

• • •

Over the next six to nine months, Bobby's resistance to change broke down. He began to question the movement's strategies, both inside and outside of jail, as he raised his political consciousness to a higher level. Gerry Adams encouraged all of the young prisoners to participate in an intensified program of political education that promoted debate and political self-awareness. He gave them new confidence to develop their radical political ideology and protected them from the camp officers as they did so. Adams and Hughes also won their loyalty by demonstrating solidarity with them rather than demanding obedience. Personality conflicts dissolved. Soon, Cage Eleven had a more collective leadership and collective responsibility. In their military parades, everybody fell in together and ordinary volunteers got to dismiss the parade. Cage staff did menial tasks alongside ordinary volunteers. Even the distinction between cleared and uncleared prisoners was largely ignored.

Cage Eleven became the center of challenge to the established leadership as Adams built "a number of enterprises" to raise the prisoners' political awareness. Denis Donaldson simply says that Adams took his "half-assed" education program and moved it up a few gears. He introduced new classes that critically deconstructed Republican ideology and policy. He resourced them by starting a book club that provided the necessary materials for self-education. Adams used his contacts to supply the book club and to build up a cage library. Prisoners gave up their food parcels to get books, instead. Bobby Sands, says Adams, had "a more than normal interest" in these activities.

But Adams insists that his objectives were limited to critically discussing the broad objectives and policies of Republicanism and not trashing the leadership's specific tactics or strategy.

"When you're in prison you're in a sort of twilight zone," he says, "and you can't deal with what you're picking up through loose talk or gossip or conjecture. *But you could deal with big issues.*"

Thus, while the new curriculum began with fairly abstract studies of certain phases of Irish history, or radical Irish political thinkers like James Connolly with whom the prisoners would find a natural attraction, the historical discussions graduated into a general debate about what was going on in the current conflict. Adams almost surreptitiously got the men to consider whether the movement needed change. Just as important as the content of the lectures, he encouraged a new attitude toward education, emphasizing its participatory side. To get prisoners to participate, the content and method of education had to relate to their own lives.

While "political animals" like Bobby became catalysts for more intensive education, Adams also targeted some of the more militaristic prisoners.[18] Under his guidance, prisoners like Danny Lennon began giving lectures, as if they suddenly had a higher goal to pursue in their lives.[19] Adams felt that most of the prisoners were far more aware than they realized. Like Bobby, most of them were in jail because they wanted the "Brits out" after experiencing violence and harassment in their home areas.

"They knew why they were there, they were there for instinctive patriotic reasons or for broadly nationalist reasons or for a sense of national consciousness or because they were confronted with British aggression and responded to it in an instinctive way. They knew they were Irish and they knew they wanted a United Ireland. But they were not politically or ideologically schooled or perhaps *even aware of their own awareness.*"

They were in the IRA but they had no real awareness of being Republicans. The leaders of the movement were the Republicans; these young men felt like they were "just rakers." Adams felt differently. He thought they were *very* politically conscious "but they had never seen themselves as such." For Adams, one of the most important outcomes of getting them to participate more seriously in education was to get them to believe in their own political awareness. In this way, they began to identify their instinctive left ideology with Republicanism and, so doing, to realize that their point of view was as legitimate as their leaders' conservative or even apolitical thinking. Less political prisoners like Danny Lennon began to see that their militarism also *had to be political.*

Adams developed this new awareness by encouraging the young radicals to continue reading global revolutionaries but also to synthesize them with Irish Socialists like James Connolly and Liam Mellowes.

"It's all well and good talking about Che Guevara or Ho Chi Minh . . . now let's get back to what *we're* doing," he would challenge them.

He strongly believed that "you ground your politics in the indigenous . . . it's much easier to argue the validity of a position from the perspective of a James Connolly or a Fintan Lalor or a William Thompson or a Liam Mellowes or a Pearse."

Bobby threw himself into the new education regime. When he was not in classes or debating in the yard, Tomboy Loudon often found him laying on the bed in the cubicle they now shared in the Gaeltacht hut, holding a book by Che Guevara in his right hand and writing notes on the partition wall with the pen he held in his left. He began to organize notebooks on "guerrilla struggle" and "the Cuban Revolution."

Bobby and the others developed from a near-childish understanding of politics to a relatively mature political analysis. They were under the guidance of the new leadership but they achieved the transition by learning from each other. Learning came through participation and debate and not through lecturing and the handing down of "truth" by a "teacher" of superior intellect. Possibly, they read Frieire's *Pedagogy of the Oppressed,* which was published in Britain in 1972. More likely, they were discovering a wheel that has been discovered in similar ways in many revolutionary situations, all with their own local characteristics. Either way, the young prisoners were awakening their own consciousness *and* talking about how they would change the organization of life in their communities once they got out of prison.

The fundamental political lessons they explored were rooted in five basic principles, which Adams called "the five isms": Nationalism, Socialism, secularism, anti-sectarianism, and internationalism. Adams proposed that the Irish struggle was always internationalist and Nationalist, going back to 1798 and the alliance with French Republicans against British monarchic imperialism. Against the public image of the IRA as a "green Catholic army," he talked about secularism and anti-sectarianism. Adams told the men that the differences between orange and green, Protestant and Catholic, had always been carefully fostered by Britain. He cited intelligence that purportedly showed that the British and the police were behind many Loyalist attacks on Catholics and that they had armed the Loyalists who carried them out. The men began to question the IRA's involvement in reprisal attacks against Loyalists. It was up to them to turn this around. Republicanism, they learned, can only be as anti-sectarian as its volunteers.

The enemy, they decided, was not defined by religion but by politics. Adams summarized what they were saying in their discussions:

> *They must be enemies because they are anti-People and pro-Profit, not because they go to a different church or no church at all, not because they have better ghettoes or none at all. They cannot be enemies because someone else defined them as the enemy for us. If we look hard enough we will find the real enemy in behind there somewhere. In behind, making real profits out of old scores.*[20]

Defining the enemy in this way, rather than by religion and "warring tribes" as the press and government consistently did, was highly appealing to Bobby. It was just what he had been waiting to hear: an analysis that merged international anti-imperialist struggle with a practical analysis of their own struggle against British imperialism. The IRA should fight the British *because* it is anti-sectarian *and* Socialist, because the British were "armed mercenaries" and, therefore, "we must be armed revolutionaries."[21]

The prisoners in Cage Eleven also talked about how the media portrayed the IRA as "tribal" or "mafia-like." This, they decided, was part of an attempt to dehumanize and demonize their struggle.

Another series of lectures explicitly addressed the implications of the IRA truce. The men built an alternative analysis to optimistic statements about an impending British withdrawal. British political tactics was a triple strategy of Ulsterization, normalization, and criminalization. Nobody bluntly stated that the current IRA leadership was wrong but the discussions raised questions that encouraged the men to work out alternative explanations of British behavior from what their leaders were telling them.

"Ulsterization" referred to Secretary of State Merlyn Rees's stated goal of moving political and security functions to the north of Ireland, thus reducing the cost of the war to Britain. "Normalization" referred to the hope that the truce could be extended long enough to defeat the IRA through inaction. Under "criminalization," IRA prisoners would lose their "special category" status and be branded "ordinary criminals." To Bobby, the criminalization of prisoners was equivalent to the criminalization of the whole struggle.

If the questions under discussion were subtle at first, it soon became clear what Adams and his accomplices were up to. Says one prisoner from Cage Eleven, "Nobody called a spade a spade, but we all knew who the spade was we were talking about."[22]

• • •

Discussions became more forthright in September 1975 when workmen arrived at Long Kesh and started building a high concrete wall around the prison. To most people, a transition from barbed wire to concrete would seem to represent evidence that the British were digging in for the long haul. Yet the old guard watched the new structure taking shape and claimed that it was evidence of impending British withdrawal, "the death throes of the British in Ireland."[23]

After the wall was finished, Bobby and Tomboy climbed onto the roof of their hut, where they could just see some cranes on the other side, lifting concrete slabs into place. They were building a new prison, a proper one with cells and iron bars on the windows. Each of the low-profiled buildings took the shape of an "H."

"God help the poor cunt that goes into them there," Tomboy said to Bobby as they watched the building work progress from the roof of the hut.

They suspected that the new structure was part of the criminalization plan that they had discussed in their lectures. The "poor cunts" would be themselves. As soon as they saw the new prison blocks going up, the discussions in lectures and in the prison yard became more pointed.

In November, Merlyn Rees announced that anyone convicted after March 1, 1976, would lose his or her special category status and would be treated as an ordinary criminal. As a sweetener, he would simultaneously introduce 50 percent remission to the existing prisoners, which for many would mean immediate release.

Morley still insisted that the new prison structures were for ordinary criminals. Don't worry about these new prison blocks, he told them, because you'll never be in them. Bobby, Tomboy, and Seanna stood on the roof of their hut watching the men working seven days a week to get the H-Blocks up as quickly as possible. They wanted to believe Morley's optimistic messages but every day they became more convinced that he was wrong. Because they wanted so hard to believe Morley, they never forgave the old guard for misleading them once it became clear that the H-Blocks *were* meant for them. Their loyalty to Adams became absolute.

The likely effects of criminalization on the struggle were discussed inside out in Cage Eleven.

"How do you deal with it?" was the big question.

Bobby answered, "We will not wear the uniform. We will not criminalize the struggle."

They were especially concerned about how criminalization would destroy any possibility of widening support for the struggle. In a long war, the IRA would have to expand its base of support while wearing down the enemy. For this, they had to assure that propaganda and a hostile media did not blacken Republicanism. They had to fight criminalization.

As education intensified, the prisoners in Cage Eleven held "camps" where they spent weekends intensively reading, debating, and training with homemade weapons. The military and the political were one single project. Their morale rose as individuals who had never been involved in education started to see a role for themselves. Brendan Hughes watched with satisfaction as Long Kesh "became pretty well organized, a lot less tense." And his personal relationship with Sands improved. Hughes had always liked Sands because he was "a very personable fellow, a likeable guy." Now, they got along well because together they were trying to break down the conservatism that prevailed among the leadership of the IRA.

• • •

The debate that had the strongest effect on Bobby Sands began when Gerry Adams organized a series of critical discussions of Sinn Féin's central policy document called *Éire Nua*. What began with a critical analysis of existing policy ended as a full-blown radical alternative that Adams called "active abstentionism," that is, abstention from the existing structures of mainstream politics while actively creating an alternative that combined grassroots democracy with military resistance to British rule.

Adams encouraged wide-ranging discussions of people's councils and grassroots politics, always with an eye toward how a more democratic and participatory grassroots strategy could be incorporated into the Republican campaign outside of prison. The prisoners discussed how military struggle alone was an inadequate basis for bringing about progressive social change; it had also to be political struggle, a struggle to create something and not just a fight against the Brits. But how could you do this and still adhere to one of the movement's sacred cows: the policy of abstaining from elections?

Just because the movement did not participate in elections, they decided, did not mean it must avoid politics. Rather, it had to build an alternative administration, particularly in "war zones" where the IRA enjoyed widespread grassroots support *and* where the state failed to provide adequate services.

Adams incorporated the main points of these discussions in a series of articles under the pseudonym "Brownie" in the *Republican News*.[24] In time, this would be his most lasting influence on Bobby Sands, not just in terms of what he wrote but also by demonstrating that the written word could be an effective tool of struggle. If, in time, Bobby Sands became the leading Republican propagandist through his own writings—prose, essays, songs, and poetry—he was following the example of Adams. In Adams, Sands found a role model to help him complete his personal journey toward becoming a politicized militant.

Some prisoners began asking Adams some very searching questions. Adams specifically mentions Bobby Sands as someone who pressed him on political issues. As Adams turned these probing discussions into newspaper articles, he began to be more openly critical.[25] In fact, clear differences between Adams and the Republican leadership plainly emerged in his first article. "Brownie" hit the press on August 16, 1975, with a strong indictment of sectarianism, at a time when the IRA was in the middle of a sectarian war with the Loyalist paramilitaries. The article appeared a mere three days after a young IRA volunteer named Brendan "Bik" MacFarlane drove a bomb to a bar on the Shankill Road in Belfast, which killed three men and two women, all Protestants.[26]

"Brownie" wrote,

> *Taigs and orangies, Prods and micks. But it goes deeper than name-calling, as you know better than I do, and only the British reap the benefits. "Let you and him fight," sez one wily Sassenach [Englishman]. "While yez are at it I'll be left alone to impose solutions, to build new profits on the backs of old scores. Let you and him fight and me and the privileged few will see things through."*[27]

The attack on sectarianism was only the first example of how Adams took points from the discussions in Cage Eleven and turned them into articles for a broader Republican readership. The men defined a new Republican project as a concrete struggle for and with ordinary people in real communities and not just some abstract group called *"the* people." They wanted to create a positive political project that went far beyond passively abstaining from elections. They wanted to turn alienated non-participation in electoral politics into a positive program to create alternative state institutions in Republican ghettos.

As they began to construct an alternative political strategy, the prisoners started trying to impact Sinn Féin policy from within the prison. They could not affect policies directly because they had to be physically present to vote on motions at the party's annual *ard fheis* (conference). So they built a relationship with a sympathetic Belfast *cumann* (branch) of the party and sent out policy papers and proposals for them to introduce.[28]

Discussions about current policy took on a historical aspect after Adams "fell on a treasure": hardbound volumes from the Irish Government Printing Office that included the Treaty Debates of the 1920s. They read about the partition of Ireland, about the original split in Sinn Féin over the 1921 Anglo-Irish Treaty, and about the Irish Civil War (1922-1923). Adams recalls that the prisoners "were just greedy because once people started to read the stuff they were then relating it to their own situation."

Joe Barnes remembers this as the moment when he began to see the importance of political education. He read an article about an IRA cease-fire in 1920 and he saw a direct parallel between the debilitating effects of that cease-fire and what was happening to the IRA in 1975. The study of history had an immediate meaning because it clarified current processes.

Adams's education program succeeded because it encouraged prisoners to make connections between what they read and what was happening in real life.

It also gave them confidence. The debates contained speeches by people who, until then, were just abstract Republican icons. They read Liam Mellowes's famous remarks: "when men get into positions of power they will not give up power"; "the Free State idea is imperialism, the Republican idea is anti-imperialist."[29] Mellowes had also been in prison and as they read his words, says Adams, "I think we got the very clear impression that these people were just the same as ourselves."

Mellowes was the Irish revolutionary that Bobby came to admire most. He was one of four Republican leaders who the Southern Irish government executed in December 1922, in reprisal for an IRA shooting of a member of the Dublin parliament. The four were executed without trial, by cabinet decision, even though they were all in jail when the politician was shot. Mellowes, just twenty-seven years old, was the most radical Republican of his time.

Mellowes's writings contained thoughts about building alternative Republican structures as a challenge to the existing government of his day.

"Where is the government of the Republic?" he wrote. "It must be found . . . It is, and must always be, a reality."

By this, Mellowes meant that alternative structures of government had to be built, including courts, land settlements, decrees, etc. Now, the prisoners in Cage Eleven explored whether a similar opportunity to "find" the Republic existed in the north of Ireland. People in the Nationalist communities had "opted out" of the British system, providing a real opportunity to build alternative structures of local governance. As Adams summarized their discussions, ". . . the building of alternatives cannot wait until 'after the war.' It must start now." And this was not just a military war; it was also necessary to fight the British on economic, political, and cultural fronts. Now was the time to build "peoples' organizations" because they could harness the energy that "only a people at war possess."[30]

Volunteers like Bobby could build the alternative. In every neighborhood, they could work with people to govern themselves. They might even organize parallel community councils in the three or four big Nationalist areas in Belfast, complete with departments to provide services. Far from being an alternative to armed struggle, such a program of community action would strengthen the IRA's war effort. Again, as Adams wrote,

> *If we have only a local unit in an area, th[e] Brit wins by isolating or removing that Unit from the people. If the Unit is part of an aggressive Republican or People's Resistance structure (Local Peoples' Councils), the Brit must remove everyone connected, from schoolchildren to customers in the co-ops, from paper sellers to street committees, before he can defeat us. Immersed in the structure, as part of the Alternative, Republicanism can't be isolated and will never be defeated.*[31]

Bobby Sands was excited by this kind of talk. Here was the kind of project that he could work with, a revolutionary project that was Irish in character and origins, yet reflected the kind of militant politics that he had been reading about in the books by Latin American revolutionaries. In Mellowes, he found an *Irish* revolutionary spirit that he had earlier located in men and women from other countries. In Gerry Adams, he found a mentor who had practical suggestions about a way forward. Here was something that he could take from Long Kesh and put into practice back in Twinbrook.

Chapter Nine

Leaving Long Kesh

After Rees announced that internment and special category status would end on March 1, 1976, he increased the period of early release for sentenced prisoners from 25 to 50 percent. Suddenly, nearly everyone was waiting to be released. The men began to plan for life outside. Adams asked Denis Donaldson to step up the program of political education to prepare the men to reenter the struggle.

Men who intended to become active again as IRA volunteers started to work out more intensively. Bobby joined others running around the yard. They set up an obstacle course in the canteen. Yet Sands did not want to simply go back the military activities that had got him into jail in the first place. He also wanted to go home and put the books and the discussions he had worked through for the past three years into practice in his own community. He took a near-fanatical interest in the idea of people's councils.

Sands had a lot of work to do, since practically everyone in his old IRA unit had fallen away from the struggle. Yet he was hopeful. No other organization in Twinbrook was really trying to involve the community in social change. The Official IRA relied on brute force to keep people in line. If the Republican Movement could just create a real grassroots community *movement* and not just an underground military presence in Twinbrook, who knows how rapidly or how far it could grow?

Sands led discussions on people's councils that were now a feature of Cage Eleven. He developed a large folder of notes that he entitled "Development of Community Councils in Local Areas: Proposed Ideas."[1] He argued that IRA volunteers needed to integrate their army activities into the broadest spectrum of political activity in their communities. He proposed to extend their democratic practices in Cage Eleven to the context of organizing grassroots participative structures in the community. The community's alienation from the state paralleled their own alienation from the prison regime. Surely, the Republican Movement could mobilize similar activism outside of prison. Republicans had to become centrally involved in community activities like newspapers, co-ops, and tenant's associations. They had to ensure that people had access to basic services like transport and better housing, as well as cultural resources like music and Irish-language education.

Bobby combined these themes in his first known prison writing. Toward the end of 1975, he wrote a piece for the prison camp newspaper, *Ár nGuth Fhéin*, entitled "*Ag bunadh Gaeltachta* ["Establishing a Gaeltacht"]." It follows the easy conversational style of "Brownie." Yet Bobby wrote it entirely in Irish, in the old script. It is a remarkable achievement. Sands had been learning Irish for less than three years, in a context that many scholars would consider to be less than ideal. Nonetheless, according to native speakers his Irish is of a high standard.

In the article, Sands relates prison life and big political issues to a small Irish-speaking community, or *Gaeltacht*, that had recently been set up in Andersonstown, not far from Twinbrook.

> *When we live here we have plenty of time to learn and read Irish and I think that most of the people know what is happening in the country and in the world, too. And we can talk about the Vietnam War, the conflict in the Middle East, and the troubles in our own country.*
>
> *These are the things that are the usual subjects of conversation for everyone but now I would like to take this opportunity to write about something else—the small Gaeltacht on the Shaw's Road. Maybe you've often heard of this place and maybe you haven't. Maybe you think it is not important, and there's a good chance you have not heard about it until now.*

He is already trying to connect the global with the local, the radical issues that fill the world's screens with the equally important issues that affect a few people in a small neighborhood. Sands describes a real example of local grassroots solidarity and action.

I don't know how many people live there, but I think that there are about fifteen houses there, as well as a small nursery school, and the children are learning everything through Irish. And they speak in Irish all the time and their parents do, too, and they have their culture.

Then, he sets out a program of work by asking why this utopian but concrete experiment cannot be replicated more widely.

They can have little Gaeltachts in their own streets as long as people are willing. The other people didn't have much money when they started. They only had one thing and that is a lot of courage, and that is the most important thing, and I know that it is a small school but it is an Irish school at least. I think that in theory it is very easy to make a Gaeltacht but first people need information about why they're doing it and if they accept that they will be living with their real culture and language and if they use them, well then that's a start.

Finally, Bobby sets out his real program, which is to use these small experiments to promote a wider social experiment that will provide for all of the needs of the community. It may seem naïve and utopian but it is nonetheless appealing in its optimism.

But that's not all of it, it doesn't stop there, a lot of other things are happening, and they are for the people living in the Gaeltacht. They will be able to set up small factories first and then the will be able to move forward from there (a good start is half the work). Maybe they could do everything through Irish there, and other people would be able to come from the outside to the Gaeltacht to work and use their Irish there. As well as that, they would be able to make a profit for themselves and with that profit they would be able to establish a new school, or factory, or new houses, or what-ever they like.

Sands ends with a statement of voluntarism that is right out of "Brownie" (but which also reflects Che Guevara's descriptions of setting up revolutionary administration in the Sierra Maestra in *Episodes of the Revolutionary War*).

> *And it would be without help from the government, too. I know that they wouldn't get any help from any government, north or south, and that is why we must do it ourselves, and as I said already, before you do anything you need information as to why and how, as well as strong courage (hope), and then you can do anything.*

He signs the article with the Irish version of his name, Roibeard Ó Seachnasaigh.

Gerry Adams recalls during this period how Sands, "focused in more and more on me. We talked more about the struggle and things outside while walking around the cage together with some of his close friends or in one-to-one conversations in the study hut."[2] Adams knew that Sands was going back to the struggle and that he was searching for ideas about what to do when he got out, how to put the ideas they had developed into practice on the ground. Yet Adams was careful about what he said to Bobby.

"I was very chary about all of that. I was obviously very open to the politics of it but I was very chary about anyone thinking that anyone was going to come out of prison and 'sort things out.' The people outside probably thought things didn't need sorting out, that they were doing a good enough job."[3]

So things would be complex enough on a political level. On a personal level, however, "going back to the struggle" would be even harder. Bobby had a family. Gerard was now nearly three years old and Geraldine wanted Bobby to take a leave of absence from the IRA and confine himself strictly to political Sinn Féin work. He could get a job and they could build the home that they never had. Geraldine found a house in Summerhill, a new part of Twinbrook. She furnished it, mostly with borrowed furniture, and began getting it ready for Bobby's release.

Geraldine was a forceful woman and, eventually, Bobby agreed to give her and the child a year "to become a family unit." It was hardly an unreasonable request from her point of view. But it was an impossible request for Bobby to comply with because he was so politically active and dedicated in so many spheres, including his military commitments. Perhaps he wanted to let Geraldine *pretend* that he would not report back to the IRA. His comrades in Long Kesh had no doubts that he would report back as soon as he got out of prison.

• • •

As release approached in early 1976, Adams was directly challenging the prison leadership. He organized a cage *Ard Fheis* (literally, "high meeting") where Gerry Rooney proposed anti-imperialist unity among working-class groups, seconded by Tomboy Loudon. Both emphasized how imperialists maintained unity and asked why shouldn't anti-imperialists follow suit? After discussion, the assembly carried the motion that Sinn Féin should identify with *all* true anti-imperialist groups throughout the world.[4]

After months of open discussion and political debate, Sands and his closest comrades were now fully radicalized volunteers who openly questioned the leadership. Indeed, he was now of the opinion that it was a politically aware volunteer's *duty* to question a leadership that was faulty. Jake Jackson remembers him saying,

"You have to view the struggle as a train heading from A to B. The passengers on the train have a vested interest in getting there. Although there are people who drive the train and work as engineers, we're all heading along toward our destination. And the more people we bring onto the train at the different stations the more viable it will be."

But, added Bobby, "If the driver is taking us in the wrong direction, then the rest of us collectively have to move the train onto another track or take it into a siding for awhile and park it until we figure out what to do."

• • •

Sands had come a long way. He had also matured socially. He now regularly organized music sessions for the hut and, on special occasions, he organized the big events for the whole cage. His last big event in Cage Eleven was to emcee the 1975 Christmas concert. Cage alumni still talk about it. Bobby organized the entertainers—"the artists, musicians, singers, comediennes, and general head cases," he called them[5]—while Kevin "Igor" Carson did the technical production. They brought tables into the large hut to make a stage, with curtains hung across to approximate a theater. They installed all the chairs they could get and a bar served *poteen* ("soft" drinks).

The night began with traditional Irish music by Sands and Martin McAllister. Gerry Adams says Bobby "did his best to play guitar." Others played skits and did their musical bits. As the drink flowed, Bobby later wrote,

> . . . *all sorts of artists spring up from no-where, NO-WHERE??? Singers have been known to sing themselves hoarse and many a guitar string has been strained to breaking point, some have even broken. It is a time for generally making a fool of yourself and some just enjoy the drink. It all adds up to a very enjoyable evening, the best of company and entertainment.*[6]

For the finale, Stu Rooney, Danny Lennon, and Juice McMullen dressed in wigs and did their version of Queen's "Bohemian Rhapsody," which had barely been out a month. The lyrics alone were far enough over the top to guarantee a showstopper for a performer singing to a prison audience juiced up on moonshine. But Kevin Carson added to the mood by making "dry ice" out of table tennis balls that he crushed to a powder.

As the three came to the climax of the song—"Oh mama mia, mama mia, mama mia let me go; Beelzebub has a devil put aside for me; for me; for me"—Carson released the "dry ice" and enveloped the stage in a mist. It cleared the hall.

"While Igor got the visuals right," recalls Gerry Adams, "he did not allow for the toxic nature of his product. Or the smell. It was ghastly, choking everyone and bringing our concert to a fitting, farcical end."[7]

Less than a month before he was released from jail, Sands wrote another short piece on culture for the camp newspaper. The article was entitled "*Easbaidh Gaeilge ar Raidio agus Teilifis Eireann*" "(The Lack of Irish language on Irish Radio and Television"):

> *The whole world knows that yesterday was a special day (17th March) and everyone who could listen to programmes in Irish, which were on all day, was happy. It was St. Patrick's day, but at the same time I was angry.*
>
> *Usually there is only one programme in Irish on Raidio Éireann. But programmes were plentiful yesterday, everyone*

used their Irish, and when we heard everything in Irish we thought we were listening to Radió na Gaeltachta.[8]

But as I said earlier, I was angry. It is clear that people wanted to be Gaelgeoirí yesterday for St. Patrick's day but now that St. Patrick's is over they have finished until this time next year. And the programmes in Irish are finished too, and they will be very scarce from now on . . . I noticed a while ago that there were seven hours of Welsh language programmes on television in Wales each week, and don't forget that the Welsh are under British rule too.

. . . Anyway we need Irish on television, Irish from the Gaeltachts, maybe it will help everyone learn Irish and then maybe we'll have St. Patrick's day everyday. I hope so.

Finally, because of his cultural and sporting interests Sands was chosen for his first widely published piece, a chapter on "Activities" in a book entitled *Prison Struggle* that was written in Cage Eleven and smuggled out to the publishers. The book had thirteen chapters on subjects like Education, the Irish Language, Medical Facilities, and Escapes. On its cover is a photograph of Brendan Hughes giving a lecture in the use of arms while holding a homemade automatic rifle. It is full of other photographs and drawings, including a picture of some of the men digging a tunnel, which was actually a mock-up constructed from some tables covered in muck.[9]

Bobby's chapter is a general review of sporting and cultural activities. He begins by stating that some kind of recreation is essential to prison life. Some people, he says, think that "because you are in jail you can lie about the hut and have a nice easy time of it." This, he claims, is untrue and "even the laziest of men get fed up with that sort of caper" and get involved in some kind of pastime such as soccer.

Other activities are less strenuous. He mentions playing cards for a few hours but expresses a special delight in reading, from novels to political philosophy to history. Not only is it "time well spent" but it also "gives you the opportunity to catch up on Irish history which was ignored at school."

Sands describes Irish language classes at length, emphasizing how classes are organized and taught by the prisoners and how "men have come into Long Kesh without a word of Irish and in no time have learnt sufficient Irish to hold a conversation with any of the fluent speakers." Then he adds an autobiographical note:

> *I myself never had the opportunity of learning Gaelic at school nor had I the inclination or time for either serious or light reading until I was thrown into Long Kesh. Now it is the opposite and I like to think that the results of how I spent my leisure time will have the opposite effect to that intended by my captors and jailers. If Long Kesh is designed to break a POW physically and mentally these activities are our defence against such designs and, if anything, help us to become more determined in our resistance to abject defeat.*

Bobby would return to these themes in subsequent years in the H-Blocks of Long Kesh, where the twenty-four-hour lock-up and the absence of even the most basic reading or leisure materials would stretch the prisoners' creativity to their limits. Yet already, he was expressing a theme that had become central to his life and to his everyday practice: no matter what the limitations, one should seek out opportunities and take advantage of them.

• • •

On April 13, 1976, Bobby Sands was finally released from Cage Eleven. Most of the others would soon join him: Danny Lennon in four days, Seanna Walsh in a couple of weeks, and Tomboy Loudon in June.

"I can't get it out of my head about leaving all those other prisoners behind," he told Seanna.

Seanna disagreed.

"I just want out."

On the morning of his release, Bobby spoke to Tomboy and Roon about going back to his local IRA unit as soon as he got out. Roon counseled a bit of caution.

"Get out and look around ye, settle down. Don't be jumping in. Settle down and see what you want to do then."

They had all come a long way since 1973. When they were arrested, says Seanna Walsh, he and Bobby were no different from the rest of the people outside. They certainly were not the vanguard of their people. They weren't even Socialists. But when they came out of jail three years later they had *totally* politicized themselves.[10]

Chapter Ten

Putting It into Practice

Oro, se do bheatha 'bhaile!
Oro, se do bheatha 'bhaile!
Oro, se do bheatha 'bhaile!
Anois ar theacht an tsamhraidh.

(Óró! You are welcome home!
Óró! You are welcome home!
Óró! You are welcome home!
Now that summer is coming.)

—*Traditional Irish song*

When Bobby Sands came back to Twinbrook after three years in jail he had changed. Had Twinbrook? In some ways it was the same migrant community he left behind, with disputes between the newer and older residents, between Republicans and others who just thought, "don't mention the war."

But some things had shifted. There were new residents, concentrated in two new housing areas called Almond and Summerhill. Most of them quietly supported the Provisionals. A small local *cumann* (branch) of Sinn Féin had achieved limited gains. It had only three members. Keeler McCullough, a veteran of Republican politics now in his fifties, was chair.

At the other end of the spectrum, Féilim Ó hAdhmaill was in his mid-teens. They took to Bobby straight away.

McCullough remembers him coming to his house to discuss how they could organize local Sinn Féin politics. Bobby never sat. He was up and down, always on the move. He kidded McCullough about his age but he also encouraged him, saying, "Keeler, you're never too old to be a Republican."

Ó hAdhmaill was "totally mesmerized" as a kid, seeing Sands coming out of jail and figuring that he was the *real thing*.[1]

What the small group lacked in numbers they made up for in enthusiasm. They had organized a march in support of Frank Stagg, a southern Irish IRA volunteer who was on hunger strike in an English jail. Hundreds of locals came onto the streets.

Bobby moved with Geraldine and Gerard into a house at 7 Summerhill Gardens. The house was in a terrace of five boxy brown-brick houses. Downstairs, it had a spacious living room and kitchen. Upstairs there were three bedrooms. Furnishings were sparse: basic outdated furniture and a TV. One friend described it as "the very barest I've ever seen," and added, "I suppose today you'd call it minimalist but it was just barren. They had nothing."[2]

Yet Keeler McCullough always noticed the picture above the fireplace. It was a portrait of Liam Mellowes. Bobby told McCullough how much he admired Mellowes and thirty years later Keeler remembered Mellowes as the Republican to whose example Bobby Sands most aspired.

Eibhlín Glenholmes was Seanna Walsh's jailhouse girlfriend. After he got out, they were engaged. As Bobby and Seanna were practically inseparable, Glenholmes spent a lot of time in a foursome with them and Geraldine. Her first impression of Bobby was that he was "gorgeous," very fair compared to Walsh. She remembers a pronounced mole on his neck, a tiny flaw in him that fascinated her. Her other memory of Bobby is that he "smiled before he opened his mouth, you always felt that he was glad to see you."

Geraldine could hardly have been more different. She was small, thin, and hard. She went off on tirades about nearly anything while easygoing Bobby just sat there. She wouldn't take crap from anyone. If someone was talking rubbish or doing something she did not like, she would say, "Would you give your head a shaking!?"

The first time Eibhlín Glenholmes met Geraldine she came to the house looking for Seanna. Geraldine answered the door and could not have been more abrupt.

"What do you want, love?"

"Is Bobby there?"

"Why, who're you?"

Glenholmes told her.

"Well, what do you want with Bobby?"

Geraldine did not settle down and let her in until she explained that she was looking for Seanna, not Bobby.

This kind of scene was repeated with some regularity. One time, Walsh and Glenholmes were sitting in the front room talking to Bobby. Geraldine periodically came in and interrupted them with a sharp comment.

"Come on, they're fighting. Let's go," said Glenholmes, embarrassed. Seanna just waved her off.

"No, why should we leave because she's fighting. *Geraldine's* fighting, Bobby's not fighting."

Despite their differences, Glenholmes says that Bobby would look at Geraldine and anyone could see he adored her. He was devoted to Gerard, yet bonding was not easy. One morning soon after Bobby's release, Gerard found him in Geraldine's bed. He went ballistic, jumping on Bobby and making it clear that he did not like this stranger in his mommy's bed.

Bobby's small income from the movement was hardly enough to live on so Geraldine worked nights in a local chip van. She did not get off until eleven o'clock or after. That added to their family pressures since Bobby was always busy. He often took Gerard along when he was seeing people but the child also spent a lot of time with his aunts and his grandmother. "Bobby Mark II . . . her blue-eyed boy," was how one friend described Rosaleen's attitude to her grandson.

Within days of Bobby's release Geraldine was pregnant. She kept working throughout the summer, even after her thin frame was heavily pregnant. By the time she finished work most nights she was exhausted. Some mornings, when the money was especially tight, Bobby got up at five and made his way several miles down the road to the Peter Pan Bakery to line up for a few hours of low-paid work before he returned to Twinbrook to do his "real work." They were not living the "godfather" life, the image that the British media used to support their criminalization of active Republicans. Bobby Sands and his family were barely scraping by.

• • •

One day Geraldine said to Eibhlín Glenholmes, "Bobby will have to get a job." Glenholmes thought to herself that he already had a job and he worked overtime at it. She knew that Geraldine did not have a chance of "reforming" Bobby, although she admired her for the effort and wondered whether she should be trying the same tactic with Seanna.

Despite his promises to Geraldine, Bobby reported straight to his local IRA unit when he got out of prison. By the time Seanna Walsh got out two weeks later, he had already walked into a central position in the local unit of about ten volunteers. His chief objective was to reorganize not just the IRA unit but also support groups within the community: the local Sinn Féin cumann, the youngsters in the *Fianna,* and a group of older supporters that he formed into a new auxiliary unit.

"Broaden your base, republicanize your area, intensify the armed struggle,"[3] he told Seanna.

As soon as Walsh got out, he went to Sands.

"Where you going?" Bobby asked him. "The Short Strand or Twinbrook?"

Bobby explained the situation in Twinbrook. They had few volunteers, not very experienced but dedicated and with potential. There were a couple of rifles, some short arms, and they had access to explosives through their contacts in Andersonstown.

Seanna asked Bobby what he saw as their main role. Bobby said that they would emphasize attacks against the British army. The IRA's current tactic of economic bombings was a legitimate part of a complex strategy that extended to community political development. But the main enemy was the British army. Without hesitation, Seanna moved to Twinbrook and joined the local IRA unit.

But Twinbrook was a difficult place to operate as an urban guerrilla. Its wide open spaces made them vulnerable, making it easier for the army to observe their movements or track their escape routes. Attacks had to be planned well in advance. Houses had to be secured for the preparation and aftermath of the attack. Volunteers wore masks and gloves and were more concerned about alternative escape routes and destruction of forensic evidence. They hijacked cars for security and left them far away after the attack. One car would be used to take the weapon away to a secure location while another took the shooter to a safe house to wash off forensic residues. A simple shooting attack required many active volunteers and a broader support population.

Despite these difficulties, Bobby figured they could really damage to the British army. Many of their comrades from Cage Eleven were already making big noises. Surely, they could do the same. In the middle of May, the Royal Marines had withdrawn from Twinbrook and were replaced by military police.[4] Some local volunteers felt it was an insult for the army to send such a light unit into Twinbrook. Yet Bobby and Seanna were delighted to see the redcapped MPs driving through the estate in light cars. There was no end to the possibilities for attack.

"We'll give them a long hot summer," they told each other and, indeed, the sun shone continually in an abnormally hot and dry season for Ireland.

But there were operational problems. No one had much military experience. The community was not sufficiently activated. And they were short on equipment. Members of the unit mainly went along with experienced volunteers from nearby areas to raise their skills. If they planned an operation, they had to inform the battalion leadership in Andersonstown, who then provided experienced volunteers. The battalion sanctioned IRA attacks all around but other units led the Twinbrook volunteers. At the start of May, such a unit placed a massive bomb that wrecked Lisburn's main shopping district. In time, the Twinbrook unit planned more operations, but they always involved experienced volunteers from Andersonstown.

In one such operation, on May 25, ten volunteers from Andersonstown and Twinbrook arrived at the Kilwee Industrial Estate in Dunmurry in a hijacked post office van. They planted four twenty-pound bombs along with drums of fuel in businesses on the estate. The bombs caused extensive damage. These operations followed a pattern. Cars or vans were stolen from other areas of West Belfast and brought to Twinbrook where the men and materials were assembled. Then the group went to the target of the operation and, after their escape, the vehicle was burned out in another area.

Things rarely went according to plan, however. Operations were planned every couple of weeks but they rarely came off. Then it would be another few weeks of planning and waiting until they could try again. In military terms, Bobby's return to Twinbrook hardly got off to a resounding start.

● ● ●

Sands did not put all of his marbles in one barrel. While some of the IRA volunteers were frustrated because they were not progressing rapidly enough, he was busy trying to build a political movement.

As soon as he was back in Twinbrook, Bobby organized discussions about how to mobilize supporters. He reinvigorated the small group of Sinn Féin activists because it was still rare for such a well-known IRA prisoner to get directly involved in the *political* side of things. Most encouraging to the handful of Sinn Féin members was Bobby's opinion that the Republican Movement was already very popular in the area, despite its low profile. Many people repeated the old mantra that Twinbrook was a "Sticky area." But Bobby refused to engage in such defeatism and his unflagging enthusiasm infused energy to the other party activists.

Sands argued that once people began to identify with the movement in small ways, they could then be emboldened and mobilized to support the movement in more open ways. Their public support would demonstrate that Republicans were not a criminal gang, as the British media portrayed them.

Bobby told Seanna Walsh that a mere military campaign would always be vulnerable. If you had five or ten of the best volunteers in an Active Service Unit, the Brits could arrest them or kill them; at best they would have to go on the run and Republicanism would be wiped out in the area. But if you backed up your IRA unit with an auxiliary unit and the Fianna and a Sinn Féin cumann and a group to collect money for prisoners and sell *Republican News*, and if all of these people were involved in community affairs, then even if the Brits shot dead the whole unit of active IRA volunteers, they couldn't kill Republicanism in the area. Other people would step into their shoes.

Sands was also acutely aware of the importance of how the media "framed" the conflict. The British were able to criminalize the movement in the public eye because of its conspiratorial nature, because there were not enough public demonstrations of support. Bobby wanted to get the people of the community involved in running their own lives, in a parallel administration to the British State structures, and he wanted to be able to reflect these grassroots expressions of support and self-administration in public statements that would counteract the prevailing media image of the IRA.

Sands immediately suggested that the local Sinn Féin cumann should set up a newspaper to raise their profile and bring new supporters into the activities of producing and selling the paper. He suggested that they call their newspaper *Liberty*. It was crudely produced. Articles were usually typed but the masthead was crudely drawn. Some issues were completely written out in block letters, as neatly as possible. The paper was reproduced in secret on a Gestetner.

Sands wrote the whole first issue of the paper. But he encouraged others, especially Féilim Ó hAdhmaill, to write articles for subsequent issues. They produced and distributed *Liberty* underground, like *Samizdat* in the Soviet Union of the time. Although Sinn Féin was not illegal, they knew that the security forces would stop and arrest anyone they caught with the paper.[5]

To maximize the paper's political effect, they decided to distribute it free to Twinbrook residents. They produced two thousand issues and put one through every door. Then they sold the rest in other areas to raise the money for ink and paper. Danny Morrison and Tom Hartley first met Sands in May 1976 when he walked into the offices of the Republican Press Center on the Falls Road and asked for duplicating paper and stencils. They asked him to work in the press center but Bobby replied that he wanted to work in his own area. They knew from his response that he was not just organizing Sinn Féin but was an active IRA volunteer.[6]

In line with his optimistic populism, Bobby proposed that Sinn Féin should rename itself "Sinn Féin—the People's Party." He even put his new party name on the masthead of *Liberty*. His choice of "people's party" instead of "worker's party" reflected the political awareness he had achieved in jail. He continually talked about street committees and popular politics. He tried to bring young people, women, and the elderly into the movement. His broad definition of "the community" showed that he was quite aware of the social structure of Twinbrook: with such high unemployment, most people were hardly "workers" in the traditional Marxian sense. Nor were housewives or young students "workers" in that sense. In his identification of "the community" and "the people," Bobby was articulating the kind of movement that social scientists have only recently recognized as "identity movements."[7]

Besides selling *Liberty*, local Sinn Féin supporters put leaflets through doors, pasted posters, and painted slogans around the community. The Sinn Féin cumann organized collections for prisoners' families while simultaneously increasing their contact with the local population. All of these efforts created a belief that Republicans were everywhere in Twinbrook and were not afraid either of the British state or of the Official IRA.

• • •

Encouraged by his early successes, Sands considered how to increase the movement's profile in Twinbrook. In June, he got his chance when the Twinbrook Tenants Association (TTA) elected a new board of directors. It would prove to be his biggest political victory and would make him a formidable local figure long before he became well known within the broader Republican community.

When Sands first suggested involvement in the TTA, he encountered more scepticism than enthusiasm. Local Republicans had experienced too many squabbles with the TTA to think about it as a resource.[8] Every time the IRA attacked the British army, the TTA Committee issued a press statement condemning them. Bobby used their argument against them. It was crucial, he said, to transform the TTA into a sympathetic institution. In May, Bobby and other IRA volunteers were already mounting gun attacks on military police patrols in Twinbrook. After one of these attacks, the TTA condemned them on the grounds that they were "creating animosity between the two communities in Twinbrook." Bobby struck back, issuing a statement through Sinn Féin that attacked the "hypocrisy" of the TTA, claiming that the TTA and residents of the neighboring Loyalist estate wanted to build a "Berlin wall" between their communities.

"To our knowledge the IRA has never been involved in sectarian attacks, but only attacks on military and economic targets," he asserted.

He asked why the TTA were so one-sided in their condemnation of violence. Young boys and girls had been lifted by the British army from their very premises, yet they had never issued a statement of condemnation or concern. "The TTA should be at least as much concerned with what happened to innocent people as with the safety of foreign mercenaries," he wrote.

Sands ended the statement with a repetition of the political analysis that he had gone over so many times in Cage Eleven, arguing that the introduction of British MPs into Twinbrook was a "stepping stone" toward the reintroduction of the RUC. It was a central part of the strategy of "Ulsterization, normalization, and criminalization."

Sands argued that the best way to stop these anti-Republican messages was to get sympathizers elected onto the TTA Committee. Then, by using the resources of the TTA with respect to housing issues, social events, and cultural life they could mobilize further support and deepen their ties to the community. If they could mobilize new supporters in campaigns for housing rights, if they could draw them into regular Irish cultural events, then they would eventually draw them into active Republicanism.

"Get the people out and it will give them the confidence to support us in other ways," he argued.

McCullough, and Ó hAdhmaill helped Sands identify a slate of twelve candidates who were quiet supporters of the movement. Only two (including Bobby) were members. On the night of the election, the Officials and the Social and Democratic Labour Party packed the meeting. Bobby and his crew packed it better. Nine of the new committee members were from their slate. Only one sitting committee member was reelected. Until that night it was accepted wisdom that Twinbrook was a "Sticky area." The result was a big shock for Provo supporters and opponents alike.

Sands had uses in mind for the TTA's public hall. He asked the committee if they could have a folk night every Sunday. It was a clever move. None of the committee wanted to run the event so they agreed to Bobby's folk night as long as he would organize things. Bobby put together a series of programs that combined socializing with cultural and political messages. He put together the entertainment more or less single-handedly, hiring well-known folk groups. As emcee, he played guitar and sang Irish rebel songs that eventually had the whole hall singing along. He promoted the Irish language by singing traditional songs like "*Oro se do bhatha bhaille.*"

The local IRA unit supplied more direct politics to the folk nights. Masked IRA volunteers came on stage dressed in combat gear, carrying guns. They read out political statements that Bobby had written about community politics, British army actions, and the need to be vigilant against Loyalist sectarian attacks.

Sands also helped organize a children's clinic, a preschool playgroup, and training for local boxing and soccer clubs. On Friday nights there was a youth disco that the Fianna organized as a tool to mobilize young people. On Saturday afternoons there were social clubs for senior citizens and in the evening there was an adult dance. There was a women's night and a men's night. Bobby set up an Irish language society where he taught Irish classes once a week.[9] By midsummer, the TTA Center was being used practically all the time, whereas the old TTA usually sat empty.

Sands and his comrades had made remarkable progress in turning Twinbrook into a consciously rebellious, Republican district. The locals viewed him more and more as someone to call on if they needed help. They came to his door or they stopped him on the street, asking for help on all kinds of social issues. If they needed the plumbing or heating fixed, a broken window replaced or rats exterminated they came to Sands, who organized "unofficial" fixes through his contacts in the community. Bobby *was* finding Mellowes's "real Republic" in Twinbrook. By all accounts he was intensely happy.

• • •

Sands still found a bit of time for his favorite leisure pursuits. As soon as he got out of prison, he started playing soccer on a local team, Brookville, in the amateur Andersonstown League. A team picture shows Bobby standing on the back row next to one of the coaches, smiling and fully at ease. At one match he ran into an old friend from Star of the Sea in Rathcoole. Denis Sweeney, now a doctor, was surprised when Bobby approached him to talk.

"I didn't like him that much. I don't think he liked me," he recalled.

But something had changed in Bobby. Sweeney thought that prison had made him "a far nicer person . . . a warmed person and a more sincere person, far more sincere person." In the old days, he never thought of Bobby as someone with high moral principles. But now, after he came out of prison, "he seemed to be a lot more settled person and someone who would have been the type of person who would have gone all the way with something."[10]

Bernard Fox, who worked with him at Alexander's factory, also saw big changes in Bobby after prison. He was "a very aware and politically-minded person [rather than] the young lad who took dog's abuse from his workmates and said nothing."[11]

Bobby Sands had changed so much that is hard to remember that it had only been four years, the time it takes in most countries to get a university education.

There were big changes in Bobby's social circle, too. Seanna Walsh and Eibhlin Glenholmes were engaged and were moving into a flat around the corner from Bobby and Geraldine.

"We all thought it was the start of everyone's life," she recalls. "We just thought the four of us were gonna be friends forever, watch our kids grow up. When I look back, that was the best time in my life."

Twinbrook was a nice place to live; people took pride in their homes. The weather was fine that summer, the nights were late. Life was good.

Even bad things seemed to turn out good. Glenholmes only remembers one time when Bobby lost his temper. He had organized a folk night fund-raiser for one of his pet schemes in the PD Club in Andersonstown. It was a great venue and he was very excited that he had gotten permission to use the club. He hired a good band and expected a big crowd.

When the big night came, Bobby and Geraldine went to the PD with Seanna and Eibhlín. The band was there but they waited and waited. No one came. Bobby couldn't understand it because he at least expected all his friends in Andersonstown to come and support him. They tried to figure out where the people were.

"I can't understand this. We put an ad in the paper. Where the fuck is everybody?" said Bobby.

They talked a bit longer and Bobby said to Geraldine, "You did put the ad in the paper didn't you?"

"What do you mean did I put the ad in the paper?" she shot back at him. "Sure, you said you'd put it in!"

It turned out nobody had placed the ad and for a few minutes Bobby was fuming. But then they sent the band home and went to the Chinese take-out restaurant around the corner and got a lot of food. They went back to Bobby's parents' house and ate out the back with some tins of beer. The weather was beautiful. Bobby got out his guitar and he sang for quite awhile into the night, while they ate and drank. The last song he sang was Woody Guthrie's "Plane Wreck at Los Gatos."

• • •

As the remarkably hot summer wore on, political successes under Bobby's direction continued to be matched by military shortcomings. The British government was on an offensive that nearly neutralized the IRA's plans to reemerge from the truce as an effective guerrilla army. The IRA had successes in its economic bombing campaign but at a considerable cost in terms of volunteers arrested and killed.

In July, the losses hit close to home.

After his release, Danny Lennon moved back to Andersonstown, just around the corner from his childhood friend John Chillingworth.[12] A militant through and through, Lennon was one of the most vociferous opponents of the IRA's 1975 cease-fire. Back on the streets, he was frustrated with the terms of the ceasefire and appalled at how certain people in the IRA leadership encouraged retaliatory sectarian attacks against Protestants while forbidding attacks on the security forces.

"We should be hitting the Brits," he told Seanna Walsh, "*they're* the enemy, not the Protestants."

Lennon was soon "*very* active" in one of the busiest units of the IRA in Andersonstown. Like others there, Lennon worked with the Twinbrook IRA when they needed help. On Sunday night, August 8, he went to see Bobby Sands. He had explosives that he agreed to exchange for the loan of an ArmaLite for a few days. Bobby was delighted. He had plans for explosives.

The following Tuesday afternoon, Lennon took the wheel of a stolen Ford Cortina. Chillingworth sat in the passenger's seat with the ArmaLite from Twinbrook tucked in beside him. It was a beautiful sunny afternoon.

They had not got far before two or three Jeeps full of British soldiers surrounded them. They knew that they should stop and surrender but Chillingworth fired the ArmaLite at a British soldier. He was sure that he hit him. Lennon floored the Cortina. For a moment they thought they got away. But as Lennon turned, screeching onto the Shaws Road, more British soldiers fired on them. He sped down the hill and turned left. The soldiers kept firing. Just as they came to the junction with Finaghy Road North, Lennon's head went down. Chillingworth knew instantly that he was dead. The car, effectively driverless, went out of control and mounted the footpath in front of St. Michael's church. The soldiers kept firing.

Annie Maguire was walking along Finaghy Road North, pushing her six-week-old son Andrew in a carriage. Her eldest child, eight-year-old Joanne, was on her bicycle a little bit ahead of her mother. Six-year-old Mark and two-year-old John Maguire were walking next to her. Andrew kicked his foot up into the air and his toy went flying out of the carriage onto the road. His brother ran onto the road to get the toy. Perhaps that is what saved him. The Ford Cortina, Lennon dead at the wheel, crashed directly into the children. Joanne and Andrew were killed instantly. John died in hospital a few hours later.

The story went around the globe. Two brave women started a campaign that brought thousands more onto the streets of Belfast in direct defiance of the gunmen and in favor of peace. They won the Nobel Peace Prize for leading the "Peace People" at the end of that hot summer in Belfast. Yet the reaction to their campaign in the streets of West Belfast was more ambivalent. Some people held pickets for peace; others refused to join in. To many, Danny Lennon was a hero who had bravely taken on the British army and paid the ultimate price for his actions. Everyone was horrified for the children and their grieving mother. But they wondered why the British army acted so recklessly.

When word got to Twinbrook that Danny Lennon was dead, Bobby and Seanna Walsh were both in shock. The local movement immediately mobilized people to protest a "state killing." Young people burned buses to build barricades and block the road. In response, some local women blocked the main road leading into Twinbrook with their own bodies, calling on the young people to stop the violence and to leave them in peace. They were visible and vocal enough to challenge Republicans, who had emerged so strongly out of recent community struggles like the campaign over the TTA.

Some Republicans wanted to force the peace people off the streets. Ó hAdhmaill suggested that they should confront them and discuss their grievances in a constructive way. Bobby agreed. A high-handed and violent approach was inconsistent with his intentions of winning broad-based community support. So he took a small delegation of Republicans and arranged a meeting with the women. The meeting never took place because of developments in rest of Belfast, where the Peace People mobilized huge rallies and marches against the IRA.

Gerry Adams wrote a letter entitled, "In Defense of Danny Lennon," and Bobby later remembered him, from jail, in a poem.

● ● ●

Once again, as happened years before with the death of his three comrades when their bomb exploded in Bawnmore, Lennon's death shook Bobby from a sort of unreality about the struggle. It gave Bobby and Seanna a sense that "this thing is for real." They felt that they had to rededicate themselves to the struggle.

They determined to "get one back" at the British army for Danny Lennon. Bobby immediately put into action his plan for the gelignite that Danny Lennon had given him just a few days before he was killed. He took a squad of men to dig a landmine into the bottom of the Summerhill Road, not far below his own house, where he had often observed the MPs slowing down for a sharp curve. The hedgerow beside the road was a perfect place to dig in the mine and hide the wire while volunteers lay under cover behind it in wait. (Years later, the site would become known for the ill-fated DeLorean factory, which produced fancy stainless-steel cars for export to California.) Days passed but the MPs' car never came. On the third day, a heavily armored pig came. It drove directly over the landmine several times as the men watched. Finally, they lost patience and hit the button. The mine blew the pig onto its side but none of the soldiers was seriously injured.

Ironically, the landmine gave Sands an opportunity to demonstrate how political and military action could be combined. The explosion broke windows in nearby houses and the neighbors came to Bobby to get their windows repaired. He spent the next few days organizing glaziers to fix the broken windows in his neighbors' houses. It was parallel government in action, but not quite as he had envisaged it.

• • •

Having failed to extract their revenge by landmine, the unit went back to shooting attacks. In early August, they secured an SKS rifle to replace the ArmaLite they lost when Danny Lennon was killed. The following Sunday was another glorious day. Bobby had to go away on business that afternoon. He knew that Seanna was anxious to try out the new rifle but he was concerned about security. The last thing he told Seanna before he left was not to take it out.

But the lure of "getting one back" for Danny Lennon was just too much.

After Sands left, a local volunteer brought a car and took Walsh and the local OC across the estate to an area where new houses were being built. They took the SKS out of the boot and began test firing it.

When they were finished, Seanna carried the rifle back to the car. Just as he was about to put it in the boot he looked up and saw a British army Jeep coming toward them. The three jumped into the car to make their getaway but there was no acceleration. They had no chance of getting away.

Sands arrived back in Twinbrook with Eibhlín Glenholmes just as the British army was taking the three men away. They ran to the top of hill. The car was still there with its doors lying open and the army Land Rover was moving off. There was absolutely nothing anyone could do. Bobby saw a friend watching the commotion.

"What's up, Eilish?"

"Bobby, it's a rifle."

His heart sank. He knew right away that it was Seanna.

"Oh, God," he said to Glenholmes, "everyone just wants to shoot a Brit after what happened to Danny Lennon."[13]

Bobby took her straight to Seanna's house while he went around to find out what had happened. Glenholmes just sat there crying. It was two weeks before their wedding. It was to be the biggest day of her life and now everything had gone wrong.

When Bobby returned he came into the kitchen and sat down beside Glenholmes. The look on his face confirmed that it was Seanna. Bobby took her hand and squeezed it.

"I told him not to go out and test fire that rifle. I told him not to do it."

Bobby was crying. He was thinking about what Walsh was going into; not the fact that he was going into jail but that he would be going to the new H-Blocks that they had watched being built from atop the huts in Cage Eleven.

Later that night, Bobby went out to get Geraldine and bring her home from work. The ground was uneven and Geraldine tripped and fell over a broken pavement slab. She was four months pregnant. Something went inside of her.

● ● ●

With his best friend arrested, Sands turned his attention back to rebuilding the local movement. Now, it was more important than ever to build a structure that would be intact if more volunteers were caught or killed. He put a special focus on the young people and encouraged a group of them to take on more political activities like publishing and distributing *Liberty* and organizing community-based projects. They regarded him as a sort of guru. Not only did he lead by example, he also made them feel like he was "just one of them." Jennifer McCann, who was just sixteen, was in awe of Bobby, not just because he'd been in jail but because he talked to her like he really cared about her. She looked up to him because he listened to what she had to say.[14]

He stepped up their political education with a view to making some of them IRA volunteers. He made a special point to encourage women to join the IRA. Sands organized a series of lectures for the *Fianna* (the organization of Republican youth) about respecting the community and gaining respect from the community.

"The Republican Movement is nothing without its people," he told them. "Our main objective is to keep that support and build on it."

He went out and sold newspapers with them. He went door to door with them collecting for the prisoners, when most other IRA volunteers felt that was below them. According to Féilim Ó hAdhmaill,

> *Bobby's attitude was different from other IRA men. He believed strongly in Socialist revolution and political mobilization. Political mobilization and debate was the number one thing for him. Take on board what people can do. Some other volunteers might have said, "This is daft." Bobby wouldn't have forced them to do [political activities] but he would have been involved himself.*

Sands was in a fight against time. By September, the movement in Twinbrook was coming under intense pressure from the British army and the police. In mid-month, a local newspaper reported on the government's "new policy line to step up harassment in Twinbrook" against party members and the residents at large. The British army and the police were constantly raiding houses, arresting young people, and interrogating them about Sinn Féin activities in the area. They wrecked homes, pulling up floorboards and punching holes in walls. In one incident, the British army stopped a group of young people selling *Liberty* and confiscated their papers.

Local Republicans were defiant. They released a press statement saying that "we are here to stay and if the Brits don't like it then it's just hard luck."[15] In private, though, some of them were more cautious, especially about Bobby Sands. He was too valuable as a political activist, said some, to continue his military involvement in the IRA. They could see the noose closing in on him.

Yet Bobby Sands simply would not ask people to do anything he was unwilling to do. So he continued to sell Republican newspapers *and* he went on military operations, now as officer in command of the Twinbrook IRA.

Chapter Eleven

A Bad Day in Dunmurry[1]

The weather was stinking on the morning of October 14. It would be one of those cold, gray Belfast days with an on/off heavy rain. At 8:15, N— left his house in Twinbrook and climbed into his dark green Bedford van to begin his working day. As he drove toward Gardenmore Road, which runs parallel behind Laburnum Way where the Sands family lived, he saw two young men at either side of the road. They wore masks, one dark blue and the other khaki. In front of him in the middle of street was a third man wearing a green anorak, with a khaki mask, large brown boots, and a pistol. The man with the pistol waved him down.

"Provisional IRA. Nothing will happen to you. We only want the van."

The men got inside the van along with a fourth man, two in the rear and two in seat beside N—. The man with the gun gave directions. He made N— drive up the street, do a U-turn and then drive to a quiet cul-de-sac on the other side of the estate. There, they told him to get into the back of the van and lie down. After half an hour he heard gunshots nearby. Then the men told him he would get his van back after lunch. They blindfolded N— and two of them stayed with him in the rear of the van until 11:15, when they brought him back to his own house. They removed the blindfold and ordered him to walk into his own house and not look back. He was to stay there until he heard further. N— did as he was told.

The weather stayed nasty, as the men took the van to a safe house nearby. They loaded it with four blue and green plastic bags. Each bag contained twenty pounds of gelignite, a detonator, and a box timer. They also loaded some five-gallon tins of gasoline into the van.

Shortly after 2:00 P.M. a woman and five men got into the van and drove off. Two of them carried .357 Magnum revolvers, and another a 9mm automatic pistol. Behind the van were four men in a stolen blue Ford Granada. Next to the driver of the Ford, Joe McDonnell sat wearing a blue anorak, carrying the bag lunch his wife Goretti had given him that morning as he left on his way to work. One of the two men in the back of the Ford wore a black waterproof coat. It was Bobby Sands, who had planned and coordinated the operation. He carried two plastic bags, one from Stewart's supermarkets and the other a red, white, and blue bag with no name. Inside were several pairs of gloves and some woolen masks. The other man in the back seat wore a blue anorak and carried a black Colt .45 automatic.

The van and car turned right into Upper Dunmurry Lane and drove along the winding street, under the Train Bridge, toward Station View. In the Ford, Sands passed out the masks and gloves to his companions and then scrunched up the bags and put them into his trouser pockets.

Station View Street is a short narrow cul-de-sac, one hundred meters long. It is tucked between the Lisburn Road, the main road south from Belfast, and the Belfast-Dublin railway line. As you turn into the street, there is a block of seven tiny terraced houses, fronted straight onto the footpath with no gardens. They are rendered with dirty gray pebbledash and roofed with blue-gray Bangor slates. Then, set back further from the road, is a block of nine bigger houses, with small front gardens, brick-faced ground floors, and white stucco above.

On the left-hand side of the street was a complex of old and new buildings that comprised Balmoral Furnishings. They included furniture factories, warehouses, and showrooms. An eight-foot high white-metal-picket security fence, topped with barbed wire, spanned the length of Station View on the left, with a gate into the office halfway up (employees only) and another at the top end, leading into the showrooms. As you entered the top gate, a security man checked you out before you drove into a small car park to the right or walked to the left and entered the main showroom. To get into the showroom, you entered a stone-clad porch at the front of a yellow-brick two-story building. A white sign across the top read:

WHOLESALE BALMORAL FURNISHINGS SHOWROOMS

Inside the entrance door was a platform with a small office off to the side. A short staircase led down to the ground-floor showroom, a few feet lower than the entrance. Some employees called it "the basement." Another set of stairs led upward to the first floor showroom. The showrooms held furniture for any room in the house, as well as carpets and other furnishings. Behind them was a furniture factory and storerooms. The complex was the biggest business in the small suburb of Dunmurry, between Belfast and Lisburn.

At about 2:15 P.M., the Bedford van turned into Station View, followed by the blue Granada. In front of the van, B— and his girlfriend Margaret were in their brown Ford Cortina, out shopping for furniture.

The van stopped and out got a young man and woman, both in their twenties. The woman was five foot six inches, slim build and slim of face, with dark brown hair that was parted in the middle and tied back. She was plastered with thick makeup and wore blue-tinted glasses with heavy blue frames. She wore a moss green calf-length shiny nylon raincoat with a tie-belt and dark brown boots. The man was taller, perhaps as tall as six feet, also of slim build, with sharp features and medium-length fair hair. He wore a gray checked sports jacket and a long bluish raincoat.

The security guard at the gate moved toward the brown Ford Cortina to check out the couple inside. As he did so, the woman in the nylon raincoat walked through the gate and the security guard turned away to meet her. As he began to speak to her, he felt a jab in his back and he heard the tall man's voice.

"Move on into the office or I will blow you in two."

Inside the showroom, they met the showroom manager E—. The woman drew a Browning semiautomatic pistol from her coat and put it to E—'s throat.

"Don't panic," she told him. "Just get down on the floor."

Then she saw G— working in the office.

"Get out here," she ordered, waving the gun in her left hand.

As G— followed her orders, a tall man in a dark knee-length overcoat came through the entrance door carrying a blue plastic bag. He put the bag down while he took a mask out of his pocket and placed it over his head.

The woman with the gun asked E— where were the rest of his staff before ordering the group downstairs to the showroom.

"Lie down and don't move or I'll blow your heads off," she told the group once they were downstairs. Then she rounded up the other staff and customers and left them lying flat on the floor with their arms outstretched and their heads down.

J— was attending to two customers in the downstairs showroom when a tall masked man at the entrance pointed his pistol at him. The gunman was wearing a blue anorak with stripes on the arms.

"Everybody freeze or you're dead," he said. "Lie down facedown or you'll fucking well get shot."[2]

The three lay down on the floor between two rows of Chesterfield suites. Others soon joined them. The tall masked man grabbed another salesman from the showroom floor and made him lie down with the group. Two other workers were moving mattresses from the top end of the showroom to the storeroom.

"Get down, get down," the gunman shouted at them.

They lay on the floor, as they were told. One of them was too afraid to look at anything but as they lay on the floor the other noticed that a man passed carrying a green plastic bag.

"Stretch your hands above your head and crawl back up the passage on your belly," the tall man ordered, sending them crawling over to the other people who were already lying at the front of the showroom.

Then there was the sound of a woman's voice. "Keep your heads down or you'll get shot. If you all lie there you'll be alright," she said, calmly.

Outside, as the green Bedford van backed up toward the entrance of the furniture showroom, K— was crossing the yard from the main office block some twenty yards away. At first, K— thought the van was filled with schoolchildren coming to view the factory. The three people he saw in the back of the van seemed to be very small. He thought the van would hit the showroom but someone in the back shouted, "Stop!"

He realized that these were not schoolchildren when a man jumped out the back of the van. He wore a green jacket and a knit mask and was carrying a gun in his right hand. As he ran into the showroom the man looked at K— and ran on. This was a big mistake.

K— ran back to the general office to tell the office manager what was happening. The manager ran to front door and saw the green van. There was someone inside with an anorak hood pulled over his head. That was enough for him and he immediately phoned the police at the Dunmurry RUC barracks, just around the corner.

I— and his wife drove from the town of Portadown to Balmoral Furnishings to look at furniture. It was their first time there so they did not know their way about. They turned into Station View and parked halfway down the street, behind a light colored car with a reddish van parked along beside it. I— remarked to his wife that the cars were badly parked and then they walked toward the entrance gate to the furniture showrooms. As they approached the building they noticed some men waving at them. They were not sure whether the men were waving them in or waving them away. The couple proceeded to the entrance, where a young masked man appeared and pushed them into the showroom. Inside they saw three masked men and an unmasked woman with a handgun. The woman and one of the men were covering a group of people who were lying on the floor between rows of Chesterfield suites.

The couple in the Ford Cortina soon joined I— and his wife. They were oblivious to what had been happening in the showroom after the security guard turned away from them to talk to the couple that walked in behind their car. They just drove through the security gate and parked their car as the green van backed toward the showroom entrance. They got out of the car and entered the showroom behind the couple from Portadown, who had parked their car on the street. By the time they saw the man inside the door wearing a black mask and carrying a gun, it was too late to turn back. He pointed his gun at them and ordered them into the building.

"Lie down on the floor," he ordered them.

"Lie down with your arms out," added the woman. "If you don't move you'll be alright."

The couple from the Cortina lay with their hands outstretched, just as they were told to do. The man from Portadown was not as quick. He bent lower and the woman shouted at him to lie flat.

"Get down or I'll blow the fucking head off you."

At that, the masked man came over. The others heard a couple of thumps as if someone was getting hit. They lay completely flat and did not look up to see what was happening.

The masked man had a deep voice. He sounded older than the rest.

"Keep your heads down," he said.

Another salesman entered the showroom and an armed man made him join the others on the floor.

As he lay on the showroom floor, the showroom manager was curious about what was happening. He could see the entrance to the showrooms and he watched two more masked men coming in the front door. One had a blue plastic bag. The manager watched him take it into the main showroom before he felt someone put a foot on the back of his neck.

"Lie down."

He put his head down.

G—, who was lying still, afraid to move, felt the man step on his back and, with his other foot, jab him in the back of his head and neck to make sure that he, too, kept his head down.

Masked men were carrying blue plastic bags containing twenty-pound bombs and five-gallon tins of gasoline from the green van into different parts of the showrooms. One of them was Bobby Sands. The woman and man who were guarding the group on the floor shouted out to the men to find out what was happening.

"Is that ring complete?" the woman shouted.

"They haven't finished upstairs," came the reply.

Then the man with the deep voice said, "Did you do the circle upstairs on the first floor?"

"Are they all down?"

"They're all down, they're standing out there," replied the woman.

As they started to leave the showroom, the woman turned to the group on the floor.

"Nobody move."

"Don't move for two minutes or you're dead," added the man with the deep voice.

After calling the police, the office manager had gone back to the front door of the office block to watch what was happening. He saw a man in a full mask, wearing a dark raincoat and jeans, move from the showroom to the front gate and look up street as if waiting for someone. He did it two or three times.

Then the company secretary approached the office in his red Ford Cortina. As he drove toward the office one of the secretaries ran out to him and informed him what was going on. He backed his car across the road and parked it, adding to the congestion of parked cars on the narrow street. Then he ran toward the RUC station to summon more police. As he got to the main road, a police Land Rover and an army Land Rover passed him, on their way to Station View.

Back in the showrooms, some of the people lying on the floor heard glass breaking and a roar.

"A puff, not an explosion," was how one of them described it.

They saw a red glow in the back of the showroom and smoke started to fill the area. Someone looked around and the gunmen and woman were gone.

"Are we going to lie here and get burned to death?" someone asked.

They lay there for a few seconds. The smoke was getting thicker. They heard voices and footsteps as another group began to leave.

"Is everything alright?" one of them asked.

"Everything's alright," came the answer.

They got up to leave the building.

Outside, the office manager continued watching. Eight men emerged from the showroom, some masked and some not. They ran up Station View. He saw some of them stop at a light colored car that was parked at the railings. After a moment, they got into the car. He did not see the other four men get into the blue Ford Granada that was parked further up the street.

Seamus Finucane jumped in behind the wheel of the Ford. He ripped off his black woolen mask and his gloves and threw them onto the floor. The other three jumped into the back, Bobby Sands in the middle, Joe McDonnell behind the driver, and Sean Lavery on the passenger side of Sands. They also removed their masks and gloves, scattering them in the rear seat and the back window shelf. A Colt .45 lay on the floor at Lavery's feet.

The four might have escaped had they driven away immediately. But they knew the others could not get the van out of the street due to all the parked cars. They stayed where they were in case some of the others needed to jump in beside them.

In the meantime, a young couple had driven their white Datsun down the left-hand side of Station View. They were hoping to price a kitchen for their new house. They stopped at the first gate to the office where they saw a sign instructing them to go to the next gate. So they drove toward the main gate and stopped in front of the fence railings, now totally blocking the road because of the vehicles parked all along the right-hand curb. Four masked men came over to their car. One put a gun to the driver's head.

"Get out!"

The couple got out and ran toward the furniture showrooms.

As soon as he saw the others get into the Datsun, Seamus Finucane started to back the blue Granada out of Station View. The road was too narrow, so there was no chance of turning round. The four men in the white Datsun began to reverse behind them. They were too late.

A car sped round the top corner of station view and halted across the road, blocking their way. As two British army MPs, nineteen-year-old Nicholas Victor Tennant and twenty-one-year-old Bernard Maguire, drove into Station View, they saw a blue Ford Granada reversing toward them. Maguire stopped the car across the road and the two MPs got out.

"Fuck it, that's it, we're caught," exclaimed one of the three men in the back seat of the Granada as he looked out the rear window at the MPs' car and then at a police land rover that pulled in behind. Finucane, knowing that this escape route was hopeless, stopped the car.

Tennant ran up the left-hand side of road toward the Furnishing Company while Maguire ran toward the Granada to cover its occupants. Finucane tried to open the car door to make a run for it but Maguire was already standing in his way.

"Sit still and don't move," he shouted.

Finucane quietly sat back in his seat.

None of the four had ever been in such a situation before.

"We were terrified to say the least but our discipline and our focus got us through it. There was very little we could do about it, we just took it in the chin," Finucane later recalled.

The four men exchanged words of encouragement.

"Keep your chin up."

"Don't be saying anything."

"We'll get out the other end."

"Don't anybody admit to anything and maybe we'll get out of this."

They quickly assembled a story. They were just there looking for work.

What happened then is disputed. The two MPs told one story. Both of their accounts agreed . . . too well, perhaps. The police who arrived behind them told a different story, again suspiciously consistent. Survivors from the Granada tell a third version. Like Kurosawa's film, *Rashomon*, the scene is told in three different and incompatible ways.

The MPs were first on the scene. We know from the testimony of witnesses that some of the escaping IRA volunteers tried to hijack a white Datsun. Yet the soldiers never mention the Datsun. Instead, they begin their story with a crowd emerging from the Balmoral showroom.

Tennant claims he then saw about six people separate from main escaping crowd and run toward him.

"Halt!" he called on everyone in the crowd.

Those nearest the premises did so.

"However, the other group kept coming toward me. This group then seemed to panic and run separately and I then saw two men, each carrying handguns, in this group. At this point the men in this group started to turn around as if to run away from us and after I had called on them again to halt I fired four or five aimed shots at one of the gunmen. I wasn't able to see what kind of gun he was carrying. I fired quickly and I saw the man I had fired at fall to the ground. When the man fell two of his companions went to his assistance. They didn't help him at all and they too ran down the road away from us. I remained where I was and fired a further four shots at the other gunman who was then running down the road. He then disappeared from view running round the end of the houses situated on the right hand side of the roadway."

The shot man was Seamus Martin from Twinbrook. The "other gunman" was Gabriel Corbett, who was later arrested some distance away with a bullet lodged in his back.

Tennant then saw a man assisting Martin. His partner Maguire ran up and tackled the man, thinking he was one of the gunmen. When he found out that the man was a civilian, he sent him away. Maguire "dragged [Martin] back along the road toward our car."

By now there were more police on the scene. The other IRA men and the woman had disappeared. Tennant helped the police clear the houses in the street and went back to the car. Maguire had placed Martin in the back of the car and decided to take him to the hospital because he was bleeding badly. An ambulance arrived and Maguire accompanied Martin to the Royal Victoria Hospital.

MP Maguire tells the same story as his partner, again leaving out the white Datsun. He saw a crowd emerging from the showrooms and they called on them all to stand still. Most obeyed, but a group of "about six males and at least one female carried on running toward a red Cortina car which was parked unattended in the center of the roadway . . . I then saw that one of the six men was carrying a handgun and I then shouted at them to halt. Corporal Tennant also shouted for them to halt, and at this point the group started to turn away from us back along the street. I then saw Corporal Tennant fire a number of shots at the man carrying the handgun. One of these shots must have hit him, as he fell to the ground."

Two companions stopped, says Maguire, knelt beside their wounded comrade, and then ran away. Tennant fired more shots at the escaping volunteers. Maguire told a policeman to cover the occupants of the Ford because he saw a man tending to the wounded person and thinking that he was also involved, tackled him. Only after the man identified himself as an employee of the Balmoral Furnishing Company did Maguire let him go and tell him to move away.

Then, Maguire says he asked Martin, "Are you a gunman?"

"Yes, I am," Martin supposedly replied.

He asked Martin who his companions were. He replied that he didn't know.

After Maguire heard that there were bombs in the showroom, he dragged Martin to the MP car. An ambulance came and Maguire stayed with Martin until he handed him over to an arrest team at the hospital.

The police story differs from that of the MPs in crucial respects. It conforms more closely to the accounts of civilian eyewitness, although it differs from these accounts in important ways.

Constable Douglas was driving an RUC Land Rover, along with Constables Craig, Moss, and Wilson. At about 2:20 P.M., they received a call and as they parked the Land Rover across the top of Station View, Constable Wilson claims he saw a blue Grenada and a white Datsun, both with their reversing lights on. Both cars were moving. A green van was parked beside the white Datsun.

As they got out of the Land Rover, Wilson saw three persons get out of white Datsun, and "two carrying handguns began firing at us and RMPs." Wilson returned fire, discharging three shots. One man fell to the ground. The other two, one of whom was armed, ran through the gates of the Furnishing Company and got away.

Wilson then approached the blue Granada and saw Seamus Finucane in the driver's seat and Lavery, Sands, and McDonnell in the back.

". . . Lavery, had a cocked Colt automatic pistol at his feet," said Wilson. He lifted the gun and a pair of gloves and covered the men in the car along with Constables Moss and Craig.

Constable Craig, too, saw three men emerging from the Datsun and he dived for cover before "returning four rounds at these gunmen." He then went to the Granada and saw the cocked Colt automatic at the feet of Sean Lavery.

Douglas also saw three persons getting out of the White Datsun. Two of them turned around and shot at them (the MPs had these gunmen as part of a group of six who came running out of the crowd that was escaping from the furniture showrooms). Douglas "returned" one round and then went back to the Land Rover to call for assistance. When he saw that one man was hit, he radioed for an ambulance.

Constable Moss also observed the white Datsun and blue Granada "both with their reversing lights engaged." He jumped out and drew his Walther, ran toward the showroom, and stopped about twenty-five yards from the white Datsun.

"Three persons then got out of the car all carrying handguns. Two then turned and fired at the Police and RMPs who had arrived at the same time as our patrol. I then fired six aimed shots at these persons."

With his gun empty, Moss ran for cover behind the blue Granada. He did not see anyone hit by any shots. He insists that he only fired at two gunmen who were firing at him, and not at the third man who did not fire and who ran off.

"There was not [sic] other person in my line of fire other than these two persons who were firing at me and my colleagues," he claims. "None of my bullets could have possibly hit anyone other than one of the two gunmen."

Moss concludes by saying that the two gunmen fired "about two or three shots at us."

What did the other witnesses see, including the four men who watched the shooting from the vantage point of the blue Granada?

Seamus Finucane "saw everything" from the front seat of the blue Granada. He insists that the MPs jumped out of their car and just started firing without warning.

"I know as a matter of fact that as soon as the MPs got out of the car there was no warning shouts, no yellow cards or anything like that there. They could have shot anybody but it was fortunate for them that they shot three volunteers."

Martin, he says, never had a gun. He was shot unarmed. The other volunteers escaped by running through a crowd of people and any shots at them must have endangered civilians. All four men in the car were shocked at the recklessness of the firing MPs and police.

The civilian witnesses also tell how they emerged from the showroom and there was gunfire all around them. They dove for cover, back into the burning showroom, behind cars and vans, anywhere they could find. By the time the shooting began, civilians were scattered all around the place.

H— ran out "and then shooting started." A few men got out of a Datsun car and started to run behind the houses. About six shots rang out and H— went back into the showroom and threw himself on the floor.

I— ran out and saw police and army at top of street. Someone was wounded and lying in the street. The woman and one of the men who had been holding them inside were "running up an entry at the far side of the street."

Whether or not these civilians were in real danger from gunfire, they clearly *felt* they were in danger. Another civilian witness, however, directly contradicts the police. J— ran out of the showroom as soon as he realized that the bombers had left. As he went through the door, he says, "five or six shots were fired which seemed to hit the wall beside us."

Later, in the committal hearing for their trial, Sands asked the British MPs a "number of questions" on this point. He wanted to know what evidence they had that anyone who they shot at was armed. Had they ever found any weapons on them or connected any weapons with them? (They hadn't.) Had they not recklessly endangered numerous civilians by firing into the crowd at some alleged gunmen?

Of course, many people would find it hypocritical for Bobby Sands to call British soldiers "reckless" when he had just been involved in placing bombs in a furniture showroom. He would have argued, in return, that his unit made every effort to ensure that only property, not people, was damaged as a result of his actions, whereas the security forces were purely reckless in pursuit of their enemy.

As the firing went on the couple from the white Datsun ran down an alleyway at the right-hand end of Station View. They jumped into the back garden of the end house and tried to hide in a garden shed. They were startled to see the three masked men who hijacked their car in the garden behind them. The three men ran away to the main road and ran across it into the car park behind a Crazy Prices supermarket, where they hijacked a car and escaped.

Gabriel Corbett was shot in the back, near his spine. By the time he got to the parking lot at Crazy Prices he was alone. He jumped into a car and asked the driver to take him to the hospital. But when she screamed, he got out of the car and asked a cab driver to give him a lift. The driver took Corbett to the military hospital at Musgrave Park in Belfast, where a British soldier arrested him.

After the shooting ended, policemen returned to cover Sands and his comrades. They pulled them from the car and spread-eagled them against the front wall of the terraced houses. Finucane says the police kicked them about for a couple of minutes while they were spread-eagled against the wall. Then all hell broke loose. The twenty-pound bombs began to go off in the showroom and the windows came flying out of the houses. They exploded into small shards that, along with the slates dislodged from the roofs, pelted into parked cars, policemen, and soldiers. The spread-eagled men and their handlers immediately dropped to the pathway as the bombs went off one after another. The showroom and its contents were soon ablaze.

Two policemen were blown through the door of one of the houses and fell to the ground. As they got up, another explosion again threw them off their feet. They got up again and took Joe McDonnell by the arms and just as they got him to the land rover another explosion blew them down again.

Finucane says the explosions angered the police, who then *really* began to manhandle them. It was then, he says, that they searched the car and found the .45 automatic (the police said that they found the gun while the men were still sitting in the car). Constable Wilson lifted the pistol, along with a pair of gloves.

The discovery of the gun incensed them further and they frantically shouted questions at the four men, asking what else was in the car.

The four were only on the street for a couple of minutes, but, "For us, it was an eternity."

Finally, the police handcuffed them and put them into the Land Rover. They took them around the corner to the RUC station and handed them over to Detective Constable King, who placed brown paper bags over their hands. He would see some of them again over the course of the next few days in Castlereagh interrogation center.

Chapter Twelve

Castlereagh[1]

From day to day in Castlereagh
The hours tick by like years,
While to and fro men come and go
To play upon your fears.

—Bobby Sands, "The Crime of Castlereagh"

A fter four hours in Dunmurry RUC Station, the police took Sands away for interrogation under the British Prevention of Terrorism Act. This usually meant going straight from the police station to Castlereagh Holding Center, the north's main full-time interrogation center. But the police were arresting people by the boatload as Secretary of State Roy Mason tried to "squeeze Republicans like a tube of toothpaste." Castlereagh was packed. Instead, they took Sands and his comrades to the Crumlin Road Jail.

They were fingerprinted, photographed, and processed. A forensics man took the paper bags off of their hands and made swabs to test for traces of explosives or handling weapons. Then, they started the interrogations. It was a dreary, wet, stormy night that matched their feelings at getting caught. Sands had it worst: he had a terrible cold.

Bobby's old friend Jimmy Rafferty was also in the jail awaiting interrogations that night. Bobby asked Rafferty how he was doing and would he get out. Rafferty was just in on the usual seven-day detention; he told Bobby that he expected to be released after the detectives finished their "fishing trip."

"What about yourself?" he asked Bobby.

Bobby just shook his head and said that he had no chance. Rafferty was struck by his generosity. Bobby had just been caught redhanded and was clearly in for a rough time and probably a long prison term, yet his first thought was to ask how Rafferty was doing.

There were no heavy interrogations that night. The four suspects stuck to their stories about hunting for work and their interrogators did not press them hard. The *real* interrogations would start the next day in Castlereagh, a new purpose-built two-story brown-brick building. It had thirty-eight holding cells upstairs and twenty-one "interview rooms" downstairs. There was a medical room where suspects got a cursory check before they were sent to interrogation. Lawyers and human rights groups complained that it was located upstairs instead of downstairs, where doctors could observe ill treatment by the detectives.

Police violence was a rising concern. On July 26, the chief constable issued a memo on that seemed to indicate that violence during interrogations could be justified if it led to confessions. The memo distinguished between an "interview" and an "interrogation" and said that the rules which safeguarded suspects against police violence only applied to the former. When a suspect entered Castlereagh, the detectives decided whether to use interviews or interrogations.[2] Complaints of assaults during interrogation rose from July 7 to August 21, despite the fact that many detainees refused to lodge complaints. In September, the European Commission found the British government guilty of "torture, inhuman and degrading treatment" of detainees.

Down in the interrogation rooms, teams of detectives questioned their suspects. They worked in groups of two so that they could try to break their man in shifts. Interrogation sessions usually lasted about two hours, but with the team system, one session could follow another and they could stretch for hours on end. The strategy was simple: try to break down one suspect and then use his admissions to extract statements out of the rest. As one detective boasted, "even strong wills crack when they hear that their associates have confessed, and most suspects crack in the first two days."[3]

Castlereagh had such a bad reputation that many detainees broke and signed a statement before a hand was raised. Detectives described the atmosphere in the interview rooms as "indescribable . . . only the Provos knew what it was like, because only they had been through it." IRA suspects alleged beatings and detectives admitted that "many of [the allegations] were true."[4] Getting results was what mattered.

Bobby was placed in a bare, windowless cell. It had a big round light that the warders brightened and dimmed from outside. It could glare at full brightness through the night or they could turn day into night, a form of sensory deprivation. Sands wrote later, in his epic poem "The Crime of Castlereagh,"

> 'Twas ten to nine, for that's the time
> I heard the Watcher say.
> But was it light or was it night
> I ne'er knew either way.

In the cell was a hard prison bed with sheets and blankets. A chair. White walls. The food was too cold. The room was too hot. The air vent rattled incessantly overhead. White noise. To Bobby, it all seemed to be designed to break their spirits.

> White walls! White walls! Torturous sprawls,
> With ne'er a window space.
> And so confined a quaking mind
> Goes mad in such a place.

Bobby sat and waited to be called for interrogation. The wait was one of the worst parts of detention.

Dinner came but he was not hungry. He set his paper plate aside and drank his mug of tea. Then, a clink of key in lock.

"Interview!"

The warder took Bobby from his cell. He signed his name into the logbook and took him to the doctor, who certified that he was fit for interrogation. Bobby's savage description of this ceremony shows his strong distrust of prison doctors.

> He glared at me begrudgingly,
> He asked if I were ill.
> I shook my head, for sickening dread,
> Could not be cured by pill.

I quaked like swine on slaughter line
As he said, "You're quite fit.
So send him on, he's good and strong,
And roast him on the spit."

With the doctor's approval, the warder took Sands down to the interrogation rooms. Bobby later described in detail his experiences in Castlereagh, in a hand-written account of the interrogation sessions that he smuggled from jail to the Association for Legal Justice, a human rights organization. He said that the beatings began almost immediately. He stuck to his alibi. The detectives took the interrogations in double shifts of four to six hours at a time. This part of Bobby's testimony is consistent with the police records of interrogations, which were collected in the file of evidence for the subsequent trial.

On Friday, there were two two-hour sessions. From 7:00 to 9:10 P.M., Sands was interrogated by Detective Sergeant W— and Detective Constable McA— of the Criminal Investigation Division (CID) in the Castlereagh CID Office. Bobby claims that he was repeatedly punched and kicked by the two detectives, yet he admitted nothing. He gave his particulars: name, address, where he was coming from and going to. He told them over and over that he was looking for a job and he accepted a lift from the others in the pandemonium of the bombing. Detective W— gives a similar account, although leaving out any suggestion of physical contact:

> *I . . . saw the accused Robert Gerard Sands at Castlereagh CID Office . . . I told him that I believed he had been detained by uniform police whilst in a car, together with others, one of whom was armed. That this car was in Station View outside the bombed premises. I cautioned him that he was not obliged to say anything and that anything he did say may be given in evidence. Sands remained silent for a short period of time. I then informed him that I required him to give me an account of his movements on the 14 October 1976. He then stated that he left the house at 2 o'clock or 10 to 2 o'clock P.M. He walked from Twinbrook through Areema Drive down Dunmurry Lane and into Station View. Waa [sic] going to Balmoral Furniture Place looking for a job. When he arrived in Station View he saw a lot of men with hoods and weapons at the end of the street. Didn't know how many men*

*there were, wouldn't even attempt to guess how many. He got
scared, turned round and ran back towards Dunmurry Lane. He
then heard shots and he ran and jumped into the back seat of a car
parked in Station View. There were others in the car but there was
too much shooting going on to remember exactly. There were two
others already in the back seat but doesn't know if there was anybody in the front of the car. Sands stopped talking at this stage. I
then asked him if he saw a gun in the car and he replied, "No."*

No sooner was the first interview over at 9:10 P.M. than Detective Constables H— and McC— took over for a further two-hour interview. The
session got off to a bad start when Bobby refused to talk and complained
that he had a sore stomach and wanted to see the doctor. They granted his
request and forty minutes later the interrogation resumed. It covered the
same ground as the first session. Again, Bobby claimed that he was
punched and kicked. The detectives asked him to account for his movements at Balmoral Furniture Showroom. He repeated the same story about
looking for a job and then jumping into the car.

The second interview ended at 11:15 P.M. Sands had been under interrogation for four hours straight, including the short interval to see the
doctor. But he was not finished.

Within five minutes a third interrogation started. This time the leading
interrogator was M—, a detective from Dunmurry, accompanied by
McC—, another detective from Dunmurry. According to Bobby, this is
when the real hard times began. We have both Bobby's and the lead
detective M—'s accounts of this one-hundred-minute session, which
went on until one o'clock in the morning, by which time Sands had
endured six straight hours of interrogation. The two accounts, interrogator and interrogated, are reproduced side-by-side, below.

M—, Detective Inspector, RUC Station Dunmurry, April 9, 1977	Bobby Sands
"At 11:20 P.M. on 15 October 1976 accompanied by D/Constable McC— I saw the accused Robert Gerard Sands at the Police	"I was brought into a new room where there were two new detectives awaiting me. This was the third interrogation and was to

Office, Castlereagh. I identified ourselves to the accused and pointed out to him that he had been detained at the scene of an explosion at Balmoral Furnishing Company the previous day. I invited him to explain to us the circumstances in which he had been detained. He was then cautioned. The accused refused to answer. He was asked to account for his presence in the blue Granada car. Sands then stated that he had already given his story and did not wish to answer any further questions. He was then questioned about his family connections. He at first refused to answer but eventually stated that he had a wife and one child, his wife was six months' pregnant. Asked again about the bombs planted in the Balmoral Furniture Company but he again refused to answer. He was questioned about his employment. He stated that he used to be a Coach Builder in Alexanders. He was asked if he knew the identity of the others who were detained along with him. He again refused to answer. He was asked to explain why he had been down in Station View, and he said he had been down for a job. He was asked if all his companions had likewise been down about a job and he refused to answer. He was questioned fur-

prove worse than the other two. A detective stood behind me and one on the other side of the table. The detective to my left had been drinking, and was very aggressive and violent.

"I was sitting on the chair no more than five minutes when he grabbed me by the throat with both hands and said 'Before you leave here you will talk alright, you will even make up fairy stories.' I was told to stand up. The person on the other side of the table stood up and started asking questions. After each question the detective who had the drink would slap me heavily on the head, ear, or face and say 'tell him' or 'answer him.' I would not reply. This sort of thing went on for half-an-hour roughly with kicks and punches thrown in occasionally. I was spread-eagled against the wall with my fingertips only high up against the wall and my feet spread apart and back as far as I could manage. The detective who was reeking with alcohol was punching me in the kidneys, sides, back, neck, in fact, everywhere. The other detective was holding me by the hair and firing questions into my face. This continued until I stood up straight as I was exhausted and said I was not standing in that position again. I was told to sit down, given a cig-

ther about the planting of the bombs but he refused to answer any questions. Interview terminated at 1:00 A.M."

arette and soft-soaped with promises, deals, etc. The tactics and atmosphere changed two or three times while I was sitting. I was threatened that my wife would get what I got even though she was pregnant. I was threatened, with all sorts of things. They tried to degrade me, humiliate me and demoralise me. Although my stomach was painful and I was cold I was still mentally, and to a certain extent physically fit.

"I was once again hauled up on to my feet, beat about and made to take my boots off. I was spread-eagled again although I tried to resist this. I was punched on the head and neck and I felt dizzy. The detective who was still reeking of alcohol was standing on one side of me and he was leaning into my face screaming abuse. I could smell the alcohol. He put his arms around my neck and pressed his two fingers in under my jaw which was very painful.

"He also repeated this tactic on my sides and various other parts of my body. I was still spread-eagled. When he sat to the front of me, on my left hand side, he was swinging his foot between my legs and kicking me in the privates. He hit me about 4 or 6 times like that which sickened me and took the breath from me. I fell twice only to be hauled to my feet in the same position again. The same person was chopping me on the back of the neck, the individual blows heavy and continuous, about 20 or 30 times; I am not sure as the other detective was punching me in the stomach and yelling questions. I don't even remember falling, but I must have because I was being hauled off the floor and put on a chair when I regained my senses. I was given another cigarette and asked if I was all right and told it was early days yet, so I could make it shorter and easier for myself if I just put my name to a piece of paper.

"This interview ended at either 12:50 A.M. or 1:10 A.M. I am not sure but I had been beaten and interrogated for about seven hours or so with only a break for the doctor to examine me. When I was told I was going back to my cell I asked to see a doctor, but they just laughed and said, 'You have some chance.' They also said, 'So has your fucking solicitor.'"

Years later, Bobby wrote of this interrogation, the techniques of violence and the good cop bad cop routine:

Now some will say in sweetest way
They do not wish you harm,
They try to coax, they try to hoax
They murder you with charm.
They give you smokes, they crack you jokes,
Allaying all your fears,

Then beg you sign that awful line
To get you thirty years.

. . .

Some bear the stain of cruel Cain,
These are the men of doom.
The torture-men who go no end
To fix you in that room.
To brutalise they utilise
Contrivances of hell,
For great duress can mean success
When tortured start to tell.

At one in the morning, Sands was taken back to his cell. He was unable to sleep for two hours because the bright white light shone in his eyes and reflected off of the walls. He kept waking up during the night because of the noise of the ventilation system. Then, when it was turned off, the room became very warm and his sweat collected on the plastic cover of the mattress, until he was soaking. The next day was Saturday and, according to Bobby, there was more of the same.

"I was brought down the stairs into the interrogation building again. This interrogation lasted about two hours and was followed by another which lasted two hours. During both of these I was slapped, punched, threatened, etc . . ."

The detectives admit no such thing. Once more, both accounts are available for comparison.

F—, Police Officer, Regional Crime Squad Belfast, April 8, 1977

"I am a Detective Sergeant of the Royal Ulster Constabulary attached to the Regional Crime Squad, Castlereagh, Belfast. On the 16.10.1976 at 2:50 P.M. I saw Robert Sands, DOB 9.3.1954, unemployed labourer, of 7 Sum-

Bobby Sands

". . . After dinner at about 3:00 P.M. I was taken to the last room on the right of the interrogation building. I can remember this very clearly. I was brought into the room and I was standing there not saying anything or being asked anything.

merhill Gardens, Twinbrook, Belfast, at Castlereagh Police Office where he was earlier brought by other Police. Detective Constable McB—, Regional Crime Squad, was also present. We introduced ourselves to Sands and told him that we were making enquiries regarding the bombing attack earlier that day (14.10.1976) at Balmoral Furnishing Company, situated in Station View, Dunmurry, when a number of armed terrorists held up the staff in the premises and then planted bombs in the building that caused widespread damage on exploding. We went on to tell Sands that we had reason to believe that he could assist us in our enquiries into this matter. Sands was then cautioned. He replied, 'I'm saying nothing.' Sands was asked questions about himself, his family and background. He stated that he had got married about 3 years ago and has a child aged 3 years. Sands went on to say that he disagreed with the activities of the Provisional IRA and that he was not in that organization. On the day of the explosion at Balmoral Furnishing Company, Sands stated that he was in Station View near the premises following the explosions. He insisted that he had nothing to do with the attack

"I was then set upon by two detectives. I was punched very heavily across the head, ears, face and eyes. I was kicked on the legs, my head was smashed against a wooden wall; I was punched on the body as well. After this beating which lasted 4-5 minutes I was calmly told to sit down. A few things were said when they were beating me. I did not hear what they were. I was given a cigarette as if nothing had happened. I was completely taken unaware. I was very shocked. I was then told that what I got was only a taste of what I would get unless I gave the right answers to their questions.

"The questioning began. I gave my particulars, repeated my verbal statement, asked for a doctor and a solicitor and said that I refused to answer any other questions, until my requests were granted. I was hauled out of my seat and spread-eagled against the wall. Again I was beaten all over. I refused to be spread-eagled. I was thrown down on the floor and told to do press-ups. I refused. I was kicked several times so I started doing press-ups. I was only able to do three or four; I just lay down. I was then hauled up and beaten and beaten and beaten. I was disorientated . . . During this particular interrogation my two arms were twisted up my back so that I

but that he was walking along Station View on his way to the Furnishing Company to try and get a job there. As he was walking along Station View near the premises he saw men with guns. Sands went on to say that he then jumped into a parked car in Station View. There were men in this car but he knew nothing about them. That was all he knew about the incident and he strongly denied any involvement in the bombing attack. Sands was told that it was hard to believe his story and that in the circumstances of how he was detained it was not acceptable to us in that he only got into the car when the shooting started. Sands continued to deny any involvement in this matter. The interview terminated at 4:50 P.M."

was unable to move and because of the pain I was just led towards the wall with simple jerks to my arms and my head hammered against the wall. My arms were twisted up my back for about ten minutes or maybe longer. I don't know what position they were in but they were being held together by just one person at one time while the other concentrated on hitting me. I was in a great deal of pain and defenceless.

"When my arms were released from this position I could just bring them down round to my front with considerable pain. I was unable to move them ... I was spread-eagled again but I fell right away every time because my arms were so painful. A chair with a cushinoned seat was put in front of me so that when I fell I did not hit the steel pipe coming from the radiator. I was also made to stand with my eyes closed and punched in different places where I was not expecting to be hit. I only closed my eyes once, the rest of the time one of the detectives held his hand round my eyes from behind. The interrogation ended at approximately 5:00 P.M."

After the interview was over, Bobby was exhausted and in pain. The bright light and the white walls depressed him. He began pacing his cell, four steps each way. He was exhausted, pained, and demoralized but he kept pacing to keep his mind going, so that he would not break and sign a statement as he had done years before.

Finally, on Saturday night, he was interrogated again. Uncharacteristically, he could not remember whether it was one or two interrogations. There were two. They covered the same ground. When the detectives could not get Sands to talk about the bombings, they tried to loosen him up by talking about his "family circumstances." Then they returned to the bombings. He stuck to his story about looking for a job. The detectives tried to get him to at least admit membership in the IRA but he refused.

Neither the police nor Sands mention it, but the evening's interrogation sessions were punctuated by a couple of muffled explosions from somewhere, not too far away. The lads were up to something. This gave Sands and the others encouragement.

Sunday morning came and Bobby waited for the first interview. The waiting was now unbearable.

> *The light burned bright was day now night*
> *Or was night turned to day.*
> *Forty hours, I'd sweated showers*
> *In panic-stricken fray.*
> *This waiting game was greatest strain*
> *And though I knew their ploy,*
> *It did not ease nor did appease*
> *But helped more to destroy.*

When the first interview finally came, at 10:20 A.M., the police tried a new and gruesome tack.[5] The two detectives came into the interrogation room and set the *Sunday News* down on the table, facing Bobby. Across the top was a banner headline:

Two Men Killed in City Gasworks Bomb Horror

Underneath the headline the article told how two men died when an IRA unit left a bomb in the gasworks the previous night. It was aimed at a British army billet in the gasworks complex. About twenty minutes later, while the firemen fought the blaze from the first blast, the big gas tank exploded, sending them diving for cover as a huge pillar of flame shot up and lit the city. Hundreds of families ran in panic from their nearby homes. Children ran screaming, terrified, through the brightly lit streets.

The report said that police and troops searching through the debris found two badly burned bodies beside the massive tank that exploded. Police believed they had died while planting a bomb. They recovered one male body and a leg from the debris of the explosion.

The detectives told Bobby that it was not two but three IRA men who died in the explosion. They showed him pictures of the dead men. He was shocked. Two of them were friends from Cage Eleven, Patrick Fitzsimmons and Joseph Surgenor.

"There's two of your fuckin' mates blew up all over the place. We need you to tell us their names so that we can identify their bodies and tell their families."

Bobby thought that the newspaper might be a mock-up that was meant to trick him into admitting that he was a member of the IRA. But he'd heard the two explosions the night before. It all rang true and the thought of two comrades dying in such a way broke his heart. In the disorientating conditions of Castlereagh after a couple of days of hard interrogations, the story about needing to identify the bodies seemed credible. Should he tell them the names, "do the right thing" so that the families could be told? Seamus Finucane went through the same ordeal in his interrogation. Both men struggled with their conscience over whether there really *was* something they could do for the families of the dead volunteers. In the end, they kept their mouths shut.

The detectives' account of this interrogation makes no mention of questioning about the explosions. The subject of IRA membership is mentioned, however, and it is conceivable that this is the point where they brought the gruesome line of questioning into the interrogation.

After lunch, Sands had another two-hour interrogation. The detectives' account of the session is quite unremarkable, and follows along the same lines as the others.

Then, a final one-hour session took place late that night. Sands told the same story. When one of his interrogators pointed out that the car he was in was reversing when the police arrived, Bobby stated that he had nothing further to say. When they pointed out that the others in the car were either from Twinbrook or the surrounding area, he continued to deny knowing them.

The last interrogation session was on Monday morning, Bobby's fourth day in Castlereagh. It did not get the interrogators any further than the first. Bobby repeated his story again. His last interview terminated at 11:30 A.M.

Sands had been through thirteen interrogation sessions, lasting from twenty minutes to two hours. In total, he had been under interrogation for seventeen hours and thirty-five minutes. He came from his last inter-rogation having signed nothing and admitting nothing. The detectives could have kept him and the other three in Castlereagh for another three days but they must have decided it was useless.

> *All things must come to pass as one*
> *So hope shall never die.*
> *There is no height or bloody might*
> *That a freeman can't defy.*
> *There is no source or foreign force*
> *Can break one man who knows,*
> *That his free-will no thing can kill*
> *And from that freedom grows.*

• • •

Bobby Sands was not alone in Castlereagh. What happened to him was also determined by what happened to the others.

Sean Lavery's interrogations were straightforward. A tall and thin but tough character—"a big long fellow, you couldn't miss him," was Joe McDonnell's description—he just sat through the sessions and said nothing. Detective H—'s notes of one interrogation simply state that, "Lavery refused to answer any questions and sat with his hands folded."

Other detectives give similar accounts. They would get nowhere with him. Seamus Finucane behaved more like Bobby. He had a simple story and stuck to it. He was at the Furnishing Company looking for a job. He was approaching the showroom when he saw people running out, so he turned and went the way he'd come. As he passed the blue Ford, one of men asked if he wanted a lift. Somebody asked him if he could drive and he said he could. Somebody told him to go ahead and drive.

McDonnell's story contradicted Bobby's and Finucane's, which seemed to give the police some hope that they could use him to crack the others. McDonnell had been in Castlereagh before and he was tough as nails. Per-haps this is why, by all accounts, the detectives never gave him a hard time physically. Instead, they concentrated *mentally* on him, trying to trip him up on the details of his story. He contradicted assertions by Sands and Finucane that they had not previously known each other. McDonnell's story placed the other three men in the car with him before the bombing.

Perhaps the police felt they were getting somewhere with McDonnell, or at least wanted the others to think so, because they interrogated him into the early hours of the next morning. Later, they put further pressure on McDonnell. But by then, he was reluctant to say anything.

After the first day of interrogations, the detectives got nothing further out of any of their suspects. Lavery continued to sit quietly with his mouth shut and his hands folded. Sands and Seamus Finucane stuck to their improbable stories about walking to Dunmurry to look for work. Joe McDonnell talked only about his family and about his job as upholsterer and he refused to say anything more about the fourteenth of October. The detectives even tried to sweeten up McDonnell by giving him "two cigarettes, a cup of coffee and some chocolate." He happily took them but then said nothing. When McDonnell later told the others about taking chocolates from the detectives, it became a standing joke between them.

● ● ●

Although Castlereagh was dominated by interrogation and waiting for interrogation, the men did little things to keep up their spirits. When Bobby passed Finucane in the hallway coming to and from interrogations they shouted encouragement to each other. Bobby played games with his interrogators. Each game was a little battle that enabled him to win small victories over his captors, thus building confidence and diverting himself from what was happening and fears of what *could* happen. Bobby was a master at these games. He had built up his skills over the years, particularly in the cages of Long Kesh but even earlier when he had to dodge the tartan gangs. Now he played dodge 'em with the detectives.

"There's all sorts of wee battles you'll fight in Castlereagh without so much as raising a hand," he said later.

Bobby's favorite games involved cigarettes and matches. He took advantage of good cop, bad cop. A detective would offer him a smoke during an interview and leave the packet of cigarettes and the box of matches on the table. Bobby would wait patiently for that split second when they turned their backs and then he would palm his prize and hide it in his trousers. Later, when they were in a cell together, Bobby told Seamus Finucane about smuggling matches and cigarettes from the detectives and the jailers. He wrote about it in "The Crime of Castlereagh":

I'd torn my jeans twice at the seams
And hidden matches there.
For men must use each little ruse
And take each passing dare.
If one had luck a lousy butt
Could calm the nerves no end.
For cultures taste takes second place
When you're in hell, my friend.

Sands had other ways to get at the interrogators and the jailers. He turned their own tricks against them: silence when they wanted him to talk, co-operation when they were not expecting it, smiling at times when they found it most frustrating. Other tactics were more overtly disruptive: constantly requesting to go out for a wash or to the toilet, asking to see the doctor. Bobby even drove his warders crazy by singing in his cell.

The others played games, too. Joe McDonnell made games around food. One day a man made himself vomit in a futile attempt to get the doctor to force his release from custody. As he left the cell to see the doctor, he set his dinner on top of the rubbish bins by the toilets. McDonnell asked to go to the toilet and as he passed his neighbor's dinner he ate the sausages. Everyone found it very funny that they were going through hell and Joe McDonnell was stealing sausages.

Finally, on Tuesday afternoon October 19, the four were fingerprinted and photographed again before they were transferred back to Dunmurry police station. At 4:00 P.M. Detective McK— charged them. When he preferred the charge, each of them replied, "No." After five minutes with their legal teams, the four appeared in a special court in the RUC station and were remanded in custody on charges of possessing four bombs, possessing a weapon, and possessing a weapon with intent to endanger life.

It was over quickly. After their five-minute hearing, they were whisked back to the Crumlin Road Jail. By 6:00 or 7:00 P.M. they were in cells in the basement of the jail for their first overnight stay. Bobby and Seamus Finucane shared a cell with a man from Scotland who had been returned for a crime in Belfast. They would not communicate in front of the Scot, so it was a long night. There would be longer.

Chapter Thirteen

Back to Prison

I'm sitting at the window, I'm looking down the street
I am watching for your face, I'm listening for your feet.
Outside the wind is blowing and it's just begun to rain,
And it's being here without you that's causing me such pain.

—Bobby Sands, "Sad Song for Susan"

The next morning they took Bobby and the others to see Governor Truesdale in Crumlin Road Jail.

"We're political prisoners and we want to join our comrades in A-wing," they said.

"There are no political prisoners here," was the governor's terse reply.

Still, the governor put them in A-wing. He sent Bobby and Seamus Finucane to a cell on "the twos," the first-floor landing. Sean Lavery went onto the same landing. But they put Joe McDonnell on "the threes," which Republicans hoped to avoid because it housed mostly notorious Loyalist prisoners, including some who would later become known as the Shankill butchers.

Crumlin Road Jail was completely different from when Bobby left it in 1973. Under the new policy of criminalization, what the warders gave the prisoners had to take. The jail was overflowing with young prisoners, some packed three to a cell. Seamus Finucane was only nineteen years old, yet he was considered an "old hand."

Bobby faced the prospect of twenty years or more in the H-Blocks, *without* political status. As a family man, the initial shock of being back in jail was not easy. Not only did he miss Gerard, Geraldine soon let him know how mad she was at him for breaking their "agreement" that he would not be involved in the IRA. She had never really had any chance at a family life. Even during the six months that they were together she was working and he was always busy. Now she was on her own again, a single mother and pregnant.

Bobby was barely two weeks back in jail when the worst possible tragedy struck. On November 6, Geraldine gave birth to a baby boy. She named him Liam after Bobby's hero, Liam Mellowes. But the baby was over a month premature and he had no real chance of survival. Friends who saw him in the incubator were shocked at how small he was, no bigger than your hand. Liam Sands died after one week, on November 13, of terminal bronchopneumonia and pyloric atresia.[1]

Bobby got a forty-eight-hour compassionate parole to spend time with Geraldine. Despite the tragedy, it was a critical breakthrough as he was the first IRA remand prisoner to get parole after a personal tragedy. When he got to the house in Twinbrook, he was shattered but still Bobby. Mary McGinn, an old friend from Rathcoole, went to the house to convey her sympathies to the grieving couple. She was amazed to find Bobby in the kitchen organizing support for an IRA volunteer from the area who had just been caught.

"Did you get his Green Cross[2] organized?" Sands asked her.

He's still organizing, she thought, even though he's just out for a few hours. She didn't think that Bobby ever really took time to grieve. Even though McGinn nearly put Bobby on a pedestal because she admired him so much for his community work, she could also see that his political commitment carried a high cost in personal terms. Geraldine, of course, bore the brunt of that cost.

On his second day of parole, Bobby took Geraldine across the city to the Short Strand to visit Roon, who was finally out of jail. Roon's brother, Philip, thought that Geraldine seemed shattered, vulnerable. Bobby, as always, was composed.

Seamus Finucane remembers Sands coming back to the cell two days after he left. Bobby said that he could not connect to what happened. He couldn't mourn or find closure. Finucane remembered when his own father died and he was not allowed to attend the funeral. It was as if his loss never happened, like his father went away but he would see him sometime in the future. How much more confusing it must have been for Bobby; he had not even seen young Liam.

In the following few months, people saw a big change come over Geraldine. She told people that Bobby should have been there for her but instead he had gone off doing his IRA business. She told Bobby that she felt betrayed because he had broken solemn promises to her and she said that she would not be coming on any more visits; she would send young Gerard on visits with his family. Her sense of betrayal was not helped by the lack of sympathy from the local community, which always took the side of their prisoner and barely recognized the emotional needs of the woman who was left behind. As a friend put it, "[the IRA] being a macho dominated organization, nobody ever took on board what Geraldine had gone through. I mean, this girl was married in prison, she'd struggled to find a home, Bobby came out, they were going to have a life, and Bobby had failed to keep his promise to her. She felt a terrible sense of betrayal and she was also in deep mourning . . ."

For a time, Bobby fought off depression. Seamus Finucane says he was still "a bouncy character" and life in the cell with him was always interesting. He was always talking about the struggle, politics, history, nature, birds, about their families, and just about things in general. Then he would sing songs.

Sands organized things in the canteen and the exercise yard. He was always on the move. If he wasn't playing soccer he was having meeting after meeting with different people, having discussions, organizing protests. Seanna Walsh was often in the meetings. He remembers walking around the yard with Bobby, discussing British strategy. It was like they were continuing a debate from Cage Eleven, picking it right up as if they had never been out of jail.

Bobby kept up on his reading and music. He was not allowed a guitar, so he made friends with some orderlies and charmed his way into getting a loan of theirs. He continually astounded the others with his repertoire of songs in Irish and English.

Life in A-wing was relatively relaxed because the Loyalist prisoners were refusing to come out of their cells in protest after a big fracas with the warders during the summer. This gave the Republican prisoners control of their periods out of the cell: an hour of exercise in the morning, another hour in the afternoon, and two hours in the canteen in the evening.

Bobby spent much of this free time doing army work. Seanna Walsh immediately brought him into the jail command structure. Then, when Walsh was sent to Long Kesh just before Christmas, Bobby became adjutant (second in command) of the wing. Bobby's main job was to try and improve discipline among the young volunteers. He organized drills and parades, trying to recreate the regime of political status they had experienced in the cages of Long Kesh. And he debriefed the new prisoners to ascertain whether they had given up information under interrogation that might compromise the IRA's activities.

One scared young IRA volunteer who had not broken was seventeen-year-old Colm Scullion, from Bellaghy in County Derry. Scullion was from the most legendary unit of the IRA in the 1970s, led by Francis Hughes. He was caught in October 1976, after a bomb that he and three comrades were transporting exploded prematurely in their car, killing Yvonne Dunlop, a local shopkeeper. Scullion lost a couple of toes and most of an ankle while Tom McElwee lost his right eye. In hospital, Scullion endured multiple operations and skin grafts and learned to walk again. He was transferred to A-wing just before Christmas.

The first day in the Crum was hard for a shy seventeen-year-old from the country. The place was "bursting apart with raucous city men." When Scullion went into the canteen he didn't know anybody. He was on crutches and couldn't even walk well enough to get his tray of food. Then, "this figure with long blonde hair" came over. Scullion thought he looked like a rock musician with his long hair and bell-bottom trousers. The man introduced himself, "I'm Bobby Sands."

"Colm Scullion, from Bellaghy."

"You're one of the Ballymena bombers."

"That's right."

"Has anybody given you anything to eat?"

"No."

Bobby got a tray with food to bring back to Scullion. He sat down beside him and began to talk in his easy way, asking him was everything okay? Had he been debriefed yet? Did he need a radio or anything? It was the first kindness that Scullion received in jail, from a city man no less. He began to look on Sands as a sort of "father figure."

Bobby organized political lectures and Irish classes. He began by teaching Seamus Finucane in their cell. He also taught classes in the canteen. What impressed the other prisoners was how he and Seanna Walsh demonstrated the usefulness of the Irish language by speaking it in their everyday conversation. Finucane remembers exercising with Sands in the yard while Walsh was in his cell up in the threes. When they shouted back and forth in Irish, it really impressed the others because, for the first time, they saw Irish as a living language.

Gino MacCormaic tells a similar story about how Sands influenced him to learn Irish. One day, when trouble was brewing, Bobby called out the window of his cell to another prisoner and they started a conversation in Irish about what was going on and what to do about it. Gino was spellbound, "because for the first time Irish wasn't just a dry school subject."[3]

Soon, other prisoners began speaking Irish. It enabled them to talk freely in front of the warders and it gave them a sense of control over their surroundings.

"It was really a weapon," says Seamus Finucane. "It wasn't just our culture or our language. And we employed it very effectively."

Sands and Walsh organized lectures on history and politics even though the authorities banned books with an Irish or political dimension (Bobby tried to get *Trinity* by Leon Uris, a bestseller at the time, but the prison authorities would not let it in). They gave the lectures using material that was still fresh in their mind from the cages. Bobby gave lectures on guerrilla warfare and on Republicanism since the late 1960s. Finucane was impressed. He hardly learned anything as an internee and was surprised at how productively Sands and Walsh had spent their time in Cage Eleven.

The criminalized jail system aimed to stop this kind of political organization. As a result, Bobby became a target of abuse from certain warders. A warder who had been in the cages during Bobby's time bore a special grudge against him. The prisoners nicknamed the warder "Marley Mouth."[4] He was always shouting at Sands, "We run the jail now, we take no more orders from you."

To back up their control, they regularly put the prisoners "on the boards," in punishment cells on a "number one diet" of bread and water.[5] Bobby later described the diet in the following terms,

> *It is a starvation diet. It consists of*
> *1. For "breakfast," two rounds of dry bread, a mug of black tea.*
> *2. "Dinner," two small scoops of potatoes and small ladle of watery soup.*

3. "Tea," same as breakfast.
4. "Supper," nothing! [6]

Bobby spent a considerable amount of time on the boards. Despite the punishment, he continued gathering information for political propaganda, sending out statements from the jail to the media. He wrote about the "conveyor belt," where suspects were moved through interrogation in Castlereagh, conviction in juryless Diplock courts and then into the new H-Blocks of Long Kesh. The experiences of all the prisoners around him were a mine of data on the government's new strategy of criminalization through arrests, interrogation, and detention.

Soon, they begin to hear news of the conditions in the H-Blocks, where a "blanket protest" was gathering momentum. Kieran Nugent, the first prisoner to be refused political status, was sentenced and put into the H-Blocks on September 16, 1976, just a month before Bobby was caught in Dunmurry. Nugent purportedly sent a letter to the Republican Movement saying, "The only way the Brits will get criminal garb onto my back is to nail it on."[7]

For a long time, the other prisoners knew little about Nugent's conditions of imprisonment. Those who were still awaiting trial knew that he was naked and had only a blanket to wear, thus originating the term "blanketman." But since he was not allowed to take visits unless he wore a uniform, even his own family was unaware of the full degradation of his conditions.

More Republican prisoners followed Nugent into H-Block number two (or H2), refusing to wear the uniform and ending up clad only in blankets. The authorities put them in the same wings as conforming prisoners, who soon told their families horror stories about what the young blanketmen were enduring. The prisoners in the Crum began discussing how they could support their comrades "on the blanket." They had nearly always won their prison struggles, so they thought an effective protest could win political status within a few months.

• • •

Christmas 1976 was a sad time. Bobby had not spent a Christmas with his family since 1971. All the hopes he had after he was released from the cages eight months before were now dashed. Not only had Geraldine lost young Liam, Bobby knew that he was losing Geraldine as well. He reacted by hardening his attitude toward the authorities. He began to grow a beard. The warders threatened to charge him with trying to change his appearance before his trial. He refused to shave.

In response, they moved him to "the threes" in an attempt to isolate him, since most of the political activity was on the ones and twos. Bobby joined Joe McDonnell and a handful of other Republican prisoners on a landing that was dominated by Loyalists.

It was difficult to fulfill his duties as adjutant on the threes. But Bobby was not one to be deterred. He set up a communication system where they passed notes up and down the landings. When men from the other landings were in the exercise yard he shouted to them in Irish from the top floor, using every opportunity to keep the lines of communication going.

In January 1977, communication was critical because trouble was brewing with the Loyalist prisoners. Part of the British government policy of criminalizing political prisoners was to forcibly integrate them. "There are no Loyalist or Republican prisoners, just criminals," said the Northern Ireland Office.[8]

The Republican prisoners devised a novel protest. They had to appear in the courthouse at Townhall Street every week while they waited for their indictments. Before their weekly hearings, they were left together in holding cells. To protest the fact that Kieran Nugent and the other blanketmen were kept naked in the H-Blocks, the prisoners decided that they would appear in public court without their clothes. While they were in the holding cells, the prisoners stripped down to their underwear. The remand hearings became a battleground, often leading to fights with the prison guards or police. Not all of the incidents were so serious. One day Pat Livingstone appeared before the judge dressed only in a tie and his boxer shorts. As he stood in the dock he told the judge, "This is another fine mess you've gotten me into."

At one remand hearing, Bobby ran into Jim Gibney, OC of the Republican prisoners on C-wing. While they sat in the holding cell, they discussed the worsening problem of integration. Gibney told Sands that Lenny Murphy, who would later be identified as leader of the notorious Shankill Butchers,[9] was creating a lot of trouble. Ever since he came on the wing, there was fighting whenever the Loyalists met Republicans in the exercise yard or the canteen.

The two groups of prisoners tried to work out an informal system. If one went to the exercise yard in the morning, the other stayed behind until the afternoon. If one went to the canteen for the first hour, the other took the second hour. On Christmas day, however, the warders tried to forcibly mix the Loyalist and Republican prisoners in the canteen. A fist-fight broke out. Over the next ten days, the warders tried again to mix them, each time with the same result. As punishment, all of the prisoners in C-wing were locked up for twenty-four hours in their cells.

Sands and Gibney discussed how to handle the escalating situation. They suspected that the screws were turning a blind eye to Loyalist violence, hoping that it might frighten younger prisoners away from joining the blanket protest once they got to Long Kesh. They agreed that winning segregation was a crucial part of the battle to win political status. But how could they fight for segregation without getting further punishments?

The battle for segregation came to a head at lunchtime on Thursday, January 6. Colm Scullion, still in severe pain and unable to walk without crutches, shared a cell with Jimmy Burns, a leading Republican from Belfast. They were both special hate figures for the Loyalist prisoners because they were in jail for killing Protestants. As they made their way into the canteen, about thirty Loyalist prisoners came at them, throwing their steel dinner trays at them and apparently ready to jump them. A warder closed the canteen gate behind them so that they could not escape. When they finally got out of the canteen Burns was beaten up and Scullion's leg was severely injured.

Seamus Finucane immediately wrote to Bobby with details of the attack. Sands consulted the other Republicans and they devised a simple plan to retaliate that afternoon. Usually, the odds would have been heavily weighed against them but twenty-eight Loyalists on their landing were away on trial that day, leaving the numbers more even. That afternoon, when the two groups were together in the canteen, Bobby went up to head of the UVF and scolded him for attacking a man who could not walk. The UVF man threw his hands up and tried to talk but before he could appeal, Bobby hit him as hard as he could in the jaw. That was the agreed signal for the rest of the Republican prisoners to attack. Sands didn't take much more of a role in the melee, however, since he thought he had broken his hand hitting the UVF leader. By the time the riot squad arrived to stop the fight, the Republicans had already secured their reprisal and withdrawn.

Bobby issued a press statement claiming that, "The chief screw informed us that their instructions were to let both sides fight it out and that this had come from the Northern Ireland Office."[10]

Scullion was given aspirin for his pains and the next morning he was finally taken to the hospital. Bobby joined him in the transit van on his way to have his hand X-rayed. Despite his obvious pain, Bobby was on a high, telling Scullion in great detail about the battle of the canteen. Scullion remembers him laughing but he felt that Sands was not really that cheerful about the event. He was just trying to make Scullion feel better since his legs were in such agony.

The battles and their implications were debated in the Irish press for some time after the event. A Republican prisoner made a public statement about the incident from the dock of the Magistrate's Court. "The wee lad who was injured is now in hospital," he said, "and if the solicitors want to verify that they can go up to the prison and see for themselves. The screws set him up."[11]

The next day, Republican prisoners resumed their public protests. Thirty of them appeared naked in the dock of Belfast Magistrate's Court, this time not just in solidarity with the blanketmen but also to demand the segregation of Loyalists and Republicans in Crumlin Road Jail.[12]

The Loyalist prisoners made their own public statements, claiming that they were "in fear of attack" by the IRA prisoners.[13] "It is just a plain and simple fact," they said, "that the two factions will never see eye to eye, and want to be segregated from each other as quickly as possible."[14]

Both Loyalist and Republican prisoners laid the blame firmly at the door of secretary of state for Northern Ireland, Roy Mason. "[He] is the man who took away political status, classes us as ordinary criminals and yet still persists with Diplock courts when each man should be entitled to be tried by a judge and jury," they said.

Unionist politicians supported the prisoners. One member of parliament asked why remand prisoners in Crumlin Road Jail could not be separated for their own safety. "Education and housing are segregated in Northern Ireland," he said. "Why not prisons, where violence could result?"[15]

• • •

While the weekly court visits were an important stage for protests, they also presented opportunities to escape. Sands and Joe McDonnell were on a constant lookout for ways to escape while in transit to and from the courts. The usual plan was to smuggle explosives into the jail and to place a charge on the doors of the van that took them to court. They would jump out of the back of the van and into nearby escape vehicles.

Fra McCann first met Bobby just after Geraldine lost their child. McCann was at a bail hearing and Sands was trying to get a compassionate parole. The guards took them into a large room with high ceilings and sat them down next to a table. The two began talking about the jail situation while they waited to be called. But Bobby kept looking up at a skylight in ceiling. Finally, he could take no more. He got up on the table, jumping to see if he could reach the skylight. McCann was amazed. The window was several feet above Bobby's outstretched arms and there was no possible way of reaching it. Yet he would not let even the remotest chance of escape pass him by.

On another occasion Bobby tried to get to the hospital by using a drug that mimicked acute appendicitis. Once he was taken to the hospital for treatment, a squad of IRA volunteers would be standing by to break him out. On the prearranged night, the squad were in the hospital waiting on him, but when he took the drug the medical officer refused to send him to the hospital. Bobby lay in his cell vomiting blood while the screws sat by and let him suffer. Under the old prison regime, the plan might have succeeded. But these were changed times.

• • •

In March, Sands and his co-defendants had a preliminary inquiry and were reclassified as "awaiting trial." Their solicitors demanded that the case be dropped for lack of evidence, which Bobby thought was funny since they were caught red-handed. But the police had no forensic or eye-witness evidence to connect them with the bombings. No one had broken under interrogation. Although the reasons they gave for their movements may have been bizarre, they still cast doubt on the charges against them. Since they claimed that they had all jumped into car in the pandemonium and no one admitted owning the gun, there was no direct connection of either the bombs or the gun to any specific defendant.

The four debated about whether someone should take the rap for the gun. Typically, Joe McDonnell offered to take the rap right away. The others wouldn't let him because he was married and had two kids. Sands and Sean Lavery were eliminated on the same grounds. That left Finucane as the only single man. But *he* was in front seat and the gun was in the back of the car. In the end, the idea of having one man claim possession of the gun never came to anything.

At the hearing, a military policeman gave eyewitness testimony. He admitted that he shot Seamus Martin as he ran away from the bomb scene. He claimed there was an exchange of fire. Yet no weapons were found on Martin, nor was forensic evidence presented to indicate he had handled weapons.

Bobby jumped up to cross-examine the MP.

"You say you shot Seamy Martin because he had a gun in his hand. Did anybody go near him from the time you fired at Seamy Martin to the time you went up to him."

"No," replied the MP.

"Well, where did the gun go to?" asked Sands.

At that point the judge intervened.

"What has that got to do with you, Mr. Sands?" he asked, and ruled Bobby's intervention out of order. Yet, to this day, survivors of the Dunmurry operation insist that Seamus Martin had no gun. Neither was any connection ever made between the gun that was recovered in the car and Seamus Martin or Gabriel Corbett.[16]

Following the inquiry, Bobby was transferred to C-wing of H-Block 1, Long Kesh. He now found himself in the place he had heard so much about since Kieran Nugent began his blanket protest. What struck him most about the H-Blocks was the attitude of the screws. In the cages, it was, "Hello, Bobby, what about ye." Now, the very same screws called him by a number. And they wanted "sir" in return.

Bobby inevitably replied that he wouldn't call him "sir" so he got threats and sometimes a slap in return. The prisoners figured that this was a part of a policy to break their spirits right away. Yet a prison governor of the time, who eventually became governor of the whole prison, insists that the screws' violent behavior was not part of any plan. Instead, they developed a deep culture of sectarianism and violence. The problem, he insists, was a *lack* of managerial control, leaving the prison warders in each H-Block to develop their own cultures of control. In place of management, sectarianism led warders into abusive behavior against the prisoners, which fell into an upwardly spiralling dynamic—when one warder got away with violent behavior without being punished, the others gained confidence to engage in even greater violence and abuse.[17]

Despite the increased abuse from screws, there were fewer hassles with Loyalists, who were segregated on separate wings. There was plenty of time for activities like soccer, sometimes played in violent indoor matches with a ball made from paper bunched up in a sock. And quieter activities filled much of the day. Bobby finally got a copy of *Trinity*, which he devoured with great delight. He particularly liked a character called Long Dan who, at one point in the novel, gives a rousing speech where he tells his men, "Remember that the British have nothing in their entire arsenal or imperial might to counter a single man who refuses to be broken."[18]

Bobby committed the speech to memory and adopted Long Dan's motto as his own.

• • •

By summer, the breakup with Geraldine was definite. It was one of the few times that Bobby did "hard time." His general depression over the breakup was intensified by his fears that he would not see his young son Gerard because Geraldine was talking about moving away from Belfast. At one point, after relations between the two deteriorated badly, Bobby got a letter from Geraldine. Seanna Walsh watched Bobby read the letter. When he was finished, he tore it up and threw it away. He never told Seanna exactly what was in the letter but Geraldine generally had told him that any hope of a relationship was over and she wanted to part on some kind of amicable terms. By tearing up the letter, thought Walsh, Bobby was drawing a line and putting that part of his life behind him.

To make things worse, Bobby was split up from his best friends when he was transferred to D-wing. He took his isolation hard because there was no one in D-wing whom he could trust about intimate matters such as his split with Geraldine. He turned to music to help him get through his depression. He borrowed a guitar from a friendly orderly and wrote a song that many prisoners remember more than any other. He called it "Sad Song for Susan." Close friends felt it was inspired by the breakup with Geraldine.

> *I'm sitting at the window, I'm looking down the street*
> *I am watching your face, I'm listening for your feet.*
> . . .
> *You're gone, you're gone, but you'll live on in my memory.*

Christy Moore, Ireland's most popular folk singer since the 1970s, performs several songs by Bobby Sands. He considers "McIlhatton," a song that Sands wrote a couple of years later, to be one of the finest songs he's ever heard. But he never sang "Sad Song for Susan."

"No. I learned it and I tried to sing it but I couldn't fuckin' sing it because it was so . . . emotional. It was just a song I couldn't . . . it's so . . . . sad. Oh, there's lots of sad songs, you can get through them but this one was too much for me to sing."

● ● ●

Bobby began preparing for his September trial. Seanna Walsh had already been sentenced and was now a blanketman. In the days leading up to his trial, Bobby helped organize a one-day hunger strike in support of Kieran Nugent, who would be a year "on the blanket" on September 14. All 102 of the Republican prisoners who were awaiting trial in H1 signed their names to a statement, published in *Republican News*:

> *We, the undersigned Republican prisoners-of-war held in H1, A, B, C, and D Wings, Long Kesh, take this opportunity to send our congratulations and support to our comrade Kieran Nugent on his tremendous display of dedication approaching his 365th day in solitary confinement and to all our comrades in H5 who are protesting for recognition as political prisoners. We have one simple and straightforward message for you, we will all be joining you shortly. VENCEREMOS.*

The final salute, à la Che Guevara, was typical of Bobby. Alongside the message, he scrawled a note, which read, "A 24 hour token hunger strike will be held on the 14th September down here as a gesture of our support for the protestors. Signed, P.R.O., H.1, Long Kesh."[19]

Chapter Fourteen

Solitary Confinement

B obby Sands never joined the token hunger strike. His trial began on September 5. He was taken, along with his co-defendants, to the Crumlin Road Jail just before trial, enabling the authorities to transfer them between the jail and the courthouse by way of an underground tunnel that ran beneath the Crumlin Road.

Tomboy Loudon was also in the Crum awaiting trial for placing a bomb in the offices of the *Belfast Telegraph*. Bobby told him that he expected to get fifteen to twenty years for the Dunmurry bombings, although their solicitors thought that they could beat the charges if they fought them in court. The movement even told them to fight their case if they wanted to but Bobby said, "No way, I'm not recognizing the court." Fighting the case would have been a compromise and Sands and his co-defendants all agreed not to contest the case.

With the trial approaching, Bobby began to confront the likelihood that he would be sentenced to the H-Blocks. He had heard tales of rough treatment that the warders meted out to the sentenced blanketmen and he asked around to find out what it was like in the H-Blocks.

"Is it really as bad as you read in the *Republican News*?" he asked a priest. "What's the reception committee like?"

It was a common story that the first thing you got when you arrived in the blocks as a sentenced prisoner was a beating.

"No, I don't think it is. They don't get beat up," replied the priest, reassuringly. "It's just now and again they get a slap across the face, no more than you'd get at a Christian brothers school."[1]

The day of the trial arrived. Four prison warders led Bobby and his co-defendants through the brick-lined tunnel beneath the Crumlin Road. From the tunnel, the prison officers took them through a warren of corridors and stairs to the courtroom.

It was one of the smaller courtrooms, but still had high ceilings with fancy chandeliers. As he was led into the dock, Bobby saw wooden compartments on either side. These were the "box seats," where witnesses, policemen, and the legal teams sat. Straight in front of the dock was the judge's bench. It was Judge Watt. The lawyers said he was notoriously "orange." They could expect little positive consideration.[2] Bobby's family sat alongside the other families in benches at the back of the court.

The court official read out the charges and tried to get the defendants to stand up. They sat passively, ignoring him. Then the counsel for the defense asked for leave to withdraw their representation of the six because they were refusing to recognize the court.

During the trial, the defendants talked among themselves. Sean Lavery read a novel throughout the whole trial. Sands and Finucane, however, listened to the evidence, to pick holes in it, and embarrass the court if they could by shouting out. They expected the trial to last at least a week. It only lasted a day and a half.

To their surprise, Judge Watt found them not guilty of the bombing charges due to lack of evidence. They went down only on charges seven and eight, possessing a firearm and ammunition with intent, and possessing firearm and ammunition under suspicious circumstances.[3] The sentence was fourteen years each, a lot for possessing a quarter of a gun! As soon as the judge finished reading out his sentence the guards moved in to take the men out of the courtroom and back to the holding cells in the basement. Bobby's mother shouted to him as he was led away, "Good-bye, Bobby."

He turned and spotted Rosaleen standing next to Marcella. As he raised his hand in a wave, one of the guards smashed his baton onto Bobby's head, driving him to the ground.

All hell broke loose.

There were only four guards in the dock. Sands, Finucane, and McDonnell immediately laid into them with punches and kicks. The one who hit Bobby got "a busted face and a sore pair of balls." When the other defendants came over to join them, McDonnell called a halt to the fight. You quit when you're on top; no point in getting anybody else in trouble.

The guards handcuffed Sands and Finucane and brought them down to one of the holding cells in the basement. They sat nervously in the cell, waiting on the screws coming in to "beat the crap clean out of us." After about ten minutes they heard steps and the jangle of keys.

"This is it," Bobby told Finucane under his breath.

The key turned in the lock and Joe McDonnell came bouncing into the cell, still handcuffed, with a smile on his face. The three waited there until some guards led them back through the tunnel to the jail, giving them "a bit of a kicking" along the way. Despite the beatings, they were relieved. So far, the consequences of their little fracas in the court were less severe than they feared.

● ● ●

Their relief was premature. The others were taken straight to Long Kesh to begin their sentences in the H-Blocks but Sands, Finucane, and McDonnell were put in solitary confinement in the punishment area of the Crumlin Road Jail. The punishment block was a row of twelve old Victorian cells running along the left-hand side of the ground floor of "B"-wing; five cells, then a kitchen, then five more cells including a padded cell on the end. Past the padded cell was a toilet with a filthy basin for "slopping out" chamber pots. The punishment cells were isolated from the other prisoners by a chicken wire partition.

Bobby called them "filthy ancient concrete tombs."[4] They had thick walls like the other cells in the ancient prison. But the barred window in the back of the cell was too high up to see out, except momentarily if you jumped up and held on by your fingertips. Anyway, there was no view because the windows were overshadowed by other wings and walls. The cold of the cell was intensified because the panes were broken out of the windows and the wind howled in through them. Behind the cells, a generator constantly droned. Bobby said it "would drive you insane." Furnishings were sparse. They were denied books, radios, or other personal items, just like the blanketmen in the H-Blocks. No food parcels or cigarettes. There was a bed, a mattress, a water container, and a chamber pot. Reading material consisted of a Bible and some Catholic pamphlets.

Sands and his two comrades had company in the punishment block. Four Republican prisoners had been there for months, although hardly anyone knew about it because the authorities kept them incommunicado.

They had a cell between each of them so that they could not communicate easily. They were there because they were serving short-term sentences but refused to wear the uniform. Had they been "young prisoners" (YPs, meaning under nineteen), they would have been in the H-Blocks. Instead, they were doing their sentences in the punishment block of the Crum.

The men in the punishment block were kept naked in their cells. They were only allowed out to slop out. Once a week they got a shower. This was a treat, but at the cost of an extra bit of degradation. To get to the showers, they were marched out, stark naked, past the remand prisoners, and up the stairs into the administrative circle, where they passed dozens of screws who laughed and cracked jokes at them as they went by. Sometimes there were women screws there. They tried to avoid embarrassment by looking straight ahead. Then, they prolonged the showers as much as possible because it was the only place where they could have good conversations with each other. One decent screw, a Protestant, let them stay in the shower as long as possible. A Catholic warder took delight in cutting them very short.

Every fourteen days the men went before the governor to be punished for breaking prison rules by not wearing the uniform or doing work. One by one, they were quick-marched naked the length of the wing to the circle, with one screw in front and one behind. When they got there they stood with a screw on either side while the governor read out their sentence: "Three days cellular confinement on a number one diet, fourteen days loss of privileges, fourteen days loss of remission."

It was as quick as that. Then they were marched back to their cells. The screws took their bedding away from 7:30 A.M. to 8:00 P.M. for three days. During this time they exercised and ran around their cells to fight the cold. After a while they fell into the habit of talking to themselves, thinking out loud. They were constantly walking, constantly on the move. To make matters worse, they were on a "starvation diet."[5]

Sands, Finucane, and McDonnell were in adjoining cells at the opposite end of the punishment wing. Sands was in the middle. They were bored and extremely cold. To keep warm, they played handball against the walls with the religious pamphlets, crumpled into their socks. They sang to each other to keep going. Bobby sang a new Rod Stewart song, "The Killing of Georgie."

On the sixth day, the screws brought the three to the prison governor for adjudication.

"We are political prisoners and we will not be wearing a uniform or doing prison work," they told him.

The governor informed them of the consequences: cellular confinement. As for the courtroom fight, they lost six months remission effective immediately and the governor put them on a number one starvation diet for nine days, three days on and three days off. This would be the routine for the next fifteen days.

That afternoon, the screws came into Bobby's cell and made him take off his clothes. He would be completely naked for the rest of his time in the punishment cells and thereafter in the H-Blocks. The screws gave him a prison uniform. He threw it in the corner. They took away his bedding until 8:30 P.M. From then on, for twenty-two days, they took his bedding away at 7:30 A.M. and gave it back at 8:30 P.M.

The Crum is cold at the best of times. But it is "real North Pole stuff" when you've no clothes on. Bobby took the socks from his uniform so that he could continue playing handball to keep warm. Even after the bedding was returned he could get no heat in his body until about one o'clock in the morning. The only break in his routine was when he went to slop out. Then, if the screw was okay, he got a quick yarn with one of the blanketmen as he passed on the way to the toilet.

"How the fuck do you stick this?" he asked Fra McCann through the peephole.

On the weekend the three took their shower together and "talked the heads off each other." They talked gibberish because that's the way you go when you're in total isolation. On Sundays they received their only visit, from an alcoholic priest who they called "Captain Black"[6] because he brought them tobacco. But he was not overly generous. The prisoners got half of what he had and the priest kept the rest.

Soon after he left the Crum for the H-Blocks, Bobby wrote about his experiences in the punishment block. He wrote the piece in the most challenging conditions, with a smuggled ballpoint refill on bits of toilet paper. He had to write it with a constant eye to the prison warders, who would punish him severely if they caught him writing. Despite this, Bobby's account of his time in the punishment block is, arguably, one of the finest pieces of prison reportage in the English language. His description of the conditions of punishment is sparse and matter-of-fact, yet eloquent. By avoiding exaggeration, it is moving to a degree that transcends mere propaganda.

Sands begins his piece, *Four Forgotten Blanketmen,* by describing the conditions endured by the prisoners with whom he shared the wing for a little more than three weeks. The most moving and graphic passages of the article refer to the three-day punishment periods that followed their appearances before the governor.

> *Having appeared before the Governor and received your sentences, your punishment really begins. The next morning you are woken at 7:00 A.M. by a bang on the cell door. It is now December and the mornings are dark and very cold. You must rise naked and shivering and fold up your bedding and mattress (no bed for the next three nights, just the hard mattress on the floor). The Screw opens the door at 7:30 A.M. and you leave your bedding out in the corridor. Again head for the toilet, naked as usual, to empty the Chamber-pot. When you return and the Screws slam the door shut you are left there standing naked and freezing, with the wind howling in through the holes in the windows. There is only one thing for it and that is to do exercises to keep warm, but your feet stay blue with cold, no matter what you do.*
>
> *. . . To pass the time you try to read a page or two from the bible, but it's too cold, so you sing a song or two to yourself, periodically continuing your exercising to keep warm, right through to dinner time.*
>
> *By dinner time you are thoroughly frozen and starving. The dinner arrives at 11:30 A.M. It's two small scoops of potatoes covered with a ladle of soup. You "wolf" this down you in less than a minute with the plastic spoon they give you. You have to stand with a steel tray in one hand and eat with your other hand. When the steel tray is too hot to hold you must set it on the ground, get down on the floor on your knees, lean over your dinner like an animal and eat it as best you can. You must eat everything, leave nothing or you will really feel it later on.*
>
> *Having eaten your dinner you still feel hungry as ever and equally as cold and miserable. You know you could simply end it all by putting on the prison garb and calling for a screw but you don't. You know that this torture is geared to make you do just exactly that, to break your resistance. You know that you are a POW no matter what they may try to do to you.*

. . . Your morale is ebbing drastically. When you hear a few thumps on the wall, one of your mates giving you encouragement, you remember that he too is in the very same predicament. So, encouraged by a few thumps on the wall, you snap out of your depression and rally yourself for the final hour or so until you get your bedding back in at 8:30 P.M.

It seems like hours but you make it. It's the greatest feeling in the world, when the door opens and the screws tell you to take your bedding in. You throw your hard horse-hair mattress into the corner on the floor. As soon as the door shuts you arrange your bedding and sheets into some sort of order and get underneath them. After a few minutes you feel yourself warming up. You're exhausted, and tomorrow will be much worse. You say a quick few prayers in gratitude for surviving that day, and ask for assistance in the coming battle. You drop off to sleep thinking of better days and your family.

But it seems only a few minutes when the door bangs again and it all starts again. The next two days seem like an eternity. The cold, the hunger, have almost defeated you several times, but you've made it. You've survived again. You look forward to a full meal again and a bed for the next 11 days But at the end of those 11 days it will all start again, a torturous nightmare.

The four blanketmen endured this every eleven days for more than a year. Bobby Sands endured it over a period of twenty-two days.

On the Blanket

B obby Sands began life in a utopian village. He now found himself in a utopian village of a different kind. The H-Blocks of Long Kesh were built to modern specifications, although rapidly and on the cheap. They were called "H" Blocks because each cellular block was in the form of an H, with an administrative center in the crossbar and four wings of cells that formed each leg: "A-," "B-," "C-," and "D-" wings. For speed of construction, each block was made of prefabricated cement slabs that were set into place by crane to form the walls of the cells that ran down each side of each wing. They were single-story blocks, with yellow-brick external walls, flat roofs, and barred windows. The utopian village of Bobby's childhood, Abbots Cross, had precisely one hundred houses. Each H-Block had precisely one hundred cells.

There the similarity ends. Abbots Cross was built on an open plan, characterized by its lack of fences and walls. The H-Blocks were *defined* by their fences and walls. Every eight-by-ten-foot cell had a small barred window and a heavy steel door. The doors had a horizontal slotted window that was covered by a latch. Each wing was separated from the central administrative area, known as "the circle," by bars with electronic locks. A concrete wall topped with razor wire surrounded each block. Exit from and entry into the block was through a double air-lock gate. The eight blocks that were eventually built were set out in two groups of three and one group of two; around each group was another wall topped by razor wire. Around the whole thing was a perimeter of four parallel chain-link fences about five feet apart, with coils of razor wire strung between and, finally, a fifteen-foot high corrugated iron outer wall, punctuated by dark green sentry boxes. And just to be sure, there was another, shorter razor wire fence around the whole camp, reinforced with corrugated iron.

Needless to say, the architects of Long Kesh did not give much consideration to special modern design features incorporating a "restrained use of neo-Georgian detail." The clean lines of Long Kesh were neither white nor Mediterranean. There were no upmarket features like glazing bars, although there were four thick, vertical reinforced concrete bars in each window. Nor were there triangular pediments over the doors, just a plain metal grille that covered an air vent.

The cells were simple and bleak. Cell walls were punctuated only by two heating pipes that ran along the back wall, a metal switch-plate by the door with "panic buttons" to call the warders, and the air vent above the door. The floors were solid cold black bitumen, kept shiny in the corridors by the occasional pass with a floor-polishing machine. When Sands first came to the H-Blocks, he had some simple furniture: a bunk bed, chair, desk, and locker. The locker contained his only clothes apart from the towel he wore around his waist and the blanket he draped around his shoulders: a prison uniform and boots (a few blanketmen "cheated," wearing the boots on cold days to keep their feet warm). His only reading materials were a Bible and a few religious pamphlets.

Interpersonal relations were simple. If a prisoner had a cellmate he spent twenty-four hours a day with him, minus a few minutes twice a day when he slopped out in the bathroom, had a wash, and scoured the rubbish bins for cigarette butts. He communicated with other prisoners on the wing by talking out the windows, through the cracks around the heating pipes and by shouting out the door. At night, prisoners in cells facing the inner courtyard shouted across at those in the opposite wing of the H. The best shouters, called "scorchers" (from the Irish word *scairt*, meaning "to shout"), bellowed messages to prisoners in the adjacent blocks. From his cell in H5, Bobby could shout across in Irish to comrades in H3 or H4.

The only people the prisoners saw regularly were the prison staff: a governor ("number one") and his deputy governor ("number two"), about twenty-five assistant governors, and the uniformed prison warders. The warders included principal officers (PO), senior officers (SO), and ordinary warders. Each H-Block had an assistant governor, a principal officer, a senior officer, and twenty-five to thirty ordinary warders. These were the "screws," with whom the men had most contact. They came on the wing at 7:30 in the morning and left at 8:30 in the evening, leaving a skeleton night crew behind. In between, they got two breaks, from 12:30 to 2:00 P.M. and 4:30 to 5:30 P.M., during which time they locked everybody in their cells. This made no difference to the blanketmen because they were locked up all the time, anyway. But the breaks gave them time to communicate freely without the screws listening in. They also provoked fear; some warders spent their breaks in a bar that was, astonishingly, located in the prison for their use. The time after lock-ups was when the drunken screws were most aggressive.[1]

The prisoners dubbed the screws with nicknames that, often savagely, focused on physical or mental characteristics. "Red Rat" was the "bad screw" in H5. Decades later, prisoners still recite his sadistic activities. "The pipe" (*píopa*, in Irish) was an older man who walked slumped over and always smoked a pipe. He sat outside of a cell at night and made a stream of savage comments about the prisoners inside. L—, on the other hand, was the principle officer of H5. The prisoners liked him because he tried to improve their conditions. The men in H5 even credited L— with small comforts. Sometimes they got jam or fruit with their dinner. Blanketmen in other blocks kidded the men in H5 about living in "the hotel" because of L—'s relative generosity.

Later on, when Brendan Hughes came to H5 and took over as commanding officer, L— was the only warder who gave him any sort of recognition.

"I draw a difference between a screw and a prison officer" says Hughes, "and L— was a prison officer."

L— told Hughes that he wanted a transfer from the H-Blocks but he stayed because he thought he could lessen the brutality there. He also told Hughes that the police warned him to check his car each morning for bombs because some prison officers were using their Loyalist connections to attack him for being "too liberal."

A priest who was a regular visitor to the H-Blocks found "sectarianism everywhere" there. One time, he spoke to an English warder who was visiting the prison and he mentioned his misgivings about the brutality and the sectarianism of the prison officers.

"Everywhere you put your hand you touch it here," the Englishman replied.

A prison officer who later became the number one governor in charge of the whole prison confirms that "there was drunkenness on the wings all the time. And, yes, there were severe beatings all the time." The mindset of the prison officers, he says, was territorial. As long as the prisoners were locked up in their cells, the warders were in control. But when the blanketmen got out of their cells or even when they tried to communicate from cell to cell, they were challenging the control. The prison warders turned any interaction with a prisoner into a confrontation because it was about control and loss of control.

Prisoners also played violent games. They refused to obey orders, knowing that this would invite violence upon them. Their environment was one of extreme power imbalance: they had no clothes, no control over where they spent their time, much less any real instruments of violence or even defence. Under such circumstances, passive resistance was often the only effective recourse short of acquiescence. Yet they also fought back with words and sometimes with their fists. Despite their defiance, one emotion dominated their lives: fear. They feared the violence that *might* visit them. Anticipation of violence was their greatest enemy. *Actual* confrontation left them bleeding and bruised, yet raised in spirit by a sense of resistance and control.

On a higher level, relations between warders and prisoners reflected the conflict that raged beyond the prison walls. The warders were mostly Loyalists who considered themselves to be at war with the IRA. The blanketmen were mostly IRA members who made no secret of the fact that they could pass on intelligence about hated prison officers. Prison officers were killed in brutal circumstances: seventeen of them died at the hands of the IRA between the time Kieran Nugent went on the blanket in September 1976 until the the Hunger Strike of March 1981. For all of the above reasons, day-to-day relations between prison warders and prisoners became a constant game of violent confrontation.[2]

The game was observed, but largely ignored, by the higher-rank officials. The prison doctor dropped in once a fortnight to pronounce them fit to remain in the cell. One young prisoner was amazed that a doctor faced with a young naked lad, shivering and obviously frightened, could routinely ask if everything was alright and on receiving the uneasy reply "yes," return to whatever he was doing and completely ignore the evident fact that everything was not alright.[3]

Having been pronounced fit, the number one governor came onto the wing, to the accompaniment of an unholy racket of prisoners banging their pisspots against the cell doors. He went from cell to cell, informing each prisoner that he was sentenced to three days of "cellular confinement" for "breach of prison discipline" and, in addition, that he would lose all of his privileges.

The only regular visitors from outside were priests. On Sundays, most prisoners put on their uniform bottoms and went, half-naked, to the unused dining room for mass. Stauncher prisoners refused even this luxury. Bobby went to mass because of the opportunity it gave him to communicate with his comrades and to beg cigarettes and ballpoint pens from the priests. Priests also went round to individual cells to hear confessions. And a priest could make a special arrangement to visit a prisoner from his parish on a "pastoral visit." This allowed prisoners to discuss special problems like an illness in the family or a broken relationship. If the priest was considered trustworthy, prisoners gave him messages to take out of the jail in his socks or in the rolled up sleeve of his jumper.

When Bobby came to H5, few blanketmen took visits. To do so, they would have to put on the prison uniform and it would have been anathema to appear before loved ones wearing it. So week after week they remained in their cells without even the slightest usual human contact.

The number of blanketmen was growing rapidly. They now had their own block and most of them were doubled up two to a cell. They devised new ways to communicate with each other and to distribute supplies like tobacco. Most of these techniques required creativity and patience. A simple note written on a piece of toilet paper could be sent up and down one side of a wing by placing it in a folded bit of a religious pamphlet for stiffness. Then they could pass it to the next cell through the crack around the heating pipes at the back of the cell. Larger items like tobacco, cigarette papers, or extra food went by a method called "swinging the line." A prisoner tore a strip from his blanket, six feet long and a couple of inches wide, and tied a deadweight on one end. A toothpaste tube or a bar of soap would do nicely. He put his arm out the cell window and swung his "rope" until the prisoner in the next cell caught it. Then, the item to be passed was tied to the other end and pulled in by the prisoner in the next cell. After meals, men who had extra food put it into a cup and swung it to the wing's "seagulls," the men who were never full. They passed their extra rice, potatoes, and peas this way and particularly "nuclear waste," the foul yellow cake that passed for dessert.

To get things across the corridor, the blanketmen had to devise a more complicated technique that they called "shooting the button." They unravelled the ten to fifteen feet of fine wool stitching from the tops of their blankets and tied a button to its end for weight. There was a small gap at the bottom of each door and the shooter would flick the button toward the door across the corridor. After a few tries, the shooter usually got the button close enough for the other prisoner to fish it in with a mass sheet folded into a paper hook. Button shooting took place at night, after the screws left the wing. The items that could be moved this way were restricted in size and weight, and the button was used to move things like notes and, most importantly, the nightly round of cigarettes that were rolled in Bible pages and distributed to the smokers on the wing.[4]

• • •

They took Sands to the "circle" of H5 when he arrived at Long Kesh at the end of September 1977. The principle officer told him to put on the prison uniform. He replied that he was a prisoner of war and would not wear the uniform of a criminal. The PO made him take off his clothes and stand naked before him. For the younger prisoners this was an embarrassing and psychologically scarring moment. While it was no picnic for Bobby, he had been through this degrading ritual for the previous three weeks in the Crumlin Road Jail. After stripping, he got his two blankets, which he wrapped around himself as he walked to his cell. They put him in cell 14, D-wing, with Tony O'Hara, a volunteer of the Irish National Liberation Army (INLA). The screws slammed the cell door and put a card in the metal holder beside it. On the card was his number: 950/77.

Tony O'Hara saw "a wreck of a man, pale, thin and drawn—but with a fire inside him—a sense of purpose backed by tremendous energy." He used other words to describe Bobby, including "intense," "ardent," "political revolutionary."[5] Sands spent the first day learning songs from other men and memorizing them. He organized a plan for reading the Bible and another plan for reviewing his Irish. He made a schedule for his exercises. Tony could not believe it, "he seemed to have his whole day worked out."

Bobby had to learn the basics of living life "on the blanket." How to wear his blanket: fold it in half, fold the top down three or four inches to make a waistband, put it around your waste and tuck the waistband into itself, leaving your hands free. If it was cold you draped the second blanket over your shoulders. Washing: a prison orderly put "hot" water into a basin in the cell and he washed as best he could. To go to the toilet, you shouted to the screw, who accompanied you to the toilets at the bottom of the wing. At night, you used the chamber pot.

The next morning when O'Hara awoke Bobby was already up doing his exercises. After breakfast at eight, O'Hara went back to sleep. At midday Tony woke up for dinner and then he went back to bed again. Sands sat in his chair looking at his new cellmate.

"I can't believe it, Tony. What do you do all day?" he asked.

"I sleep," was Tony O'Hara's reply.

"It's a waste of your opportunities, isn't it?"[6]

So there was Bobby Sands, a physical wreck after twenty-two days in the punishment cells of the Crumlin Road Jail, fifteen of them naked. He found himself in a bare cell with no exercise, no clothes, and nothing to read. And he spoke about *opportunities!* He spent his first week talking to the other men on the wing, finding out their attitudes about the blanket protest, where it was going and what their strengths and weaknesses were. He told O'Hara what he thought of their situation. His point of view was different from anything O'Hara had yet heard. Bobby thought that the authorities were happy to have them lying around doing nothing. They had plenty of blankets. They had successfully isolated and silenced the prisoners. There was only one way to get political status back, he argued, and that was to organize an effective campaign. They had to let people know what was happening in the H-Blocks. They had to raise public awareness, sympathy, and support. Only British propaganda was getting to the media, that they were criminals, suffering needlessly in the most modern prison in Europe. The blanketmen had to break through the walls and let people on the outside know what was going on.

Bobby suggested that they had to make bridges of information to people who would pass it on to others. The best place to start was with their families and friends. They had to come out of their cells and stop hiding their suffering from their families. Everyone should take visits to open up lines of communication. Once these were established, they had to write letters, as many as they could and smuggle them out through their relatives. Sands talked about the resources they would need to do this. They needed pens or pen refills, which they could pickpocket from the screws or take from the priests in mass. They needed writing paper; cigarette papers or toilet paper would do.

Bobby practiced what he preached. He had been thinking back to Gerry Adams and his "Brownie" articles. Adams began transforming the whole Republican Movement from within the jail. Bobby figured they could do the same thing to get the message out to the public about the H-Blocks. Brutality was an important message, but more stylized and humanized writing could spread the message more effectively. They needed to write prose and poetry that spoke of the humanity of the prisoners as well as the inhumanity of their situation. Danny Devenney, an old friend from Cage Eleven, recalled Bobby's attitude: "A statement will pass by, people will forget it, but if you write a wee story about it, a wee poem, a wee moral coming in there somewhere then people are educated by it."

Bobby began writing such articles almost immediately. He wrote his first article on October 23, 1977, within three weeks of arriving in the H-Blocks. He wrote about life in the H-Blocks, both the good and the bad. He told of the depression and comradeship. He wrote surreptitiously, with a ballpoint pen refill on slick prison toilet paper, one ear cocked for approaching screws who would confiscate his writing and send him to the punishment cells if they caught him. When he finished, he signed his Irish name, Roibeard Ó Seachnasaigh, folded the paper into a tight wad, and took it to his mother on his next visit. He told her to get it to Roon in the Short Strand.

Rooney was by this time on the run again because the police suspected that he was involved in some bombings. He took the package to Danny Devenney, who was a layout artist for the *Republican News*. Devenney took it to the editors and they published it in the November fifth edition, under the title "On the Blanket." It was the first public eyewitness account of life on the blanket.

The article began with an explanation: "The following article was smuggled out of H-Block, Long Kesh. It was written on a tiny piece of paper and tells the story of conditions for the men 'on the blanket.'" They removed Bobby's name "for fear of 'disciplinary action' being taken against him by the prison regime."[7] Then, the words were all Bobby's.

It's Sunday the 23rd of October and it's tea-time here in H-Block 5, Long Kesh Camp. It's one of those depressing days with the wind howling and the rain lashing against the window. The

lads in the adjacent "A" Wing are up at their windows. I can't
really make out their faces, but I can see the white forms with
long beards gazing out into the yard.

Sands wrote about how the men were watching the food trolleys being wheeled into the block. They were hoping for a hot meal. They got cold salads. He wrote about going to mass and how much the men had changed since they went on the blanket.

Everyone with the exception of the latest arrivals has a beard
of sorts. When I first arrived here I noticed that a lot of the men's
eyes seemed to be sunk into the pits of their eyes, and everyone's
face was a pale yellowish complexion.

He put their condition down to their lack of exercise or access to fresh air. He wrote of the absence of reading material and how few of the men took visits. A lot of them had not seen their families for almost a year. In place of visits, they longed for their two allotted monthly letters (heavily censored) and relied on rumors for news.

It's seven o'clock now and the supper has arrived: a half cup of
lukewarm tea and a small slice of cake. That means no more food
until breakfast at 8:00 A.M. tomorrow morning.

After dinner, for entertainment, they would have a quiz and converse with their neighbors by shouting out the door.

Bobby describes their general conditions of imprisonment. How boring it gets having "the same old worn-out conversations" with your cellmate. How he will see the governor during the week and have his bedding taken away. The lack of cigarettes. The lack of reading materials. Of course, he could have these things if he put on the prison uniform. But he would not do so. He finished the article with the main punch line:

We are all Republican Prisoners-Of-War here, and there is
nothing that the Prison Authorities, the Northern Ireland Office,
or the British Government can say or do to change this. They can
keep us incarcerated and naked, they may use everything and every
means at their disposal to try and break us. We have lived in terrible

conditions under constant harassment, through a freezing winter and a sweltering summer locked up in our cells like animals.

But there is one thing that we remember always, and those who torment us would do well to listen: "You have nothing in your entire arsenal to break one single man who refuses to be broken."[8]

Bobby continued to write. He sat in his cell, with his cigarette papers or toilet paper on his knee and wrote with the smuggled ballpoint refill. When he was not writing, he paced the cell, stroking his wispy beard, which would never achieve the fullness of other blanketmen. When he was not pacing, he talked with his cellmate, with Eoghan MacCormaic in the next cell to one side, with Seamus Finucane on the other. Out the window or through the pipes, they talked and talked and talked.

Sands devised other activities to pass the time. He played chess with Tony O'Hara, using a hankie for a board and bits of paper for men. Bobby used his pen refill to mark the pieces: K, Q, B, etc. He hated to lose. When they got bored, they devised new rules. Bobby continually won until one day the tide changed. They had been playing for hours when Bobby made a mistake and O'Hara lifted his pieces one after another. With each man he lost, says O'Hara, Bobby's temper rose. When Tony took his queen and made a victorious remark, Bobby hit the ceiling.

"You can't play chess like that, Tony," he said. "When you're playing a friendly game with someone, you shouldn't be rubbing salt in the wound. And that's what you're doing!"

Despite these occasional spats, O'Hara admired Bobby's dedication and commitment. He called Sands a "twenty-four-hour-a-day revolutionary." Practically every prisoner who spent time with Sands agrees: he was a constant builder of morale. Gino MacCormaic found that Bobby had "an instinct for knowing how morale could rise and fall." He tried to get his fellow prisoners to improve their situation by organizing education, debates, and singsongs. When he could do nothing else to keep up morale he stood at the door for hours, singing. This almost inhuman ability to keep going would become an important part of life in the H Blocks.[9]

• • •

Soon it was Christmas. Bobby described his first Christmas on the blanket as "one massive disappointment after another." A few days before, several men were sent to the punishment block for smuggling cigarettes. They spent Christmas with a board for a bed, a cement block for a chair, and bread and water for their Christmas dinner. On Christmas Eve, the authorities took everyone's beds away. Although the governor gave them back on Christmas Day, he said they had to wear prison uniforms to go to the canteen for Christmas dinner. The prisoners refused and said that they would eat their dinners in their cells. Just as they were reaching a low point in morale, hundreds of Christmas cards appeared. Bobby wrote that it was the biggest morale booster they had had in fifteen months of the blanket protest.

The men got their Christmas dinner in their cells. It was lukewarm, "nothing to tell your grandchildren about."[10] But they did enjoy a Christmas Mass, after which they sang Christmas carols "in such a hearty fashion that a few tears were seen on a few faces." Then they organized a "super concert" where every man had to sing a song, recite a poem, or tell a joke out the quarter-inch gap between the door and door frame.

Perhaps the joy that the prisoners expressed in their Christmas concert provoked the authorities into action. First thing in the New Year, some workmen came onto the wing and welded strips of metal onto the door frames to cover up the gaps. It was a big blow to the prisoners. The gaps provided a small window where they could see each other on the way to the toilets. From then on, they rarely saw each other apart from mass. Other prisoners were *just* disembodied voices that came through the crack in the pipe, out the windows, and in the doors.[11]

After Christmas, there was a flu epidemic among the blanketmen. The worst hit were Bobby Sands and John Nixon. Their suffering worsened when the authorities took two of their three blankets away during the day and turned off the heat in their cells. On January 2, after three days on his back with a high temperature, they carried Sands and Nixon on stretchers to the prison hospital. According to a smuggled press statement (possibly written by Bobby himself), he "was tossed up and down on the stretcher like a pancake [and] dropped to the ground a few times before being thrown into the back of a van" on his way to the hospital. In the hospital, Nixon lay for some time, naked and shivering, dressed only in a towel. Then they were "forcibly bathed, scrubbed, and had buckets of cold water poured around them."[12]

A week later, Bobby wrote a statement outlining the conditions in what he called "Britain's Siberia":

Today (Wednesday 10th January) we rose once again naked, freezing cold and hungry, to face yet another nightmarish day. It is so cold that we are unable to walk upon the concrete cell floor in our bare feet; the water in the drinking container has frozen and my filthy foam mattress upon the ground is wet with the snow that came in through the window during the night.

I had no sleep again last night, my three flimsy blankets being no match for the biting bitter cold. I spent last night huddled up in a corner listening to many of my comrades coughing and groaning, whilst scores of men lay shivering from flu, fighting against high temperatures and severe pain.[13]

February brought more flu and colds. Others had eye trouble and headaches, which they attributed to constant bright lights shining against their white cell walls. When they asked for treatment, the authorities refused unless they wore prison uniforms to the hospital. *Republican News* published a list of the health complaints among prisoners in H5. Sands was first on the list, with "pains in legs, continual cold, and cough."[14]

• • •

After three new H-Blocks (six, seven, and eight) were opened and the number of blanketmen increased, the authorities started moving prisoners around. Bobby, Seamus Finucane, and a few others were moved to A-wing, directly facing their old home in D-wing. A-wing was known as the "cynical wing" because of the attitude of some of its occupants, like Joe McDonnell. Sands and McDonnell, says Gino MacCormaic, "were as different as day from night." McDonnell was always ready to pull some practical joke while Sands was seriously engaged in jail politics. Where Bobby was "a bundle of energy" McDonnell was "a stick of dynamite" waiting to be primed. Bobby was a dedicated revolutionary, McDonnell a dedicated cynic.[15]

Their cynicism created a strong bond of solidarity. The wing took pride in the low numbers among them who left the protest compared to other wings. Many, like McDonnell, were staunch protestors, who never even went to mass because it would be "giving in" to put on prison trousers. A-wing was the only wing that did not do the rosary and it also had the fewest men learning Irish. They were "too tough" for all that. Gino McCormaic tried to get Irish classes going and Joe McDonnell gave him dog's abuse. Whenever Rab McCollum tried to start a singsong, Joe McDonnell told him to "knock that on the head!"

But Bobby continued unfazed, still exploiting "his opportunities," even if A-wing was not the ideal place to do so. He organized tobacco hunts. Sometimes the orderlies brought them tobacco and one even hid cigarettes in their mattresses. A priest would bring them four ounces of tobacco from the men in the cages, squeezed tight in a vice so that it would fit neatly in his pocket along with song sheets and history lectures. But it was never enough. So Bobby made a game of getting tobacco. The warders emptied their ashtrays in the bin next to the showers. Bobby was frequently seen ("or rather his legs were frequently seen sticking out of the bin") looking for "Reverend Strutts" or "Revs" as the men called cigarette butts. He was an expert at picking up cigarette butts with his toes while walking up the corridor.[16] He told the others that it was not just a treat but also as a way of "beating them at their own game."

Yet, for all the tricks of getting a cigarette, sometimes nothing worked. Bobby got severe headaches when he was short of tobacco and tied a towel tightly around his head to fight the pain. One night, in sheer desperation, he sent a note through the pipes to a prisoner two cells away who he thought had a bit of tobacco. Seamus Finucane intercepted the note and when he read it out the door, Bobby got dog's abuse from the others for sending "begging letters."[17]

• • •

Entertainment was already organized before Bobby arrived in the H-Blocks. Gino Mac Cormaic described the activities of the wing in a letter to a friend:

> We play bingo every week in here. The cards are made of toilet paper. The prizes are shampoos, soap, paper hankies, and sometimes a roll-up (made of toilet paper, of course). It's a real laugh hearing a bar of soap being described, the smell, colour, size and its name . . . It's a better laugh when somebody with his head shaved wins the shampoo. Anyway, it's a change from the singsongs and quizzes or discussions that are held on other nights.[18]

Typically, Sands dove in and took a central role in organizing the nightly events, especially if there was singing involved. He sang Freda Payne's *Band of Gold* and Cat Stevens's *The First Cut Is the Deepest*. Leonard Cohen's *Suzanne* was another favorite. But he also sang Irish songs like *Gleanntan Glas Gaoth Dobhair* and *Baidin Fheidhlime*, to encourage more men to learn the language.

Bobby took a leading role in education. The teachers of history and politics relied mostly on memory, which gave an advantage to those who had been in the cages. Sometimes, they got priests to bring them lectures that the prisoners in the cages wrote out for them in tiny print. Irish was easier, since teaching depended mostly on fluency. When Bobby started teaching Irish in the blocks about three or four others were fluent. Within eighteen months nearly four hundred blanketmen would speak Irish. The language was taught constantly and spoken constantly.

Most prisoners learned Irish by "picking up half-baked sounds from out the door," as Seanna Walsh describes it. There were no blackboards so the teacher introduced a new word by shouting its spelling phonetically. For the infinitive verb *tabhair* (to bring), for example, the teacher shouted: "*T* for Thomas, *A* for Alfred, *B* for Barney . . ." Most prisoners got a lot of words wrong and the end product was a strange approximation of the real language.

Outside of class time, debates about politics, history, and sport lasted "for days," with Sands always at the center. He seemed to enjoy arguing just for the fun of it. He distinguished between "sporting" arguments that were for fun and political arguments, over which he was deadly serious. He argued so intensely that some prisoners could hardly distinguish a real argument from one that he was having "for the craic." Either way, he generally had to get in the last word.

As PRO, Sands used the discussions to identify other prisoners who had a good head for language and encourage them to follow his example. "Straight away" after coming into H5, Bobby had Gino MacCormaic writing poems and articles for *Republican News*.[19]

Despite these advances, Bobby was still unhappy with the protest. Its nature was quiet determination. Under Tom McFeely, their OC, the men remained staunchly in their cells, refusing to budge to British pressures to wear prison clothing or do prison work. The protest was solid but stagnant. It needed new energy.

Chapter Sixteen

Escalating the Protest

B obby Sands was right. The protest needed changes. Yet most of the blanketmen embraced a naïve faith that if they just held out they were bound to win. They would come back from a half-hour visit with three hours of news. "Bishop so-and-so says we'll be out in months." A rumor went around that the Swiss dockers had thrown their weight behind the protest and were refusing to unload all British ships coming into that country![1] But the main reason that the men thought they would win was their deep belief in the rightness of their cause and of the inability of the system to keep them in such deprived conditions.

The impetus for this staunch but ultimately reckless strategy was the OC, Tom McFeely. His cellmate, Sean Glás, says that McFeely "was like the country he came from—granite. You just couldn't break him. He had no concept of fear." McFeely was hard on prisoners who were less able to maintain the protest. If he gave an order, he wanted it followed to the letter, without discussion. His stern leadership produced a sort of negative solidarity that held the protest together.

Yet the British authorities knew that *they* were winning. Week after week, they put dozens more young Nationalists in jail. Judges handed out big sentences that would keep them off of the streets for years and make them think twice about returning to armed struggle. Roy Mason, the British secretary of state for Northern Ireland, thought he could crush the ideology out of young Republicans.

A few prisoners like Bobby soon realized that the prison administration could manage the ongoing protest. It was "becoming institutionalized."[2] Things might have continued in that vein but early in 1978 two things changed. First, Bobby's old comrade Brendan ("the Dark") Hughes was moved to H5 from Cage Eleven. Second, Sands was moved back to D-wing and placed in a cell next to Hughes.

When the Dark arrived everything began to change. For Bobby, it was the chance to get his teeth sunk into the protest. He had already been PRO of H5 under McFeely, but the Dark drew him onto a higher level. He gave Bobby more ways to exploit "his opportunities."

It all started several months before, in Cage Eleven, when Joe Barnes got into a fight with some prison warders. Although eyewitnesses insist that the Dark was not involved in the fight, he was charged nonetheless. In the ensuing trial, his political status was removed and he was transferred to the H-Blocks.

"That morning I was negotiating with the screws and they were calling me OC or Brendan. Brought back to H-Blocks, threw in, and then I was Hughes 704. So from the morning I was OC of the camp, the afternoon I was Hughes 704, threw into a cell and told to put on a prison uniform. Obviously, I didn't. I went on the blanket."

• • •

The Dark came to the blocks with a heavy burden of expectations. Sean Glás regarded Hughes as "the messiah who had arrived to alleviate us of our burden . . . our Lord had intervened, got him sentenced just at the right time to help us with our problem."

The Dark saw things from the other direction. The prison authorities put him into Tom McFeely's cell while he was in punishment for hitting a screw. To the Dark, this was a clear provocation, an attempt to create internal divisions by getting them into an argument about who was in authority.

The prisoners pressured the Dark to take over as their OC. Much to his surprise, McFeely also pushed him to take over. Hughes was the choice of the outside IRA leadership, who were ultimately responsible for his appointment. It seems the only one who did not want him to be OC was himself. His lawyer advised him to appeal his sentence because a lot of witnesses would say that he was not in the fight back in Cage Eleven. But the Dark was already feeling a sense of responsibility. He dropped his case and stayed in the H-Blocks.

Then, he did something that none of the prisoners expected . . . or wanted. He suggested that they put on the prison uniform and go into the system, to wreck it from within. The other blanketmen rejected this suggestion out of hand. They began to wonder what they had got themselves into by making the Dark their OC. Hughes was not really surprised at the hostile reception that his suggestion received. These guys had been suffering for a couple of years and here he came telling them to give it up and put on the uniform.

In hindsight, many blanketmen admit that they were mistaken to take such a rigid line against Hughes. They were not thinking strategically, their thinking was reactive. Every time something was taken from them and every beating they endured convinced them that they had to continue their protest.

Only Bobby tried to put a positive spin on the Dark's proposals. He told the men on A-wing that they could make the system unworkable by burning workshops and disrupting the routine. No one was sure whether Bobby supported the Dark or was just playing devil's advocate. But no one supported him, either.

This left the Dark with the problem of how to move the protest forward. How could he create a dynamic that could bring them victory and, in so doing, increase public support for the whole movement and the war effort? This is where Sands came in. He was one of the few blanketmen who the Dark knew and trusted, a veteran of Cage Eleven. He was willing and able to work and think on the same level as the Dark. He was already writing articles to publicize the conditions in the H-Block to people outside of the jail. And he was already trying to organize better communications through visits and to raise morale by organizing classes and entertainment.

● ● ●

In March, with three hundred prisoners now on the blanket protest, they moved Bobby back to D-wing, into a cell next to Brendan Hughes. It was the beginning of an intimate working relationship. From then on, they were always next to each other. They never shared a cell but every time they were moved, they were put in adjacent cells.

Hughes says that the importance of Sands's constant location next door is indisputable.

"We discussed everything. *Everything* we done I discussed it with Bobby . . . I never made a decision without consultation with Bobby."

Hughes promoted Bobby to PRO for all of the H-Blocks, although he effectively served as his adjutant. Bobby was the Dark's "public voice." Hughes sent Sands the outline of a statement and said "put beef on that." Bobby beefed it up. Sometimes he went over the top through his enthusiasm and Hughes had to edit his statements. The other prisoners quickly noticed the budding special relationship. They saw Sands as the open, enthusiastic voice while Hughes was the "wily old man" who sat back in his cell and took in everything until he was ready to make a decision. Joe Barnes says that Hughes had ideas but Bobby gave life to them. He was "prolific," "full of beans," "constantly on the go."

Sands and Hughes started right away to discuss new strategies to move away from inactive protest. Since Hughes was so close to the Republican leadership, he knew how weak the IRA had become after several years of widespread arrests. Before he was arrested he had been among a handful of leaders who began restructuring the IRA from its old brigade system toward a cell structure, where secrecy and revolutionary discipline were central. He knew that the other side of the new army discipline was the creation, under IRA direction, of a more dynamic political party that would agitate around social and economic issues, as Bobby had tried to do in Twinbrook. But it would take years for the new structures to take effect. In the meantime, he felt that the prison protest could provide a popular platform that would enable the Republican *Movement* (not just the IRA and not just Sinn Féin) to mobilize support while the IRA regrouped.[3] So for him, and then for Bobby, the prison protest was not just a matter of prisoners' rights; it was central to the whole process of rebuilding the IRA.

"What I was doing at the time and Bobby knew it, I knew it, a lot of the people in the jail did *not* know it . . . I knew the leadership on the outside were rebuilding. We had an issue here that could give some help to the leadership on the outside. I knew that was the situation, and that's what we were doing."

The first move was to implement Bobby's ideas about creating a communications infrastructure, to keep the prisoners in constant contact with the IRA and with an emerging group of activists who were beginning to organize a public campaign. The prisoners had to stop relying on outsiders to carry sensitive information about their strategies or plans. In particular, they had to stop relying on priests to carry communications ("comms"). Bobby, in particular, was highly suspicious of priests.

Most prisoners still refused visits. The Dark told them to start taking them, to open new lines of communications and get pens and other materials, even if it meant putting on the prison uniform. The Dark was acutely aware of the mental and physical difficulties involved.

"It was quite tough at the time to go out of your cell and put on that prison uniform. Initially it was symbolically very *very* difficult and then it became brutally difficult because obviously they realized what we were doing, bringing in the lines of communication and so forth and bringing stuff in and getting stuff out. So they began to make it tougher for us by physically abusing people."

Once they got over the symbolic issue of wearing the uniform, most prisoners realized that taking visits actually lightened the protest. They got to see their loved ones *and* they felt like they were doing something positive.

Bobby had been taking his half-hour monthly visit all along, even while the vast majority of the blanketmen refused theirs. His family visited him regularly, particularly his sister Marcella and his mother. Hughes was amazed when Rosaleen turned out to be a magnificent smuggler, just like her son.

"The stuff Bobby used to bring back. Tobacco, pens, papers. It was fantastic," he marvels. "Bobby's mother was the best, she was the best at getting stuff in. He *never* came back without any, he *always* managed to do it."

Rosaleen also took Bobby's writings out. She was so good that Sands and Hughes called her "Old Faithful." If Bobby had a visit with Rosaleen, the men all knew that they would have a smoke that night. This taught them that visits were not just an important source of communications, but they were also a source of luxuries.

Smuggling was not easy. The visitors, usually women, had to carry their packages into the jail through a rigorous search procedure. Then, they had to pass their message and receive one in return, all while sitting at a table in a visiting box with a prison warder watching. The passing usually took place during an embrace and a kiss. A small message, tightly folded and wrapped in cling wrap, could be passed from mouth to mouth. A larger item, such as a package with tobacco and pen refills, had to be passed by hand. Once the prisoner had the package, he discretely slipped it into his mouth or up into his anus, through a hole that he had ripped in the uniform trousers for that purpose. Sometimes prisoners had to swallow comms, hoping to retrieve them later by vomiting or simply by waiting until nature took its course.

The prisoners went to great lengths to hide their comms. Some carried them in their mouths but the guards could easily find a note hidden under a tongue or between the cheek and gum. Some prisoners slipped their comms inside their foreskins, transferring them into their mouths only moments before they reached the visiting box. Others slipped the comm up their rectum with an extra layer of paper and a string round it. When they were past the searches, they would pull out the string and take off the outer layer of paper and then stick the comm in their mouth to pass across with a kiss.

The kiss was repulsive for the visitors. One prisoner recalls how his kids would shrink back from the smell of his breath. Without toothpaste, their teeth were in terrible shape and their breath stank.

Another problem with visits was their infrequency. One visit a month was hardly enough to establish a reliable stream of communication. So Hughes got prisoners to take "appeal visits." Every prisoner had the right to appeal his sentence and while it was being processed he received daily fifteen-minute visits with anyone he nominated as long as they talked only about the appeal case. This increased the frequency of communication but the warders strictly enforced a rule that nothing could be discussed but the appeal. If the visitor or the prisoner said anything that was not directly relevant to the case, they immediately stopped the visit.

One time Sheila McVeigh was visiting her husband on an appeal visit. It had been snowing and when she got to the visiting box she discovered she had snow on her trousers.

"Jesus, it's snowing out there and I've snow in my trousers," she said, inadvertently, while shaking the snow out of the cuff.

"That's not about the case. Visit over," the guard cut in.

• • •

Visits soon turned from capitulation to *confrontation*. The act of going on visits unexpectedly stepped up the intensity of the protest. Once the prison warders realized that messages and tobacco were being smuggled, they started strip-searching the prisoners, probing their hair, mouths, and rectums for messages or tobacco. If they were lucky, prisoners merely had to go through the humiliating procedure of "touring full circle with [their] arms raised in the air."[4] But forced squatting, bending, and probing became common and, with them, beatings increased as the prisoners resisted procedures they regarded as sexual assault (the issue of strip-searching would become even more controversial for women prisoners in Armagh jail).

Hughes and Sands were trying to intensify the protest. They wanted to increase publicity about their conditions of detention and, in doing so, were quite aware that they would provoke further repression by the authorities. Yet they had little control over the escalating pattern of confrontation that followed.

On both sides, action and reaction combined in a creative process of confrontation. Although both sides planned and discussed their strategies, they also made things up as they went along. They were not doing so entirely out of the blue. Rather, they called upon their considerable past experiences of protest and repression, much of it from the distinctly different environments of the cages and the Crumlin Road Jail. Even familiar tactics had to be adapted to the new conditions of the H-Blocks and there was no predictability about the outcomes of a new initiative or a new reaction.

The immediate cause of the next escalation of the protest was a conflict over the conditions under which the prisoners could leave their cells. They were not allowed to wear their blankets outside of the cell but the authorities reached a sort of compromise by allowing them to wear their hand towels around their waists. By the end of 1977, however, as the numbers on the blanket protest swelled, the warders reduced the regularity with which they allowed prisoners to go to the washroom. Some prisoners complained that they were brutalized on the way to and from the washroom. The corridors became a battleground for control.

The worst trouble was in H3, where Joe Barnes was OC of mostly young prisoners (YPs). He claims that they were treated worse than the older prisoners in H4 and H5, as several screws did their best to break them. They got fewer showers, little or no milk in their cornflakes, less bread with their dinners. One warder boasted about how many YPs he had driven off of the protest.

Barnes sent word to the Dark telling him how the YPs were being brutalized. Hughes and Sands immediately decided that if the YPs were not allowed to wash then no one would wash. If the screws were trying to control the pace of their lives, they had to take back control by acting together.

On March 20, 1978, all of the blanketmen refused to wash, shower, or clean their cells. They knew it was a momentous step but they did not know that it was the beginning of a long process that they would call the "no-wash" protest. The authorities and the media would it call the "dirty" protest.

"We basically slid into it. It wasn't a conscious decision," insists the Dark. "Well, initially it wasn't. It was because of the situation, people getting brutalized going to the shower and so forth."

Yet a temporary response, even a defensive one, can have unintended consequences. It may provoke unexpected reactions or be so effective that it becomes a weapon. "No-wash" became a tactic because the warders' repressive reactions boosted the prisoners' morale. It gave them a sense of control over their relationships with their jailers.

According to a statement Bobby smuggled out of prison, the warders reacted to their no-wash strategy by arbitrarily picking out a dozen men and sending them to the punishment block. So the following Monday, the prisoners notched up their protest by refusing to "slop out" or fill their water containers. This was a more serious challenge to the prison authorities. For a few days the screws took it as a laugh and went around in gloved hands emptying the pisspots.[5] But soon they reacted more strongly. Some emptied the pots and then passed out dinners with the same hands. Some "accidentally" spilled the contents of the pots over the cell floors and the bedding.

Bobby described what happened on his wing. The men set their dirty dishes and water containers outside of their cells and the screws threw them back in. Some men received minor injuries; others got burst water containers and soaked bedding. Then the screws handed out a mere "half a sheet of toilet paper" and stopped emptying the pots altogether. Things rapidly deteriorated from there.

> We received our dinner cold—it was served half an hour late. Dishes which we left out were used as missiles against us, before being later removed. Another comrade was taken hostage and shipped off to punishment block.
>
> At 8:30 P.M. lock-up there was no point in putting out our water containers. The chamber pots were overflowing: We uri-

*nated into the boots, which are part of the criminal uniform, and
then threw the urine out the window. On top of this the men had
to leave excrement lying in a corner of the floor.*

Bobby continued,

*My own cell is stinking and my body has a sickening smell
about it. We expect more beatings and more harassment because
of this stage of the protest. Our strong convictions that we are
Irishmen struggling for Ireland, and that Englishmen have no
right to treat us like this, will see us through our long protest. All
that we ask of the media is coverage of a statement made by 300
Irish political prisoners suffering the worst jail conditions known
about in the world.*[6]

The instrumental act of urinating in their boots was also a strong symbolic gesture. It was, simultaneously, a use of black humor to raise their
morale under difficult circumstances.

The screws responded to each new act of resistance with informal punishment. In return, the prisoners escalated their protest each Monday. The
third Monday they refused a partial change of sheets. The authorities
changed just one of their two sheets with a clean one each week. The prisoners threw the remaining dirty sheet onto the landing when the screws
gave them their clean one. The screws kicked the sheets back into the
cells. After a few days, the prisoners threw all of their sheets and pillowcases onto the landing and demanded a full change of bedclothes. The
warders refused and this time they did not even give the sheets back.

One might expect that such intensification of their privations would
make the prisoners reconsider their actions. But every time the screws introduced a new form of repression, they interpreted it as a sign of weakness,
an indication that they were winning. They began talking about "victory
around the corner" and reckoned that they had the authorities on the ropes.[7]

"Morale was sky high," recalls a prisoner. "We felt that we were winning and for a change that we, not the screws, had control over our lives
because we dictated the pace of events. The screws for their part were
demoralized because they had no control over what happened next. They
dreaded Mondays because that was the day that we kept upping the
tempo of the protest by introducing something new."[8]

The prisoners had to solve the little matter of what to do with extra food. They threw it into the corner at the foot of their beds. It piled up. They threw their leftover tea on the walls and ceilings, staining them brown. Hughes and Sands began talking about the state of the cells and their likely effects on prisoners and authorities. They recognized a potential in what was going on.

"It soon became a tactic."

Not only did they feel that the authorities were having a hard time dealing with the mess that their modern prison had rapidly become, they speculated that the no-wash protest would escalate to a stage where the authorities would be unable to deal with it and would be *forced* to grant them political status just to bring some order back to the prison. Hughes had a specific scenario in mind:

"The idea I had was when we stop washing, we stop going out, we dump the food in the corner . . . the idea was to start an epidemic. Yeah, we believed we could do it that way, an epidemic . . . It would wreck it."

Bobby predicted such an outcome in May:

> *The danger of a health risk here at present is no longer a possibility. It is inevitable. A major outbreak of disease would devastate these blocks. As has been said, the physical and bodily resistance of each man here is practically nil. Our chances of survival in such an event are not worth even mentioning.*[9]

The epidemic never happened. In fact, the prisoners remained remarkably healthy despite the foul conditions in which they were living.[10] Some medical warders noticed that the blanketmen got sick *less* often than the men who were not on protest.[11] Rather than an epidemic, they got further escalation and more miserable conditions, beyond a point that any of them could have imagined when they first refused to wash or clean out their cells. Once the warders stopped emptying chamber pots, the prisoners had to throw their contents out the window. Bobby described how he did it in an article.

> *We put our human waste out the cell windows as we were put in this position by prison authorities. When pouring out urine we have to use the lid of the poes as funnels between bars which is both degrading and embarrassing.*[12]

The administration answered this new practice by making the warders hose down the prison yards with high-pressure hoses, followed by more warders in white protective clothing who sprayed disinfectant around the windows and the walls. The next development was surely inevitable. As summer approached, the men left their windows open to get a bit of air into their stinking cells. Water from the high-pressure hoses wound up in the cells, soaking the prisoners' bedding and leaving pools on the floors. The prisoners ran to close their windows but they hardly ever got there in time.

As summer progressed, the cells got hotter and the piles of rotten food got more disgusting. They grew "beards" of mold. Then, they began to move. Maggots were wriggling in their thousands throughout the piles. Some prisoners sat and watched, disgusted, as they wriggled around and climbed up the walls. Sometimes a maggot got one of a prisoner's filthy matted hairs twisted round its body; he had to burst it in his hair to get rid of it.

Bobby was disgusted on the first morning when,

> *I woke up and my blankets and mattress were a living mass of white maggots. They were in my hair and beard and crawling upon my naked body. They were repulsive, and dare I say it, frightening at first.*

But he soon got used to them, even to their rustling about the floor at night and the crunch they made when he stood on them in his bare feet. He gathered them up in his hands and threw them into the yard for the birds to eat. He stood at the open windows and chatted to other prisoners while they watched the birds gorging themselves.

> *The wagtails came fluttering about in a frenzy, their quick little legs darting them from one maggot to the next, feasting upon what to them must have been a delicacy.* [13]

As their physical situation worsened, the prisoners used any means they could to raise morale. Around May, someone discovered that the cell walls had round holes toward the bottom where they had been lifted into place by crane. The holes were filled with a soft plaster that could be chipped out with whatever tools they could fashion. They enlarged the holes around the heating pipes in the same way. All of this made it easier to communicate between cells.

When they were not talking about the protest, Sands and Hughes talked about their kids. They had gone through similar experiences. The Dark's wife left him when he went to jail and his sister brought his kids to see him on visits. Sands told Hughes about life in Rathcoole and the hills of Carnmoney. His sister Marcella sent him a big postcard of a river in the mountains. They traded it back and forth through the pipe to brighten up their cells. Bobby put it on his wall for a few days and then passed it over to Hughes to put on his wall. Eventually the screws took it away but "for them few days it added a bit of color to the cell."

• • •

As the mess became unbearable, the authorities introduced new restrictions. One day, they started taking the furniture out of the cells. Upon hearing this, the Dark ordered the men to smash it before the screws could take it away. They smashed everything but the beds and threw the pieces out the windows onto the catwalks that ran along the outside walls. The next day, the warders removed the beds, leaving the mattresses on the floor. Since the cell floors were soaking wet, so were the mattresses and blankets.

Then the authorities changed the rules about monthly parcels. Each prisoner had been allowed one monthly parcel with a bar of soap, three shampoos, three small packets of tissues, and two religious magazines. The authorities limited them to three packets of tissues only. The screws searched the cells and took away all the magazines, toothbrushes, toothpaste, and combs. They even took rosary beads. If anyone wore religious medals, they could only keep only one of them.

Threat is opportunity. Every time the authorities intensified their punishment the prisoners found a way to turn their behavior back on them. Eventually, the prison authorities took away all of the prisoners' material possessions.

All that was left was the food and the human waste.

When the prisoners tried to get rid of *these*, the warders gave them back. After the episodes with the hoses and windows, the prisoners began slopping their urine under the doors or out the door hatch. The screws squeegeed it back under the doors at night so the prisoners woke up on sopping wet foam mattresses, swimming in pools of piss.

Each side tried to outwit the other. The prisoners squeezed wet bread into rubbery dough to build dikes at the bottom of their cell doors. The screws came along with coat hangers and punctured them so that the urine flowed back into the cells. On and on went the battle, usually ending in a wet cell in the morning. Bobby had to squeeze out his blankets each morning and lean the mattress up against the heating pipes to dry out.

Solid waste was the biggest problem. First, the prisoners threw it out the window but the warders threw it back. Hughes and Sands talked about spreading the shit on the walls. *That* would certainly draw attention to their conditions. Most of the prisoners dreaded the thought.

Despite all this, morale constantly improved. A rumor went around that the prison authorities had until December to break the blanketmen; if they failed, political status would be granted. Most prisoners had enough Irish to hold conversations and they spent more time talking to their neighbors. They organized entertainment every night. If there was to be a singsong, Bobby would sit in the cell from six in the evening, planning out what he would sing and making sure he got the words right. He would sing the words, over and over, constantly clearing his throat. His new cellmate, Ginty Lennon, heard the song a dozen times before the wing heard it.

The men invented new forms of entertainment. Their favorite was the "book at bedtime," where the best storytellers recited a book from memory after the screws left the wing at night. There were good book tellers and bad ones. Bobby was regarded as one of the best. He "researched" *Trinity* for weeks, sending out requests for information on visits and asking orderlies to get information from the other blocks. He told the whole epic, coming to life especially when Long Dan Sweeney gave the rebel monologue that he had committed to memory like the words of a favorite song. It was just a popular novel but Uris's words must have sounded eerily contemporary in the H-Blocks of Long Kesh:

> *If you remember nothing else, remember this. No crime a man commits on behalf of his freedom can be as great as the crimes committed by those who deny his freedom . . . Sure, we'll never see the day we can meet them in open warfare and match them gun for gun, so they'll denounce our tactics as cowardly. But we are not without weapons of our own. Remember that the British have nothing in their entire arsenal or imperial might to counter a single man who*

refuses to be broken. Irish words, Irish self-sacrifice and, ultimately, Irish martyrdom are our weapons. We must have the ability to endure pain to such an extent that they lose the ability to inflict it. This and this alone will break them in the end. Martyrdom.[14]

Bobby also told a tale about a Parisian who was on death row for killing an Algerian. For years, he had driven down an avenue of cherry blossoms but he never really noticed them. Now, from his death cell, he could see the tops of the cherry trees and the blossoms became the most important things in his life. The cherry blossom comes into its own, said Bobby, when you know you'll never see it again.

● ● ●

By May, the cells were utterly disgusting. The warders shoveled out the rubbish on Sunday mornings while the prisoners were at mass. The stench was unbearable. Life became a sort of routine, punctuated by conflict between prisoners and screws. It was only when he was released from this environment for a few days that Bobby realized how oppressive it really was.

His temporary release came in mid-May, when he was taken for an appeal hearing in the Crumlin Road Courthouse. He was woken up by the rattle of keys.

"Right! You better get up, you're for court this morning," the screw told him, setting a breakfast of porridge and tea by the rubbish pile at the foot of his mattress. As he slammed the cell door, says Bobby,

> *I wrapped one of the blankets around me and braved it to the perimeter of the rubbish heap to lift the mug of tea. The stench hit me immediately. I grabbed the mug of tea and retreated to the far corner, dismissing the bowl of cold porridge as being uneatable as usual. Finishing my tea I folded my two filthy, shabby blankets and set my damp mattress against the heating pipes that run through each cell.*

The idea that he was actually leaving the prison left him "unsettled and nervous." The sensation of wearing clothes again was "very strange but tremendous."

I suppose you could say I almost felt human again. The short walk to the van which brought me to reception left me a bit light-headed and sickly.

He was taken to the court in a blue van with small windowless cubicles, just a small vent through which exhaust fumes entered and made him sick while he bounced back and forth. It left him physically shattered. The courthouse was even more disturbing. He was left in a holding cell with other remand prisoners. He was unaccustomed to being around other people and felt nervous and ill at ease. But he got a few luxuries: cigarettes, chocolate, and a newspaper. He was brought to court through the crowded foyer of the courthouse. Everyone looked at him like some kind of alien; he had not showered or washed in two months and had long straggly hair and a wiry beard that "did not cover the pale yellowish complexion of my face." He got even more embarrassed when he overheard people whispering to each other that he must be one of the blanketmen. When he got back to the cell he was glad to be away from the crowds.

Then, when he got back to the prison he was sent to the punishment block for arguing with the prison doctor. Vomiting and dizzy from the fumes in the prison van, he started to tell the doctor that he was sick. But before he got the words out the doctor approached him with gloves on and said that he was going to inspect his anus. Sands refused to let him, saying that it was extremely degrading. He had suffered enough humiliation for one day and this measure was going too far.

He was charged with breach of prison discipline and taken to the punishment block for four days. When got back to his cell,

The stench that hit me was almost overwhelming. A multitude of flies departed from the piles of decaying rubbish on the floor. The heat in the cell was extreme, my mattress lay on the cell floor in a pool of water . . . My quick appraisal of my living conditions was brought to an abrupt halt when the screw slammed the cell door shut behind me.

Back in his cell, Bobby began to note some unnatural things about their way of life. The stench was obvious but the other thing he noticed was the noise. The constant slamming of cell doors reverberated throughout the wing. If someone hammered on his cell wall, the noise carried throughout the wing. He felt claustrophobic because he had no real view of the outside world. "One is meant to see out and see nothing and even then the nothingness is restricted to barbed wire," he wrote. The strong bright cell lights bothered him; even at night the prison was light. He had become so used to these things that he only noticed them after being out of his cell for a few days.

"The long-term effects are inconceivable," he wrote. "It has taken me two weeks to recover to what can incorrectly be termed as my normal self."[15]

On one of those nights, a few cells down from Sands, Sean Glás was at the window looking out at nothing. It was about 1:30 in the morning and things were eerily quiet. Bobby was awake in his cell, pacing and thinking. Sometimes, he would come up to the window and look out. Bobby watched two screws walking past with massive dogs. He looked past the dogs at the wire and fences. And he began to think out loud. Sean Glás heard him through the early morning silence.

"How do you fight all this?" Bobby asked no one in particular. "The watchtowers, the guard dogs . . . how do you break out of this?"

He paused, then he spoke again.

"If you can't break out of it physically, you have to break out of it mentally."

Thereafter, he began to talk about how important it was to transcend the wire. He wrote about it a couple of years later in a prose piece he simply titled, "Barbed Wire."

"There is perhaps a couple of thousand miles of it spread all over the place, rolls and rolls of it winding its way throughout the camp," he wrote. "It's just one large barbed wire jungle. That's what makes the largest part of my limited scenery each day: cold, gray wire."

Even the birds perching on the wire could not make it any less gruesome.

"Maybe someday I'll have the pleasure of trailing every single piece of this ungodly material down for good."[16]

● ● ●

"Bobby was a typical poster of a blanketman," says his cellmate, Ginty Lennon. "If they'd have walked in and said they wanted to take a photograph for a poster outside, I'd have nominated Bobby because he had that dilapidated look about him."

Lennon immediately adds, "But in saying that, his morale was high, he was the life and soul, I don't ever mind Bobby Sands being down."

Just after they moved in together, Sands argued with Lennon about the 1916 Easter rising. He quoted James Connolly, who said that the rising was as much about class struggle as Irish nationalism. Lennon thought Bobby was talking nonsense. He said that the Easter rising was a Nationalist rising, the same as today. The only way to beat British colonialism was to fight for an independent Irish nation.

They argued the whole day, stopping only for dinner. The debates turned into a political education for Lennon. When they were not debating, they did quizzes, asking each other questions and awarding points for the right answers. Lennon hardly ever got the answers right. Bobby taught him Irish and persuaded him to keep studying and talking Irish whenever he began to waver. Bobby played battleships with other prisoners in the surrounding cells. They drew grids on the wall and moved their ships as they called out their moves to each other. Then he talked all night at the pipes or at the window.

But most of the time Sands spent writing. He was a "compulsive writer" who had his pen out at every opportunity to write poems, songs, and articles.

"See the whole time I was in the cell with Bobby, he just wrote and rewrote. He was constantly writing. Bobby would get up in the morning and just started writing, that was him."

Bobby paced the cell like a caged animal. He walked up and down the cell, constantly stroking and pulling at his beard while he thought. Then he would sit down and jot some quick notes for that night when the screws would be gone and he could write safely. Then it was back up again, pacing and pulling at his beard. He scribbled on the wall with whatever was to hand, perhaps the tab from a zipper that he had ripped from the baggy uniform pants on a visit. As soon as the screws left the wing, out came a pen refill and he was putting the scribbled points together into articles. Lennon never saw Sands reading the Bible but it was *always* in use because he needed it to write on.

Sometimes Lennon was asleep when he heard a rustle and then scraping. He could see the outline of Bobby's figure in the light that came in through the cell window.

"What are you doing, Bobby?" he would ask.

"I've an idea here. I'm just scraping the wall to write notes so I don't forget it."

As summer came on, Bobby wrote about an especially hot day. This article was considerably more depressing than his first article about life in the H-Blocks, written the previous October. "Today has been a very long one. As my old cellmate says, it's one of those days that never ends," he began. The heat, combined with the stink of their bodies and the trash, meant that they could hardly breathe. Most depressing to Bobby, however, was the fact that they had little to talk about.

> With the heat being what it is and after 20 months of being out of contact, we have nothing of interest to talk about. It is depressing just to wake up and see what we live in (concrete tombs).[17]

He describes their horrific conditions in detail:

> When we awaken, it's not unusual to see maggots crawling across the bedding and us. They crawl from the rubbish heaps in our cells, remember we have to sleep on the floor . . . Bloating flies are everywhere and they pester us . . . There is room to walk only five steps and then turn five steps, then turn again. Ten minutes of this and we are dizzy.

Bobby described how degrading it was to go to the toilet in front of each other. He wrote about the poor quality of the food. But, as usual, he ended on a note of defiance.

> This type of treatment will always be resisted. We will never conform to criminal rules like common thieves. All we ask is to be treated like P.O.W.s. That is what we are.[18]

The weather got hotter. The cells got stuffier. It was especially bad when the screws threw disinfectant around the rubbish piles. The ammonia burned Bobby's eyes and he could hardly breathe.[19] Hughes and Sands discussed the situation and sent out the order to smash the windows. Again, taking control over their environment was "exhilarating." And with the windows broken out communications were easier.

One night, Bobby sang "Sad Song for Susan" out the cell window.

"Who wrote that one, Bobby?" asked Ginty.

"I wrote that myself," he said, in a voice loud enough for the other prisoners to hear. No one believed him. Could one of their own have written such a moving song? They would change their assessment in time as they sampled more of Bobby's poems and songs. As for that particular song, Bobby did not sing it very often, just the odd time when the mood was quiet and slow.

It was not long before the maintenance men installed Perspex windows. Someone got the bright idea to burn them out to let the air back in. Sands and Lennon set a fire and the Perspex began to melt, filling the cell with a thick acrid smoke. They were delighted when the warders came because the smoke was choking them. But they succeeded in getting the windows out again.

The downside, however, was getting drenched by the high-pressure hoses. One warder who they called Fat Geordie seemed to take great pleasure in pointing the hose through the windows and soaking them. Whenever Geordie was near, everyone ran to the corners of their cells to avoid a soaking. One afternoon, Bobby decided he'd had enough. The governor was scheduled to come around the wing that evening to sentence them to cellular confinement and Fat Geordie was in the yard with his hose. Everyone else ran away but Bobby stood at the wide-open window, just staring at the warder as he soaked him. That night, when the governor opened Bobby's cell to sentence him, a wall of water came rushing out and Sands lay shivering on his soaking bed. They had to stretcher him to the hospital.[20]

● ● ●

Inevitably, the prisoners started putting their shit on the cell walls. Initially, most of them slapped it on as quickly as possible, hoping that it would stick. But eventually they perfected a method where they tore lumps off of their foam mattresses and used them to smear the shit on the walls and ceiling, leaving a two-foot square clean spot near the pipe for writing. As the wall filled up, they hoisted each other onto their shoulders to cover the high places. No one ever got comfortable with it but the dread of putting their shit on the walls was worse than the reality. Some worried about the effect it would have on outside opinion.[21] Their plight was worsened by the constant comments of the warders, who called them names and said that even animals would not live in such filth.

Like everything else, their new conditions eventually became routine. Morale heightened once again as they found strength to endure conditions that would have been unimaginable a few months previous. Best of all, their enemy, the screws, could not handle it.

Looking back, Hughes remembers how he and Sands had predicted that living in the dirty cells with maggots and flies would lead to some kind of epidemic.

"Yeah, that was the general idea . . . uh . . . it didn't happen . . . didn't happen!"

He gives a big laugh at their miscalculation. Then, matter-of-factly, "so the thing escalated to the shit going on the wall."

• • •

The "no-wash protest" had become the "dirt protest." A public campaign was now more important than ever. Relatives of blanketmen and others who were concerned about prisoners' human rights had organized local Relatives Action Committees (RACs). Bobby knew that it was important to feed more information to these supporters.

On the fourth of July 1978, he lodged an appeal on his conviction. It was a ruse to increase his ability to smuggle messages in and out of the prison. Eilish Carlisle, a friend of his old comrades from the Short Strand, took his appeal visits until he abandoned the process five months later.[22]

Gerard Rooney's brother Philip, now remanded on charges of causing explosions, often saw Bobby on his way to see Eilish Carlisle. His overriding memory is how confident Bobby was. "Every time you seen him he looked like he owned the place." The other guys on the blanket "looked like shit." They clomped around in boots that were too big for them, in uniforms that hung off of their rapidly emaciating frames. But Bobby took care to straighten his hair as best he could and he wore the blue prison shirt collar outside the denim jacket, "John Travolta–style." He walked with a confident stride and talked to everybody, prisoners and screws. He'd put his arm around the other prisoners and ask about their people, giving them the feeling that he had a special interest in their personal details. As for the screws, Rooney almost thought they were working for Bobby, as he seemed to have control.[23]

Perceptions depend on your point of reference. Perhaps Sands seemed confident to other prisoners but his visitors saw a different man. Eilish

Hamill from Twinbrook was shocked when she ran into Bobby in the visiting room as he was returning from an appeal visit. He was much thinner than he'd been in Twinbrook, with a long whispy beard and unkempt straggly hair. His trousers were too baggy, his shoes too loose. His complexion was pasty and his eyes sunk. He shuffled along like an old man. When they hugged, the prison guards sneered at her like she was hugging a leper. Yet, despite his appearance, she noticed that his morale was high.

• • •

As the summer wore on, the heat got worse and the stink of shit and rotting food was matched only by the disgusting flies that emerged from a steady supply of maggots. Some prisoners organized fly races, placing them on a "race track" and betting on which fly would win. Others organized more civilized entertainment. At the end of July, Bobby organized the First Annual Talent Competition in the wing. The first prize was six cigarettes rolled in toilet paper. In their present state, this was like gold dust. On the big night, Bobby was MC. The Dark opened a betting book on who would win first prize and acted as referee. "Red" Mickey Devine reported the event, assisted by his cellmate Sean Glas.[24] Under Bobby's encouragement, Devine was enthusiastically beginning to write.

The competition began after the warders left for the night. Practically everyone joined in. Between acts, Bobby sang "Band of Gold" and "Suzanne." Joe Corey from Derry did a stand-up comedy routine about the Queen. John Nixon bopped out a Buddy Holly song. Others did renditions from Frank Sinatra to Little Richard. Seando Moore even did a whistling act à la Roger Whittaker.

Finally, the voting started, each judge giving a score out of ten.

"Can I have your attention, please," Bobby finally announced. "Here it comes."

And then he told a joke, leaving the prisoners hanging until, at the announcement of the winner, the whole wing erupted. Mickey Devine's report ends with a few words that encapsulate what Bobby Sands was trying to achieve:

> *At various times during the acts I looked at our surroundings,*
> *here we were in the dirt, urine, and maggots, and things we have*
> *endured fresh in our minds and indeed which are still happening.*

> *At face value it seems to be just a simple singsong, but it really demonstrated to me more than any political article just how determined the men in the H-Blocks are.*
>
> *I personally feel proud to be with men who have the courage and spirit to laugh and smile no matter what the circumstances and never allow themselves to be grinded down by Britain or her lackeys in Black Uniform.*

Bobby knew, however, that courage and spirit were not enough. Despite his efforts, public relations were still the missing key in the escalating protest. A local journalist noted that, far from eliciting sympathy for their degrading conditions, "the dirty protest was instead widely condemned as grotesque."[25] Bobby's articles had helped to mobilize opinion in Republican communities but few people outside of these communities ever saw them. Even the *Irish News*, the daily "Catholic" newspaper, failed to explain what the protest was about. The prisoners had to convince a broader audience that their degrading conditions were forced on them by government intransigence. They needed support from sources that had moral credibility in society at large.

In July, Archbishop Tomás Ó Fiaich of Armagh, soon to be cardinal of Ireland, requested a visit to the H-Blocks. It would be the beginning of a long relationship between the prisoners and Ó Fiaich, who would later act as their intermediary to the British government. The prison authorities were concerned about Ó Fiaich's visit. They knew that he was more than just a cleric. They tried to get his parishioners to see him in groups in the wing canteens, wearing prison uniform, rather than allowing him to go from cell to cell where he would witness the extent of their degradation. The prisoners refused. They reached a compromise; all of the archbishop's parishioners would gather in one cell but not wearing any part of the prison uniform.

When he got to H3, Ó Fiaich was directed to Martin Hurson's cell, where the men from his diocese were assembled. Hurson, a devout Catholic, joined the others for nearly an hour in a discussion with the cardinal. They told him that they were determined to break the British criminalization policy and discussed their conditions of imprisonment, although a lot of what they had to say was readily apparent.[26]

In H5, the meeting was in the Dark's cell because his cellmate was from the archbishop's diocese. Ó Fiaich came into the cell, opened his cassock, took out hundreds of cigarettes, and handed them around. The Dark noticed that he was visibly upset at their conditions. Again, the men expressed their determination to remain on protest until the British government recognized that they were political prisoners. The visit backfired on the authorities in a big way. The following day the archbishop released a statement to the press that expressed his feelings about what he had seen:

> *Having spent the whole of Sunday in the prison, I was shocked at the inhuman conditions prevailing in H-Blocks 3, 4, and 5, where over 300 prisoners were incarcerated. One would hardly allow an animal to remain in such conditions, let alone a human being. The nearest approach to it I have seen was the spectacle of the hundreds of homeless people living in sewer pipes in the slums of Calcutta.*

He described the conditions in the H-Blocks in detail and then, as if this it was not enough, he went on to express his admiration for them:

> *I was surprised that the morale of the prisoners was high. From talking to them it is evident that they intend to continue their protest indefinitely and it seems they prefer to face death rather than submit to being classed as criminals. Anyone with the least knowledge of Irish history knows how deeply rooted this attitude is in our country's past. In isolation and perpetual boredom they maintain their sanity by studying Irish. It was an indication of the triumph of the human spirit over adverse material surroundings to notice Irish words, phrases, and songs being shouted from cell to cell and then written on each cell wall with the remnants of toothpaste tubes.*[27]

For Sands, it was a PRO's dream. Their protest finally had mainstream support. This was something on which he could build a campaign, one of the highest moral voices in the land making a public statement that he could nearly have written. Only a few weeks before, Sands had smuggled out an article to his movement's newspaper that ended with the words: "This type of treatment will always be resisted. We will never conform to criminal rules like common thieves. All we ask is to be treated like P.O.W.s. That is what we are."[28]

It was also a considerable morale booster for him personally, as the archbishop had singled out his own pet project, the use of the Irish language, to illustrate their spirit. From then on, a support campaign no longer had to rely on Bobby's descriptions of "concrete tombs"; the phrase "sewer pipes in the slums of Calcutta" became part of the lingua franca of the Irish political conflict, even in the mainstream media.

After Ó Fiaich's intervention, the blanketmen really became optimistic about their chances to win political status. In a protest campaign that had its ups and downs, its rumors and its disappointments, here was a tangible expression of support that had unquestionable moral authority. Now they *had* to keep on going and they had to find ways of building on the new foundation that the archbishop had given them.

● ● ●

Conflict continued to escalate through the summer of 1978. The cells got dirtier; the authorities reacted. Their solution was the "wing shift." Until now, they had attempted to maintain a sort of order by keeping the blanketmen in the same cells on the same wings as far as possible. After the embarrassing publicity surrounding the archbishop's visit, this changed. At the beginning of August, the authorities decided to clean the cells periodically by keeping three wings full of prisoners while one wing was being cleaned. The wings were cleaned in rotation, by moving the blanketmen in one wing into a wing that had just been cleaned while they steam cleaned the newly vacant cells for the prisoners from the next wing. In this way, the prisoners could be shifted into clean cells about every two weeks.

It should be no surprise that the wing shifts became arenas of violent confrontation. As usual, the prisoners used the violence of the shifts for propaganda while the authorities tried to deny undue brutality. The first wing shift was a "pretty relaxed affair." One by one, the cell doors opened and the two occupants of a dirty cell picked up their mattresses, blankets, and personal property and walked to the corresponding cell in the wing that had just been steam cleaned. On the second shift, they were stopped at the top of the wing while the screws gave their bedding a quick search. On the third shift, they were told to set their bedding down and were then directed toward a table where they had to take off their towels while they were inspected.

On the fourth wing shift things became unbearable. More screws directed each prisoner to go the table and take off his towel. This time, they ordered him to bend over. If he hesitated, four or five screws jumped on him, grabbing his arms and legs. One grabbed his hair. The others turned him upside down while one screw spread his legs and pulled his buttocks apart with his thumbs. The pain was bad, said one prisoner, but nothing compared to the humiliation.[29]

The wing shifts became extremely violent affairs, where the struggle for physical control over prison spaces turned into bloody boxing matches. The violence overflowed into the cells as warders raided them to find pens, tobacco, and other contraband. None of it would be serious in another context but to the jailers it proved how far they had lost control over the spaces of the H-Blocks. Thus, wing shifts and table searches were accompanied by cell searches which often ended up with the contents of the chamber pots thrown all over the prisoners' bedding.[30]

Visiting families and priests were soon aware of the violence. On arriving at mass, priests began to notice marks on the half-naked prisoners. Nonetheless, many prisoners agree that their morale heightened even more as the violence escalated. After each wing shift, they took stock of everyone on the new wing and, upon realizing that they had achieved another move without permanent damage, they broke into songs and rebellious chants.

Morale was sky-high on Bobby's wing. In October they organized a second talent contest. It went very much like the first, although Sands competed this time. According to Devine's report, "silence reigned" as Bobby "Every Voice" Sands got up and sang "like a true professional." His choice of song for the event was an interesting throwback to Cage Eleven: Loudon Wainwright III's sacrilegious hymn, "I Am the Way." His voice "echoed as he hit the high notes":

> *I can walk on the water & I can raise the dead*
> *It's easy,*
> *I-I-I am-m-m the wa-a-ay*

Bobby followed this up with a self-composed piece about life on the wing. When he was done, "the noisy applause seemed to upset the screws who indulged in a bit of heckling but soon got fed up and went back to mumbling things (like 'Why can't we break them?' and 'Why does everybody hate us?')."[31] As usual, Bobby was raising morale to new highs, giving the prisoners a sense of agency against the "enemy."

Brutality rose with morale. In November, the authorities replaced table searches with mirror searches. The screws took a prisoner out of the cell, walked him up the corridor, and forced him to squat over a mirror. Most of them refused, so they were physically forced over it so that the screws could look up their anuses.

The prisoners asked their leaders what to do. No one wanted to accede to the searches but resisting inevitably meant a severe beating. As usual, the YPs were most intimidated since the screws recognized their fear and singled them out for especially rough treatment.

Hughes discussed the YPs' predicament with Sands. He ordered them not to squat for the search. "Let them physically force you over the mirror. Don't put up too much resistance but physically, symbolically refuse to go over the mirror," he told them.

This worked for a time but a new procedure soon enflamed the conflict again. In early December, the warders took Muffles away from the Dark's cell. He was gone for some time and when they brought him back Sands heard all the warders giggling. Muffles had been forcibly shaved and washed; he was totally covered in scrapes and red welts from the hard brush they used. Hughes and Sands saw it as a sign of what was coming and began to discuss what to do about the new threat.

A few days later, on a Friday, the screws started giving forced haircuts to the YPs in H3. Many prisoners sat down in their cells when the warders came to take them away. So groups of screws dragged them out of their cells by their long straggly hair, which they cut forcibly with sheers. They told the prisoners that they would be back on Monday to wash them.

The YPs feared that if they resisted, they would be beaten to a pulp and then scrubbed even rawer than if they had not resisted. Joe Barnes, their OC, shouted in Irish to Bobby, asking him what to do. He said that the YPs were all cowering in their cells, trembling in fear.

That night was one of the longest nights they ever spent in the H-Blocks. Says Hughes, "One of the hardest orders I gave in my life and, again, through consultation with Bobby, was that we had to resist this. Because [the forced washes would] wreck morale throughout the whole blocks."

Hughes and Sands "debated and talked and talked and talked." Eventually, in the early morning hours, Bobby shouted the order to them, *"Moill iad."* ("Hold them back, resist them.")

Barnes could not believe his ears.

"Is that what they said? I don't think that's what they said," he told himself. He gave no response.

Bobby thought maybe Barnes had not heard the order so he shouted again and again, four or five times. All he got in return was silence.

After a couple of hours of deep soul-searching, Barnes decided to disobey the order. He shouted to the men, "If they come in, just passive resistance."

Bobby sat up all night, talking to Hughes about what might happen when the screws came to start washing. They had already instructed the men on their wing to resist. If any of them felt that they could not go through with it, said the Dark, they should leave the protest first thing in the morning, no hard feelings and no disgrace. No one left.

Sands and Ginty Lennon decided to stay alert the next day whenever the screws were on the wing. They would keep just a towel around their waist and a blanket around their shoulders to keep warm as they waited. If the screws came, they could throw off the blanket to gain freedom of movement. They would get their backs to the wall, facing them as they came rushing in, and take it from there.[32]

The next morning the screws started the forced washes in H3. Sands and Hughes sat listening. First there was total silence. Sands and Lennon felt the tension even though they were locked in their cell. Lennon walked the floor, waiting for them to come, while Bobby lay still at the pipe listening and ready to consult with the Dark. No one ate. Soon, they heard squealing and scuffles from H3. They assumed that the YPs were being badly beaten. After a couple of hours, the squealing stopped.

The men in H3 had not resisted. One by one, they were pushed into lukewarm water while the warders scrubbed them and shampooed their hair. When the scrubbing stopped, the screws threw a bucket of ice-cold water over them. One man thought his heart would burst. That was where the screams came from.[33]

When they were done with H3 the warders started in H4. There, the men resisted. The whole morning was a melee of yelling and screaming, kicking and punching. The men at the top end of the wing sat in their cells and listened to the screams and the punches at the bottom end, waiting in fear for their own turn. Then, with five cells left to go, the noise stopped. The cell doors were opened and the warders handed out bowls of rice. Nothing else happened. After a long time one of the prisoners, Kieran Doherty, called everyone up to their cell windows.

"It's a week to Christmas lads," he said. "How about a few Christmas carols?"

He began singing "Silent Night," to break the fear. His leadership was all the more remarkable, since no one had ever heard him sing before.[34]

The washings were over and the prisoners were higher than ever. A new blanketman in H4, Brendan "Bik" MacFarlane, listened as the men shouted victory slogans and sang Republican songs. They laughed and yelled and made fun of each others' sheared heads, bald spots here and tufts of hair sticking out there. MacFarlane took particular pleasure in the fact that the shears broke as soon as the warder stuck them into his thick beard. They took a tally of how many screws each of them managed to hit before being battered into the ground. "There was great satisfaction that we had stood firm and fought against impossible odds."

It was like the cages again, after the burning. The prisoners had taken a physical beating. By most standards their resistance was in vain, if not insane. Yet they felt that they had taken back some control over their lives and reestablished some sense of humanity under the most inhumane circumstances.

"It was our victory. Morale was high in those last couple of weeks of 1978."[35]

The warders never came to H5. If they had been attempting to demoralize the blanketmen, the victory celebrations in H4 surely convinced them that they had failed. Perhaps, as the Dark felt, the brutality of it all was too much, even for the screws.

• • •

The period of escalated violence affected Bobby's writing. Between July 1 and late November, *Republican News* did not publish any of his articles. According to Ginty Lennon, he was still writing constantly. But he concentrated on press releases and coordinating information that was coming in from different blocks and wings. When a new article finally appeared at the end of November, it marked a significant new phase of Bobby's writing, reflecting both a transition in his own consciousness and the beginning of public awareness of his stature as a writer, poet, and propagandist. Bobby was now in solitary, in a cell on the outside of the H-

Block at the bottom of the wing. On November 25, 1978, *Republican News* published an article entitled "The Window of My Mind." Bobby signed it, for the first time, under the pen name "Marcella," after his sister. In time, "Marcella" would become synonymous in the public mind with Bobby Sands. He was becoming an increasingly influential voice in the Republican struggle, like the young "Brownie" had been three or four years earlier.

> *When one spends each day naked and crouching in the corner of a cell resembling a pigsty, staring at such eyesores as piles of putrefying rubbish, infested with maggots and flies, a disease ridden chamber pot or a blank disgusting scarred wall, it is to the rescue of one's sanity to be able to rise and gaze out of a window at the world.*

It was a common theme with which Bobby began his first writing as Marcella, the theme of the condemned Frenchman staring from his prison cell out to the cherry blossoms. But the blanketmen had no cherry blossoms. The "world" that Sands described as he gazes from his barred window was,

> *. . . a view of nothingness, unless a barbed wire jungle and rows of faceless tin timbers offer an artificial appreciation unknown to me.*

Nonetheless, Bobby wrote about how he could brighten up a dreary wet November afternoon by pressing his head to the window and watching the birds at play in the prison yard. He describes the scene in a sort of soap opera that unfolds outside his window, as if he was watching it on TV. A dozen starlings bicker over crusts of bread, "continually on their guard, all their tiny nerves on edge, feuding amongst themselves." The greedy one tries to take all of the bread but the sparrow sneaks in while the starlings fight among themselves and grabs some. Over the whole yard, however, rules the seagull, who periodically sweeps in and "dominates, steals, pecks, and denies the smaller birds their share." The seagull "takes it all."

Sands cannot pass up the chance to make a political point about the lack of solidarity among the people outside of jail. "I dislike the seagull," he writes, "and I often wonder why the starlings do not direct their attention to the predator rather than each other, perhaps this applies to more than birds."

Bobby's view then expands. He thinks back in time to when the summer birds were in the yard: finches and the lark, which would later become the symbol of freedom that people would associate with the name Bobby Sands.

> *. . . the music of the lark a constant symphony of sound and a reminder of life.*

He lets his thoughts soar outward to the skies and the blanket of stars under which "one can dream a thousand dreams of yesterday, of childhood and happiness, of love and joy, escape through make believe and fantasy."

"How do you fight all this? How do you break out of this?" Bobby had asked on a night some months before. And he had answered himself, "If you can't break out of it physically, you have to break out of it mentally."

It is significant that it was not the physical abuse—the wing shifts, the beatings, the searches, the forced washings—that provoked Sands to write again. It was the threatened loss of his last visual contact with normal life, the free birds in the prison yard and the stars in the heavens above. In the last paragraph of his article, Marcella tells of the latest episode in the blanket struggle. In the midst of the violent struggle over space, searches and resistance to searches, shit and maggots and urine-soaked mattresses, the prison authorities began something that, to Bobby, was even worse.

> *Today the screws began blocking up all the windows with sheets of steel, to me this represents and signifies the further torture of the tortured, blocking out the very essence of life—nature!*

They had not yet blocked Bobby's window,[36] but he knew his turn would soon come and that darkness would prevail over his own cell and his own life.

> *A few words I once read came echoing back to me today—"No one can take away from a person his or her ability to contemplate.*

> *Throw them into prison, give them hard labour, unimaginative work to do, but you can never take from them the ability to find the poetry and music in life"—and I realised that they, here, my torturers, have long ago started and still endeavour to block up the window of my mind.*

This last paragraph signals a transcendence from the physical world of the H-Blocks into a new reality. Everything has been stripped away except his last source of inner strength and sanity, the window of his mind. Some men say that being a blanketman was an out-of-body experience. In his article, Bobby moves through the physical window of his being and out the window of his mind. He is transformed, from caterpillar to cocoon and now to butterfly. No longer is he a faceless "young West Belfast Republican." He is now Marcella, on his way to becoming the enigma the world knew as Bobby Sands. He is freed from his existence as spectator, from watching the lark and longing for its freedom. He begins to dig deep inside of himself to discover *his own* freedom, to intensify *his* struggle. On the day the screws began to physically block the H-Block windows they unwittingly played a role in the birth of Bobby Sands, hunger striker.

Abbots Cross. The Sands family lived in the second house when Bobby was born.

The Stella Maris youth soccer team. Bobby Sands is seated in the front row, fourth from the left, between his best friend Tommy O'Neill (holding trophy) and Michael Acheson, who later joined the loyalist Ulster Volunteer Force (UVF). Terry Nicholl (standing, second from left) also joined the UVF. Others in the picture include Dessie Black (standing, middle) and Willie Caldwell (seated, far left).

The Sands family house at Doonbeg Drive in Rathcoole. Note the Union Jacks. This neighborhood now has one of the highest concentrations of loyalist flags, murals, and graffiti in Northern Ireland. [Agnieszka Martynowicz]

The Willowfield Temperance Harriers on a training trip to the Mourne Mountains. Bobby Sands is kneeling, second from left and Paul Scott is on the guitar player's other side. [Courtesy of Larry Fox]

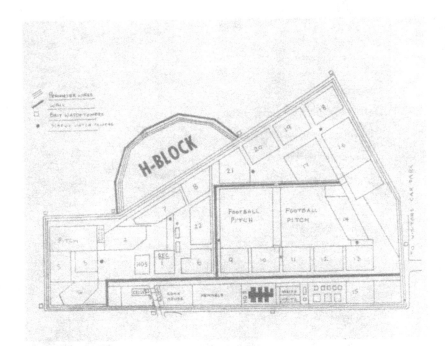

Map of the cages of Long Kesh, drawn for Gerry Adams's memoirs of Cage 11. Cages 1-8 and 22 housed internees. The other cages housed sentenced prisoners. [Reprinted from Gerry Adams, *Cage Eleven*, Dingle, Brandon Book Publishers Ltd., 1980]

Tomboy Loudon, Gerard Rooney, Denis Donaldson, and Bobby Sands in Cage 17. Donaldson painted a replica of Anderson Street in the Short Strand, where he and Rooney were born, in his cubicle. This is probably the most famous picture of Bobby Sands because it was used in hunger strike campaign posters. [*Coiste na n-Iarchimí*]

Cage 17 after the burning of Long Kesh, October 1974. The canteen and washroom remain standing. The British army, in a semicircle to the left of the picture, have the prisoners corralled in the corner of the cage.

"Poteen party" in the Gaeltacht hut, Cage 11. Bobby Sands is in the back, wearing hat and holding a guitar. Tomboy Loudon is third from the right and Kevin Carson is far right. [*Coiste na n-Iarchimí*]

Ag bunadh Gaeltachta

Seo ált faoí choinne gach duine, ác go h-áiríthe
na daoine atá ar an taob amuig, nuair a bíom muid
in ár gcónaí anseo tá tán ama againn a beit ag
foġlaim agus a léam agus sílim go bfuil fios
ag an chuid is mó se na daoine anseo caidé a
tá a tárlú so tír seo agus san domain freisin
agus tá muid ábalta a trácht ar an cogad i
Vietnam, an coimlint san meán oirtear, agus
an trioblóid in san tír seo.
Is iad na rudaí seo atá mar gnáth cómrá agus
caint i mbéal gach duine, ác anois, ba maith
liom an fáill seo a glacad an scríob faoi rud
eile — An Gaeltacht beag ag bótair Seoige
(Shaw's) Bfeidir gur chuala tú faoi an áit seo
go mion minic no bfeidir nár chuala, is feidir
nach síleann tú gur rud tábctacht é agus tá
seans maith nár chuala tú faoi go dtí anois,
bail ní raib morán eolas agam ác an oiread,
go dtí cupla mí ó sóin. Ní raib fios agam
caidé a bí a tárlú ann no caidé mar a
bí sé ag obair ác tá amáin teis mé áit
a bí scríobta san Irish Times faoi an
ceantar seo, agus bí iontais an domain orm
a feacáil go raib sé ag obair, com maith, agus
a bí sé, níl mé fíor cinnté có méas
daoine a tá in a gcónaí ann, ác sílim go
bfuil tart fá cúig teach déag ann, com maith
te sin tá naoí scoit beag acú, agus tá na
páiste ag foġlaim gach rud trí Gaeilge. agus
bíom siad ag caint inghaeilge i gcónaí agus
a dtuismuiteorí freisin agus tá cultúr féin
acú. ác freisin tá cultúr a difriúil ar an
taob eile sen bótair, bail seo mo ceist
anois.
Cad tuige nach bfuil níos mó ná Gaeltacht
amáin i mbéal Heirste? bail leis an fírinne
a insint sílim go bfuil na Gaeilgeoirí ró
fatha, chuala mé tán teitsceol cosúil te seo,
níl na daoine te Gaeilge ábalta Gaeltacht
a déanam se tairbe nach bfuil aon airgead
acú, ní fíor é agus ní teitsceol é tig
teo Gaeltacht beag a déanam in a sraideanna
féin fás as tá gach duine tiotlcednóc.
Aí raib morán airgead ag na daoine eile

In front of the "generals' hut," Cage 11. Back row: Seanna Walsh, Gerard Rooney, Jim Gibney, Brendan "the Dark" Hughes, "Tomboy" Loudon, Bobby Sands. Front Row: Tom Cahill, Tommy Tolan, and Gerry Adams. [*Coiste na n-Iarchimí*]

Bobby Sands (standing, second from left) on the Brookville amateur soccer team, summer 1976. [Courtesy Richard Caldwell]

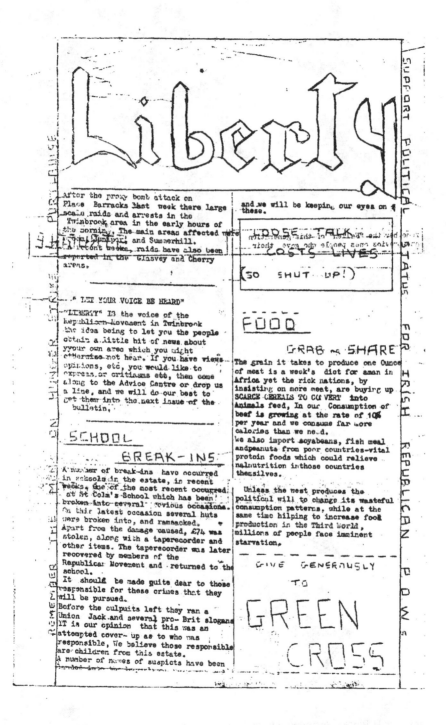

A rare surviving issue of *Liberty*, the newspaper founded by Bobby Sands in Twinbrook, summer 1976.

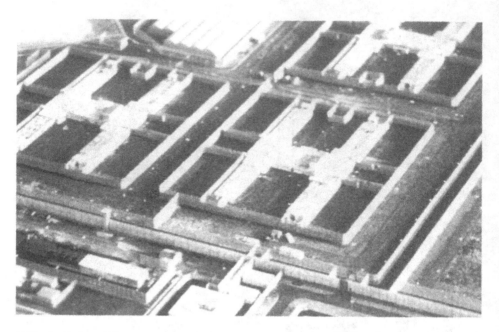

H-Blocks 3, 4, and 5.

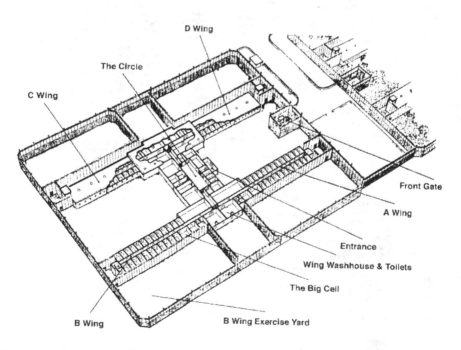

Diagram of an H-Block. [Reproduced from Brian Campbell, Laurence McKeown, and Felim O'Hagan (eds.), *Nor Meekly Serve My Time*, Belfast, Beyond the Pale, 1994]

Blanketman's depiction on toilet paper of search procedure. Note "Government Property" watermark on paper.

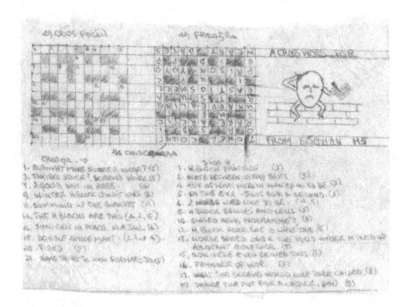

Crossword on toilet paper by Gino MacCormaic.

Two blanketmen during the no-wash protest. This photo, from a short BBC film, was one of the few times the public ever saw blanketmen in the H-Blocks. [Courtesy of *An Phoblacht*]

"Resistance," unpublished article on toilet paper by Marcella (Bobby Sands), H6, 1979.

Resistance!

The present atrocity being perpetrated upon hundreds of naked Republicans prisoners of war in the H Blocks of Long Kesh is nothing new in the long horrendous history of British treatment and torture of Irish freedom fighters. Men and women alike who have been held in the dungeons of the numerous British hell holes and prison camps down through the years. British institutionalised violence with its brutal tortures and vile inhumanities has being perennially perpetrated upon every generation of captured and incarcerated Irish freedom fighters for the sole purpose of breaking the men's spirit of Irish resistance and freedom. We have too many sorrowful examples of tortured Irish patriots to ever allow us to forget this. There have been O'Donovan Rossa's, McSweeney's, Clarkes and Ann Devlins in every Irish generation that has dared to defy the imperial might of Britain. But, the first seeds of Republican resistance sown by Tone, have through the centuries grown and spread into a forest of resistance that to the present day and throughout the preceding ten years of war has remained solid and immovable in the face of massive oppression, not only in the dungeons of the hell hells but on the streets of the war torn occupied north.

The callous drastic steps to torture hundreds of naked Republican political prisoners of war into submission, while escalating the status of a common criminal has been applied before. Many times, and May 3 add, failed many times. The torture and dungeons have not changed they remain with us and what Thomas Clarke strove for and struggled to overcome is at this very minute being struck for and the Monster is still being faced by the naked young lad who languishes in one dark corner of a bomb like H-Block cell.

The terrible bathing and hair cutting of P.O.W.s the beatings, brutalities and humiliation are all geared to demoralise break the spirit and of the P.O.W in order to depolitise him. But we Republican P.O.W's have alike to our forefathers refused to be broken! Our life is miserable and each day is a daily fight for survival. But to arise with the dawn, naked and cold in the dimness of a bare filthy prison cell, hungry and weary, to be fed on restricted diets and stand shivering after the high pressed hose has bruised one body and saturated bedding, to rise from your knees after the immerciful beatings, to fight the continual boredom, depression and despair and to face your torturers every minute of every day with no retreat, with no where to hide or to run, and with no other weapon than your spirit for to face all this and more and to carry on unbroken, is resistance! The resistance that is instilled only in the freedom fighter, the resistance of O'Donovan Rossa, Terence McSweeney, Thomas Clarke and Ann Devlin the resistance in the H-block Blocks of Long Kesh is the resistance of a risen people the Republican Spirit of freedom that can never nor will ever be broken by any Gods amount of British brutality or torture. Alike to Thomas Clarke never shall we ever forget for one minute that we are Irish Political Prisoners of War!

Left: Poster from the 1981 hunger strike.

Below: Marcella and Rosaleen Sands after Bobby's victory in the Fermanagh-South Tyrone by-election. [*An Phoblacht*]

A British intelligence document containing pictures of all of the hunger strikers, including the dates on which they began their strike and the dates of their death or withdrawal from the strike. [Courtesy of Corbis]

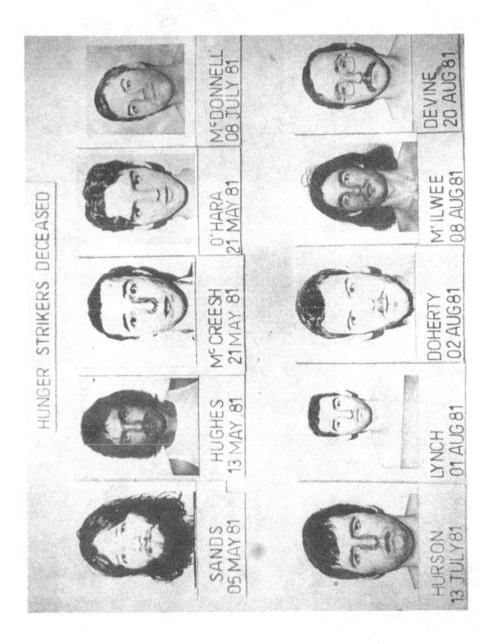

The hospital room where Bobby Sands died, taken in 2005 after Long Kesh was closed as a prison. [Ronnie Close]

Bobby Sands's funeral leaving St. Lukes Chapel Twinbrook, close to the Sands family home, with IRA color party. Bobby's brother Sean and father John carry his coffin. [*Andersonstown News*]

Above: Supporters of the hunger strikers demonstrate at the visit of Queen Elizabeth to Oslo, Norway, on the day of Bobby Sands's death. [*An Phoblacht*]

Left: Massive street protest in Lisbon, Portugal, on the day after Bobby Sands died. [*An Phoblacht*]

Belfast women banging bin lids and blowing whistles to protest the death of a hunger striker. [*An Phoblacht*]

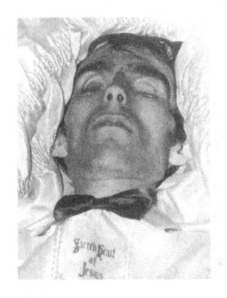

Tom McElwee, before he was imprisoned and after he died on hunger strike. [*An Phoblacht*]

Chapter Seventeen

H6: Building Solidarity Within

B y the end of 1978, the prison authorities must have been totally bewildered. At the start of the year, the blanketmen were a pretty tame lot, willing to endure amazing deprivations without trying to move their protest forward. Then all hell broke loose. Everything was a battle. The prisoners were smuggling tobacco and writing materials into their cells. The warders tried punishing them. Yet through every deprivation the prisoners bounced back and asked for more. Now they were spreading their shit all over the walls and living in twenty-four-hour confinement without any physical comforts at all.

Yet their morale was higher than ever. Every night they organized entertainment. Most of them had enough Irish to speak freely without fear of being overheard. Even the harshest winter in memory was not getting them down. Their windows were broken out and their water was frozen when they got up in the morning. They took turns sleeping. One of them put a blanket in the window to keep the room warmer while the other man slept for a while. Then they traded the extra blanket so that the first man could sleep. Some screws went around and pushed the blankets from the window. Yet the blanketmen abided. They even made running jokes about how cold it was.[1]

Bobby continued to write. Early in December *Republican News* published another short piece by Marcella called "Rats," a simple "human interest" story about the scores of rats that infested the prison. Bobby told how a few nights previous a rat jumped onto his blanket and then scurried to the foot of his cellmate's bed. He hurled his water jug at the rat, which scurried out the window as quickly as it had entered.

"Rats" was accompanied by his first published poem, "Poetic Justice," which was signed "Roibeard, H5 Block." In it, Sands tells the humorous tale of a dream where he and Roy Mason, the British secretary of state, died and went before their maker. Sands went first and got a warm welcome. Then Roy Mason came before the throne and Peter began to question him.

> *"And what about those H-Blocks, Roy, and all those naked men*
>   *you kept?"*
> *"Don't you know the Lord and I watched them and every night*
>   *they wept?"*
> *"Roy, you tortured them and you kept them all those years."*
> *"Naked and suffering, they wept a million tears."*
> *"What is to be done?" said Peter. "My Lord, you must contrive."*
> *"Poetic justice, Peter," said the Lord, "send him down to H-Block*
>   *Five."*

In January, the paper was publishing weekly articles and poems under both Marcella and Roibeard. The articles, with titles like "Alone and Condemned," "A Break in the Monotony," and "A Battle for Survival," described in detail both the physical conditions of life on the blanket and the psychological tensions of fear and boredom. A poem, "A Bright Star," which the actor Stephen Rea recited on an LP about the H-Blocks, repeated his theme about the connections between the loss of physical beauty and the gain of spiritual strength through resistance. "Modern Times" was a biting critique of what we now call globalization, in which he connected his own struggle to those of oppressed people around the world.

> *As the bureaucrats, speculators and Presidents alike*
> *Pin on their dirty, stinking, happy smiles tonight,*
> *This lonely prisoner will cry out from within his tomb*
> *And tomorrow's wretch will leave its Mother's womb.*

But Bobby had his mind on bigger things. He wanted to write a definitive record of life on the blanket. On a cold and snowy day in December 1978, he began to write what would in time become his longest and best-known work, a detailed story of life on the blanket that he called *One Day in My Life*. It was an ambitious project for someone living in his conditions. When it was eventually published it would be ninety-four pages long. Bobby kept the manuscript, written on dozens of sheets of toilet paper, stuffed up his anus, carefully folded like an accordion to keep it as small as possible.

One Day is a relentless journey through a "normal," terrible day on the blanket. It was a "good day" for Bobby even though it began with a frightening wing-shift and a beating that sent a prisoner to the hospital. He received a letter from home and two packets of tissues that he could lay out on the floor to keep his feet warm for a moment until the urine soaked through them and they disintegrated. It was also the day of his monthly visit with his family, his half-hour of comparative happiness each month.[2]

He had to endure humiliation by the warders before they handed over his letter; an obstacle course of strip searches and insults on the way to and from his visit; abuse when he hugged his mother in the visiting room; intense fear that he would be discovered smuggling back a short note from his sister and a quarter ounce of tobacco. In between were "petty" annoyances. He waits in his new cell, shivering, for the warders to deliver his blankets while the wind and the snow blow in through the open window. A warder steals his fish, his only substantial bit of food that day. He battles with the warders to clear the urine from his cell floor.

Through it all, Sands punctuates his terrors with small victories. He refuses to beg for his package. He will not bend for the mirror search. He rolls cigarettes and delivers them around the wing. He participates in a hastily organized singsong to recover their morale after a shattering attack by buckets of disinfectant. He shares good news from his visit.[3] Sands ends the book on a hopeful note, reflecting on the events of the day.

> It was cold, so very cold. I rolled onto my side and placed my little treasured piece of tobacco under the mattress and felt the dampness clinging to my feet.
>
> That's another day nearer to victory, I thought, feeling very hungry.
>
> I was a skeleton compared to what I used to be but it didn't matter. Nothing really mattered except remaining unbroken. I rolled over once again, the cold biting at me. They have nothing in their entire arsenal to break the spirit of one single Republican Political Prisoner-of-War who refuses to be broken, I thought,

*and that was very true. I rolled over again freezing and the snow
came in the window on top of my blankets.*
  "Tiocfaidh ár lá,"[4] *I said to myself. "Tiocfaidh ár lá."*

One cannot know exactly what purpose Sands intended when he
wrote *One Day in My Life*. If he wrote it to achieve immediate publicity,
he was taking a big risk for himself and his family. He made no attempt
to hide any of their identities as he had in his articles. He was quite
explicit about techniques for smuggling and hiding contraband, and for
passing items between cells. Had the document been discovered, it could
have had terrible consequences. Perhaps he was more concerned about
making a lasting record of life on the blanket, even if it could not be published for some time to come. If so, he succeeded. *One Day in My Life*
appeared in print in 1983, two years after his death. It was compared with
One Day in the Life of Ivan Denisovich, a book that was possibly even a
model.[5] If it never achieved the international status of *Ivan Denisovich*, it
is less because it has inferior literary value—*One Day in My Life* is doubt-
less a magnificent piece of jail literature—than because it served the
opposite side in the then-raging cold war.

• • •

During the second week in January, as Bobby was finishing *One Day in
My Life*, the prison authorities decided to isolate the prisoners' leaders
by moving them into H6. Looking back, many prisoners who were sent
there are puzzled by the move. H6 became a cauldron of resistance. It
had a higher degree of sharing—Bobby said it was the closest they would
ever come to Communism—than anyone experienced before or since. It
also became an officer training school where new men were trained in
leadership skills and gained confidence as they participated in the constant debates on the wing. Slowly, Hughes and Sands brought younger
prisoners like "Bik" MacFarlane, Jake Jackson, and Pat McGeown into
their inner circle. MacFarlane says that by the time the authorities finally
transferred everyone back out of H6 "they had made leaders for the
whole prison."
  But at the time, isolation must have seemed like a way to break the
protest. "Cut off the head and then break what's left," is how Seanna
Walsh assessed their strategy. At the start, things *were* a bit disorganized.

The move took place in the middle of the week and some residents of H6 hardly knew any of the others. MacFarlane remembers a blur of unfamiliar voices discussing what was happening until, finally, they all saw each other at mass. They went into the canteen and looked at each other with puzzled faces, thinking to themselves "who are these guys?" They introduced each other and began building things from there.

Building things was hard for the first few weeks because of their brutal treatment. The screws constantly shifted them from wing to wing, sometimes twice a day. The potential for violence rose when the warders told them that they have to wear uniform trousers if they wanted to go to the doctor and they would also have to wear them for wing shifts. The men refused. In response, the warders trailed them by the hair into the circle, where they forced them over a mirror to search their anus before taking them to a new wing.

Sands was moved into a cell with Gerard Hodgkins, a young man from Turf Lodge in Belfast. Despite his age, Hodgkins was a veteran of the blanket protest. He went to the H-Blocks in November 1976 after he was sentenced to fourteen years for possession of a pistol. There were only about a dozen men on the blanket.

It was not long before Bobby took out the manuscript to *One Day in My Life*. Hodgkins was fascinated as he watched the bulky package unfold into a sheaf of written pages, all filled from edge to edge with Bobby's tiny left-leaning writing.

"It's like a science!" Hodgkins thought to himself as he watched Bobby fold and unfold his writings.

One night, Sands asked him to read the manuscript.

"What do you think?" he asked Hodgkins, excitedly.

A few nights later, he was called for a legal visit. He went into "a whole fucking panic" because he was worried that his manuscript would be discovered on the way to the visit. But he succeeded in getting it to his lawyer and he came back in a relaxed mood.

Even after he was shod of *One Day*, the constant wing shifts bothered Bobby since each mirror search was a threat to the considerable library he carried around in his back passage. Finally, he could take no more. He kicked down on the mirror and broke it. Everyone expected retaliation for his act of defiance but to their surprise, the wing shifts simply stopped. Life on the wing reached a level of stability that they had never experienced in the other blocks. For the next nine months they were practically left alone. It seemed like if they were there for a hundred years nobody new would have come in to bother them.

Everyone soon realized Bobby's centrality to the life of H6. Richard O'Rawe first heard him rather than seeing him. He couldn't help it. The minute they got to H6 Bobby was talking out the door. O'Rawe listened in amazement as he organized the social life of the wing and built strategies of protest with the Dark.

Joe Barnes was taken aback by the changes he saw in Bobby. He was so much more self-assured than he had been in the cages. He had "grown up in a lot of ways."

His energy seemed unending. Says another prisoner, "Bobby was always doing something, writing something, getting it out. Every day he was achieving something. This guy was just bouncing, doing this and doing that. You even heard it in his voice."[6]

The main problem in H6 was food. Not only were the portions tiny, the quality was poor. Joe Watson counted his breakfast one morning and there were thirty-five cornflakes. The water was "gray," five or six parts water to one part milk. The regulations stated that each man should get ten rounds of bread a day. The warders could not cheat on the quantity, so they gave out moldy bread. In *One Day in My Life*, Bobby writes about an incident where the screws tricked him into taking his dinner in the dark cell after a visit. For some reason, he threw his bread onto the food pile in the corner. Only later, when a warder opened the door and the light shone in, did he discover that the bread was blue with mold.[7]

Some orderlies were even worse than screws. They put things in the food, pissed in it, spat in it. The worst offender was an orderly from Derry, a former Republican who they called "the Renegade." Sands and Hodgkins decided that even Father Toner hated the man because he had converted to Protestantism.

Bobby wrote a story about him. He speculated that the man felt guilty for turning on his comrades but that he comforted himself by pretending that he was getting back at them for the hatred they showed him. He laughed when the screws beat the men. He watched the forced washes with glee. But he was also deeply troubled by the blanketmen, their "stone-like eyes" and their unyielding spirit. Behind his façade of hatred, he concludes, "I wish I were one of them!"

Along with the food, the scenery took a change for the worse. Soon after they arrived, workmen attached grilles and "dog boxes" of frosted

Perspex to the windows. Bobby could hang onto the expanded metal grille on the inside of the windows and see out. But the metal ate into his hands after a few seconds and, anyway, all he could see was a bit of sky and the top of the wire around the prison.

• • •

The men responded to adversity with novel forms of resistance and solidarity. They stepped up their tobacco smuggling, Irish language education, political debates and discussion of strategy, writing/propaganda campaign, and their program of entertainment. All of these provided new opportunities to win small victories over their jailers.

Tobacco was the *bia beatha* (food of life). Bobby was a fanatical smoker but the importance of tobacco went beyond the smokers. If someone came back from a visit with tobacco, everybody was happy, including the people who didn't smoke. If not, everyone was depressed. Initially, H6 was well off for tobacco. A sympathetic orderly got tobacco from prisoners in the "working blocks" and supplied them with as much as nine ounces at a time. Eventually, he got caught and the supply dried up.

The ensuing tobacco drought mobilized the prisoners to smuggle more of it. Some "hard men" who had been refusing to take visits found new principles. Once they began taking visits to get tobacco, they also became couriers for comms and supplies. Jackie McMullen, one of the cynics from H5, thought that it was kind of pathetic to be writing out begging letters to movie stars like Jane Fonda. But he was "programed to get tobacco." Once he started taking visits he reassessed his attitude. The importance of keeping open a line of communication began to dawn on him and, with others facing mirror searches going to and from visits, he began to feel like he was copping out by refusing to take visits.

The amount of tobacco a man could smuggle was limited. Even when it had been pressed tight in a vice, it was hard to smuggle more than an ounce and a half. The biggest package of tobacco anyone remembers was a three-ouncer. Bobby usually came back from visits with two. At that rate, the smokers on the wing got two cigarettes each the first night and one the next.

Getting the tobacco into the block was not the end of the struggle. Cigarettes had to be rolled and the extra tobacco had to be stored. Then the cigarettes had to be distributed to the smokers. They went up and down one side of the wing through the cracks by the pipes. They were sent across the wing by "shooting the button." Then, they had to be lit. The prisoners made a fire, a *splunk,* with a ball of wool from a blanket or a bit of cotton teased from a towel. They fluffed it up and lit it by striking a flint against metal. Once lit, the splunk was passed from cell to cell by swinging it out the window, or even by shooting a line across the corridor. It was a tricky process that did not always work. Sometimes it took a long time to get the wick lit and then there was always the danger that it would go out. Jackie McMullen recalls a night when another prisoner spent half an hour shooting a splunk across the corridor to light his cigarette. Just as he pulled the light under the door, *pssssshhh* . . . the fire went out. It was one of the worst nights he ever spent on the blanket.

• • •

Nighttime belonged to the prisoners. Once the warders left, they began their nightly routine of cigarette manufacture, button shooting, news broadcasting, and general entertainment. After the religious prisoners said the rosary and everyone distributed cigarettes and messages, there was debate and discussion.

The men told the time by the night guard's "bell checks." He came on at nine o'clock and every hour he pushed the security grille at bottom of wing to show that he had checked the cells. Time was measured by the first bell check at nine, the second at ten, and the third at eleven. After the third bell check the last business of the night was entertainment, including the "book at bedtime." The storyteller pulled his mattress up to his cell door and shouted out a story while the rest of the men lay, listening. All the surfaces in the prison were hard, with nothing to dampen sound, so noises traveled. When the book was a good one and the storyteller was engaging, everyone got lost in the story.

Bobby told an array of stories. His speciality was epics. His story of Geronimo and his Apache guerrillas "epitomized everything that he thought a human being should be," says Richard O'Rawe, "compassionate but unbreakable, fighting the whole of America on his own." There were other stories, all about struggle. Bobby told *Trinity* several times and *How Green Was My Valley*, about the Welsh miners. He told *Doctor Zhivago*. The other prisoners began to learn political lessons from the stories.

"Bob's stories was all about heroes . . . It was always about the individual against the establishment and how the individual no matter what happened couldn't be broken. If he had to fight them all on his own, so be it. If he had to die, so be it. That's just the way he was, that was his mentality. Bob just had a spirit that couldn't be tamed, and he wasn't going to allow it to be tamed. If it came to it, he was going to fight them on his own, he was going to carry the burden of everybody."

It was not long before Sands told a story that became legendary among the blanketmen. He said that he had read a novel the last time he was in the prison hospital. Its title was *Jet*.

Like all of Bobby's books, *Jet* was a story of someone pursuing and winning freedom in the face of all the oppression that the forces of reaction could muster. *Jet* was about a man who took on the U.S. military-industrial complex and achieved his own personal freedom through struggle. To the prisoners, it was a story about *them*, about how they could achieve an inner freedom even as they lay isolated in their grim cells, surrounded by barbed wire and concrete and a hostile force of screws. For a couple of hours a night as they listened to Bobby tell his stories, they *were* free. Their mind's eyes took them beyond the walls, beyond the razor wire, wherever Bobby chose to take them. Each prisoner latched on to his words and created a vivid image of a place where, at that time, they most wanted to be . . . free, in struggle. Bobby was their travel agent and their guide and these stories, perhaps more than any other aspect of his seemingly tireless efforts to organize the prison struggle, turned him into their leader. They followed him because he could take them to the most special of places. He never let them down.

Jet was a young American named Jonathan Eisenhower Truman. He was the son of a fanatically militaristic colonel in the U.S. Army who named him after his two great commanders-in-chief, President Dwight David Eisenhower and President Harry S. Truman. Growing up in the 1950s and 1960s, the young boy rebelled. But he could not avoid the plans that his gung-ho father had for him. War was raging and his father made him enlist and ensured that he would serve a tour in Vietnam. Jet was wrenched away from his music and his teenage parties, from the girl he loved.

Jet went to Vietnam and everything he saw fed his sense of rebellion. After a time, he began to hatch a plan of escape. He faked his own death by leaving his dog tags where his comrades would find them and think the Vietcong killed him. After a series of dangerous adventures, Jet finally made his way back to the United States, where he took the pseudonym John Earnest Thornton . . . Jet. He bought a Harley, grew long hair and a beard (like a blanketman), and met his old girlfriend. They set off for the open road.

The blanketmen lay on their foam mattresses, miles away from the maggots and the shit, imagining Jet as he rode the American highways on his Harley, his girlfriend on the back with her arms around him and the wind blowing through her hair. They loved it when Bobby interspersed the narrative with music, adding a new dimension that made the fantasy even more real. As they rode along the open roads, Jet and his girl listened to music, loud, on the radio. They rode down the highway at seventy miles per hour, the sun beating down on them, when Bob Dylan came on the radio. Bobby broke into song, his husky voice turning book-telling into concert.

> Go lightly from the ledge, babe
> Go lightly on the ground
> I'm not the one you want, babe
> I will only let you down
> . . . it ain't me, babe
> No, no, no, it ain't me, babe
> It ain't me you're lookin' for, babe.

But somebody *was* looking for Jet. His father learned of his son's treachery and vowed to take his revenge by having him court-martialed and executed as a traitor. He hired a renegade gang of Hell's Angels to find Jet and bring him in. The head of the gang, a big militaristic guy called Hoss, had been a drill sergeant in Vietnam.

Jet took many nights to tell, "a bit of a record" since most books lasted only a couple of nights. At 2:00 A.M. on the last night, when Jet made a dramatic escape from the pursuing motorcycle gang, handing a decisive defeat to his father and (figuratively) to the oppressive forces of the state, the wing erupted into applause and whistling.

"It was an absolutely terrific story," recalls Richard O'Rawe. "And it was a story that you could relate to because Jet was a free spirit and he was rebelling against conscription, he was rebelling against his father who was the establishment, he was on a big Harley with the hands up and he was on that road, hair flowing and the world was out there and he was going out to get it." Jet was "even spiritual, in the sense that you were actually on the passenger's seat with him when he went down the highway."

Joe Barnes says that *Jet* really *was* an out-of-body experience. "The boys absolutely adored it because it was everything you wanted to be. You wanted to be free, you wanted to be your own man on that Harley Davidson and the world's your oyster and any worries you have are back there and you're just heading forward."

Jet was so popular that Sands had to retell it again and again by popular demand. Dixie Elliot later shared a cell with Bobby. His first memory of him is hearing him tell *Jet* in H6.

"It had everything which we hadn't got at the time and which we wanted. It was better than any experience at the pictures or any video. Guys used to structure their lives around it. They had a sleep during the day so they wouldn't miss the book at night. He was just whacking it out and the flow was as if he had the book in front of him!"[8]

• • •

Sands approached his creative writing as he approached his political propaganda. He often called the Dark to the pipe to sing a new song or recite a new poem before he performed it in public. Sometimes Hughes told Sands that he had gone "over the top." Bobby listened to his criticism and the Dark often felt that his response was "not good." But Hughes figures his critical attitude must not have hurt Bobby too much "because he kept coming back."

Joe Barnes also thought Sands had a tendency to overdo; the enthusiasm with which he threw himself into things sometimes created the wrong impression. Barnes remembers the first time Bobby sang "Sad Song for Susan" in H6. He got up one night, announced that he had written a song and sang it at the top of his voice, a bit off-key because of the effort he was putting into it. Barnes's first reaction was, "that's a load of balls, sort of pretentious saying he wrote a song and getting up and singing it." But the more he thought about it the more he realized that there was "much, much more there" and he even came to think that Bobby's off-key singing added to the effect of the song and its sadness. He was in an environment where he would never have to fear embarrassment. They all trusted each other and each man knew that anyone else on the wing would do *anything* for him. Bobby was contributing to the whole atmosphere of trust, thought Barnes. He was "singing *for* people, not to people."

There is a big difference between a song and public relations. A public relations statement is only as good as its immediate impact. The potential damage of going "over the top" is great, because it invites disbelief. In time, Sands became more aware of the impact his writings could have and he even began to censor his own stories for their political effects. One day he wrote a true story about a mangy stray dog back in Rathcoole. Nobody wanted the dog so eventually some of the kids took it to the dam and drowned it. He wanted to make a point about how society discards the things no one wants, they put away things that challenge their social morality or remind them of their lack of charity or justice. In the same way, he wrote, the prisoners had been discarded in the H-Blocks and Armagh Jail. The authorities tried to keep their situation out of sight, to cover up the fact that their society could not deal with these men and women.

Bobby showed the story to Gerard Hodgkins but at the last minute he tore it up and threw it onto the food heap in the corner. He was worried how someone might use the image of Republican kids killing puppies.

"Nah, I'll not send that out," he told Hodgkins. "Some fucking Unionist would probably read that and say, 'I told ye, psychopaths from the day and hour they're born!'"

Other works, too, were never published. Hodgkins remembers a poem that Sands wrote about coffin ships leaving Ireland during the famine. He still considers it to be one of Bobby's best poems. Yet it is, apparently, lost.

By now Bobby was reading as much poetry as he could get. He constantly requested people to smuggle poems and song lyrics to him so that he could commit them to memory. He wrote a letter in Irish on toilet paper to his best man Diarmuid Fox, who was now in Cage Nine. He wrote about their common friends and his breakup with Geraldine. But his main reason for the letter was that "we're looking for a couple of songs in English," including "Jesse" by Janis Ian, "Ben" by Michael Jackson, and "Soldier Blue" by Buffy St. Marie.[9]

In H6 he got the words to "Brian Boy Magee" by his favorite poet Eithne Carberry, a nineteenth-century Irish Republican who came from County Antrim near where Sands grew up. "Brian Boy McGee" told of the 1641 massacre of nearly all of the inhabitants of Islandmagee (now a fiercely Loyalist area of County Antrim) by English and Scottish troops. In the poem, Brian Boy Magee sees his mother hung and his brothers and kinfolk butchered while he and his father fight off the troops. After they dispatched the men folk, the troops drove the women and children over a cliff to their deaths on the rocks below. Magee pledged to his dead kin-folk to kill as many of the enemy as he could.

Bobby was a borrower. He used Brian Boy Magee as a model for a poem about Bold MacKillen of Abbot's Cross, in which compared his own role in the Republican struggle with that of a Republican hero of 1798 who came from his home village of Abbot's Cross.[10] A year later he would write his own version of Carberry's most famous poem, "Roddy McCorley," about another Republican hero of 1798 who the British hung at the bridge at Toome in Country Antrim.

By now, Sands was seeking out other prisoners who could make intel-ligent comment on his writing. The man he went to most often was "Bik" MacFarlane, who was two cells away. MacFarlane had drawn closer to Sands as his regular chess partner. They scraped out boards on the floor of their cell, the scratched black bitumen turning gray for the white squares. Chessmen were sculpted out of dough (a bit of dirt thrown in for the black pieces), then dried on the pipes. They shouted their chess moves out the window or sent them through the pipes. Sometimes, Bobby slipped poems through the pipes. Soon, every time he wrote a poem he sent it to Bik. He wanted to know how it scanned and what Bik thought of his use of words and images.

MacFarlane especially remembers a poem where Sands used flowers as a metaphor of the women in Armagh Jail. MacFarlane decided to wind him up. He got down to the pipe and told the man in the cell between him and Bobby, "Now, see when I get up and say, 'Nah, that's a bit too sweet,' you go along and stick the knife in."

MacFarlane heard Bobby jump up onto the heating pipe in his cell before he had even finished reading the poem. He knew Bobby was anx-ious to hear his opinion. MacFarlane felt that the poem was really special but he had decided on his course.

"Ah, it was too sweet. You didn't really get it right that time, Bob."

The man in the middle cell pitched in and agreed that the poem was a bit too sugary, that he could have been subtler. Finally, after a bit of back and forth, MacFarlane suggested, "Why don't you just . . . uh . . . throw it in the corner."

At this, the man in the middle cell burst out laughing and Bobby caught on that the whole thing was a joke at his expense.

• • •

One result of the stability and solidarity in H6 was that spoken Irish improved by the week. Prisoners like Bik MacFarlane came to H6 with spotty Irish but were soon fluent. Gerard Hodgkins had poor Irish so he and Bobby conversed in it as much as possible and Hodgkins learned the language quickly, as if he was on an immersion course.

The teaching materials improved when the prisoners in the cages sent A4 sheets of rice paper with Irish grammar and vocabulary. Later, supporters photocopied Celtic mythology in Irish on rice paper and smuggled them into the block. By May Bobby was pretty happy about the level of Irish in H6.

"The Irish is going fantastically in the blocks," he boasted to Diarmuid Fox. "Maybe it's true to say that we hear more Irish than English, well that's what it is like in this wing."

The constant informal arguments during the day and organized debates at night continued and Sands was always in the middle. Daytime arguments were about anything and everything. There were arguments about the birds in the yard. There was a classic argument about the size of the cell doors:

Joe Watson: What size do you reckon them doors is?
Sands: I'm five foot nine and a half . . . over six foot, six foot one or two.
Watson: You're full of shite! They're six foot three.
Sands: What do you mean six foot three?
Watson: It stands to reason they have to be six foot three.
Sands: What do you mean it stands to reason?
Watson: It stands to reason they have to be six foot three.
Sands: Why?
Watson: Well, your average screw is six foot.
Sands: Wha'! What screws is six foot?
Watson: Well they mightn't be now because they're trying to get as many screws as they can but screws are meant to be six foot.

The argument raged for days until someone discovered that the King

James Bibles in each cell had their size on the inside cover: nine and a half inches by five and three-quarters inches. They measured the doors and everybody agreed that they were exactly six feet. Even Watson gave in and agreed that the doors were six feet. But Sands held out. "In the name of fuck," he said, "sure that's a Protestant Bible there, you don't believe that!"

The nightly debates out the door were more serious and could be quite intense. The lectures on Republican ideology, Irish history, community politics, and political theory all generated intensive debate. There were practical debates about moving the protest forward. The Dark used these to create consensus. Bobby moderated the debates, taking them in directions that he had already discussed with the Dark, while Hughes sat back and listened, taking in what was said and thinking about how it affected their strategy.

The radical politics of the wing were reflected in the discussions. Everyone was to the left except "Blute" McDonnell, a dedicated blanketman who still refused to put on uniform trousers even to go to mass. Sands and Hughes lived yards away from him for nearly a year before they ever saw him. When McDonnell found out that Gerard Hodgkins had scraped a hammer and sickle on the back of his door, he wrote a long letter to Hughes complaining about the propagation of Communism on the wing. They had important visitors of all kinds, he said, and they had to be careful about the image they projected.

Hughes discussed the complaint with Sands. They were annoyed at McDonnell both for red-baiting and for sowing dissension on the wing. Bobby reassured Hodgkins.

"Blute's put in a complaint about you propagating Communism," he said. "I just told him it's a load of bollix. Forget it."

But McDonnell insisted on pursuing the matter. So one night the Dark got up and called Hodgkins and Blute to the door. His first question was for Hodgkins, "What do you have on your door?"

"A hammer and sickle," replied Hodgkins.

"What does it represent to you?"

"Well, it's power to the workers and Socialism."

"That's okay," said the Dark and then he turned on McDonnell.

"Blute, there's no grounds for a complaint. There's all sorts of stuff gets out of here. You have American flags. Does that endorse Vietnam? Now if you want I'll send [your complaint] outside, but I reckon they'll put it in the waste bin."

In retrospect, Hughes concedes that they probably created their right-wing image of McDonnell as a mechanism for enhancing leftist solidarity among the others. The rest of the wing "publicly flailed" him out the door for his politics. But, "that was the politics on the blanket, it was left-wing politics. There was no real argument in that wing, just shades of left-wing thinking."

Chapter Eighteen

H6: Extending the Protest

In their own way, the blanketmen were intent on building an ideal world, if one could use such a term in such miserable circumstances. In their interactions with the screws, they resisted. Among themselves, they built a shared community. Yet it was not enough to build protest inside the prison. At its core the protest was about legitimating armed struggle *outside* of jail. They were fighting for social recognition that they were a political army, resisting injustice and fighting for a new and better society. Thus, they had to win their struggle *not* primarily for themselves but to validate the right of oppressed people to resist. Obviously, their belief in the legitimacy of armed struggle was not the majority position in Irish or British society. But if they acceded to criminalization, their movement would never achieve a mass following. If their prison struggle gained popular support, *that* could be a vehicle for building broad support for the Republican struggle.

Thus, the blanketmen felt that their struggle was part of the war effort. Given the recent weakness of the IRA, perhaps it was even the vanguard. Bobby said, "make no mistake, what's won and lost in these blocks is won and lost for the struggle. If the Brits succeed in criminalizing prisoners they succeed in criminalizing the struggle."

The Republican leadership did not agree. They left the support campaign to prisoners' relatives and independent activists like Bernadette (Devlin) McAliskey, who made her name fighting in the Battle of the Bogside and as the youngest member of British parliament. Together, these groups and individuals set up a series of local Relatives' Action

Committees (RAC). Their tactics were mostly direct action. They interrupted meetings, shouting, "What about the blanketmen?" They held
demonstrations. Any way possible, they got their message across. People
began to talk about the H-Blocks and even made bridges between their
troubles and the conditions of the blanketmen.

"The conditions in them houses are as bad as the H-Blocks," a local
woman would say to her friend. "H-Block," "blanketman," "on the
blanket," and "dirty protest" were entering the public lexicon. Slowly, the
public became aware that something was happening, even if the H-
Blocks were not yet on the nightly news.

Other groups sprang up to support the prisoners, including the Trade
Union Campaign against Repression (TUCAR), the Student Campaign
Against Repression (SCAR), and Women Against Imperialism. With
McAliskey's sponsorship, the groups organized a conference for January
1978 in Coalisland in County Tyrone.

The Republican Movement remained ambivalent about these developments. As long as the support groups were small and local they
retained autonomy of action. But once there was a threat of a larger support movement, particularly one that was led by a political maverick like
McAliskey, the movement began to take notice. They criticized any broad
front campaign that did not explicitly support the armed struggle. Sinn
Féin put its position succinctly if crudely in a document prepared for the
Coalisland conference: "Repression condemned on moral grounds isn't
good enough. For while it brings sections of the population into opposition it rarely brings them into Resistance."[1] The conference rejected the
idea that one had to support armed struggle and it backed a policy of
assembling a broad front based on human rights for the blanketmen. It
sent a wake-up call to Sinn Féin with an attendance of more than eight
hundred people.

Prisoners' rights were surprisingly low on the Republican Movement's
agenda, even as the prisoners sank into the depths of the no-wash protest.

"I would have a view that prisoners should always take second place,"
says Gerry Adams of the movement's instinctive priorities between
prison protest and struggle on the outside.

The IRA leadership told the prisoners that they could not afford to
divert resources from armed struggle into a prison support campaign.
Apart from diverting resources, says Adams, building support for the
prisoners was difficult because this was a time of extreme repression:

*People were being shot in the streets. People were being arrested
on sight. The legislation was used at will to allow the British or
the RUC to almost do anything. And these areas were under very
heavy occupation and people were living underground. So there
was enough to be getting on with and those of us who wanted to
try and build some sort of a popular movement, it was very difficult to do. It's very difficult to build open and democratic politics
if you're on the run or if you're not able to meet and debate and
have public manifestations and so on and so forth.*

The movement supported the prisoners through Sinn Féin's POW
Department and the IRA added concrete support by attacking prison officers.[2] But as far as a public campaign was concerned, the blanketmen had
to rely on their own resources.

They were helped by exceptional public incidents like Archbishop
Ó Fiaich's "sewers of Calcutta" speech. In October 1978, they hit international headlines when the U.S. syndicated columnist Jack Anderson
compared the H-Blocks to "the most barbarous regimes of Communist
commissars or tinhorn Latin American dictators."[3] Then, at the beginning of 1979 Frank Maguire, an independent member of parliament from
the Fermanagh-Tyrone constituency, spoke out against conditions in the
H-Blocks.

Maguire had been a thorn in the side of the prison administration since
he was elected MP in 1975. His main claim to fame was that he single-
handedly brought down the British Labour government that created the
H-Blocks. In March 1979, the government went into crisis and needed a
single vote to survive a no-confidence motion led by the rising conservative leader Margaret Thatcher. By a bitter irony, Labour needed Maguire's
vote. Maguire said he would support Labour if they improved conditions
in the H-Blocks. But political status was too high a price for the Labour
government to pay to stay in office. Instead, they pulled out all the stops
to defeat Maguire. The Social Democratic and Labour Party (SDLP) stood
against him in an effort to split the Nationalist vote. The police harassed
his election workers, on one occasion detaining him for ninety minutes at
gunpoint while he was on his way to an election meeting.[4]

In the May elections that brought Thatcher to power, Maguire doubled
his majority. Within weeks, he announced his intention to tour Long
Kesh. He intended to investigate whether the blanketmen were getting

their proper allocation of food, saying that he suspected that the authorities were attempting to starve them into submission.[5]

The elections had another impact on the blanket protest. Besides being a staunch Unionist, Thatcher had a personal grudge against Irish Republicanism after the INLA blew up her close friend and advisor Airey Neave outside the British parliament in March 1979.

After the British election, another election soon impacted the blanket protest. In June, the first European parliament was elected. Bernadette McAliskey stood on an independent anti–H-Block platform, much to the annoyance of Sinn Féin. McAliskey received 33,969 votes, a respectable showing although far less than she needed for a seat and considerably less than she could have got with Republican support. Her electoral intervention provoked an extended debate in H6.

Bobby Sands led a faction that favored using the H-Block situation to gain electoral advantage. "If we're afraid of our political opponents then we should withdraw from the struggle," he argued.

He was *not* calling for candidates to take office but rather to use the elections to prove they had community support and then to use that as a base to launch grassroots community politics of the kind he tried to promote in Twinbrook. Sinn Féin, he said, had a responsibility to capitalize on the gains that the prisoners had made and not let others take advantage of their sacrifice.

Some blanketmen went further. Jake Jackson drafted an angry comm to the Republican leadership, asking, "Is the leadership asleep? We should have been in there. We should have been standing candidates."

Others were against elections. They put forward arguments that ranged from "Lie down with dogs you'll get up with fleas" to "Elections are a path to reformism" to, simply, "There is no unarmed strategy."

The debates continued throughout the summer. Bobby summarized his position in a comm to the Republican leadership in August. He suggested that the leadership should run blanketmen in local council elections. His suggestion, however, was subject to two conditions. First, the movement had to build enough mass support to ensure that its candidates would be elected. Second, they would *not* participate in state institutions like the parliament or city councils but rather stand to gain legitimacy to organize *against* those institutions. It was an extension of Gerry Adams's argument about setting up parallel (anti-)state institutions at the community level. The novelty of Bobby's position, however, was his argument that electoral victories could provide the popular legitimacy that would enable such a strategy to work.

He wrote,

> *Well here's the last idea for the time being—going on the supposition that our massive push sparks off a large emotional reaction. We gauge the three best areas, say for the sake of talk, Crossmaglen, Bogside, and Short Strand, we call on people to show their opposition to H-Block end Brits representation in Ireland which means Brit repression. By coming out and voting for a Blanketman as being the representative of the people . . . those voting, the oppressed, make him not a figurehead but a representative of the people in that area.*

Sands was not advocating conventional electoral politics. He was rather proposing a radical use of electoral tactics to legitimate *alternative* political structures.

> *This is a launching pad to community councils. The Blanketman cannot administer the local affairs of the area where he is and while he is in H-Block, the people have decided to run their own affairs and undermine the oppressor—the best substitute can stand in for him while he remains in H-Block, preferably an RAC person or tenant association chairman, who must be red minded or at least nationalistic . . . When time is ripe, we build & move on to other areas doing the same thing. We bring all those standing together and build a provisional type government, we move south to places like Leitrim and Kerry and Wexford and do likewise, we seek international recognition similar to what Arafat done, we get Basques, Bretons, and every other person and group to back and recognize these Blanketmen as the true representatives of the nationalist oppressed people . . . take everything that I've said and tie it in with the IRA and the War effort and we are on the right track comrade. That's about it on that for now!!*

• • •

Bobby's opening phrase, "going on the supposition that our massive push sparks off a large emotional reaction," reflects concern about the future of the blanket protest in the summer of 1979. While public support had increased, it had not built adequate pressure to impact governmental policy. The prisoners perceived a distinct lack of mass support among the wider population and they realized that they would have difficulty achieving political status without it. Later in the year, Bobby wrote a letter to the leadership that reflected the realism of his thinking. "As you know," he wrote, "we have failed to reach a broader base of support, therefore we have failed to engage any active support outside of our immediate hardcore, friends, relatives, etc."[6]

The prisoners began to talk bluntly about ensuring that they would not be lying in their own filth on soggy mattresses for another several years. Sands knew that they could not maintain morale much longer under such conditions, especially in blocks like H3, where young prisoners were concentrated. Philip Rooney was put into H3 in early January 1979. As a new blanketman, he thought that the next best thing to being outside was playing your part in the struggle inside. But he was horrified to hear other prisoners saying, "this can't go on." Rooney struggled to come to terms with the lack of enthusiasm on the protest. The place was a "shambles." The leaders were all in H6 and the rest of the guys were just "trying to keep their act together." For them, "there was definitely no light at the end of the tunnel" and little was happening outside the prison to encourage them.

By spring, things even turned grim in H6 when some surprising prisoners started "squeaky-booting." Initially, they got verbal abuse for leaving the protest, but as time went on the abuse stopped because no one knew when he might break. In the middle of May, Bobby's old mate "Cleeky" Clarke, left the protest for personal reasons. He talked it over with Joe Barnes and said that he felt as if he was going back on everything that had meaning for him. Hughes was deeply hurt by Clarke's move because he was such a close and trusted comrade.

Bobby tried to hide his concern.

"Big Cleaky left for H-Block 8 a fortnight ago but don't be concerned," he wrote Diarmuid Fox at the end of May. "The Dark is here and Joe Barnes and a lot of other people who were in the cages before."[7]

His confidence must have shaken, however, when Joe Barnes considered leaving the protest. Hughes and Sands talked him out of it by convincing him that his departure would have a big depressive impact on morale.

• • •

Threats to morale became acute during 1979 precisely because the men were becoming more realistic about events outside of prison. They had always believed their well-meaning supporters when they tried to raise their spirits. The head of Sinn Féin's POW department came on visits and exaggerated about street protests: "The crowd was electrifying, blah, blah, blah." Looking back, they began to realize that they needed a dose of reality instead of false encouragement. As the main leaders of the protest discussed their situation in H6, they slowly began to realize that their internal victories did not always transfer into popular support outside of prison.

After Thatcher took office in May, they knew that there would be a hardening of British attitudes. By the summer, therefore, the prisoners began to debate the most extreme form of protest: hunger strike. Hughes and Sands were the most vocal supporters of a hunger strike. They said that they had a moral responsibility to ensure that the extreme conditions of the protest were not long term.

Only a few blanketmen opposed a hunger strike. Joe Barnes wouldn't advocate anyone doing anything that he wouldn't consider doing himself. Jackie McMullen opposed it on strategic grounds, although he would later become a hunger striker. Jake Jackson was against it because he thought there were still other avenues to explore.

To get the pulse of the blanketmen, Hughes ordered discussions in all the blocks. In one wing of H3, only two or three men took part in the debate, all strongly in favor of a hunger strike. The OC called every prisoner individually to see why he was not debating. Some said they were not willing to go on hunger strike and thus did not think they had a right to state an opinion. One prisoner said that they had never been asked their views before. He felt a sense of pride that he was being asked but he was not confident enough to express his opinions.[8]

By early summer the issue was settled in favor of a hunger strike and Hughes wrote to Gerry Adams advising him of their intentions. Adams wrote back "a very strong letter" saying that Thatcher would simply let them die. While Adams "was mostly against [a hunger strike] because I didn't think it would work," he was also against it for strategic reasons, "because once again this was the prison butting in on outside, so the entire struggle was going to be put on these prisoners."[9]

The prisoners in H6 continued to debate. Hughes and Sands said that if someone had to die for them to win their rights, so be it. Bobby made an impassioned speech, saying that, at certain points in the struggle it takes a few good men to do a major deed in order to turn fortunes around. He made bleak references to 1916, when the leaders of the Easter Rising in Dublin seemed at first to be taking a senseless course of action but, once they were executed, the Irish people rallied to their side and supported the independence struggle. "It's highly unlikely that the Brits are going to move this side of a death," he said, but hunger strike deaths could mobilize enough public pressure that even Margaret Thatcher would be moved.

The Republican Movement and particularly the IRA leadership remained firmly against a hunger strike. The Army Council told the prisoners that it had a duty to prosecute the war and to use army resources in the most effective manner. They could not allow the fortunes of the struggle to be held hostage to a group of hunger strikers. Bobby turned their argument back on them. The IRA, he said could not survive *unless* the prisoners won their struggle. He used the analogy of the "breaker's yard," the area behind the Crumlin Road Jail where for decades prisoners were consigned to break stones day after day, week after week. The purpose was not to break stones but to break men. It left them dispirited and dehumanized.

"We cannot allow the Brits to turn the H-Blocks into the breaker's yard for the Republican struggle," he said.

The Republican leadership remained opposed to a hunger strike but they also knew that the IRA would always have to be replenished from within the jail. The "breakers' yard" argument had its effect and the movement struck a bargain with the prisoners to postpone their hunger strike while they intensified their efforts to organize popular opposition and put pressure on the British government to resolve the prison conflict. They argued that a reinvigorated national campaign, with real Republican support and participation, might bring positive results short of a hunger strike.

Indeed, some things had changed in the movement during the previous year. Gerry Adams had been arrested on a charge of IRA membership and he was held in the H-Blocks until the authorities released him due to lack of evidence. This was different from his previous experience of prison and it deeply affected his understanding of the prison struggle. Before he was in the H-Blocks, he believed that the blanketmen had unilaterally and voluntarily started putting their shit on the walls to draw

attention to themselves. Now, he came to believe that the horrid conditions in the H-Blocks were forced on the blanketmen by the actions of the
prison warders. Adams gained real admiration for their spirit. On his
release, he immediately went to Ruaraigh Ó Bradaigh, president of Sinn
Féin, to plead for a higher profile for the prison campaign. Although the
party was still considerably underdeveloped and had little capacity to
run a protest campaign, it reorganized its POW Department and gave it
more resources. Adams brought in a cadre of Sinn Féin activists like
Danny Morrison, Tom Hartley, and Marie Moore to give practical support to the blanketmen.

Adams says that the movement "started to handle [the prison protest]
better, motivated I think by two concerns; one was a genuine concern for the
plight of the people in there and the other one was to illustrate to the world
and to our own people that here was a manifestation of British rule."[10]

In other words, he began to realize that building support for the prisoners was not just a diversion; it *could* build support for the overall struggle.

Adams had another card up his sleeve. Tomás Ó Fiaich was elevated
to cardinal at the end of June and he offered to negotiate with Thatcher
on behalf of the prisoners.

"Give the cardinal some time and see what he can do," Adams told the
prisoners.

They responded sympathetically because Ó Fiaich's "slums of Calcutta" speech had been so beneficial. Moreover, the priest they trusted
most, Alex Reid, was acting as personal emissary between them and the
cardinal. He continually told them that positive things were happening
"behind the scenes."[11] The announcement that the pope would visit Ireland at the end of September provided a target for a mass publicity campaign in support of the blanketmen. Perhaps, some said, the pope might
even follow Ó Fiaich's example by giving some message of support
during his visit.

The prisoners agreed to postpone their hunger strike. In the meantime,
they discussed how escalate their protest. Over in H3, the OC read out a
comm that Bobby wrote in the Dark's name. It said that the leadership
was exploring ways of escalating the protest. The young men listened in
disbelief, thinking, "How can you escalate this? It's bad enough already!"
Maybe they would throw out their mattresses, but that was the only comfort they had left.

• • •

Frank Maguire finally visited the H-Blocks on July 16, 1979. Bobby was in the middle of his second retelling of *Jet*. The visit got off on a bad foot when Maguire entered H6 just as Rab McCollum was caught smuggling tobacco.

"Look at what we have to put up with here," a screw told Maguire, showing him a lump of tobacco wrapped in cellophane. "Believe it or not he had this in his mouth and he was trying to smuggle it into the prison."

Maguire's response was unexpected.

"Maybe if they were allowed tobacco they wouldn't try to smuggle it."

The prisoners did not yet know who the visitor was but they knew "it wasn't an ordinary NIO yes-man."[12]

Maguire asked to see a couple of blanketmen and he was directed to Sands and Hughes. Bobby shouted to the rest of the wing who their visitor was. Maguire talked with glee about his recent election win. In turn, Bobby and the Dark showed him the new wire mesh grilles that had been placed over their windows, obstructing their views to the outside. They showed him their soaked mattresses and described how the warders put hoses under their cell doors. They spoke about the lack of food. And they described how they were forced to squat over mirrors while their backsides were searched. They told Maguire that they called this position "Humphrey's Hump," after Thatcher's new secretary of state, Humphrey Atkins. The issue of hunger strikes came up. Maguire said that he had visited Frank Stagg, the 1976 hunger striker, before he died in Wakefield prison in England. As he was leaving, Stagg asked him to sing a song. He sang "Help Me Make It Through the Night." Maguire stayed in H6 about half an hour and Bobby made sure he did one thing before he left: replace some of their lost stash of tobacco. Seanna Walsh recalls that they puffed well for several nights, "courtesy of the member from Fermanagh/South Tyrone."[13]

That night, Maguire called a press conference to describe his visit. He told the press that the blanketmen were in danger of being "smothered in their cells." The prison governor, he said, was "trying to break their spirits" by covering the windows and depriving the men of "both light and air." He accused the governor of trying to turn Long Kesh into a "deep litter prison." He said that he would contact the International Red Cross and ask them to undertake an official investigation of the conditions in the H-Blocks.[14]

• • •

Sands and Hughes were not long in holding the movement to its word about boosting the support campaign. Bobby led a discussion in H6 about how to mobilize a publicity campaign. He summarized the discussions in a series of comms to the Republican leadership. The first of these, an extremely long and detailed letter, has survived.[15] It began with a humorous understatement, "This will be pretty long, so get comfortable, *cara*."[16] Bobby then outlined an ambitious and detailed plan to win support.

> *There are two major things we have got to do. One, we must make more people aware and engage their help. Two, to get to these other people, we must organise our own people effectively and massively on the ground.*

In the absence of sufficient movement activity, he wrote, the prisoners had already begun the process of building a campaign themselves.

> *We are preparing an army of propagandists on the ground. It will depend on you and your team comrade to ensure their co-operation at a later date, whether through the central body of the RAC, or whoever.*

Bobby then outlined a plan for the campaign.

> *The idea to reach people is to pass a simple message to them. Our simple message to everyone will be "Smash H-Block" . . . This wee message then "Smash H-Block" will be what we will build around. We want to get this message to everyone, we want to make it impossible for people to forget it, no matter who they are or where they are, they shall see it, hear it, backing this will be material on H-Block to stir people's emotions and to arouse them and activate them.*

Having presented the message, Sands drew on his own experiences as PRO for the blanketmen to outline how it would be spread.

> *Now to tackle this broad spectrum of people in which we'll be plunging we must create our own mass media, The Brit mass*

*media being unreliable but we can use it whenever possible and
through time they'll be forced to cover us, through what we are
going to stir up . . .*

His idea of a mass media comes directly out of his street politics,
where direct action is the most effective weapon.

*. . . passing the message can mean or be through painting a
Smash H-Block on a road or wall or sticking a poster on the side
of a bus or lorry that is stopped at traffic lights or whatever,
now I'll be giving you ideas on this later, but consider these two
wee things I mentioned—a Paint and Poster Campaign. A massive effort on a national basis, through organised workers on
the ground.*

So far, so good. Yet Bobby's readers must have nearly fallen out of their
seats at the scale of what he was proposing.

*In one weekend we move and distribute one million posters
North and South—a million is not aiming too high, we stick
them everywhere on roads, bridges, walls, trees, windows, we
want one in every window in a nationalist area, we must work
on people to get them to put them up, we must put them on
everything that moves to carry them for us, at traffic lights we
stick them on vehicles, they'll be carried into towns, Loyalist and
upper-class areas.*

The agitation had to be maintained and intensified until "Smash H-
Block" was literally on everyone's lips.

*Shortly afterwards we back this up with another massive coor-
dinated painting spree (Smash H-Block) cover the countryside
with it . . . We can keep repeating this every three or four weeks.
By doing this we create our own mass media, we can advertise
forth from us "Big Parades" in this manner, we must work hard
and make it big, we want people to see H-Block everywhere. We'll
do a door to door canvassing in every area, our people being
armed with facts and details of H-Block.*

Bobby's personal energy and his innate optimism shone through in his certainty that they could win mass support if they only kept hammering away at people. He thought everyone could be turned into an energetic activist like himself, a deeply held belief that was encapsulated in his oft-quoted statement that "everyone has their part to play, no matter how small"[17] Speaking of the role of canvassers and supporters, he recommended that,

> *They give our material and put our case, emotionally breaking people down into giving a commitment, put them on the spot there and then, offer them ways in which they can help, come to a march, put a poster in their window, buy a paper, do the whole lot, join the RAC, etc. We want parades the like of which have never been seen before. By continuing pushing "Smash H-Block" we believe we are pushing a small message and making people aware through their wee jobs and those who they reach will learn something if it's only that H-Block exists. They will help and support. We'll pick up as we progress!!*

Sands summarized his proposal for a campaign in four simple steps:

> *It sort of boils down to this Cara:*
> *1. Organise the people that we have already got.*
> *2. Attack through mass media propaganda, through an army of propagandists, you out there and we in here . . .*
> *3. Make our message simple—"Smash H-Block," some details, a call for action, plenty of emotion.*
> *4. Broaden our battlefield, locally, nationally, and internationally, the field is limitless . . .*

Bobby did not expect the movement to create a campaign while they sat in their filthy cells and cheered them on. Rather, he outlined an active part for the blanketmen. He requested resources so that they could play their part.

> *We need a list of names, a who's who, what's what in Ireland, all those who have influence, here's a few to start with, trade unions . . . social conscious groups, left-wing groups, churchmen*

> *Catholic and Prod, with influence, newspaper and tv and media list of people who write or produce political or social programmes and articles, etc. Anybody who's anybody—also a list of people who allegedly have made some sort of statement on the H-Block favourable to us ranging from organisation leaders to important individuals those doctors made statements last year, etc!! The idea is this, one of us in here can write to one of those above or whoever, in a very emotional and distressing letter (in the case of an organisation our workers can back it up with a publicity brief, where possible give us as much background so that we can make the letters individual).*

In case the Movement had any questions about the purpose of this mass writing campaign, Bobby put it bluntly that, ". . . personally I envisage creating an atmosphere of mass emotion trying to use it as best we can and as soon as we can." He even went into detail about how to heighten the emotional impact of the campaign by suggesting that their posters "must be eye-catching, thick black type with 'Smash H-Block' small run down on blocks and the call for action." He suggested a,

> *Poster with a child on it, emotional The Year of the Child "Don't Let my Daddy Die in H-Block." Get them up everywhere (I'm wrecked). Get those "Smash H-Block" posters up everywhere for Pope coming on the vehicles we can do it on the continent and USA. Also England. Paint "Smash H-Block" all over the major motorways in Britain—God knows how many we will see before it's obliterated. We want H-Block more common than Shamrock and we can do it (read on Cara). Black hacks[18]—we want posters stuck on every door so as we have "Smash H-Block" sailing in and out of every District every minute of every day up and down the Falls so that thousands see them . . .*

In all, said Sands, "you'll probably need about 10 million for what we've planned." Just in case they did not get the message, he added, "Deadly serious, comrade."

Finally, Bobby listed suggestions for chain letters, pirate radio stations, school boycotts, "token industrial strikes," demos at sporting events, sending kids wrapped in blankets to the pope's youth mass, an H-Block flag ("booby trap a few in Crossmaglen"), an International Committee headed up by a team of sympathetic priests and others. "All that I have written here came out of an hour's discussion from one wing. By next week we'll have more when we discuss it deeper."

Then, after an extended argument about standing in elections, Sands asked, "Can you urge priests to bring lots of pens into us, also cages—to send as many as possible. Well that's about it, the screws are throwing buckets of disinfectant under the doors at the minute so I'll see ya!! Regards to all. —Marcella."

The recipient of the comm surely had a headache by the time he finished reading it, probably wondering where this Sands guy was getting amphetamines in the H-Blocks! Yet over the following months many of Bobby's suggestions were put into action, if on a scale of "tens of thousands" rather than "millions." Once the National H-Block/Armagh Committee was launched in October 1979, its campaign *was* centered on the simple message, "Smash H-Block." Within months the slogan appeared on walls, bridges, and hoardings across the island. Posters *did* appear with the slogan "Don't Let My Daddy Die in H-Block." Perhaps most significantly for the prisoners, Bobby succeeded in organizing a veritable letter-writing factory, where the prisoners wrote hundreds of letters each week to practically every supporter and potential supporter with any kind of influence.

• • •

If the blanketmen were to coordinate a mass campaign, Bobby had first to create a more effective communications system. They needed regular channels of communications to get writing supplies, addresses, and other information into the prison and communications out of the prison.

Bobby Sands organized the communications network inside the prison, while women from Sinn Féin's reorganized POW department coordinated it outside. Their leader was Marie Moore, a fortyish woman with impeccable Republican credentials. Working alongside her was Mary Hughes, another trusted Republican organizer. Bobby and the Dark called them by code names. Moore was *An Ban Uasal* (the noblewoman). Hughes was "the kitten" (not because she was soft and cuddly but "because she had a hiss, and she had claws that she would sink into you"[19]).

Moore visited Bobby in jail to help him arrange the network. She remembers feeling sorry for him because his lovely blonde hair was all dirty and matted, despite his attempts to look as good as he could for her. Yet her feelings of pity soon vanished because of his personality. He came in with "a jaunty walk," not like so many blanketmen who entered the visiting room with their heads down, reeling from the humiliations along the way. Bobby practically sprang up to the visiting box and greeted her with a pleasant remark. He always had a joke, always had something to say about her appearance, even if it was "you're weathering well with age." He sat down and looked at her with his "very piercing blue eyes," smiled with his "very happy smile" and showed a set of teeth that somehow were not as bad as the other prisoners (in spite of herself, Moore always noticed their teeth because she had to kiss them).

Bobby spoke to other prisoners even though the screws told him not to. His exchanges always ended in a laugh that spread. He had a very infectious laugh and others laughed along with him even if they didn't catch the joke. As a result of this confident air, says Moore, she found that the screws seemed to have a high regard for Bobby, even those who treated other prisoners badly. Instead of "Sit down!" or "Don't move!" they asked Sands, in a civil tone, "Do you mind sitting down?" Bobby had a charisma that Moore can only compare with Gerry Adams.

In response to Bobby's requests, Moore formed a team of young women, who "were in jail nearly as long as the prisoners."[20] They went back and forth into the jail, twice a day every day, smuggling comms and supplies. On most days, Bobby could send out messages in the morning and receive a reply that afternoon.

It is hard to imagine what it was like for the young women who went in to visit the men. They were women of dating age, visiting men of a similar age. They tried to look their best in an effort to keep up the prisoners' morale while they did their job of carrying communications.

And the men?

"It was very heartbreaking going in to see them because their hair was long and dirty, their faces were dirty as well and the smell of them was unbelievable . . ."

It was hard for the young women to go into jail day after day and kiss somebody who was completely dirty to get communications coming from all parts of his body. "Sometimes you felt like being violently sick before you got out with the communications," says Moore, and sometimes they had to swallow them and wait until it they came back out again.

The women swallowed their pride as well as the comms. They were doing things that went against much that they had been taught. Not only had they to receive items that the men had been holding internally,[21] they also had to secrete comms, supplies, and even miniature radios and cameras on their bodies.

The job got harder as the prisoners' demands increased. As the women became known, the prison authorities held them back for special searches.[22] After the searches, packages had to be passed to the prisoner. The visitors were always in the visiting booth first, where a warder sat at the table to observe the visit. Usually, the prisoner passed his comm from his mouth during a kiss while the visitor slipped hers into his jacket pocket during the embrace. On a good visit, it happened right away. Then they could relax and have a good chat. If not, both parties visited anxiously, knowing that they only had one more chance to pass their precious cargo. If there was something bulkier to pass, three women went together. One sat beside the prisoner while the others diverted the warder's attention so that they could, eventually, slip the package to the prisoner.

But the ordeal was still not over. The women still had to get their comms back out. They stank because the smell of the communications was unbelievable. Even the Sinn Féin office back in Belfast stank from the comms that were open and transcribed there. A local businessman gave Moore a bottle of expensive perfume to spray the comms before she opened them.

Despite the ordeal, day after day, month after month, the women kept up their visits. None of them ever stopped working for Marie Moore.

"They all just carried on."

The women stayed in the Sinn Féin office well into the night, transcribing and packaging the next day's communications and making up endless packages to satisfy the prisoners' seemingly insatiable demands for supplies. Keeping them supplied with cling wrap alone was hectic. Bobby always had a *beart* (parcel) up his anus containing comms, writings, a stock of cigarette papers, cling wrap, and two shortened ballpoint refills. Other prisoners said that he was so organized, he could reach up into his backside and pull out the comm or writing he wanted among the dozens that were there. He used so much writing materials that his cellmates had to keep a second *beart* for him up their backsides. The other prisoners called Bobby's cellmates his "mules."

Comms from the jail were mostly descriptions of conditions in the H-blocks. Comms went back in telling the prisoners news from the outside.

The OCs of the wings read out the comms at night, lifting the prisoners by telling them about a big demonstration or a successful military action by the IRA. Yet Hughes and Sands needed to know how things were *really* going. Bobby was especially aware of the need for accurate information. He read his visitor's mood very quickly. Moore visited him after a discouraging turnout at a public demonstration and tried to hide her true feelings.

"How did it go?" Bobby asked her.

She tried to make things look better than they were but he interrupted her.

"Wasn't a very good turnout, was it?"

Then, rather than commiserating over the failure, he began making suggestions about how they might get others involved so that the next event would be better attended.

• • •

Sands used the new communications network as a launching pad to extend the struggle. Richard O'Rawe called H6 "a production factory for comms." Bobby gave the men lists of names and they each had to write four or five letters a day. Bobby drew up sample letters, explaining the conditions in the H-Blocks and why they had been forced into the no-wash protest. Each letter contained a section where the prisoner introduced himself and personalized the message. As time went on, Sands customized the templates for different kinds of people. It would take a different message to move an academic or a politician than an actor or an artist.

One prisoner wrote to the U.S. journalist Jack Anderson about how his founding fathers had fought the British for independence and the Irish had as much right to fight for theirs. Then he wrote to *Pravda* about the working-class struggle against imperialism and called his reader "comrade." In time, they got hundreds of names and addresses and wrote to trade unionists, actors, writers, and musicians in various countries. Bik MacFarlane wrote letters to Jane Fonda and the dean of Westminster Abbey (he framed it and hung it on his wall). Muhammad Ali, Vanessa Redgrave, and Jean-Paul Sartre all got letters.

The prisoners seldom heard back from anyone; they had to assume that their letters were having an effect. Some people *were* deeply affected.

Christy Moore, one of Ireland's most popular singers, became one of the strongest supporters of the blanketmen after receiving a number of letters from them.

"At the time the name Bobby Sands didn't mean anything to me," explains Moore. "In actual fact I had received quite a lot of stuff from the pen of Marcella, and I think it was only when he came to national attention that somebody pointed out to me that Marcella was Bobby Sands . . . the quality of stuff that was coming out in the comms and the quality of the writing certainly was inspirational."[23]

Moore soon began incorporating their messages in his songs. Anywhere he went he sang about the blanket protest and subsequently about the hunger strike. It remains part of his music to this day. Moore says he moved from being a "bar-room Republican" to an active political performer. In return, he got "a feeling of working side by side with people who were on the blanket and people who were in prison." He felt a "very direct contact" with the blanketmen so he became more and more involved.

Soon, Moore formed a group called Moving Hearts that became the most popular band in Ireland. The group's concerts generated huge support for the blanketmen, so much so that the national Irish radio and television network censored their songs. The Special Branch, a political force within the southern Irish police force, followed the band and harassed Moore. They raided his house several times and stopped and searched him on the streets.

If the letter-writing campaign brought big returns from Christy Moore, other appeals were less successful. In one legendary episode, Bobby decided to write to his favorite poet, Eithne Carberry. Surely, he thought, it would be great if they could get her to support the blanket protest. Bobby requested her address but it never appeared among the hundreds of addresses they received. Finally, he wrote her a letter even though he did not have an address. The prisoners on the wing were all listening one night when Bobby shouted across the landing to Brendan Hughes:

"Hey! Dark!"

"Yes, Bobby."

"I've just written a letter to Eithne Carberry outlining the conditions of the blanketmen and I've told her how much I admire her poetry. Would you like to hear what I've written?"

"Hold on a second, I've a wee bit of news for you first."

"You have? And what's that?"

"Well, have you got an Ouija board in the cell? Because you're gonna need it to get in contact with her as she's been dead over a hundred years."[24]

• • •

As the summer ended, the prisoners worked overtime in their propaganda factory, getting ready for the pope's visit. Monday, August 27 changed all that.

In the west of Ireland, it was a sunny day with hardly any wind. At about 11:30 in the morning, Louis Battenberg (Lord Mountbatten), the last Viceroy of India and Prince Charles's favorite uncle, who was holidaying in his summer castle near the fishing village of Mullaghmore in County Sligo, set off in his boat with a small party of family and friends. As he stopped in the harbor to inspect his lobster pots, an explosion blew the boat to smithereens, killing Mountbatten and three of his party. A few hours later, on the other side of Ireland, a three-vehicle convoy of paratroopers, the regiment infamous for its role in Bloody Sunday in Derry, was driving along a highway beside a stretch of Carlingford Lough known as Narrow Water. As the convoy passed a trailer load of hay that was parked beside the road, an IRA unit detonated a huge bomb, blowing a three-ton army truck across the road. The surviving paratroopers radioed for help and a helicopter full of British soldiers came to their aid. The IRA detonated a second bomb. Some surviving soldiers opened fire across the water at two passing Irish civilians, killing one of them and wounding the other. By the end of the day, eighteen British soldiers were killed along with the Irish civilian.

Prime Minister Thatcher immediately flew to Ireland, where she met shoppers in Belfast and soldiers at Crossmaglen, a few miles from Warrenpoint. The IRA reacted to her condemnation with a terse statement, "The Iron Maiden's declaration of war is nothing but the bankrupt rattling of an empty tin."[25]

On Wednesday of the following week, Mountbatten was buried. That same day, the prison authorities moved the men out of H6. They just came in without warning and moved Sands, Hughes, MacFarlane, and some others to H3. Others were scattered throughout other H-Blocks. Another phase of the prison struggle, of the life of Bobby Sands, was ended.

Chapter Nineteen

Toward the Inevitable

"McIlhattan, you blirt, where have you gone?" cry a million
    choking men.
Where are your sacks of barley? Or will your likes be seen again?
Here's a jig to the man and a reel to the drop and a swing to the
    girl he loved,
May your fiddle play and poteen cheer your company up above.

—*Bobby Sands, "McIlhattan"*

T he prison authorities put Bobby Sands in a cell with a Derryman named Dixie Elliot. Sands had known Elliot in H6 but they were never close. In the next cell, the Dark was now with Ricky O'Rawe. The first day in H3 they went through a rough mirror search. When they refused to squat some of them got a beating. The young prisoners told them that this treatment was normal, it simply had not been happening to them in H6.

"H3 was a terrible, terrible, terrible place," says Colm Scullion, the young prisoner who Bobby had befriended as a scared, limping country boy back in Crumlin Road Jail. It was so bad that "Teapot" McMullen used to say, "When I get out of jail, if anybody ever asks me was I on the blanket I'll say, 'No, I was in H3!'"

Bad relations with the screws matched the bad morale in H3. The blanketmen gave the warders nicknames. "Jimmy Clawhammerhead" had hair that he greased back with a bit sticking out behind; if you saw him sideways he had the profile of a claw hammer. "Dried-Up-River-Bed Face" had a particularly rough complexion. "Noddy" resembled a famous baby-faced cartoon character. There was *Buachaill Bo* (the cowboy), the "Red Rat," "Ronnie the Moron," and "Vinegar Face." Even the doctor had a nickname—"Dickie-Bow Wellington"—because he always appeared on the wing in a bow tie *and* Wellington boots, the latter to avoid the pools of urine in the corridors and cells.

A particular hate figure for the prisoners was *Sron Dearg* (Red Nose), whom they also called "Rudolph" (after the reindeer). Later on, when Bobby discovered that the word for "scabby" was *gearbach*, *Sron Dearg* became *Sron Gearbach*. The blanketmen called another screw *Cupan* (Cup) because they didn't know the Irish word for "mug." "Crocodile Face" looked like a crocodile. "Vomit Face" looked like Paul Newman but he made such a thing of his good looks that they had to call him something derogatory.

Teapot, who handed out most of the nicknames, had been badly shot up before he was caught and imprisoned. But that was war and British soldiers were the enemy. H3 was the first time he really *hated* someone. Teapot sat in his cell and fantasized about killing a screw. When he realized what he was doing, it scared him. He never hated anyone before or since.

A few screws were not so bad. H— was "Okay." Jimmy B— was "alright," they "couldn't say a bad word about him, to be honest." And they quite liked white-bearded "Captain Birdseye," who gave Sands the nickname "Charlie," which Bik MacFarlane used as Bobby's codename.

H3 was a revelation for Hughes and Sands. Not one man was smoking, such was their fear of getting caught smuggling tobacco. No one was writing comms. During the day, the men spoke in whispers. The screws "had squeezed the life juices out of them," said one prisoner from H6. "They were no longer functioning human beings. They were cowed . . . total demoralization."

In their midst were a couple of prisoners with some hope. "Hector" and "Teapot" were two resilient characters who did their best to inject some spirit onto the wing through their incessant cynical commentaries.

The first night the new men were on the wing Teapot addressed the Dark.

"What are you going to do about this?" he asked him.

Hughes talked to Bobby about how they could raise morale. They ordered the young blanketmen just to bend for the mirror search instead of resisting, a simple measure that immediately lifted pressure off of them. Bobby got the young prisoners involved in smuggling tobacco and opening lines of communication on the wing. He told the stories out the door. Political discussions started. Guys started writing letters to celebrities.

The wing came alive at night. The first week in H3, Bobby organized a singsong. He sang an early Bee Gees song and the Dark did his imitation of Barry White crooning "You're the First, the Last, My Everything." Bobby's new cellmate, Dixie Elliott, sang "Jailhouse Rock" and the wing went crazy, banging their pisspots on the door.[1]

Veterans of H3 joined in. Teapot did "Skibbereen," a song about the Irish famine. It was the only song he knew. Hector got up to vent above the door, which he called his "echo chamber," and sang "They Shoot Horses, Don't They?" a 1977 one-hit wonder by Racing Cars that Teapot called "a real sad, dour fucking song." Martin Hurson sang the rebel song, "Sean South." Everybody was amazed at what a bad singer he was.

The book at bedtime became an immediate favorite. Bobby told *Trinity* for seven or eight nights and even the night screws sat down and listened. Soon, young prisoners started telling books and the older men began to see them growing in confidence. The young INLA prisoner Kevin Lynch, who they called Barabbas because of his thick black beard, particularly stood out.[2]

For the first time in H3, they held political debates. They debated whether Republicans should stand in elections and the younger prisoners began to find a voice. Tommy McKearney gave a series of lectures on Irish history. Others began to sing, to recite poems, to learn Irish. Bobby's old friend Tomboy Loudon was in the next wing and they impressed the younger prisoners by shouting to each other in Irish.

Bobby was not teaching formal Irish lessons anymore but he contributed to the development of the language in informal ways. He took nursery rhymes like "This Old Man" and turned them into Irish mind games. He taught the YPs a whole repertoire of songs in Irish during the afternoons, singing a verse, over and over, until they memorized it. He organized competitions around the songs, one side of the wing against the other.

Then Bobby started translating names. He got a list of Irish names from the Cages and even collared Cardinal Ó Fiaich during a visit to the H-Blocks and probed him about the Irish equivalents of certain names.

Ironically, Bobby's own name was of lowland Scots origin but he admitted privately that he picked "Ó Seachnasaigh" because it sounded romantic; its nearest English translation is the "descendant of the seventh fairy." Soon, everyone wanted his name translated. Teapot was *Mac Muilleoin*, "the son of the bald man." After the others got their names translated, one prisoner who "wasn't overly courageous on the blanket" spoke up.

"Bobby, what's my name in Irish?"

Bobby studied his Irish materials for a minute or two. He could not locate the man's name on his list. So he improvised.

"It means 'he who has nothing between the legs.'"[3]

From then on, the man's nickname was either "no balls" or "he who has nothing."

• • •

Hunger strike was still on the agenda. The prisoners threatened to go on hunger strike in September but Gerry Adams again persuaded them to postpone the action. Again, in early October, they announced that they would go on a hunger strike "to the death" unless their demands for political status were met "within the next few weeks." The IRA added its own statement, threatening that there would be "heavy civilian casualties in Britain" if any prisoners came to harm.[4]

Again, the movement made promises about stepping up its support campaign. As part of a renewed publicity campaign, leading up to the promised establishment of a national H-Block committee, the POW Department and Bobby coordinated a media blitz for early October. On a single day a number of journalists were invited to visit blanketmen on their regular monthly visits. Joan Boyd of the *Sunday News* was assigned to visit Bobby Sands.[5] She found the atmosphere of the prison and the search procedures "hostile and unfriendly." They led her to her visiting cubicle and after a few minutes Bobby entered. Boyd was shocked, clearly unprepared for this "grotesque looking figure with filthy shoulder-length hair and a long scraggly beard." The screws hovered and listened to their conversation, which was half in English and half in Irish. According to Boyd, "throughout the 30-minute visit [Bobby's] hands shook and his whole body trembled. His eyes darted back and forward at the slightest movement or sound, and his face was deathly pale and sunken." He chain-smoked, hardly taking time to snub one cigarette out before he started another.

Despite Bobby's appearance, his thoughts were clear and firm. He said that they would accept "absolutely no settlement or compromise short of political status." Asked about the pope's appeal for an end to violence, he simply said that he had full confidence in the leadership of the Republican Movement. He was sorry that people had lost lives but, "the British created the climate for political violence . . . their actions created the IRA." And Lord Mountbatten, did he have any sympathy for him? No, replied Bobby, Mountbatten was part of the "British war machine" and had been "responsible for perpetrating injustices in other British colonies throughout the world." Bobby was resolute on this point, saying that, "I don't want to see anyone getting hurt or dying but so long as injustice reigns in this country I feel it is my duty to fight it whatever way I can." Even if he was released tomorrow, he said, he would go right back to the struggle just as he had done before.

Finally, Bobby told the journalist about the conditions in the H-Blocks and explained why they were protesting and might go on hunger strike. He said that there were daily beatings and many prisoners were sick. Several had worms from eating their food with contaminated hands. One man, he said, had been taken to hospital after spending the day vomiting hundreds of worms.

"If one of us doesn't die through starvation and disease in this place," he said, "we'll die from the beatings we get."

He even told Boyd that he expected to die. "I know I'm dying. I'm prepared to die on the blanket. I will never, never accept criminal status. All the prisoners have the same determination as myself, and we will never give up.

"I'll admit that I'm afraid," said Bobby. "I lie in my cell and wonder if the footsteps I hear will stop at my door and it will be my turn next. But the harder the prison authorities lean on us, the more determined we are that we're right and we'll never back down."

Boyd left the visit and compared notes with other journalists who visited other prisoners. She seemed convinced by many of the stories, especially after the other journalists reported hearing "remarkably similar" stories of ill-treatment. Journalists would often debate whether these stories were so similar because they were true, or, perhaps, because they were rehearsed.

Within a month, however, the stories of the blanketmen were supported by an unexpected source. A group of prison officers announced to the press that they intended to set up a breakaway union called the "Progressive Prison Officers' Committee." A spokesman for the group, who claimed that they had strong support among the prison officers, said that Northern Ireland Office (NIO) policy, or, more accurately, a lack of a constructive policy, was forcing them "to subject prisoners to a brutalising and intolerable way of life." Moreover, their existing association, the Prison Officers' Association (POA), encouraged a policy of "blanket reprisal" against prisoners who flouted prison rules. This attitude, said the spokesman, simply "ape[d] the destructive attitude of the NIO," and was turning prison officers into "cannon fodder" in the Northern Irish conflict.[6] Although the threatened breakaway never materialized, it shows that there were prison officers who opposed the daily brutalities that they were experiencing and inflicting in the H-Blocks.

• • •

Dixie Elliot, Bobby's new cellmate in H3, was in prison for shooting a British soldier. Elliot was from a mixed background: his father a Protestant and his mother a Catholic. That was probably why he and Sands hit it off right away, talking about their common experiences of growing up in mixed communities. Bobby talked at length about Rathcoole. In turn, he wanted to learn everything about Elliot's community.

Elliot's main memory of Sands was a man who was constantly on the move, pacing up and down the cell, stroking his beard and thinking. His long blonde hair swung from side to side. Bobby cut a hole in the middle of a blanket and wore it over his head as a pancho. He traded songs and stories with Elliot, giving him early Bee Gees songs like "Massachusetts." By speaking Irish constantly, Elliot became fluent.

Elliot did not write much on his wall but he drew. In one cell he drew a mural of Custer's Last Stand. He created a group of cartoon characters that he called the Gretí, small Yeti the size of a leprechaun. He had read an article where a Russian scientist argued that there was a connection between the Yeti and the Irish leprechaun and it fired his imagination. He made up children's tales in pictures on the wall.

"They'll make you money some day," Bobby told him.[7]

Sands was at the height of his writing energies, often using material he collected from other blanketmen. Elliot thought of him as a magpie, with a capacity to take things in and turn them to his own use. "The Rhythm of Time," one of his most often quoted poems, was modeled on the Rolling Stones classic, "Sympathy for the Devil":

> *There's an inner thing in every man,*
> *Do you know this thing, my friend?*
> *It has withstood the blows of a million years,*
> *And will do so to the end.*

> *It was born when time did not exist,*
> *And it grew up out of life,*
> *It cut down evil's strangling vines,*
> *Like a slashing searing knife.*

Just as the Jagger/Richards song follows the Devil through key historical events, Bobby's poem runs through Babylon, the crucifixion, the uprisings of Spartacus and the Paris Commune, the indigenes' endurance of the Conquistadors, U.S. westward expansion, and British colonialism. Yet, Sands uses the form of the Rolling Stones song to turn that song's dark message of unspeakable evil on its head. His is a message of hope, of resistance rather than capitulation to evil. The "inner thing" in every man "knows no bounds nor space."

> *It lies in the hearts of heroes dead,*
> *It screams in the tyrant's eyes,*
> *It has reached the peak of mountains high,*
> *It comes searing cross the skies.*

> *It lights the dark of this prison cell,*
> *It thunders forth its might,*
> *It is "the undauntable thought," my friend,*
> *The thought that says, "I'm right!"*

Bobby wrote stories about things around him and things the other prisoners told him. "The Captains and the Curs" was about a young prisoner who was beaten by a big screw. Captain Birdseye, the "Captain" of the title, tried to stop the beating but was unable to do anything.

To improve the Irish vocabulary of the wing, Bobby told folktales. He made up a story about a farmer who chopped down a thorn tree. That night he was haunted by bad dreams. When he woke up the next morning, everything was gone in his house, furniture and all. The thorn tree was home for the fairies, who came into the man's house during the night and took everything away for revenge.

One of his favorite songs was the "Lonesome Boatman," a traditional Irish air. One day Bobby sat looking at a stain on the wall. Later that night, he wrote a poem. He told Dixie that the stain looked to him like the lonesome boatman. The poem began with Bobby's common theme, of longing for the countryside.

> *In the middle of the sleepy lake*
> *The lonesome boatman dwells.*
> *Around him rise the bracken hills*
> *The dreamy glens and dells.*

He spoke of the scarecrows and the birds, the beauty that surrounded the boatman. But, in the end, the boatman was sorrowful and forlorn. "Why?" asked Bobby. Were the stars above him only tears that he had shed? Such sorrowful thoughts jolted Bobby back to his cell.

> *Oh, lonesome boatman, the birds are here,*
> *The morning shadows fall.*
> *Oh, friends, why must you be*
> *But a dying shadow on my lonely cell wall.*

Soon, Bobby turned conversations with Elliot into a song about Derry. Dixie told him about his native city's history of forced emigration to Australia during penal times. Bobby asked him about common Derry names and colloquial sayings.

Philip Rooney remembers the day when he heard Sands walking up and down his cell, singing. There had just been a wing shift—they were moved about every two weeks now—and they were without mattresses. Rooney could not make out the words but the tune was "The Wreck of the Edmund Fitzgerald" by Gordon Lightfoot, one of his favorite songs.

That night there was a singsong and Rooney spoke to Sands.

"Bobby, go ahead and sing 'Wreck of the Edmund Fitzgerald.'"

"I've been putting me own words to it," answered Bobby. Then he sang "The Voyage," a song about United Irish rebel prisoners who were transported to Tasmania on a ship called the *Gull*.

> *It was 1803 when we sailed out to sea*
> *And away from the sweet town of Derry*
> *For Australia bound and if we didn't drown*
> *The mark of the fetter we'd carry.*

The men listened, mesmerized by one of Bobby's most haunting songs, punctuated by constantly pleasing yet often frightening turns of phrase.

> *The Gull cut the sea carving our destiny*
> *And the sea spray rose white and came flying*
> *O'Docherty screamed, awoken out of his dreams*
> *By a vision of bold Robert[8] dying.*

Another verse could have been autobiographical. It tied the United Irishmen with the blanketmen, nearly two centuries later,

> *In our own smelling slime we were lost in a time*
> *Hoping God in his mercy would claim us.*
> *But our spirits shone high like the stars in the sky*
> *We were rebels and no man would tame us.*

"The Voyage" is perhaps Bobby's most famous song. Christy Moore made it wildly popular in the years following his death. Thousands of fans sing the song's chorus in unison at Moore's concerts. Writings like "The Voyage" impressed Bobby's cellmate. One day Elliot said to him, "I wish I could write songs like you, Bobby."

Bobby turned and stared back at Dixie for a minute. "Well, I wish I could draw like you."

● ● ●

Shortly before Christmas, Sands was moved in with Colm Scullion. At Christmas each prisoner got a couple of cards and a turkey dinner. Scull will never forget the dinner coming through the door that year and the two of them looking at it, amazed. It looked as if the cook had taken a butcher knife and whacked the turkey into squares. Scull got a bit of breast with some wing and a quarter of a leg attached. The odd feather stuck out here and there.

Bobby quoted Oscar Wilde: "A prostitute would degrade herself by doing business with a screw."

Despite the dinner, morale was high and they had a Christmas concert. To the young prisoners in H3 the amount of talent was "unbelievable." Philip Rooney lay on his sponge mattress and listened to the men singing and telling stories. He looked out the grille in the window and thought what a lovely night it was. For the first time since he was put in H3, he asked himself, "Even when you *do* get out could you ever have an experience as good as this?"

The next day a bad sickness came into the wing. Some men ended up in prison hospital with vomiting and diarrhea. They blamed the turkey dinner.

In the cell, life was the usual routine. After breakfast, Bobby walked up and down either thinking or asking Scull endless questions about his background in rural County Derry. It was now winter, so they both walked and talked, trying to keep warm. They folded one of their blankets into a foot-wide "path" from the front to the back of the cell. Up and down they paced, talking and talking, even though it was painful for Scull since he had lost the toes and part of the ankle of his left foot. Sometimes Bobby ran to write something on the wall. Other times he started singing and it seemed to Scullion like he would never stop. But then he would take a break and write a poem or send some comms up to the Dark.

When Bobby first came into the cell, he told Scullion that embarrassment over your mistakes was the greatest barrier to learning Irish. So they should begin using Irish right away before they became friendlier and it was more difficult to "get over the barrier." They immediately began speaking only Irish all day long, speaking English only between eleven o'clock and twelve o'clock at night to figure out things they had not fully understood during the day.

Jake Jackson gave formal Irish classes in the afternoon. He gave exercises from the Bible, their only reading material:

"Go to the Bible, find Ezekiel 23:19-20. Colm, translate it into Irish for me."

The Bible was a good resource for Irish except when specialized words went beyond their vocabulary. The prisoners made up "provisional" Irish words until they could get the proper translation. Their phrase for "palm tree" was *cran leamh*, literally "hand tree," since a hand was the closest thing they could think of to a palm. Dixie Elliot was disappointed years later when he found out that Bobby's word for "wren," *rio na mona* (king of the bog), was made up.

Since Scullion was religious, they argued about the Bible. Bobby said he liked John because he "was a true Socialist" and Revelations for a bit of a scare. Scull enjoyed St. Martin de Paor's magazine for its articles. Bobby liked it because it had the best paper for rolling cigarettes. As soon as Scull finished the articles, Bobby recycled them. But their conversations were mostly about country life. Bobby wanted to find out about Scullion's people. "It was almost as if he was a countryman at heart," thought Scullion. "He could see the richness in it."

Scullion told Sands about places around South Derry, like Crosskeys with its tradition of Irish music, or Largy and its ancient oak woods. On hearing that the girl's name Aisling was a Derry name, Bobby told Scull that it had always been his favorite Irish name, and that if he ever had a girl he would name her Aisling. Bobby made plans to visit Scullion in his townland of Ballyscullion, beside Lough Beag on river Bann, after they got out of prison. To Scullion, Bobby was not like the other Belfast men. He was always asking about farming. He wanted to know about quality of life on the farm and security of tenure.

Scullion told Sands about fishing for eels on Lough Beag, near his home, and how his father poached salmon in the streams nearby. This was grist for Bobby's mill. *He* would like nothing better than to go fishing on Lough Beag, he said. He wanted to know everything about fishing for eels. Scullion told him how eels run by the dark of the moon. It's pitch black and you're out on the lough in a boat and you've no lights (if you did the bailiff would see you). How he hated it, said Scull, all those dark nights in the miserable rain in a boat out in the middle of the lough.

Bobby scolded him for not realizing when he had it good.

"I think country people are in a rich situation compared to the ones in Belfast," he said. He thought of his friends in Ardoyne whose idea of a good time was to go to the gasworks with a bottle of wine. "It's sad," he said. "It reflects on the whole struggle."

Right enough, thought Colm, he had never really appreciated nights on Lough Beag until he talked to Bobby and saw what it meant to him.

Scullion told stories and Bobby took notes, trying to visualize it all "as if he was there." One day he told Bobby about Rodai Mac Corlai, the Protestant United Irish leader who was hanged at the bridge in Toome for his part in the 1798 rising. Mac Corlai was from Duneaney, Tom McElwee's townland. Bobby's favorite poet, Ethna Carberry, had written a poem about him that was later made famous as a hit song by the Kingston Trio. That night Bobby sat down and started to write on the wall with the lead of a pencil. He wrote for several evenings and would not allow Scullion to look at it. Finally, he finished the poem and memorized it. That night after the screws left the wing he called on everyone to keep quiet. He shouted to Thomas McElwee, who was across the landing and a few cells down.

"*Tomás, ag an doras.*" ("Tom, come to the door.")

"*Cad é, Bobby?*" ("What is it, Bobby?")

"This here is for you and Scull."

Sands read out his new poem, "Rodai MacCorlai." It incorporated his favorite images: the birds, the hills, the beauty of the Ulster countryside.

> *I am Rodai of Duneaney—Mac Corlai—Antrim born!*
> *This day in Toome I meet my doom for an oath that I have sworn.*
> *On yonder oak in Roughery Hill a jackdaw I have heard,*
> *It waits to steal my very soul, 'tis surely the devil's bird.*

Scullion was thrilled when Bobby brought him and his father into the sixth verse:

> *And 'twas at Crosskeys the pikes gleamed white 'neath a telling*
> *   yellow moon,*
> *As the common folk (and there, there the poacher's son) went out*
> *   to meet their doom.*

Later, he incorporated the story of Mac Corlai's stay in Scullion's townland:

> *In Ballyscullion I spent some nights, in Bellaghy three or four,*
> *Then I crossed the Bann with a fisherman to my native Antrim*
> *   shore.*

Then, to drive home the political message that was rarely far away from Bobby's poetry and song:

> *Be staunch my friends and never lose faith though freedom's*
>   *struggle's long,*
> *For the common men have a common cause against England's*
>   *ancient wrong.*
> *The drum beats loud, it scares a man, and the irons bite grim and*
>   *cold,*
> *But the gallows stand in ghostly hate and with terror a hundred-*
>   *fold.*

Finally, after Mac Corlai's execution, visited by "humble folk who come with tear in eye," is a verse that foreshadows Bobby's own likely end:

> *And the sun set red on Slievegallion Brae, the jackdaw hid the*
>   *shame,*
> *The primrose wept for Rodai boy, for Mac Corlai óg was slain.*
> *And along the Largy line a woman wails and tonight she'll roam*
>   *the glen,*
> *Oh Rodai of Duneaney!—Mac Corlai! —Antrim born—will e'er*
>   *we meet again?*

• • •

One day, Sands and Scullion got a new luxury. Someone outside figured out how to build small crystal radios, cylinders the size of a couple of "D" batteries placed end to end. Tom Hartley christened the radios "Mrs. Dale," after a popular but insipid British radio show. They only lasted a short while before they broke down, so there was a constant stream of requests to Marie Moore: "Mrs. Dale has died on us. Can you send in another?"

Smuggling the radios into the jail was hard enough for the women, who brought them in between the cheeks of their buttocks or taped to the insides of their legs. But it took a special kind of prisoner to discretely take the radios off of the women and then slip them through the rip in the crotch of his trousers and up his own anus, without being detected. Tom McElwee, who had regular visits with Moore's girls was "a walking suitcase."[9]

Bobby always had a radio to keep informed about current events and how they were playing in the media. But it was usually his cellmate who had to keep it. One of the disadvantages of being with Bobby, says Scullion, was that you had to carry the radio, plus maybe three or four pens and tobacco and some Irish notes. Scull had an advantage because he had shrapnel all over him from the premature bomb explosion that landed him in prison. The screws' metal detectors went off everywhere. One time there was a wing shift and Scullion had four Parker pen refills inside of him. Bobby preferred the metal Parkers because plastic refills were hard to hold and the writing always came out shaky. But Parkers were dangerous because they set off the detector.[10] Scull's Bible was full of scribbles from a previous pen that hardly ever worked. A screw looked through the Bible and saw the scribbles.

"Well, young Scullion," he said, "I see you had a pen."

"Is that right?"

"Aye. I can see you're having a problem with it. Listen, take my advice and get yerself a good Parker!"

He started laughing as Scullion went to his new cell, full of Bobby's Parker refills.

Since the radio had a short life span and its existence was a strict secret from the screws, Bobby only took it out for a short period last thing at night to hear the news. As soon as he knew it was safe, he took out the radio and attached its wire antenna to the grille on the window. There was a BBC radio mast nearby, so they could easily tune in the local news broadcast at five minutes to midnight. As soon as the news was over, he shouted out the details in Irish. Then they had a short debate about what was happening in Ireland and the world.

• • •

By the end of 1979, the Republican Movement was slowly getting its act together with regard to the prison struggle. At a second National H-Block conference, they sought to broaden support by dropping the demand for political status and replacing it with five key demands about prison conditions.[11] Gerry Adams saw the five demands as Britain's "get-out clause," although he also contends that the British government went "a wee bit mad" under Thatcher and were never likely to take advantage of it.[12] The demands were: to be exempt from wearing prison clothes; to be exempt from prison work; freedom of association with fellow political prisoners; the right to organize educational and recreational facilities; and one weekly visit, letter, and parcel.

The meeting supported the five demands and Sinn Féin became the strongest force on a restructured National Committee. The committee was considerably broader than anything in which the Provos had been involved before. Even the leader of the Peace People, Ciaran McKeown, stood up at the meeting and publicly supported the five demands.

In late December, the prisoners asked Cardinal Ó Fiaich to help resolve the H-Block issue. The cardinal met the Republican Movement, the first of a series of meetings with him or his deputy, Father Alex Reid. Ó Fiaich's exchanges with the British authorities took the form of a series of letters and meetings over several months. Reid acted for Ó Fiaich as a liaison to the blanketmen and he accompanied Ó Fiaich to meetings with the British authorities.

Reid had been meeting with Brendan Hughes and Bobby Sands at Sunday mass for nearly three years. They knew that everything they told him would go back to the cardinal. They did not yet know that Gerry Adams had asked Reid to help them avoid a hunger strike.[13] Reid kept Hughes informed about what was happening "behind the scenes" in the cardinal's discussions with the British government. From talking to Hughes, Reid felt that certain moderate changes in the prison regime, particularly access to their own clothing, could end the prison conflict. After listening to Reid, Cardinal Ó Fiaich put a series of proposals to the British government in the form of a letter. To Reid, it was a classic example of lateral thinking. Ó Fiaich never spoke of political status but used neutral phrases—"as a matter of prison reform . . ."—to introduce proposals that he hoped would satisfy the prisoners without indicating weakness on the part of the British. You don't have to grant political status, he told them, just give them their own clothes, and it can all end.

Reid says Hughes told him that getting their own clothing could end the prison conflict, even though the protest was also about deeper issues. "This is a political conflict," he told Reid. He insisted that the British must "recognize that the conflict was at the base of the problem."

Atkins continued to meet Cardinal Ó Fiach over the following months but to the Cardinal he seemed to turn his concern off and on. On March 26, Atkins gave a public statement in Westminster that he portrayed as an initial reform that could lead to bigger changes. He announced that he would double the number of visits to two a month and quadruple the number of letters to one a week. Prisoners could exercise in sports clothes instead of denim uniforms. Sands eagerly accepted the increase in visits because it doubled his opportunities to smuggle comms and supplies. But they refused Atkins's offer of exercise on the grounds that accepting the concession would weaken the clothing demand and confuse the public, thus weakening the protest without achieving much in return.

By Easter, the prisoners felt that not much was happening to progress their case. Hunger strike was back on the agenda. Whenever Hughes went to meet Father Reid, the blanketmen asked him, "When's the brown bags arriving?" (with their own clothes inside). Every time he came back he could see the faces at the window, hoping he had good news for them. But he never did. After Atkins's limited March initiative, the men began losing faith. They wanted the protest to end. If somebody had to die to reach a solution, most of them were ready to take that road. The gloomy mood was expressed in their Easter pageant, a play about the events of Easter week 1916. Geek O'Halloran devised a bodhran from his water gallon and started things out with a roll of the drums. Bik MacFarlane gave a recitation about the things committed revolutionaries must endure. Then, he whistled the "Foggy Dew." Mixed among the songs of Republican glory were songs of doom, death, and defeat.

At the time of Atkins's statement, some observers speculated that he was making concessions to undermine a forthcoming (June) judgment on a case lodged against Britain in the European Commission on Human Rights. He need not have worried. The commission ruled against the blanketmen on each of the five demands, stating that the requirement to wear a prison uniform was "necessary in a democratic society in the interests of public safety and for the prevention of crime." The concept of "freedom of association," said the commission, did not mean that prisoners are free to associate with other prisoners. The right to exercise had not been violated, the prisoners had simply refused it. In a damaging conclusion that must have discouraged Hughes and Sands, in particular, the commission concluded that "the protest campaign was designed and coordinated by the prisoners to create the maximum public sympathy and support for their political aims. That such a strategy involved self-inflicted debasement and humiliation to an almost sub-human degree must be taken into account."

One glint of comfort for the prisoners came in paragraph forty-six, where the commission expressed "concern at the inflexible approach of the state authorities which has been concerned more to punish offenders against prison discipline than to explore ways of resolving such a serious deadlock." [14]

Still, the blanketmen were making progress inside the Republican Movement. In May of 1980 the movement announced internally that the H-Block issue was its "top immediate priority." It made the head of its POW department a full-time post and put more resources into the department. Instructions went out to local party organizations to raise the prison issue in their lists of priorities.[15] At a June conference, a new National H-Block Committee was elected. Although Sinn Féin's candidates trailed some others, the election of the three of party representatives onto the committee marked the beginning of a new phase of heightened attention to the prison protest within the party.

Their attentions would be needed. Anxieties about a hunger strike heightened in May when the veteran Republican Martin Meehan went on a solo hunger strike to protest his innocence on charges of kidnapping and false imprisonment. Meehan's hunger strike lasted more than sixty days, from May 19 to July 23. When he abandoned the strike, the prisoners and many Republicans outside were doubly angry. They feared that he had shown the British hardliners like Margaret Thatcher that hunger strike was just a bluff; they only had to hold out long enough and they would win.

● ● ●

During the summer, as talks between the cardinal and the British authorities dragged on, talk of a hunger strike became more common. Bobby was moved in with Malachy Carey, a countryman from County Antrim. Since Bobby was also from Antrim, they found common ground. Bobby depended more and more on Carey to keep things for him. During mass, prisoners came up to give Bobby writing supplies and comms. He passed everything to Malachy. Soon, Carey was carrying so much of Bobby's stuff that he was nicknamed "the suitcase." In Irish, some simply called him *másachín* (big arse).

Since Bobby had written "The Voyage" and "Rodai MacCorlai" for his previous cellmates, Malachy asked him to write a poem about the Glens of Antrim. One day, he told Bobby about a man from his area who was a local legend for his poteen (Carey's region of the Antrim Coast is well known for its moonshine). Sands immediately saw a poem in the story of McIlhattan.

He sent the poem through the pipes up to Bik MacFarlane.

"Bik, what do you think?" he asked him, as usual.

As soon as he scanned the first lines, MacFarlane felt that it was something special.

> *In Glenravels Glen there lives a man whom some would call a God*
> *For he could cure the dead and kill the live for a price of thirty bob.*
> *Come winter, summer, frost all o'er or a jiggin spring on the breeze*
> *In the dead of the night a man slips by—McIlhattan, if you'll*
> *   please.*

"To tell you the truth," MacFarlane told Sands, "this looks and sounds more like a song than a poem, just the way it comes out, the way it flows along."

MacFarlane did not expect Bobby's next request.

"Well, could you put music to it then?"

They turned the second verse into a chorus ("'McIlhattan, you blirt,[16] where have you gone?' cry a million choking men") and Bik composed a tune. A couple of nights later he sang the song out the door. Bobby loved it.

Both "McIlhatton" and "The Voyage" became popular in Ireland within a few years of Bobby's death, after Christy Moore sang them on his top-selling 1984 album *Ride On*. Moore says it was "freaky" how Bobby's two songs came to him. One night in the early 1980s he gave a concert in Bellaghy, Colm Scullion's hometown. The locals arranged for him to stay the night with Scullion, who was just out of jail. Moore sat with Scullion over numerous glasses of poteen and they talked and talked about life in the H-Blocks. Finally, Scullion told Moore about this song by Bobby Sands and Bik MacFarlane. Moore asked Scullion to sing it. When he heard the lyric of "McIlhattan," he thought it was "pure poetry . . . a beautiful piece of writing." There was only one problem. Scullion could not carry a tune. In H3 they called him the "Bellaghy Balladeer" because he sang so badly.

"He's got one fuckin' note but he can sing that one note very well," says Christy Moore.

In the end, Moore's fellow musician Donal Lunny had to write a tune for the song because they could make head nor tail of Scullion's version.[17]

The next night, Moore gave a concert in Derry. After the concert he met Dixie Elliot, who sang "The Voyage" to Moore. Like "McIlhatton" the night before, Moore was attracted to the song "straight away."

"So on two successive nights I got these two songs which are now part of the national repertoire."

• • •

After "McIlhattan," Sands started a bigger project. An internee had written out Oscar Wilde's "Ballad of Reading Gaol" and sent it to H3. The poem was quite a hit throughout the wing but especially with Bobby. He was mesmerized by the rhythm of the poem and he later told another prisoner that it seemed to speak directly to him. In truth, it spoke to all of them. Wilde was accessible and passionate; his ballad reflected their prison experience. From the very first line—"He did not wear a scarlet cloak, as blood and wine are red"—it seemed to jump right out at them.

Bobby identified with Wilde when he wrote of "that little tent of blue which prisoners call the sky." He, too, could remember walking, "with other souls, in pain, within another ring." The poem also reminded Bobby of one of his favorite songs, "The Ballad of Tim Evans" by Ewan McColl. Tim Evans was the last man hung in England. Like Trooper Woolridge, he was convicted of killing his wife and his child. Tim Evans is full of the same images as Wilde's Ballad: the walk to the gallows, the patch of sky above. And the moral was the same: execution is state murder, as bad as the crimes that individual men commit. After he heard Christy Moore sing the ballad at a concert, Bobby got the words and learned them.

Sands deconstructed the "Ballad of Reading Gaol" and turned it into his own.[18] First, he wrote about interrogation in Castlereagh; then, a second part about trial in the juryless Diplock courts. Like Wilde, the verses were drenched in autobiography. He passed the verses by Mac-Farlane and then sent them to his contacts outside. After the second part, someone wrote back, advising him to write a third piece on the H-Blocks.

"Ah, I'm gonna have to do this," he told MacFarlane, half-complaining. And away he went. The third part was about themselves: "The Torture Mill—H-Block."

The first part of Bobby's epic poem describes the physical characteristics of the interrogation center: the cold white cells with their hard furniture, their cold floors and the bright white lights. But his main topic is the fear that the captive endured while waiting for his interrogation, the horror of listening to others being beaten, and the possibility that one might break under the brutality. He uses repetition to emphasize the slow but anxious passage of time.

He describes the interrogations in detail. The most terrifying passages are where Sands comes across other wounded souls who have buckled under the strain of interrogation. On his way to the doctor, he passes a man in the corridor. The stanza directly mirrors Wilde's brief brush with Trooper Woolridge on the landing of Reading Gaol.

> *I seen him come, he looked quite done,*
> *His eyes were red and swollen.*
> *And knew I then, that this poor friend*
> *Had had his secrets stolen.*
> *I caught his eye, as he passed by,*
> *His terror-stricken form*
> *Search out the air for nothing there*
> *Like blind man in a storm.*

Behind it all, as with Wilde, lurks a ghost. In Bobby's case the ghost is that of Brian Maguire, a young Catholic who died in mysterious circumstances in Castlereagh in 1978. Like Steve Biko in South Africa, the police insisted that Maguire hung himself. But many people suspected that he *"was* hung." In Bobby's increasingly horrific telling, Castlereagh is filled with "howls of ghouls and hoots of owls" and "devil's rooks and phantom spooks." Demons, gorgons, morons, vipers. "Ugly beasts and Satan's priests." All dance and waltz and shuttle and scuffle until "was murdered Brian Maguire."

> *They danced in gloom, they danced to doom*
> *They waltzed in mortal sin*
> *Shuffling and scuttling*
> *'Fore dark and evil wind.*
> *They inched and winched and pinched and lynched,*
> *And 'pon that scaffold swung.*
> *'Twas evil fray in Castlereagh*
> *Until that man was hung.*

This Citadel, this house of hell
Is worshipped by the law.
It's built upon a rock of wrong
With hate and bloody straw.
Each dirty brick holds some black trick
Each door's a door of pain
'Tis evil's pen, a devil's den,
And Citadel of shame.

After Castlereagh comes the juryless Diplock Court. Of the three sections, this is the shortest; just thirty-eight stanzas compared to ninety-six for Castlereagh, and ninety-one for the H-Blocks. Sands describes the court with total derision.

There was no jury, none at all,
The pig-in-wig was right,
And only fools sought fit to stand
And challenge him with fight.

He describes the parade of witnesses who came forward to testify against him with a similar dismissal. At the end of his description of the court Sands justifies his own part in armed struggle: *not* that he was innocent of taking up arms, but that his course of action was a political one that had been determined by the injustices of the state itself.

And men asked why men rise to fight
To violence do resort,
And why the days are filled with death
And struggles' black report.
But see they not, these blinded fools,
Lord Diplock's dirty court.

Let all men know and know it well
That rich men judge the poor.
Working man 'fore bossman's eyes
Is just a sweating whore.
And rich man ne'er will bow to words
Of that, my friend, be sure.

'Tis but working men strong and bold
United, tight as one,
Who may hope to break the tyrant's grip
And see that splendid sun.
The splendid sun of freedom born,
A freedom dearly won.

The final part of the trilogy is closest to Wilde in style and content. Both poems address the horrors of prison and the terrors meted out by the authorities. Yet Wilde argues that we are all guilty while Sands contrasts the altruism of politically motivated rebellion "from below" with the oppression of state violence "from above." He returns again and again to the theme of "sleeping on another man's wound." It begins with the theme, in a stanza directly inspired by Wilde's first stanza.

On other's wounds we do not sleep
For all men's blood is red,
Nor do we lick to poor man's sore
Nor drink the tear he shed,
For king and knave must have a grave
And poorest are the dead.

Sands is quoting a well-known Ulster saying, used by the guerrilla fighter Ernie O'Malley for the title of his memoirs.[19] The origin of the phrase is confused. The most common version is that "it is easy to sleep on another man's wound," indicating that people are naturally cowards who prefer to sleep on the misfortunes of others than to sacrifice their own comforts in order to salve the wound. Another version comes from the sixteenth-century Fermanagh poet Eochaidh Ó hEoghus, who wrote that, "it is *hard* to sleep upon a friend's wound."[20] Ó hEoghus was referring to the wound of oppression, and to the natural impulse one feels to oppose the oppression of friends and comrades, rather than to sleep comfortably on the knowledge that the wound is not inflicted directly on oneself. It is fitting that Sands used the image of another man's wound, in all of its confused etymology. The screws and the British authorities find it all too easy to sleep on the prisoners' wounds, damages that they had themselves inflicted. The prisoners, on the other hand, were *not* able to sleep on the wounds of others and that is why they became political prisoners. A starker contrast could hardly be drawn between the unjust and oppressive violence of the state and the necessary liberating violence of the freedom fighter.

Sands puts a "torturing" prison warder at the center of this section of the poem. When the IRA executes the warder, a public cry goes up.

> *And he had tortured men no less*
> *For he was such a screw.*
> *Yet! Whinging voices cried aloud*
> *What did this poor man do?*
> *He only done what madmen done*
> *Upon the silent Jew.*

What more absolute contrast could Bobby draw than that of the Roman/screw and Christ/blanketman? He has the audacity to put the blanketman alongside the tortured Jew in Dachau. (Later, Fidel Castro would go further when he declared Sands and his fellow hunger strikers' sacrifice vastly *more* profound than that of Christ.)

The other main character, of course, is the blanketman himself. Here, Sands repeats his imagery of the tomb and, again, of the sacrifice of Christ.

> *Blessed is the man who stands*
> *Before his God in pain.*
> *And on his back a cross of woe*
> *His wounds a gaping shame.*
> *For this man is a son of God*
> *And hallowed be his name.*

As does Wilde in his poem, Sands describes in grim detail the brutal conditions of the H-Blocks. The grimness is increased by the obvious use of Wilde's poetic patterns and language, since Wilde was speaking of a time long past, when people would expect "Dickensian" or "Victorian" conditions. Yet here were the same conditions reappearing in the "modern" Britain of 1980! Moreover, to the dire conditions from Wilde are added the special conditions of the H-Blocks: the mirror search ("They grab your legs like wooden pegs and part them till they split") and the no-wash protest.

Finally, Sands returns to the subject of death. He compares death and its consequences for the prisoner, already in his "tomb," with that of the torturing screw.

> *He [the screw] will lie within the grave,*
> *The grave he dug with pain,*
> *And pain of those who wear no clothes*
> *And he dug it with disdain.*
> *So there he lies 'neath earthen skies*
> *In everlasting shame.*

Yet,

> *Endless is the fate of we*
> *Who fight within the gloom,*
> *For we have been imprisoned,*
> *Since conceived, within the womb,*
> *But freedom's fruit will blossom too*
> *In the darkness of the tomb.*

Perhaps it is this focus, his gaze upon the death of the blanketman and, ultimately, upon his own death as the only release from imprisonment, that is most frightening.

> *He stared upon nightmarish walls*
> *As if they held the key*
> *To some dark secret of his soul*
> *That would not set him free,*
> *That hidden cleft through which but death*
> *May find tranquillity.*

Yet, equally, there is another way out of the "darkness of the tomb": through the admiration of the people who are in the midst of liberation struggle. Sands not only returns to the theme of his earlier poem, "The Window of My Mind," where freedom is achieved by escaping into a higher mental plane, he also expresses the central impulse that has maintained him over all of these years as a freedom fighter and a prisoner. The one thing that he values over all else is the admiration of his community, whether in jail or outside, in short, *"the people."*

They call us "cons" to right their wrongs
They do it with a pen.
They call us "crims" to suit the whims
Of politics, my friend.
But they can call us what they want
For the people call us Men.

Sands is departing from Wilde's central theme, that *all* men are equally guilty. We *all* kill the thing we love. Richard Ellman, in his epic biography of Wilde, writes that the "Ballad of Reading Gaol" has "a divided theme: the cruelty of the doomed murderer's crime, the insistence that such cruelty is pervasive; and the greater cruelty of his punishment by a guilty society."[21] Ellman goes on to indicate that Wilde is motivated partly by his own feelings of guilt over his homosexuality and his destructive relationships with a succession of young men. Rather than expressing the guilt of the condemned as a vehicle to uncover the greater crime of the state, Sands is unequivocal in naming the good and the bad, the right and the wrong.

Bobby recited the "Crime of Castlereagh" several times in H3. Despite its length, he always got wild rounds of applause. The men waited in anticipation for one line where, after the prison warder dies, he gets the epitaph, "Here lies a stinking screw."

They shouted and banged their pisspots in appreciation. Brutal as it seems, it was what they wanted to hear. It was a prison thing but it was more than the simple gut reaction that Johnny Cash got when he sang to the prisoners in San Quentin, "I shot a man in Reno, just to watch him die." The *execution* of the screw gave them a feeling that they could recover something from those who had tried so hard to dehumanize them.

● ● ●

By August, Cardinal Ó Fiaich announced that there had been a "breakthrough" in his talks with the British authorities. Yet hopes that a settlement was imminent were quashed in a September seventeenth meeting when Atkins told Ó Fiaich bluntly that the British would not negotiate special category status.

In public, neither the cardinal's office nor the Northern Ireland office would confirm that the meeting took place.[22] When he flew to Rome for a month-long World Synod of Bishops, the cardinal released a press statement in which he tried to hold out hope. He told the press that "the H-Block impasse could be solved in the context of a general prison reform in Ireland regarding prison dress and prison work . . . However, we have failed so far to secure any substantial changes on these two central issues but our proposals have not been rejected."[23] Privately, Ó Fíach told the Republican Movement that the meetings had reached an unsatisfactory end.[24]

Danny Morrison had to take the bad news into the jail. The Dark knew that Morrison had seen the cardinal. He also knew that there had been high hopes of an agreement. So the blanketmen sent the Dark off to see Morrison in hope that they might finally hear something of the "brown bags." Hughes went to the visit hoping for good news. Morrison gave him a King Edward cigar and the Dark lit it and let out a breath of heavy smoke.

"What's the craic?" he asked Morrison.

"They shut the door in the cardinal's face. [Atkins] practically threw him out and the cardinal's shattered."

"What happens now?" asked the Dark.

"I don't know. What are you going to do?"

Hughes knew exactly what he was going to do. They had only agreed to delay a hunger strike to let the cardinal try his hand. Now, he would return to the original plan:

> By this stage, my main objective was to end this bloody protest. Men were beginning to crack up. It was getting far too much. So from the initial objective of giving the outside an issue to build on, my main objective now was to end the conditions that the men were in. And I believed we had done enough for the political issue on the outside. The objective now was to end the protest.

Hughes told Danny Morrison to get prepared for a hunger strike. Morrison objected but he did not push.

On the way back to H3 the Dark saw all the gaunt faces staring at him out the windows as he made his way to the entrance of the H. He tried not to look because he knew he had nothing for them. He went straight to his cell and Bobby was at the window right away. Hughes told Sands how Ó Fiaich's initiative had collapsed. Then he repeated what he'd told Morrison: they would go on hunger strike.

Bobby immediately agreed.

"Well, we've got no alternative now," he told the Dark.

All afternoon and into the night they discussed the hunger strike. They discussed when and how to start it, how to choose who went on it, and the strategy for the strike itself. Every now and then, if they wanted a third opinion, Hughes went to the other side of his cell to talk through the pipe with Jake Jackson. But, "It was largely myself and Bobby were the only two people that was making any sort of decisions."

That night the Dark got up to the door and announced that he wanted volunteers for a hunger strike. The men received his words with a deathly silence. They had talked about this and thought about it. Now the time had come to cross the Rubicon. Bobby shouted the announcement to the other blocks in Irish. Whether for it or against it, the men were relieved.

"At least they could see an end to it, one way or the other."[25]

Chapter Twenty

Hunger Strike

A fter the breakdown of negotiations with the Thatcher government, Bobby sent out documents to each block instructing them to debate the impending hunger strike. The exercise was really more about building consensus than debate. The consensus was that they had given Cardinal Ó Fiaich more than enough time. It was past time for a hunger strike.[1]

Sands and Hughes asked for volunteers. They only wanted six but within a few days they got a hundred and forty-eight. Now, they had to choose a final list of strikers. Hughes says "it was very, very hard . . . very, *very* hard to pick people." The volunteer had to have the right mental attitude to follow the course to the end. He had to be physically healthy, to last as long as possible to build up pressure on the government. Bobby wrote a personal letter to each volunteer telling him to seriously consider whether he was *really* willing to continue with the protest through great pain and until death. The letter was so hard-hitting that many volunteers took it personally, thinking that they were being put off volunteering. A few dropped out.[2]

The OCs debriefed each volunteer and drew up a physical and psychological profile. Then, Hughes and Sands made a shortlist, ruling out anyone who was physically or psychologically questionable or who had a past history that might harm the public relations aspect of the protest. Sean McKenna, a prisoner from South Armagh, was rejected because he was physically frail. Joe McDonnell was ruled out because, as a teenager, he had been convicted of a petty robbery. Bik MacFarlane was unsuitable because he had bombed a Protestant pub, an offense that the media would surely exploit to harm their public image.

They agreed that naming six hunger strikers, one from each county in the north, would widen public support. Then, they decided to include a seventh, the same number who signed the Proclamation of the Irish Republic in 1916. Symbolism was thick in the air.

The decision to take one volunteer from each county caused the Dark's only real argument with Bobby during their whole time together in the H-Blocks. They had talked about going on the strike together, with Bik MacFarlane taking over as OC. But the decision to make a geographic spread made that impossible, since both Bobby and the Dark were from County Antrim, which encompasses all of West Belfast. The issue had to be resolved at a staff meeting during mass. The staff—including Sands, Hughes, MacFarlane, and Jake Jackson—confirmed that one volunteer from each northern county would start the hunger strike together on a specified date. Two more "stand-by emergency squads" of six or seven each would be ready to join them whenever it was most strategically useful, probably when the first group neared death. At this point Hughes told Sands that he would not be going on the strike. Instead, he would be the new OC.

Bobby exploded.

"I'm on this hunger strike, end of story," he told Hughes.

"No, you're not," replied the Dark.

"You should not go on hunger strike. You should remain here in charge and I'll go on hunger strike."

"I'm the OC and I made my own decision," replied Hughes. "I'm going to go ahead with it and carry it out. I'm going on the hunger strike and you're taking over."

Bobby argued hotly but he finally gave in. Then they got back to discussing *who else* would go on the strike.[3] Sean McKenna was a problem. He came from an impeccable Republican background, having been interned in 1971 when he was just seventeen years old and now as OC of H5. Normally, he would have been a clear favorite for the first seven hunger strikers. But he had medical problems after physical maltreatment during his arrests.[4] Bobby wrote to tell him that he was not going on hunger strike. McKenna would hear nothing of it. He kept sending messages to Hughes, insisting that he should be on the protest. The argument wore on for weeks.

Another argument involved the prisoners from the INLA. John Nixon, their OC, insisted that there should be two INLA men on the strike. Hughes said there would be just one.

On October 4,[5] Bobby wrote to the leadership that they had pared down the list to twenty-one, enough for three "waves" of seven strikers each. But they were still unclear about the order in which they would start their strikes. Among the first seven "to be confirmed later" were Brendan Hughes, Tom McFeeley, Tommy McKearney, and Raymond McCreesh.

Bobby had already sent out a comm with a statement announcing the hunger strike but he requested that the movement hold the statement. He and Hughes felt that it would be cynical to announce the strike without a date and a final list of participants. They also feared that "perhaps we would prompt the authorities to move men to different and isolated blocks before we finalize." This concern came out in a strange incident a few days later. Hughes told Alex Reid that the hunger strike was imminent. Reid pleaded with him to call it off. He asked for more time, suggesting that they could resurrect the talks with Thatcher. But Hughes insisted that it would go ahead. Reid, in desperation, asked to see someone else.

"You can talk to Bobby," said Hughes.

On October 7,[6] Bobby met Reid. Ecclesiastical visits were held in small rooms, without the usual screws hovering about. It was one time when a priest and his parishioner could have a bit of privacy and a chat about something personal. When Reid got to the visiting room he had to wait a half an hour. Finally, they brought Sands in. As usual, Reid had a packet of cigarettes lying beside him. He offered Bobby one and laid the pack on the table. Reid immediately asked him to postpone the hunger strike. Cardinal Ó Fiaich was in the process of making some new proposals and he personally wanted them to postpone while he pursued them with Thatcher.

"We're doing our best. Hold your fire," he told Sands.

Bobby replied that events had overtaken him. The authorities had intercepted a comm about the hunger strike and they knew their plans. If they didn't move quickly the authorities could use the information against them by shifting key prisoners to different wings to disrupt their strategy. If he agreed to a postponement, the whole protest could collapse and *he* would be to blame.

Reid argued on. He felt that it was his Christian duty to stop the prisoners from bringing further harm on themselves unless there was no other alternative. But as the conversation wore on Bobby became more and more distressed. After an hour of intense discussion, says Reid, Sands "went into a state of shock." He held his hands beside his face and began to shake uncontrollably. His mouth was open and trembling. Then, his whole body began to shake. "He really lost control." Reid felt that Bobby reacted this way because he knew that he was confronted with a reasonable proposition but he could not bring himself to respond positively. Despite Bobby's clear agitation, Reid argued his case for another fifteen to twenty minutes. Sands continued to tremble but he would not give in to Reid's appeals. Finally, Reid stopped. "This isn't fair to the man to go on with him in that state," he thought.

He left the meeting feeling very "sad" and "annoyed." He felt that "we were lost, that there was nothing we could do." As he passed by some warders, he heard one say, "He's been in there for an hour and a half!"

Reid went into the prison car park for the minivan back to Belfast. As he waited, he began to feel quite ill. Within days, he was rushed to the hospital. He spent some time recovering and then his superiors sent him on leave to Italy. It was the end, for now, of his quietly determined work on behalf of peace and humanity in his community.[7]

Alex Reid is a persuasive man. It is hard not to believe him.[8] Yet his description of Bobby's behavior in that fateful meeting is so out of character that it is hard to *explain* why he acted as he did. Brendan Hughes, for one, finds Reid's story to be "absolutely unbelievable."

"I don't know what words were said to Father Reid from Bobby, but Bobby was probably more staunch than I was. Bobby told Father Reid the hunger strike was going ahead, and that was it."

According to Hughes, Sands came back from the meeting with Reid in a confident state. There was no sign of panic. He was just as staunch as ever. A few days later, Bobby expressed his commitment in a comm to Liam Og. Referring to the visit, he noted that Cardinal Ó Fiaich had asked them to postpone their hunger strike, but, "we won't, unless we get a positive guarantee that would be satisfactory to us."[9]

While Hughes is convincing in his assessment of Bobby's state of mind, there is evidence to support Reid's recollection. The journalist who visited Sands in October 1979 gave a similar description of how "his hands shook and his whole body trembled" throughout their visit.[10] Although other prisoners have described his confident demeanor on visits, perhaps this broke down when he was under certain kinds of physical or mental stress. Reid may have misinterpreted Bobby's trembling as a sign of uncertainty about the hunger strike, while it actually had other physiological origins.

It is true, however, that comms *were* caught and that the tactics of authorities were causing some concern to Hughes and Sands. On October 21, Bobby wrote to "Liam Og" that they had been experiencing "tight searches" and had lost some comms.[11] Bobby indicated that they were worried about the strategies of the authorities toward the impending strike. He noted that the number one governor came into the block on the twentieth with two visitors who "sounded like Englishmen," although "nothing [was] said." He then opined that, "I can't get any indication whether or not the screws are well prepared for this . . . either they're keeping very tight or they aren't prepared. I'm not sure which is the case."

Bobby was now writing several comms a day to his outside contact, "Liam Og" (Tom Hartley), who passed them on to the movement leadership. He got several comms in return. Sometimes, he wrote directly to Gerry Adams.[12] Brendan Hughes was still using priests to get messages to the movement but Bobby felt that such channels were not good enough. Constant and precise communication was absolutely necessary. On October 4, he sent a comm to "Liam Og" about the "confusion" of their communications. He had got four different comms that morning with contradictory contents. He suggested that they step up Marie Moore's system of communication.

"I want contact with the [Sinn Féin] center every day," he told Liam Og.

Bobby requested more names of females to use for passing comms.

"Need several addresses," he wrote, "more if possible, or the screws will hamper visiting passes."

He also suggested that two leading activists in the Sinn Féin center, Danny Morrison and Joe Austin, should visit the prison twice a week to discuss business that was too sensitive to be included in comms.

Bobby explained why the prisoners had difficulties reading and responding to comms.

"Understand and bear with us if you don't get fast replies as it stands. The boys have to swallow, then vomit the comms back up. It doesn't always work, plus some of our comms are just going out as we get yours and often our opinion changes upon your advice or information and leads to contradictions at times."[13]

A week later, Bobby was still not satisfied. He had only received "the first twelve girls' names and addresses" and he wanted the rest. Lest there be any hiccups with the new visitors, he reminded Liam Og to make sure they had "good ID" or they would not get in and, "also, they must understand how we pass and get comms."[14]

Sands was concerned that the authorities would isolate the hunger strikers once the protest began. While they were on the wing, he could send out information about how the strike was affecting them. But the more effective the propaganda, the more likely they would be moved: "it is *that* which will move them."[15] Moreover, they had heard talk about hunger strike contingency plans and worried that the authorities might isolate the hunger strikers right away. If they were isolated in H3, they would probably be put in B-wing and could shout across to prisoners in C-wing. But the authorities might use wing shifts to "keep us out of [C-wing] for important periods." Worse, if they moved the hunger strikers to the prison hospital they might have to revert to priests for information, and Bobby Sands had no trust of priests.

• • •

On October 10, the "H-Block Information Center" in Belfast announced that a hunger strike would begin on October 27. Written by Bik MacFarlane and Tommy McKearney, the announcement reasserted the prisoners' demand that they be granted "as of right . . . the status of political prisoners." This went beyond the five demands, although it left open the possibility that a solution based on the five demands could be interpreted in a way that neither side would lose face. The announcement recited the history of their struggle for political status and the hardships they had endured on the blanket. Despite the efforts of "many individuals, religious figures, political organization, and sections of the media" to resolve the H-Block protest, the statement said, "the British government has remained intransigent and displayed vindictive arrogance in dealing with the problem." Asserting that "every channel has now been exhausted," the statement concluded with the chilling announcement:

> *We declare that political status is ours of right and we declare*
> *that from Monday, October 27, 1980, a hunger strike by a*
> *number of men representing H-Blocks 3, 4, and 5 will commence.*

Our widely recognized resistance has carried us through four years of immense suffering and it shall carry us through to the bitter climax of death, if necessary.[16]

Even at this late stage, the declaration referred vaguely to "a number of men" going on the strike. Despite the looming date for commencement of the hunger strike, the process of finalizing the first seven names was still dragging on. It was not until three days after the announcement that Bobby confirmed Nixon as the INLA's representative. He also listed Kieran Doherty in the first seven[17] but wrote another comm later that day that placed him in the *second* group who would replace the first seven.

Two days later, the situation was confused again. The Dark finally gave in to Sean McKenna's ongoing pleas to be included among the first seven. Bobby wrote Gerry Adams that "we received a strong plea from Sean McKenna, OC, H5, to be reconsidered for H/S . . .We were forced to drop Raymond McCreesh."[18]

Bobby did not know it, but *that* decision would utterly change his life.

Meanwhile, a discussion was going on with the women in Armagh Jail about their participation. As IRA volunteers who had also been on protest, they wanted to participate alongside the men. Some blanketmen objected to this with arguments ranging from the sexist to the practical. Sands and Hughes favored bringing women onto the hunger strike on the grounds that, ". . . Armagh must be allowed to act in solidarity, to refuse them would be insulting." But they were concerned about how the women might be manipulated by the authorities, the press, and clergy. They were against bringing them on at the start of the hunger strike. Bobby argued that,

> *We don't wish to have them on H/S too soon. We want them well out of danger, for we believe to have any of them in the danger area is endangering the men from two points. 1. Distracting from their badly needed publicity. 2. People may say if the girls are in danger, if we can't save the men, save the girls.*[19]

Gerry Adams suggested that the women should join the strike "midway." Sands and Hughes agreed, writing, "We feel that if the girls come on, it should be between twenty-five and thirty-three days. This should depend on the then prevailing condition of strikers and state of propaganda and publicity."[20] They kept open the possibility of the women going on a hunger and thirst strike, arguing that,

> *There is also the thirst strike aspect which we view as dangerous but again as a big punch at the end of the last round . . . At the very least the threat of such an action would carry weight. The men going on H/S understand the situation and by no means do they or would they ever look to the girls, and such a tactic, as something that would save them. But we are agreed that as a tactic it may prove worthwhile.*[21]

• • •

As they neared the hunger strike, Bobby told Liam Og that, "I believe that we have the resolve in our seven comrades that will be needed to see this through to its bitter end." He also noted that the screws were under increasing strain, as indicated by "the sort of slobbering they are doing." He also noted that "the governors are very inquisitive in regard to the H/S and as usual they are trying to pull the wool over our eyes with wee fibs."[22]

A major boost to morale resulted from a clever plan that Hughes and Sands devised. They moved a blanketman, Sean Glas, in with the conforming prisoners to convince them to go on protest temporarily, to strengthen their numbers before the hunger strike began. By "a combination of cajoling, intimidation and appealing to their better senses" his efforts bore fruit. Three days after the hunger strike was announced, Bobby wrote that one hundred and thirty men had returned from the conforming blocks and joined the blanket protest.[23]

Mobilizing public support for the hunger strikers was largely outside of the prisoners' power. Yet Bobby continued to organize his propaganda factory, with the prisoners churning out letters to public figures. He invited members of the press to visit the prison and instructed the prisoners to make sure that their families and friends joined in direct protests.

"We know that if we can generate the urgency and activate the people, that we can achieve victory. The boys are spending the entirety of their visits impressing this point on their families."[24]

On October 13, Sands sent out names of two "stand-by emergency squads" of seven hunger strikers each. Each group would be held in reserve, to come onto the hunger strike at key moments when their addition might put public pressure on the British government. The second and third groups of hunger strikers included names that would later become better known than most of the men in the first group: Mickey Devine, Kieran Doherty, Ray McCreesh, Patsy O'Hara, and Kevin Lynch.[25]

Toward the start of the hunger strike, everyone was tense. There were rumors that Cardinal Ó Fiaich might return from Rome to talk with the British government. Rumors flew about moves and countermoves by the authorities and the prisoners. Bobby wrote to Gerry Adams that "there are rumors of the block orderlies being moved to Crum. Rumors of screws going to resign, rumors of not caring less, and rumors of hospital wing in H3 being used as place for strikers."[26]

Meanwhile, problems with communications still plagued them. On October 24, with just three days to go, Bobby wrote again about confusion over comms. He also needed another radio to keep up with what was happening during the hunger strike.[27] Then, the authorities sent Raymond MacCartney, the hunger striker from County Derry, to the punishment cells. He was likely to remain there until the hunger strike started a few days later. Bobby was not too worried, though, because he "took precautions to ensure he understands to go ahead on Monday morning."[28]

There were other indications of disorganization. In a second comm on October 24, Sands requested that the outside leadership send him "immediate advice" about whether salt would prevent delirium or prolong the hunger strike. Referring to Danny Morrison's advice that they would not get word about the effects of salt for a few days, Bobby revealed his displeasure. "Realize Danny's busy but can we have word in on bus tomorrow."[29]

• • •

After the hunger strike announcement, some clergy strongly criticized British intransigence. Father Denis Faul, a junior clergyman who administered to the prisoners and felt able to speak more openly about the negotiations than Cardinal Ó Fiaich or Bishop Daly, blamed the British for the failed negotiations. He advised the British government to take advantage of the roads that had been "left open" by Ó Fiaich. He added, "It is very sad that the recently arrived Englishmen who have had no knowledge or experience of Ireland before their appointments here should refuse so abruptly the leaders of the Irish church and then precipitate a situation which, if it goes to a tragic result, will bring about decades of bitterness between the Nationalist Irish who have suffered generations of ill-treatment and the British people."

Faul was saying publicly what Alex Reid had told Danny Morrison in private: that the British had "slammed the door in the clergy's face."[30] But he added that it was imperative for the two parties to restart the negotiations in order to avoid death in the prisons and on the streets.

On October 23, with just four days to go, Ó Fiaich left Rome for a meeting in London. The cardinal returned on the understanding that a document had been drafted that could solve the conflict, including a concession that would allow the prisoners to wear their own clothes instead of the prison uniform. But when the cardinal and Bishop Daly got to the government office the document was not ready. They waited. Over an hour they waited until Ó Fiaich began to get the distinct impression that "something fishy was going on." At one embarrassing point the hosts decided to offer their guests a drink. Ó Fiaich asked for an Irish whiskey but they had none. They had to send a man out to find a bottle, which amused the cardinal during his wait.

Finally the British brought in the statement. Ó Fiaich told Reid that he "could detect a certain paragraph that didn't read right." It was the one about clothing. Ó Fiaich later heard that a London radio station had leaked a story that morning saying that the prisoners would be allowed their own clothing. There was a fuss from some quarter, whether from Unionists or from a branch of the security forces or prison service, and a rush to redraft a section.

"You could detect it from the wording," Ó Fiaich told Reid.

When the British authorities released their proposal, the clothing concessions were substantially more limited than the clergymen expected. Atkins told the press that the prisoners would *not* be allowed to wear their own clothes but would wear government-issue "civilian-type clothing." Prison uniforms would be "substituted by civilian-type uniforms." The inclusion of the word "uniform" was deliberate, to allay fears by Unionists and prison officers that the government was capitulating to the prisoners' demands. Nonetheless, leading Ulster Unionist, James Molyneaux, called the provision of civilian-type clothing "clearly a cave-in to blackmail." Ian Paisley said that it "can only be viewed as a surrender to the H-Block protesters."

Ó Fiaich refused to comment at first.[31] The next day, however, he and Bishop Daly said jointly that they were "deeply disappointed that [the British offer] stops short of what is demanded in the situation." Bishop Daly practically accused Atkins of bad faith, claiming that "the phrase 'civilian clothes' was *always* understood to mean the prisoners' own clothing."[32] The clergymen said that they had met Atkins in a "last-minute effort" to prevent Monday's hunger strike. Although they stopped short of apportioning blame, their exasperation was evident. Their proposals were hardly revolutionary and a generous gesture on clothes and work could have produced "the long-awaited solution to the dreadful H-Blocks impasse that has now entered its fifth year."[33]

In one last plea, the clergymen called on the seven men's relatives to convince them to call off their hunger strike and the *Irish News* echoed this call in an editorial. Yet the paper did not hold out much hope that the hunger strikers would heed it, especially since Atkins had ended his announcement about the "civilian-type clothes" with a clumsy and incredibly insensitive confirmation that his government would not intervene to try and save the hunger strikers' lives and, "If they choose to starve to death they may well die."[34]

Back in H3, Sands and Hughes studied Atkins's statement. Bobby led a discussion that lasted all night. The clear consensus was that the British proposal was not even close to sufficient for them to call off the hunger strike. To the contrary, it was a cynical move by the British government, a last gasp effort to undermine the hunger strike without effecting real change. Bobby viewed the move as a sign of weakness on the part of the British government. The next day, the prisoners bluntly refused the government's offer of "civilian-type clothing." In one of his last press statements before he replaced Brendan Hughes as officer in command, Sands accused the government of engaging in,

> ... *a cruel piece of teasing and political brinkmanship in an attempt to defuse the momentum and growing support for the blanketmen. They know that the resolution of certain issues will end the H-Block crisis but they continue to avoid them and, to us, they remain suspect ... We the Republican prisoners of H-Blocks 3, 4 and 5, reject as meaningless the substitute, by the British government, of prison issue clothing for prison issue uniform. The wearing of our own clothes we regard as a basic human right*

and as only one of our five demands . . . We are not criminals and we are ready and willing to meet an agonizing death on hunger strike to establish we are political prisoners.[35]

Bobby told Liam Og that he was extremely confident that Atkins's offer to give "civilian-type" clothes was a sign of weakness, and that they could win everything if they just held out. Bobby counseled applying further pressure and told Liam Og to tell the movement to get the message to "the people in the districts" that "with more active support and pressure we can badger them totally." To drive the point home, he ended the comm, "P.S. Screws morale at all-time low following concessions bid yesterday. They'll be sickened before it's all over."[36]

Bobby was spoiling for a fight. Now he thought it was a fight they could win. The night before the hunger strike began the men on Bobby's wing had a singsong. They called it *"Fleadh Ceoil Buach"* ("The Victorious Singsong"). As soon as the lights went out, the Dark got up and gave a long and moving speech on unity, sacrifice, and victory. This was the final battle, he told them. Some men on the wing would probably die before the battle was won. But he said not to worry, that there were casualties in any war. "Whenever you went on any army job outside you ran the risk of dying," he told them. "The same applies in here." He spoke about how they had decided on their course of action because there was no alternative and "with full knowledge of the Brit enemy's callousness toward us." He asked the other prisoners to pray for God to give them strength to go through their course to the end if necessary. He thanked the rest of the prisoners for taking their brave stand in front of the world and said that if they kept their unity inside, along with a united people outside, surely they would achieve victory. He finished off with a phrase that the others had often heard him say before,

"Be true to your people and be faithful to the Republic."

The prisoners sat glued to the Dark's voice, many of them tearful and fearful of things to come. Colm Scullion had little doubt that the Dark would go all the way if necessary to win their goal of political status.

Then Tommy McKearney spoke a few words. He thanked the men for giving him the privilege of teaching them about the history of the Irish struggle. He ended his short speech with a phrase that the Spartan mothers told their sons before going to battle: "Come home with your shield—or on it."

Somebody shouted, "Sure, we'll be carrying you shoulder-high round
The Moy!"

Tommy laughed. "In a coffin," he replied.[37]

Then Bobby started the singsong.

• • •

Monday morning, October 27, 1980. When the warders came around with
breakfast, seven blanketmen announced that they were not eating because
they were on hunger strike for political status. The Dark's cellmate Muffles got embarrassed to eat so Hughes turned and faced the wall while he
ate. "But, God help him," says Hughes, "he wasn't eating that much."
That morning, Sands took over as officer in command of the blanketmen.
Bik MacFarlane became PRO.

The Dark decided to test Dr. Emerson and the warders by requesting
a physical examination. The PO said that he could only go to the doctor's
office "with prison trousers or prison underwear or naked."[38] Bobby
wanted the examinations to go ahead because he was worried that the
administration would start rumors that the hunger strikers were eating;
he needed daily weights as evidence against them. This public relations
threat was a greater concern to him than putting on prison trousers.

"On Friday morning I'm sending the boys out to surgery regardless of
what they have to endure," he informed Liam Og. He requested that the
movement put out a public statement about how the hunger strikers were
being forced to wear prison garb in order to get a medical examination.

The authorities harassed the hunger strikers in other petty ways. They
put their salt on the dinner plates, where the hunger strikers had to pick
it away from the food. They left plates of food in their cells until they
replaced them with the next meal. They left their supper in the cells
overnight. The volume of noise suddenly rose. The vacuum was in constant use and the screws enthusiastically battered on the doors first thing
in the morning.

"Otherwise," wrote Sands, "the boys are in good form. You know they
have to watch their cellmates eating and stick the stench when they go to
the toilet. There is also a lack of air in the cells. Continually dark. The poes
are unbelievably filthy."[39]

On the day the hunger strike began, Bobby was still rearranging its
details. They decided that if someone "dropped off," the next man on the

list would immediately take his place. Thus, seven men would remain on hunger strike at all times (the women were considered separately).[40]

Soon, there were unwelcome guests. On the fourth day of the hunger strike, the assistant governor informed McKearney and Hughes that under no circumstances would they get any concessions. As far as he was concerned, they could lie there and die if they wished. To finish, in a fit of pettiness, he informed them that they were now on hunger strike just three days, as the first day did not count.

"Proper little dickhead!" was Bik MacFarlane's assessment.[41]

Every night the governor came to each hunger striker's cell and asked him if he was continuing his protest. All he got was a "yes" for an answer and a refusal to answer anything else.

Nearly as bad was Father Toner's visit to Brendan Hughes. Toner wanted him to see a man whose son was once on hunger strike for thirty days. But he let it slip that the purpose of the visit would be to persuade Hughes to end his hunger strike. Hughes angrily sent Toner packing.

Other annoyances persisted. Warders made snide remarks. One always talked about food. Another shouted that he had some mahogany if anyone wanted it for coffins.[42] One day, as Hughes came back from his check-up, the warder shouted, "Bring out your dead!"

On the morning of Halloween, the fifth day of the hunger strike, the men were finally allowed to visit the doctor wearing their towels. But there were still petty problems. After getting their weight and blood pressure taken, they were left standing in an area between two grille doors for an hour before their examinations.

Brendan Hughes was already having heavy sweats and the doctor asked for a urine sample. When the medical officer[43] dipped the litmus paper into the sample he was not pleased with the color. "It shouldn't be like this," he said. Bobby wrote, "Dark is feeling weak, has constant headaches, has pains in his chest above his heart on both sides."[44] Three days later, Hughes still had a headache. Bobby reported that, "he looked haggard, but fairly steady on his feet."[45] Four days later, Hughes lost his headache. In its place, he had a kidney infection.[46]

As Sands feared, in early November the warders started spreading the rumor that some of the hunger strikers were eating.[47]

On November 4, Bobby got word that the warders were painting B-wing of H3 and that the hunger strikers would be moved there on the following Wednesday. He tried to get them moved to the hospital wing where communication would be easier.[48] Two days later, instead of moving the hunger strikers into B-wing, they moved Bobby's wing there and put the hunger strikers in the hospital wing. At the last minute, they took down the notice that read "Medical Staff Only." Bobby told Liam Og, "Rest assured, comrade, that they will say it is not a hospital wing but an ordinary wing that has windows, beds and more humane conditions."[49]

Later that night, Sands contacted the seven by shouting across and found that they were each in separate cells. "Seven boys are sound, no problems," he told Liam Og.[50] After the shouting, Bobby organized a singsong to cheer them up. This would be a nightly feature as long as the seven remained in H3. The Dark was not so sure about the concerts. Sometimes they "put his head away" and he would have rather had peace and quiet.

Early the next afternoon, Bobby began a long comm, explaining that their contact with the hunger strikers would improve and worsen, in cycles, as they were moved from wing to wing. Sands would have contact with the strikers until Wednesday, "then we scrape the barrel for three to four days." Then they would repeat the cycle.[51] Bobby's was worried about colds and flus because they had decided that the hunger strikers should refuse medication. (Bobby had a flu that did not seem to go away.)

"We discussed this before we refused medication," wrote Sands. "The doctor near broke his neck to find out if this was policy. This I feel helped more than anything to get the strikers moved to the hospital wing. We also discovered the damage that drugs could do to men in their condition. (We don't actually know but have basic idea. I'm not prepared to trust the doctor. He'd cut your throat.)"

Communications concerns continued. Bobby wanted ten more names and addresses of visitors for each wing. "You'll have 180 odd visits with center in December," he told Liam Og. "I'll be covering the whole month as I must consider all angles of aftermath." And then, "Back to the leaky comms. This is the crux of the matter comrade, men have to swallow 99 percent of all in-coming comms. They vomit them up on arrival back into cell. This has 40 percent success rate. The other 59 percent have to be passed through body. Body acids eat S/S [stretch-and-seal] (sometimes, and, especially, on country men. Ha!). (Dear God.) Anyway, to deflect this, put two light layers of silver paper around comms followed by the usual amount of S/S. Now you know what I've to go through to get a comm, okay. You wouldn't believe half of it."[52]

Each night at 9:00 P.M., Bobby shouted to Brendan Hughes in Irish. The Dark's headaches and dizziness raised another concern. "It's fairly rough for him to stand at the door shouting over messages," Bobby wrote to Liam Og. "I'm afraid in case he takes dizzy spells and hits the deck. I'm boxing and scheming other means. We'll see how we go. One way or the other we'll get the essentials." Bobby told Liam Og that he expected the seven to be kept in H3 until their conditions had deteriorated badly. Then, they might be moved to the prison hospital or maybe even to the Musgrave military hospital in Belfast, which would create new obstacles.[53]

• • •

Sunday, November 9, two weeks into the hunger strike, Bobby was in an anxious mood. He would see the hunger strikers during mass and also get a new radio. At mass, Sands saw all of the strikers except Tommy McKearney, who was resting from a cold. He "noticed when we shook hands that all of the boys hands were fairly cold." He made some observations. "Firstly, they're slightly lazy, that is, they're neglecting to mention important wee points." The Dark's kidney infection was gone. Now he had a pain in the testicles from shouting to Bobby every night. Hughes insisted, however, that he had "no real problems at all." Of the others, Tom McFeeley was by far the strongest-looking. "I'd trouble keeping him at peace in Mass," complained Bobby. "He near got us all excommunicated!"

But a problem was looming. "My personal opinion is that out of the six I seen, Sean was looking by far the worst . . . "

The seven were getting books and newspapers, although Sands noted that, "Screws are slobbering to us about them taking books (idiots)." The governors were coming in regularly and, according to Hughes, one of them was quite cheeky. Bobby wrote that, "The Dark told him that he was only a wee boy, the screw wasn't at all pleased." But, unlike the "cheeky" governor, most of the warders were pretty nice to them. Sands advised the seven to take advantage of the situation: "In general, the screws are overly-nice. Some are even crawling rather pathetically. I told the boys to request letters and pens."

Toward the end of his comm, Bobby suddenly interjected an excited note, "Dear God! Mrs. Dale just spoke! Weakly but audibly. Greatly thrilled and somewhat relieved!"[54]

• • •

As the hunger strike wore on, public pressure mounted on the British government to reach a settlement. Supporters plastered the countryside with "Smash H-Block." There were daily marches and protests, and constant confrontations between young people and the army/police. As the hunger strikers weakened, the crowds got bigger. An opinion poll conducted by the Irish radio and television network found that half of the southern Irish population wanted the British to grant immediate political status.[55]

On Monday, December 1, three women from Armagh jail joined the hunger strike: Mairead Farrell, Mary Doyle, and Mairead Nugent. The next day, the seven men were moved to the prison hospital.[56] Their new doctor in the hospital, Dr. Ross, visited them every day and sometimes stayed with them, speaking for hours.

The strike was moving toward its decisive stage. Bobby asked Liam Og to send him information about the "foreplay to settlement" of the 1972 hunger strike, when the Republican prisoners first won special category status.[57]

As the seven hunger strikers got weaker they spent their time in bed. After a few weeks in the prison hospital, some began to have difficulty walking. The Dark was getting weaker by the day. Pictures from the time show him and Raymond McCartney in their hospital beds, their beards and hair long and stringy, and their eyes sunk into their heads like old men. The Dark requested that Bobby be allowed to visit him in the prison hospital. He was surprised when the governor agreed to allow some visits. From then on, Sands came every other day for half an hour. They discussed the situation inside and outside of the jail. Sands told Hughes any news he had about the campaign and the Dark told him about their physical and mental conditions.

As the men got weaker, Doctor Ross came to talk more often. To the Dark's mind, he did everything he could to keep them comfortable. He brought them special mats to ease their bed sores. He gently turned them over now and then to ease their pain. But Bobby scolded Hughes. He said that Ross was trying to get inside of his mind and told the Dark to get him to clear off.

"Bobby didn't trust anyone, anyone at all," explains Hughes. "Especially the screws or anyone in authority there. And especially doctors, especially that doctor because we'd had a bad time with doctors."

• • •

Pressure grew on the British government to reach a settlement. Although Margaret Thatcher proclaimed publicly that she would "never talk to terrorists," her government reopened an old channel of communication with the IRA. A Nationalist businessman from Derry acted as a conduit between the IRA's army council and a "foreign office" man named Michael Oatley (actually an agent of the British MI6 *foreign* intelligence network). The channel was kept secret through layers of go-betweens and the use of pseudonyms. Oatley was known as the "Mountain Climber." Alex Reid's replacement, Father Brendan Meagher, who acted as a go-between, was "the Angel."[58]

Bobby knew about the negotiations in early December but the seven hunger strikers did not. By bringing Meagher into the equation, however, the IRA assured that the southern Irish government and, especially, the Taoiseach Charles Haughey, knew. Meagher was "Haughey's man."[59] His direct contact with the prisoners and, especially, with the hunger strikers, put Haughey in a position to try to "hijack" the negotiations for his own purposes. An obvious conduit of such a parallel negotiation was the moderate Nationalist politician John Hume.[60] Three days into the strike, Hume offered his services as mediator.[61] In early December, Hume met Atkins to try and push a "humanitarian" solution to the H-Block crisis that was based on the European Commission's judgement of the previous June.

Atkins's reaction to Hume was more of the same. In a parliamentary set piece, Atkins arranged for a conservative MP, Paul Marland, to ask him a question in the House of Commons: were the rights and privileges to prisoners clear and understood by prisoners and by public? His answer was designed to show that the government had *already* provided humanitarian prison reforms. Atkins claimed to be setting out the "real facts about the living conditions" open to all prisoners in Northern Ireland. If the seven were striking to demand political status, he said, then that would "differentiate them from all other prisoners" and "to do so would be to legitimize and encourage terrorist activity." On the other hand, the government had made the prison regime more "humane" and "enlightened." Referring to his October twenty-third announcement on "civilian-type clothing," he said that prisoners could wear their own clothes at night and weekends and on visits. Prison work included training and education. As for association, prisoners were already entitled to three hours free association on their wings each weeknight and all day on weekends. Allowances for visits, letters, and parcels were already more generous than the prisoners demanded. And they could already regain lost remission if they stopped their protest and conformed to prison rules.

Bobby was waiting for a legal visit as Atkins spoke. Normally, he would not risk having his radio out. But this was such an important statement that he decided to set it up. As he listened to Atkins, Bobby formed an idea. He had no faith that the Atkins initiative contained anything new. Yet, in a mood to exploit the warders' fears of a British "sell-out," he decided to play it as if this were the beginning of a process that would grant them political status.

When the screw shouted, "Sands for a visit," Bobby quickly took down the radio and put away his writing materials. As he was searched and put on the prison uniform for the visit, Bobby began.

"Well, Ralph, any word of the Hump's statement?"

"Funny you should mention it, young Sands, he's on the box at the minute, reading out a statement telling what's going to happen."

"Did Marland get up and ask him if the public were aware of our rights and privileges?"

"Jeez, I think you're right, I think he did ask him that."

"Atkins didn't mention the five demands and talk about making changes on humanitarian grounds?"

"Funny you should mention it, I think he did say something like that."

"Then did he turn around and say,'We're not going to give them political status or give into the five demands because that would give them too much control in the prison but we're gonna make their regime as humanitarian as we can'?"

"Aye, he did."

Sands related Atkins's statement to the warder in great detail. Then he went to see his solicitor, leaving the shocked screw to relate the story to the others. He had convinced them that Atkins's statement had been pre-approved by the IRA. It was typical of Bobby's devious sense of humor and his ability to take a bad situation and turn it around. Some warders went on sick leave after the Atkins statement, convinced that they had been sold out.[62]

• • •

Atkins's statement was based on a thirty-page document that was written by the NIO. The document was deposited in the House of Commons library and distributed to churchmen and other key people in the north of Ireland.[63] In a public announcement the following day, John Hume publicly welcomed the statement as "an important first step in a process that could lead to a satisfactory solution of the problem . . ." Hume called on the prisoners to stop their hunger strike and he repeated his offer that "my own good offices are available if requested to progress this matter further."[64]

At the same time, Charles Haughey was making his own direct moves to talk to Margaret Thatcher. Several days after the Atkins statement, he announced that Thatcher might come to Ireland within days, not just to talk about the prison crisis but also about the big prize in Anglo-Irish relations: a settlement on the "totality of relations" between Britain and Ireland.[65] In an editorial, the *Irish News* stated that talks between Hume and Atkins provided an opportunity for the British to handle the H-Blocks in a "more humane way." With Haughey's intervention at the highest level, there was now a real hope among moderates across Ireland that a solution could be found to the prison crisis before violence erupted on the streets.

In the wake of this speculation, John Blelloch, a deputy secretary in NIO but also a member of MI5, visited the H-Blocks on Wednesday, December 10. Sands had been expecting a visit from the NIO since Monday and he had requested to be present. But when Blelloch arrived, the prison authorities flatly refused to allow Sands into the prison hospital. Blelloch went into each hunger striker's cell and read out a four-page document that outlined the reforms that would be available to him *if* they abandoned their protest. He said that significant reforms had already been made on each of their five demands. After reading the document, Blelloch left a copy in each man's cell.

Brendan Hughes patiently listened to Blelloch. Then he asked for "negotiations." Blelloch refused to answer any questions. He told Hughes to read the document and "while [the] strike continued there could be nothing done, but if the strike ended perhaps the NIO could see about doing something." Hughes requested that they bring Sands over. The authorities refused while Blelloch was there. At 2:30 that afternoon, however, a warder *did* take Bobby to Brendan Hughes for a briefing. He said that the visit was a "one-off thing from the governor." As Bobby sat beside the Dark in his cell, a medical officer stood in the doorway, trying to listen to everything they said. They whispered so that they would not be overheard.[66]

Hughes showed Sands the document and told him what had happened during Blelloch's visit. He told him how Blelloch had refused to clarify anything. Then he said that John Hume had been in touch with him about opening negotiations and he was not sure what he should do.

Bobby informed the Dark about the secret contact between the movement and the British government. He told Hughes "not to be fooled by [the] morning's events," that there were "better offers in the pipeline." Haughey and Hume were trying to move in on the negotiations and it was of utmost importance to "hold and unite [the hunger] strikers" so that they would not be tricked into a separate and inferior settlement. Given Sean McKenna's worsening condition, Bobby felt that the Blelloch visit was an attempt to "stall for time" so that the NIO could see if the hunger strikers were bluffing and, if possible, push an inferior settlement on them.

Hughes agreed that Blelloch should have spoken to all of the hunger strikers together, along with Sands. They would insist that any future meetings with the NIO include not just the hunger strikers but also their OC. Bobby wrote to Adams, "I made solid arrangements that when they came back only he and I will talk with NIO on demands . . . if we were faced by three or four we'd ask for Bik, okay?"[67]

Bobby said that the Dark was "quick to piece things together." He was "very cool, except for one point." Hughes was "jittery" about what would happen as they neared the stage where someone might die. Bobby told him that they would have to "dig in" regardless of deaths if the British failed to move. Hughes asked how they could tell whether the British were bluffing or just not willing to move. This worried Bobby: it demonstrated a lack of willingness by the Dark to follow hunger strike to the death. At this point, the Dark asked him if he should send out a visit for John Hume, who had asked to see him.

"This gave me a shock," said Bobby.

He replied that no way could they allow Hume or Haughey to "steal the middle ground" and "not to dare sending for him."

What was the purpose of the Blelloch visit? Sands saw it as an attempt to isolate the hunger strikers and limit any eventual settlement; perhaps, even to undermine the parallel talks that were taking place between the IRA and other sections of the British government. From this point on, the threat of splitting the hunger strikers from their command structure at key moments haunted Sands.

That night at 6:45, Father Toner visited Bobby in his cell. He said that he was not satisfied with the Blelloch visit. The NIO had briefed both him and Father Meagher the previous Friday and they had expected more of a package. Toner brought guidelines from Brendan Hughes emphasizing that their response to Blelloch's visit should not be too strong because that might embarrass the NIO from coming back.

Bobby was livid. He had been trying to keep his conversation with Hughes secret and now the Dark had compromised him by discussing their strategy to a priest who they both considered highly untrustworthy.

". . . there's merit in [taking a softer line with the NIO]," Sands confided to Adams, "but now Index knows and so will the Brits."

How could they repair the potential damage? Bobby decided to put out a public statement that would not embarrass the British too much but which showed strength from the prisoners' standpoint. They would say that Blelloch's proposals were "irrelevant to the extreme" but that they indicated British willingness to bargain. To add an element of threat, they repeated that the strike would continue until they reached a satisfactory settlement. Meanwhile, Bobby told Father Toner that the blanketmen were in a militant mood and that he was under pressure to escalate the strike by putting on more men. He wanted to demonstrate their determination to Toner and, through him, to the British. He did not intend to put more men on hunger strike yet, but he asked Adams to leak the story that more men would join the hunger strike if the British did not come back to the jail and talk.[68]

Two days later, things deteriorated to the point that Sands felt he had to apply more pressure on the British. He wrote to Adams,

> We'll put the second squad on, on Tuesday morning . . . I'm thinking of making another addition late in the week—fourteen men to hit them again . . . Basically, it's to maintain pressure and heighten situation sky-high.

The escalation of the hunger strike would, he thought, break the British stalling efforts and the tampering by Hume and Haughey. Bobby was concerned that some of the men were placing too much false hope in these moves:

> Events of this week have been tricky. A second squad was furthermost from our minds on Tuesday, except as threat in bargaining.[69]

Over the weekend, Sean McKenna's physical condition worsened and Bobby accelerated the addition of more hunger strikers from Tuesday to Monday. He increased the number from fourteen to twenty-three and was clearly relieved when he wrote to Gerry Adams later that day,

> I feel a lot better having made move today. The air is now clear and skulduggery removed.

He felt the addition of more hunger strikers had reinvigorated the blanketmen.

> Our movement this morning has brought us down to earth. This is good and the atmosphere is better for it. That is, we're fir pluid aris ["blanket men again"], and not straw-clutchers.

He told Adams to make one point clear to Father Meagher and, through him, to Charles Haughey:

> For us compromise "does not exist." To do so is a recipe for disaster. Better fighting another day than doing that.[70]

● ● ●

Monday's move of adding more men to the hunger strike seemed to have its desired effect. The secret negotiations between the IRA and the British authorities stepped up.[71] On December 18, the hunger strikers met Governor Hilditch and a civil servant. They assembled in the dining room of the prison hospital. Sean McKenna was very weak and they had to wheel him to the canteen in a wheelchair. Bobby Sands was not allowed into the meeting.

According to Hughes, the authorities offered them their own clothes and free association at certain times of the day. The package appeared to be close to their demands. Hughes asked for time to discuss the proposals and the authorities withdrew while they discussed them in the canteen. All seven hunger strikers agreed in principle that the offer was acceptable. Hughes asked for the agreement in writing. The civil servant replied that they would have to go and check.

Hughes continued his daily round to collect details of the physical and mental conditions of the other hunger strikers. When he went to see McKenna, he was close to a coma. McKenna had a request: "Promise me that you won't let me die."

"You have my word," Hughes replied. "I won't let you die. We have the agreement here, we're just holding out for it to be on paper and to have a witness from the Republican Movement."[72]

That afternoon, McKenna slipped in and out of a coma. Hughes went into his cell every couple of hours to check on him. Meanwhile, he waited for the document from the British government. As evening approached, Dr. Ross told him that Sean McKenna only had a couple of hours to live. They were taking him to a real hospital. Hughes got up and went into the corridor. Father Murphy and Father Toner were supporting him by his arms. Hughes looked up the hallway and saw Dr. Ross and the prison orderlies rolling Sean McKenna out on a gurney. Hughes shouted to Ross, "Feed him."

Hughes went around and told the other five that the hunger strike was over. They would have to trust that the written agreement would be acceptable.

Hughes says that Sands arrived in his cell later that night with Father Meagher and the promised document from the British government.

"They were really excited and we hugged each other. I couldn't read the document, my eyesight was gone, and I asked Bobby to read it."

Bobby read parts of it aloud. Hughes asked Father Meagher, "What do you think?"

"It looks good," the priest supposedly replied. "The agreement looks good."

Sands and Meagher stayed with him for about twenty minutes and then they visited the other five hunger strikers. Hughes felt that the mood was "fantastic." Dr. Ross was excited. Paul Lennons, the medical officer who was sympathetic to the hunger strikers, was really excited. Best of all, "the screws were totally dejected because they seen it as, the Brits had given in and we'd won."

The doctor gave them injections of glucose, which hurt because they had no flesh left for the needle to go into. Strengthened by the glucose, the Dark began to think about things. He worried about Sean McKenna. The orderly came in with scrambled eggs and toast, their first meal in fifty-three days.

• • •

Bobby and other prisoners tell a vastly different story, which is supported by eyewitness testimony.[73] The first indication Bobby had that things were moving on the eighteenth was when Governor Hilditch sent for him at 1:00 P.M. Doctor Ross and several warders took him to the governor. The doctor spoke first. He told Sands that Sean McKenna would be beyond the point of no return that day. Some of the warders followed with "a big speech" about how serious the men's conditions were. Then Hilditch spoke.

"If you are playing at brinkmanship you had better pull out now, as it will be too late."

"We are not playing at brinkmanship," replied Sands. "Men will die."

He knew there were secret moves afoot, although exactly what he did not know. The movement had sent comms to let him know that the British government was sending a courier with a document that might be a solution. But Bobby never got the comms until the next day because "the lad had to swallow them." It would not have made any difference because the authorities refused to let Sands go to the hospital, where the drama of negotiations and pressures on Brendan Hughes was unfolding. In the absence of up-to-date information, Bobby tried to be as staunch as possible in front of the governor and to cause a "bit of a flare-up" so that they would see that the only way to avoid deaths was through a settlement. When Bobby left the governor, he was satisfied that he had achieved his purpose.

The next thing he knew, he was taken to the prison hospital at 6:45 in the evening. What he found there shocked him.

> *I saw Index [Father Toner] and Silvertop [Father Murphy] in the corridor as I walked down the wing. There were three cartons of eggs sitting in a doorway. My heart jumped. Dorcha [Brendan Hughes] came out of Tommy McKearney's room and went into Tom [McFeeley]'s room in front of me. Tom was in bed. Raymond*

and Nixie were sitting beside the bed. They were all shattered. Dorcha said, "Did you hear the sceal [news]?" I said, "No." He said it again. I thought Sean was dead. Then he said, "We've got nothing, I called it off." The MO was banging an injection into Tommy. Sean was en route to the hospital. Tom had been against it, wanting to wait and see what Atkins was going to say in the Commons. Dorcha was under the impression that Sean had only twelve hours to live.

The authorities then took Sands around the H-Blocks to tell the other twenty-three hunger strikers to end their protest. Then he went back to his wing in H3.

Bobby was livid. He had been trying to put a staunch face to the British authorities and Brendan Hughes had usurped his authority and ended the hunger strike without achieving their objective. The whole thing had been a big waste of time and emotion. Now, he felt, the blanketmen would emerge from the strike weaker than they had gone into it. A couple of days later, Bobby wrote his true feelings to Gerry Adams.

For what it's worth, comrade, we seen the move coming, but the boys just blew up. We were beat by a few lousy hours which were critical. Dorcha panicked when they rushed Sean to the hospital. If only he had realized that it was the sign that the Brits were moving. Well, that's that.[74]

• • •

Indeed, the Brits *were* moving. Father Meagher was at Aldergrove Airport outside Belfast to meet the Mountain Climber. They sat down to coffee and Oatley pulled out of his briefcase a copy of a British statement that was stamped "Draft." He apologized that it was only a draft and said that the plane with the final document had been delayed. Shortly afterward, he went off and came back with the final document, which he traded for the "draft." He made a few phone calls and then told the priest not to worry: there would be no problem getting the document into the prison.

Meagher took the document to the Clonard Monastery, where he showed it to Gerry Adams and some other top Republicans for their approval.

"It's as full of holes as a sieve," said one of the men, clearly not happy with the document.

Adams felt that "it wasn't a document that I would have negotiated for" but at least it was an advance on the situation before the hunger strike.[75]

They were about to send Meagher into the prison with the document when a door swung open and a man came in, panting, and handed Adams a piece of paper. He read it and then addressed the others in the room.

"The hunger strike's over."

• • •

At about the same time, Secretary of State Humphrey Atkins and two of his officials were waiting at BBC's television center in London. He was about to read a prepared statement about the latest offer to the blanketmen and was apparently waiting for word that an agreement had been achieved. The speech was on the teleprompter. As he waited impatiently, someone went up to him and said, "Secretary of state, there is a telephone call for you."

He took the telephone in an adjacent office and a voice at the other end told him, "They've called it off."

One of Atkins's officials hurried back into the studio and removed the speech from the teleprompter.[76]

• • •

The screws brought Bobby Sands back to his cell in H-Block 3 at a quarter to nine. He immediately told the prisoners around him that he would be starting a new hunger strike. What happened and what they said has already been related at the beginning of this book, including the prisoners' sense of anger and betrayal, and the sadness when they realized that their leader would be starting a protest that would certainly cost his life.

At 11:00 P.M., Father Meagher took Bobby back to the prison hospital. Meagher had the British document. It was not what they wanted. Meagher left Sands and Hughes to pore over the document, while he stood in the corner of the cell, trying not to impose but curious about what was being said. Meagher thought that Hughes was near tears and

Bobby, sitting beside the bed, was trying to comfort him. Bobby said repeatedly, "We can make something of it." He was trying to comfort his old friend but he was far from satisfied with the document. It stated that the prisoners would have to wear prison-issue clothing during weekdays, when they were engaged in prison work. This clearly failed to meet their bottom line. As far as he was concerned, the document was severely lacking in its provisions on clothes, work, and association, the three most important of their five demands.

Despite his comforting comments to Brendan Hughes, when Bobby rose from the Dark's bedside and came over to the priest, he told him bluntly, "It wasn't what we wanted." At that point, the warder broke in and said, "Okay, you're finished." Sands was taken away.[77]

● ● ●

That evening, the Republican Press Center in West Belfast issued a holding statement on behalf of the hunger strikers. It concealed more than it revealed.

> *Having seen the statement to be announced by Humphrey Atkins in the British House of Commons tomorrow and having been supplied with a document which contains a new elaboration on our five demands which were first enumerated upon by Humphrey Atkins in the House of Commons on December 4 we decided to halt the hunger strike.*[78]

Back in his cell, Bobby talked about the document and his encounter with Hughes. Still angry, he discussed with Bik MacFarlane, Richard O'Rawe, Jake Jackson, and Pat Mullan how they could carry the protest forward. No matter how they played it out, they kept coming back to one end: another hunger strike.

Chapter Twenty-One

Step by Step

I n a few short hours Bobby Sands learned a vital lesson. You have to control information and you have to control the actions of your key actors. The slightest failure can be fatal. States have tremendous power to control and manage information in order to influence even their most committed adversaries. For several years, the blanketmen had partly neutralized this power with their own forms of communication. Now, at the most critical moment of their protest they lost control.

Technically, as their commanding officer, no one could end the strike except by Bobby's command. In reality, the British authorities stage-managed events to remove him from key negotiations and put Brendan Hughes effectively back in control. Having done that, they played on Hughes's emotions and induced him to call off the hunger strike without achieving any of its basic objectives.

Perhaps Bobby had been right. Maybe they *had* asked Doctor Ross to talk to Hughes to "get inside of his head." If you had asked Bobby Sands beforehand whether his most trusted comrade would capitulate short of victory, he would have answered with a definite "no." Yet the British convinced Hughes that he was not only saving Sean McKenna's life but also achieving victory. Sands later wrote to Gerry Adams that,

> *Dorcha is shattered. He thought we'd still a chance after we seen sagart [Father Brendan Meagher]. The sagart coming in with the papers made it unbearable as we were almost there.*[1]

Sands took another lesson from this episode: if you say you are willing to die you must be willing to die. You cannot bluff a state that is willing to call your bluff. Now the only way forward was another hunger strike. The only way to be sure that a new hunger strike would endure to "victory or death" was to do it himself. If he could not trust his closest comrade, the only person he could totally trust was himself.

On December 19, the screws put a one-page document into each blanketman's cell. It did not even come close to meeting their demands. Some prisoners threw it back onto the landing. When Bobby saw the document, he "went nuts." He shouted to Bik. Then he shouted for a screw to come to his cell. Then he demanded to see the governor. But before the governor saw him, Bobby met with the other commanding officers, one by one, in the big cell on his wing. Maybe, he told them, they could get their own clothes and then continue struggling for more rights. He spoke to Rab McCollum, from H5, in low, quiet tones, saying that he was concerned that the cell was bugged. For half an hour they read and discussed the merits of the document that Meagher brought to the jail the previous night. They agreed that it was nowhere near what they wanted. Yet they *could* try to use its ambiguities to win some rights. If the authorities met the ambiguities without generosity, the prisoners would have to intensify their protest anew.

Seanna Walsh, OC of H4, did not believe any of this positive spin. He could tell straight away from Bobby's demeanor that there was little hope of getting anything from the document. He expected that Bobby's appeals to the governor would fall on deaf ears.

His prediction came true within hours. The governor offered little and Sands threatened to escalate the protest, implying that they would start another hunger strike.

Sands then had a second meeting with his OCs. He translated the governor's sentiments as, "Youse are beat, take what you've got out of this or you get nothing." That being the case, said Bobby, the only way forward was a second hunger strike.

Rab McCollum was "aghast" when he heard Bobby say this.

"You kidding me or what?!" he thought to himself.

Bobby said that they had to move quickly to recover their momentum. They would leave the no-wash protest on a limited basis and demand their own clothes. This would demonstrate their good will and their desire to make the agreement work. Once the authorities rejected their demand, they would smash up their cells and release a public statement about the authorities' intransigence. This would regain them the necessary momentum for a second hunger strike.

Only later did McCollum realize the movement was pushing Bobby toward this "step-by-step" policy. But where the movement saw it as a way of avoiding a hunger strike, the prisoners saw it as a way to remove the confusion that was left by the unsatisfactory end to the first hunger strike, enabling them to move them forward into the final phase of protest.

"Because of what happened in the first hunger strike," Bobby told McCollum, "they'll not take us seriously until someone dies. We're into a brinkmanship type of thing again and I'm going to have to die before they'll sit down and take us seriously. If this hunger strike goes we *have* to win."

Sands told McCollum that it was not just about clothes, it was about how criminalization affected the whole struggle, how it would discourage people who joined the IRA or wanted to join the IRA. Despite the seriousness of the discussion, Sands sent McCollum on his way with a joke. As he walked back to his cellblock, certain that Bobby would soon die, McCollum was surprised that he was actually in an upbeat mood.

It was the last time he ever saw Bobby Sands.

Back in his cell, Bobby asked Malachy Carey for a pen and paper. Malachy handed over a ballpoint refill and some cigarette papers. Bobby hunched down on his bit of filthy foam mattress and wrote a letter to Gerry Adams, the man he called *comrade mor* (big comrade). He told him what had transpired over the past twenty-four hours and gave him the "disturbing" news that they would soon be starting another hunger strike.

> So, comrade mor, we maintain, and the next part of this comm will be very disturbing.
>
> I would like you to issue a statement, pointing to the inflexibility of the Brits. The blanket and dirt strike goes on. We have done everything possible that can be done and on Thursday, January 1, we embark upon another hunger strike! . . . I don't believe we can achieve our aims or recoup our losses in the light of what has occurred. Sooner, rather than later, our defeat will be exposed. When I say, in the light of what has occurred, I mean not only the boys breaking but perhaps our desperate attempts to salvage something.

The whole thing is so bad that in here men have left already. When the situation fizzles out, which it indeed will, I will lose over three hundred men from this protest, perhaps more . . .

I'm speaking of this and I want to make it quite clear, myself and four others to hunger strike. There is one realization here, comrade, which rings clear. Someone will die. I know others told you this, but I am prepared to die and no one will call this hunger strike off, comrade . . .

The people, the movement, have taken a blow. We need out of it and if it means death then that is accepted. We stand to be destroyed, comrade. You must realize once eaten up by the present penal system you don't come out a fighter, or very few will. When you're knocked down you get up and fight back. We can do it. We've created the proper conditions for it. If we've had luck, it's that we can go at them again . . .

I'm not prepared to watch four and a half years of sheer murder be fritted into conformity and respectability. I am not taking our failure personally, or don't think I'm blaming myself, because I know what happened . . .

I'm asking you in a desperate plea to accept what I am saying . . . I'm not so naïve as to not accept that men will break again but what we're heading for now is something so disastrous that I flinch thinking on it. I believe I can get five men, men who'll die. I think we have the right to stand up and fight back. I don't want to die, but I would prefer to die than allow what will take place here to occur. Don't think I'm giving up hope or trying to find a way out of a mess from the standpoint of a disappointed or frustrated OC (it's me, comrade mor, I never felt better, yahoo!!) . . .[2]

• • •

Back in Westminster, Humphrey Atkins was in a jubilant mood. He crowed in his statement to the House of Commons at 10:58 A.M. that morning. "I can confirm that every prisoner at the Maze took breakfast this morning," he told the House. "This is welcome news. The hunger strike could not achieve its objects, and it is encouraging that the influence all those who sought to persuade the prisoners of that fact was finally effective."[3]

The members of the House roundly congratulated Atkins. Only Ulster's Unionists sounded a note of caution. James Molyneaux wanted an assurance that this would not open the way for future concessions to the prisoners. Ian Paisley complained that the document had already shown "considerable weakening" on the prisoners' five demands.

Gerry Adams was angry. Not only was Atkins unnecessarily ungracious to say that the hunger strikers had been utterly defeated, such an attitude would spur a second hunger strike, to which he was entirely opposed. Adams went home in a depressed mood. When he got there, he found a note from his wife Collette saying that she had gone out with a friend to celebrate "the victory."[4]

The prisoners were angry with everyone. The hunger strikers had wavered at the point of victory. The Brits had tricked them and then rubbed their noses in it. But what really made them angry was when they began to hear reports that Sinn Féin was trying to pitch the outcome as a victory. They did not feel at all victorious.

Sands had a visit with Morrison that day. He had heard radio reports about "a buoyant Danny Morrison" and his victory celebrations. Referring to Danny's "brass neck," Bobby said that he was going to set him straight about what had been agreed and not agreed.[5]

• • •

Over the next few days, Sands exchanged comms with the movement about a second hunger strike. His proposal was not welcome outside of the H-Blocks. Adams was not at all surprised that he wanted to lead a second hunger strike but he did not think that the movement could generate public support for a new strike after the first one ended in such an unsatisfactory fashion. Everyone was emotionally drained. Anyway, the authorities were likely to call the prisoners' bluff again. Says Adams,

> *I think the key thing was that [the British authorities had] a sense that the prisoners had been broken by the first hunger strike, so the system or those who were in charge of it or individuals [had] a sense that we've got them beat. Five years on the blanket and they tried the hunger strike and we beat them on that. So they probably thought that they had this thing in hand . . . I would say that if I was a British strategist sitting back and intent on the*

implementation of what was then their strategy and if I had been
concerned when the hunger strike started that this could escalate,
I would be sitting back in January and saying, "Well, we have
them now."[6]

To be blunt, hunger strikers would have to die this time to prove that they really *were* serious. Two days after the hunger strike collapsed, Bobby wrote to Gerry Adams, first in the afternoon and then again that night.

I'm still badly shaken but what is killing me most and everyone
here is if we get a refusal . . . to have another go. We believe we have
the ground to switch round the situation, hold what we have, and
get at it again.

Bobby described the current situation in starkly horrific terms. "The wings are like morgues," he said. A new hunger strike was the only way to turn things around. He knew, however, that he was unlikely to get approval for his chosen course of action. It was clearly affecting his mood.

I haven't eaten in days and I can't even sleep thinking about it all.
If we hunger strike then that's sound. If not I will have to ask each
block for their thoughts on future blanket protest, i.e. the best way to
hold it together. When I say that, that's the ball busted (as they say).[7]

That evening, a comm from the Army Council decisively ruled out another hunger strike. Bobby wrote the following day that, " . . . we accept army position on hunger strike, so that's out the windows. Now we are left with one feasible alternative—'compromise' . . . " Yet he was still not convinced. He warned Adams that they would have to take some kind of action quickly to recover momentum.

We lost seven men from the protest today. Time is not on our
side. Brits know this. We'll have to work quick all 'round . . .
when we reach mid-next week I'm going to have to make a deci-
sion, because if I don't we'll have an exodus from the blocks.[8]

There were only two apparent alternatives to hunger strike. They could try to make the December eighteenth "agreement" work by testing the governor on clothing and work. Or, they could abandon the protest and go into the system, trying to wreck the criminalized prison regime from within. The first option was risky. No one really believed they could get any more than Atkins had already offered. As Sands wrote to Adams, "... let's face it, comrade, Brits know they need only sit tight and most of us will go to them with our hands up. We have no banging power."[9] Adams apparently agreed. He wrote to Sands that the prison regime was "doggedly against any movement."[10] Yet he still insisted that Sands test the system. He hoped that if he put off a hunger strike long enough, he might eventually give up on it.

Support for "going into the system" came from an unexpected source: the prison hospital. Brendan Hughes was "dead set" against another hunger strike and was pressing hard for this option along with Tommy McKearney. But Hughes lost a lot of political capital when he halted the hunger strike. Sands just shut him out of the picture[11] and most blanketmen had endured too much to admit defeat now.

On December 21, Hughes sent a proposal to Sands through Father Toner: ask the governor to "hospitalize" the blanketmen for six weeks on grounds of poor health. That would give the authorities a chance to say that they were off the protest while allowing the blanketmen to save face. Then, the prisoners could move into the system from their hospitalized wings and try to achieve a phased settlement. Toner gave Sands the impression that the authorities had already agreed to the hospitalization scheme and that it was ready to begin. Bobby hit the roof at this abrogation of his authority until Governor Hilditch told him that there was no such plan. This was a relief for Bobby because he was not ready to go into the system "unless we have guarantees that there may be positive steps to a settlement or a settlement beforehand."

Then the governor took a strange new tack. He,

> ... *whipped out a set of clothing, civilian-style, to try and sell them to me. I played with him. I sounded him out on work. He'd have us sewing mailbags if he could. I took my leave by telling him all was not lost and that I held out some hope of conclusion of protest whilst asking for meeting with O/Cs of blocks again.*[12]

This last request was a ruse to make Hilditch think that Bobby was trying to drum up consensus for the agreement while he explained to the OCs that any moves they made would be solely to test the governor.

Meanwhile, the fact that the governor was again negotiating directly with Bobby was recognition of his officer status and, implicitly, of their status as political prisoners. Taking that as a gain, Bobby told the OCs that they would test the governor until they had to revert to a hunger strike.

After seeing the OCs, Bobby felt considerably better. Based on his guarantees about not conforming, they all told him that they could hold the line. "We will hold," he wrote Adams. "The boys know the crack but we will take casualties . . . Numbers should remain respectable, gives us recognition and does give some sign of hope to the boys."[13]

Bobby still made no secret of his disdain for any option short of hunger strike.

> *The Brits are not going to give us a way out. Hilditch accused me of trying to negotiate. There is no bend in them and we can't accept conformity. Should we do that or anything even so much as resembling it we'd be in big trouble. They'd move us all over the blocks, to Magilligan, Maghaberry, etc.[14] They'd remove all OCs and hardcore and isolate them.*

Nonetheless, since the IRA Army Council had definitively turned down his proposal for a new hunger strike, he tried to make the best of his bad situation. Sands wrote to Adams:

> *Realise now that hunger strike is wrong. Okay, I'm sorry. It was not irrational and we believed we were in big trouble and that we sunk the movement and that because of that the protest would break up. But we now see that we are climbing out of it rather well. So, as I said, we'll sit tight, hold. We're the rough, tough Provos, yahoo!!*[15]

He began to explore the features of a "step-by-step" strategy, where some prisoners would come off of the protest in stages to test the government's willingness to respond.

> *. . . we would move in a phased thing and let [chosen men] pioneer the way. In this sort of situation we're very open but we would move into it with unity (I'd hope) and we'd have a continual struggle on our hands.*

His willingness to explore such a strategy, however, was based on his certainty that it would fail. A short period of flexibility would give him the moral high ground when, inevitably, they fell back into preparation for a hunger strike. As he told Adams,

> *If we were to move then the least we can do is try to leave [the] Brits in no doubt that should they attempt to force work on us they will meet trouble. That is, they, the Brits, should not allow a Governor to upset the applecart. This is a very depressing alternative and . . . our only hope would be a hunger strike at a later date, but God knows what we'd be like then. That's why I was speaking on hunger strike in the last comm. So, comrade, we'll have to try to achieve something before mid-next week to stop a flight of the wild geese, "never to return" if we do move, i.e., put their clothes on and battle. After that we're on our own. Tactically, it's suicide but alternatives aren't really plural anymore.*[16]

As Bobby and his inner circle in H3 discussed the practicalities of a step-by-step strategy, his perception of political status changed. Until now, they had always emphasized wearing their own clothes as their central demand. Now, Sands began to think that the crunch issues were prison work and the right to associate. As long as they controlled their own lives on the wing rather than being herded away and separated to do prison work, they could continue to organize and politicize themselves, *even* if they did it in "prison-issue clothing." While keeping open the prospect of a hunger strike, Bobby explored a middle strategy.

> *Now, I feel we should (on the strength of another hunger strike) move first and seek a guarantee from Brits on self-education and segregation (if it's after a one month period that will do) . . . We should say that one way or another if this is not forthcoming there will be big trouble and a hunger strike once again. We'll give on the clothes, we'll come off protest to give the Brits the grounds.*

Before he moved anywhere, however, Bobby wanted answers from the movement. Would they gain anything tangible by putting on the "civilian-type clothes"? Could they remobilize the "secret channel" to get prior guarantees on work and association in return for making such a move? If there were no such guarantees, "then we sit tight and go straight into hunger strike footing."[17]

Bobby explained his reticence to Gerry Adams. "In consideration of what's happened," he said, referring to the obstructionist behavior of Brendan Hughes and Father Toner, "I've adopted the position of extreme militant . . . I have a problem here in that I won't be intimidated. But will have to try and avoid 'disunity.'" In the meantime, he said, "I'm doing my own thing and taking it that the Brits have dug in. I will dig in. I hold a wee bit of hope that hunger strike threats will budge or frighten them."

By Christmas Eve, Bobby had pretty much clarified the way forward. At 10:00 P.M. the screws left the block and the lighting and heating went off. Bobby sat down in the dark as the Christmas concert began and wrote a long letter to Adams, suggesting how they could proceed. They would negotiate with the authorities, with their five demands intact. Yet,

> We will be willing to concede clothing (so that's up our sleeve). What we want is self-education and segregation. We must have both and a guarantee of self-education that will hold, that is Brits saying change in prison rules, work will be optional.

The key was that "work" would include "self-education." During working hours, the cell doors would have to be left open for the prisoners to integrate and discuss. The only other work they would consider would be self-maintenance of the block. "We must not give on this at all," he wrote. "No work." Not even vocational training, cooking, or laundry. "So, to sum up, we'd wear their clothes during education periods, we'd want doors open to integrate."

This was the nub of the political status issue that could not be compromised. To be political prisoners, they had to be free to organize and politicize themselves. *That* and not the mere tactic of armed struggle defined their existence and their identity. It was the polar opposite of how Thatcher's government defined them, as simple criminals. Bobby knew that his chosen path would be difficult.

> . . . it's going to be dodgy. Let me mention that in the conforming blocks four or five men congregating together is regarded as an illegal assembly. So, the point is they want to stop

*men mixing freely as this leads to discussion and politicising. We must break it, **that is the point** [my emphasis].*[18]

• • •

To understand Bobby's shift of emphasis away from clothes, we need only ask why he and his comrades were protesting. As political prisoners, they could claim to be engaged in a legitimate liberation struggle; they could take that status to the world as recognition of their right to resist British tyranny. On the other hand, if they allowed themselves to be criminalized, the whole struggle was criminalized. The irony is that they sought political status from the enemy. The British regime might give them special rights as prisoners but would never cede that their activities were legitimate.

There was also a practical point. Bobby remembered his personal development in the cages. Prison had made him who he was today, instead of the relatively unaware lad he was in Twinbrook in 1972. Prison was a basis of his identity: his music, his political awareness, his poetry. The vast majority of books he had ever read, he read in prison. Thus, the only way he knew to mold young politically aware Republican activists was in jail. Yet to do it effectively, they had to be free to read, lecture, debate, and write. In short, the *prison struggle was the center of the struggle.* The key to reinvigorating the IRA was through the prison, which was the center of political consciousness, where "good operators" became political activists.

Thus, the definition of prison struggle changed dramatically under Bobby's leadership. The first hunger strike was portrayed as a human rights issue. Now, the move toward a second hunger strike was again an explicit struggle for recognition as political prisoners.[19]

Activists outside of prison still pushed the human rights agenda. Arguably, they had a broader and more realistic view. Yet, one can see how a small group of men at the apex of several years of the hardest and most isolated form of struggle would come to feel as though the world revolved around them. The whole hunger striking strategy was based on the proposition that if the world did *not* revolve around them, they would *make* it so. And, if all others failed, Bobby would make *himself* the center of the struggle. Again, writing to Adams,

Don't get me wrong, but I'm depressed writing this. It seems

*that I am among the few left here willing to fight the hard way,
but unfortunately, comrade, I think as a unit.*[20]

• • •

Bobby interrupted his letter to Adams. Despite the darkness and the cold,
the men continued their concert. The emcee had begun by telling everyone
that this was an historic event because it would be their last Christmas
concert. He meant it would be their last on the blanket protest but his
words must have carried a double meaning for Bobby, who was still convinced that he would soon die. Usually at the center of concerts, Bobby
was thinking about the coming struggle. As he wrote to Gerry Adams,

> *Comrade, I don't intend to see that the sacrifices of dead com-
> rades and four years of inhumanity in the H-Blocks is down into
> doldrums with the war in the long term because of what happens
> here in this gaol . . . I don't want to hunger strike but if I'm left
> with no alternative I will and you can take this as confirmation,
> Comrade Mor . . . The next few days will be crucial. Ó Fiaich can
> come in here if he wants to see me. If he does I'll tell him the same
> thing—this is my ninth Christmas in jail.*

Christmas dinner was "alright" the next day but the cells were still cold.
Bobby continued writing, trying to work out their difficulties by playing
them over and over on paper. He wrote several comms a day, going over
the same territory again and again. He still had hunger strike on his mind.
He continued to probe at how far they could go on the issues of work and
association. He was concerned that the British authorities would not accede
to their demands about free association during working hours.

> *So, we could form structures if we're locked up during
> working hours. Locked up but allowed four to a cell to form small
> classes, to do Irish classes, study groups, etc., etc. But what we'd
> do is set up a cell system, which can be done. Now, failing this we
> could have "lock-ups" during working hours to read and learn.*

The best solution would be to win a regime where work was optional.
The "bottom-line" acceptable situation would be where prisoners who

did not work would remain locked up during working hours. "Perhaps I'm wrong but I've always got the paradoxical impression that Brits would give on work," he wrote, hopefully, to Adams.[21]

After Sands finished his letter to Adams he wrote another comm to Liam Og. He went over the same ground. Summarising the state of morale of the men around him, he wrote,

> *Mentally and physically they're just about fucked. The collapse of the hunger strike has deducted about a year's resistance from most of them. They'll hang on to the last if all fails, but an amount will leave . . . make no mistake, comrade, we won't give an inch on work and that's 100%. Now, if Brits give on self-education we can get out, comrade. On the clothes we may have to wear them during education periods, but what are they going to do when they find out late that to supply forty million pairs of trousers per year to keep up with repairs is not practical! We'll literally rip the arse clean out of them. I mean we're not that fuckin' soft (pardon the expression).[22]*

Liam Og polled the other OCs about morale and they all agreed with Sands. Seanna Walsh wrote of a "dangerous" situation where "confusion, rumors, counter-rumors" were creating low morale. He could hold the men together for a few months but "after that, it's anybody's guess."[23] From H4, Tommy Gorman wrote that the protest was in "extreme danger" and, with it, the war effort as a whole. Hundreds of prisoners had "set themselves a date" of four weeks after Christmas when they would simply leave the protest if there was no movement.[24] A new danger to morale was the changing attitude of the prison warders. Now that they knew the truth about the end of the hunger strike, their attitude had changed from "you didn't get status but the next thing to it" to "you didn't get anything."[25]

Soon after Christmas, Father Toner came back to Bobby with another message from Hughes, who wanted to know why he had not yet compromised and gone into the system. There was an implicit threat, " . . . that if I wasn't willing to lead the men off the protest [Hughes] would come back and do it or, if need be, go to H8 to show the lead." The threat was empty. Hughes sent a request to the governor to see Sands so that he could press him personally for a compromise. When he told Sands he was allowing the visit Hilditch asked him whether there was any truth in the rumors of a hunger strike.

"Yes, there is," replied Bobby.

In his half hour meeting with Hughes and McFeeley, Bobby's old comrades bluntly criticized the way he had been handling things. They told him that the climate dictated some kind of movement and they wanted to know why he had not moved.

"I wanted guarantees with reference to work," Bobby replied. "Do you not think going straight into conforming would show weakness?"

Hughes replied that they had to give the British the opportunity to compromise. Threats of hunger striking would not move them. Hughes said that education was covered in the document they received on the evening the hunger strike ended. Bobby replied that now that the pressure was off, the British authorities would hardly be generous.

"I ran all over the place, trying to break the deadlock," he told Hughes, "but the Brits won't budge because they see the chance of breaking the protest."

Going into the system, he said, would portray weakness and desperation. It would be equivalent to "breaking the protest", doing the authorities' work for them.

Finally, Hughes gave in.

"Maybe we should leave it to you," he told Sands.

"*Sin ceart*" ("That's right"), was Bobby's terse reply.

Now Bobby was ready to be blunt. He told them that they were allowing the result of the hunger strike to dominate their thinking. They wanted to believe that they had achieved a victory rather than admitting that they had given in at the brink of victory. Now they were blaming Bobby for their own failure.[26]

The more the men in the hospital pressed to move into the system, the more pessimistic Sands got about such a move. He wrote again to Adams,

> Never trust a Brit is the most important point and should we go into a situation where we would end this protest, wear prison clothes and hope we'd woo the Brits into being reasonable because of our conformity and good will, we would, beyond any measure of doubt, meet trouble.

Sands saw his options narrowing.

*I will move but only if I get a nod that when I do move I won't
meet problems on work, that I won't have men stripped of their
clothes for refusing to obey prison rules, i.e. work!! If someone
stands guarantor I'll move right away. Again, failing this we'll
have to hunger strike. Now, comrade mor, I believe that this
hunger strike is not a simple matter of gaining demands, for as I
have said, all we can hope for is a compromise settlement before
death. The whole thing is a matter of not only attempting to stop
the slump and defeat of this protest but (and I'm serious here) the
far-reaching and very damaging effects that this will have in the
not-so-long-term upon the movement, people and war.*[27]

By New Years Eve, two weeks of indecision and indeterminacy had taken
their toll. In his letters, Bobby just went over and over the same ground. The
more he did it, the more pessimistic he got. He expressed his feelings in an
unusually downbeat note of New Years greetings to Liam Og.

*The situation is looking very gloomy for us. The only way I can
see this protest ending is by going into prison system. I'm not
going to do that. I'll hold with what's left, if necessary. This could
have equally disastrous results. If Tom and Dark were here and
in charge, they'd have moved two weeks ago . . . Well, it's been a
very eventful year and next year no doubt will be equally as
stinkin. But such is life (AHHHHHHHH!!).*[28]

On the morning of New Year's Day, Bobby's family visited him. He
intended to tell them that he would be leading a new hunger strike. But
he couldn't. Instead, he asked Adams to get someone to tell them.[29] A
week later, Bobby was finalizing the details of a new hunger strike where
he would undoubtedly be the first to die. He even sent out a short biography of himself for use in publicity.[30]

Threats of a hunger strike began to have an effect on the authorities,
however. On January 15, Governor Hilditch came to Bobby's cell to talk
to him about the situation. He said he needed some time to think about
how to respond to the prisoners' offer to come off of the no-wash protest
in order to test how far the authorities would change the regime. He
asked for a week's moratorium on any new protest by the prisoners while
he considered the situation.[31]

Bobby gave the governor one further by saying that "as an indication of our good will and willingness and sincerity" he would move ten men from his own wing and ten others from H5 off of the no-wash protest. They would wash, shave, and slop out. Bobby and Bik MacFarlane thought that they, too, could use a bit of time to reexamine their position. In the meantime, they could test what Hilditch meant when he told Sands that the "prison regime was not static and was indeed developing."

The blanketmen gave Governor Hilditch his week. A wing of prisoners from H3 (Bobby's wing) and another from H5 (Seanna Walsh's wing) moved into clean cells with furniture and beds. They began washing. Bobby sent out word to the families to bring their clothes the following Friday. If the governor let them in, things could proceed further, step-by-step. If the authorities failed this first test, protest would be back on the agenda.

Did Bobby seriously think that the prison authorities would move on the clothing issue? Clearly not. Rather, he had to prove to his own people that he had gone the last mile before calling on them to mobilize once again for a hunger strike. By taking the step of moving into clean wings and forcing the governor's hand, Bobby's primary goal may have been to move his own comrades, not his enemies.

● ● ●

After shaves and haircuts, the prisoners were new men.

"Bed's breaking my back," Bobby wrote Liam Og. "We're not used to such comforts . . . writing on a table is strange, sitting on a chair. Men saw themselves in the mirror last week for the first time in almost three years. It was frightening, especially for Rasputin, or I mean Bik."[32]

Beginning on Friday January 23, families arrived at Long Kesh with packages of clothes.[33] On Sunday, Bobby sent a message to Seanna Walsh to have his men ready for Tuesday night. If they did not have their own clothes by then, they would smash their furniture and trash their cells at 9:00 P.M. He wrote to the movement, telling them his plans for Tuesday night. They were not amused. Liam Og frantically sent comms to Bobby on Monday and Tuesday, instructing him to call off the protest. Bobby got the comms but he never gave Walsh the message.

"The sagart [priest] didn't appear," he wrote to Liam Og as an excuse for not passing on his instructions.

Technically, this was true. But the missing priest was convenient. Bik MacFarlane is definitive that he and Bobby decided to send a clear signal to the authorities that they "meant business." They also wanted to put their own people into a clear frame for action.

The movement was on a completely different wavelength. They thought that smashing the furniture was the *beginning* of a transition period back into the dirty protest. They were so opposed to the second hunger strike that they did not realize how far into that strategy the prisoners had already moved.[34]

Tuesday came and there were no clothes. Since Seanna Walsh had not heard the instruction to cancel the protest, Bobby decided he also had to go ahead. He wrote the movement that "H5 were going to move. So, rather than halt on the move, we all moved."

At nine o'clock on Tuesday night "the lads gave the furniture the message." They broke up their wooden beds, the tables, and chairs. Some tried to break out their windows. After half an hour, ten warders came to Bobby's wing. Whatever the prisoners expected, what happened was even worse. The warders moved them from B-wing to C-wing, and "they didn't allow them to walk over, instead they grabbed them by the hair and run them over, kicking and punching the whole time."

According to Bobby, six men were thrown over a table. The cheeks of their behinds were torn apart by screws.

"Comrade, this is sexual assault," he wrote to Liam Og.

The same thing was happening over in H5. The screws organized a gauntlet between the clean wing and the dirty wing. Each prisoner was beaten to a pulp as he ran from his clean cell to the new dirty cell. Men who were waiting to be moved listened to the shouting and the screaming, waiting in horror for their own turn.

Bobby described the scene that awaited them: "C-wing has just been vacated . . . The cells were bogging, covered in excreta, also puddles of water on cell floors where the cleaner had begun work."

The prisoners were left in darkness in filthy cells, with no water to drink, no beds, and "not even a bloody blanket." All they had was the towel they wore around their waist. The men who went through that night agree that it was the worst night of their lives. They were freezing. They were sore. And it was one thing to live in your own shit; being thrown into another man's shit was positively sickening.

Bobby organized a singsong to keep them going. Each man walked up and down his cell, trying to keep warm, singing along to the songs. But before long, they'd had enough. They just tried to concentrate on getting some heat into themselves—walking up and down, sitting down and then getting up, rubbing their bodies and hopping from foot to foot. But Bobby kept going, trying to take everyone's mind off of the conditions. All night long he just kept up a constant banter, singing away on his own, shouting down, "Are you all right? C'mon boys!"

All night, while Bobby kept up their spirits, prisoners rang the buzzers to call the warders. No one came. One prisoner took sick twice in the middle of the night but no one came to help. It was eight o'clock the next morning before the warders came back on the wing. When they arrived, six men had to go to the doctor.

The PO finally came at 10:00 A.M and gave the men, in Bobby's words, "half a fuckin' blanket each!" The governor came at 11:00 A.M. Each man asked for a complaint form so that their lawyer could charge Governor Hilditch with breaches of prison rules. That afternoon, the warders left the dinner sitting until it was cold and then distributed it to the men. It was nearly 1:30 A.M.when they finally received bedding.

"We sat all night naked, up until five minutes ago, before the bastards found it in themselves to give us blankets and mattresses," Bobby complained to Liam Og. "The boys are exhausted, the wing's like a morgue, all asleep . . . I'm away for a sleep, think I'm sleeping now!"[35]

• • •

Sands was willful in letting the trashing go ahead on Tuesday night. He had received Liam Og's comms requesting a postponement but he wrote back, unrepentant and defiant, of his total commitment that a hunger strike was the only way forward.

> *I believe that unless positive and militant action is taken to bring an end to the four and a half years of protest and inhumanity in these blocks, the protest herein will eventually diminish to an ineffective small group of men . . . once the majority of Volunteers opt for conformity then criminalisation is succeeding and will, through time, do severe damage not only in the prisons but to the movement and in general.*

Lest the movement was worried that a hunger strike might again collapse, he clarified his commitment to personally see it through.

> *H-Block has been brought to the forefront of the struggle, therefore the risk in fighting that struggle should be no different and is no different to that which is freely accepted by the Volunteer on the street . . . I accept this and make it categorically clear that I make this decision on my own behalf, influenced by no one and furthermore, go further to point out that should a comrade die before me on this H/S, that I am not coming off it for you or no one until death or victory decides. I've not enjoyed saying all this but I hope I've made myself clear and therefore acceptable to you to trust with such an enormous responsibility. What I've said is not bravado, egotism or foolhardy in any way. I realise and accept the consequences of death and for what it is worth I don't think we have a hope in hell of victory before death but I do believe there is victory in death. Good luck to you all, comrades, and I don't blame you for your justified cautiousness and reluctance in this matter.*[36]

On Wednesday, the men were moved to clean wings in H6. Bobby told Bik MacFarlane that, a hunger strike now being inevitable, he was appointing him officer in command of the H-Blocks.

"Why aren't you appointing Seanna [Walsh]?" asked MacFarlane. "He's senior to me and surely he's the better man."

"We've been friends too long," replied Bobby. "If it comes down to it, Seanna won't let me die."

"That's as good as saying that I *will* let you die."

"Yes."

"Thanks a lot."

MacFarlane was not sure whether this was a compliment or a damning comment. He just replied that he hoped he could live up to expectations. Sands showed MacFarlane a comm from the IRA Army Council, warning of disastrous consequences if the hunger strike collapsed again. MacFarlane wrote back to the IRA and confirmed his complete faith that Sands would follow his action to death.

> *Both Marcella and myself are of the same opinion that men will in fact die before we achieve anything. This is something I didn't*

believe during the last H/S. I personally and honestly believed the Brits would topple before a death. But that is all changed now and I know that once the lads embark on H/S I won't see some or all of them again. Just a personal observation here—Marcella is indeed fully aware that death is the key to victory and is in my opinion in the correct frame of mind for what he faces. I have also accepted this as fact, so comrade, let each of us do what is required of us and help each other over the hurdles.[37]

MacFarlane also wrote to Gerry Adams about Bobby. "I assure you that he is under no illusions as to what lies ahead . . . I also know that he is prepared for it." As for the others who would be on the strike, "I know they will die this time. Unfortunately, comrade, that's how it must be. As our statement said, H/S is our only option. In my opinion, any of the alternatives spell defeat without even the slimmest of chances. H/S is extremely dangerous for all, but it provides the only chance for victory."[38]

The Army Council was still not convinced. They warned Bobby that the IRA could not allow the hunger strike to divert them from their war effort. They might have to take military actions that would harm the hunger strikers in terms of publicity. Bobby was unmoved and wrote back, carefully using the pronoun "we," to indicate the solidarity of the prison leadership.

We have listened carefully to what you have said and we recognise and accept the spirit in which it was written. Likewise, in view of the situation, we do not deny you or criticise your extreme cautiousness, but, however distressing it may be, we regret that our decision to H/S remains the same and we re-confirm this decision now with the same vigour and determination . . . We realise the struggle on the outside must also continue. We hope that you accept that the struggle in H-Block, being part of the overall struggle, must also go on in unison. We re-confirm and pledge our full confidence and support to you and march on with you to the Irish Socialist Republic.[39]

• • •

The die was cast. The decision to hunger strike was finally confirmed. Now they had to begin planning the logistics of the strike. Bik MacFarlane wrote a statement of their intention to strike on March 1. It had now been nearly a month and a half of equivocation and uncertainty since the end of the first hunger strike. The blanketmen needed decisiveness. "We need that H/S statement out fast, comrade," Bobby instructed Liam Og. "The delay is damaging us, i.e., men will think we're telling lies. Lost half a dozen comrades in the blocks yesterday."[40]

They had to avoid the mistakes of the first strike, particularly a situation where several prisoners approached death at the same time. The outside leadership suggested that they stagger the hunger strikes; Bobby to begin first, then a new volunteer each week. Each hunger striker would have sole responsibility for his own death. That would maximize the public pressure on the British government, as the streets and the world's press erupted anew and with each successive death. Bobby said that it really didn't matter to him as the result would be the same.[41]

In early February, Danny Morrison (whom they nicknamed "Pennies") visited Bobby. He suggested that a woman should be the second person on this hunger strike. It would recognize their essential and equal role in the struggle. Sands and MacFarlane discussed Morrison's suggestion. MacFarlane was against it. The public would see it as "mercenary," he argued, since a woman would approach death quicker than a man and the press would say the blanketmen were using her to try and save their own skins. Bik proposed dropping the first woman further back—"handicapped so to speak"—so that they could be sure that she would not be the first to die. Bobby replied that it would make no difference. Whether it was a woman or a man, the second hunger striker would die the same as the first. Besides, he said, the women had been made to feel like second-class participants in the first hunger strike. They had been "completely swallowed up by events" in the H-Blocks. This time they should be given full equality with the men.

MacFarlane thought it over. After examining "all angles and arguments" he decided Bobby was right. He wrote to Morrison,

> They are comrades and they are equal and have a right to demand that they be allowed to exercise their equality. To be blatant, blunt—callous, if you like—H/S'ers are going to die, this is fact. Does it matter who dies first really?[42]

The women in Armagh began immediately to plan their participation in the hunger strike. Sile Darragh, their OC, sent out three names of women who intended to join the hunger strike. The first was Mairead Farrell, who had just come off the first hunger strike and who would die seven years later when she was shot by the SAS while walking, unarmed although on active service, in the streets of Gibraltar. Another was Mary Doyle, Bobby's childhood friend from Greencastle, near Rathcoole.[43]

Although they continued to oppose the hunger strike, the movement's leaders made constructive suggestions about how it should be run. If it was to go ahead, they suggested, the blanketmen should simultaneously end their no-wash protest. Then, regardless of what happened, they would be released from their worst misery. Sands and MacFarlane weighed the pros and cons of this suggestion. In the end, they decided that the no-wash protest had "outlived its usefulness." Eventually, it would have to end, so why not end it now?[44]

• • •

The time came to decide who would go on the strike and in what order. This time, there would be no relenting because someone insisted that he must be on the strike.[45] There would be no pulling men off and replacing them with others. This time, each volunteer would be in total control over his own fate; they had to pick men who they were *certain* would be willing to die. Eighty-two men volunteered. Sands and MacFarlane made a short list and picked the first four to go on the strike. According to Mac-Farlane, they were all obvious choices who "jumped off the page."

Richard O'Rawe found the selection process sort of mercenary. They didn't pick guys for their leadership qualities or their prison record; their only criterion was, "Will he die?" The process reeked of intent and there was a morbidity.[46]

Bobby would go first. Then came Francis Hughes from Bellaghy in County Derry.[47] Perhaps the most legendary IRA volunteer alive, he was revered among Republicans for his fearless leadership of the guerrilla campaign in the countryside. He was equally despised as a bloodthirsty and ruthless terrorist by the Protestant farmers of mid-Ulster and by the police. And he was both hated and respected by the British soldiers whom he had badgered for years before they finally caught him after a night and a day lying wounded in a ditch. The third man would be Raymond McCreesh, a devout Catholic from South Armagh who feared nothing and who had operated against British army patrols for years before they even knew he was in the IRA. Fourth came Patsy O'Hara who, as OC of the INLA prisoners, became their first representative on the strike.

Francis Hughes and Raymond McCreesh wrote short biographies for publicity and then they told their families that they were going on the strike. Hughes told his family that he would be starting a week after Bobby Sands and wrote a letter to people of South Derry.[48] Ray McCreesh told his brother Brian, a priest, before he told the rest of his family. The brother went to see McCreesh with the impression that he could convince him to give up on the strike. But after listening to his brother, he decided that he knew exactly what he was doing.[49]

Now that the decision to hunger strike was made, the atmosphere on the wings lightened up considerably. There was even banter again, which crept over into Bobby's and MacFarlane's comms to Liam Og.

"By the way, Charlie is well into poetry," MacFarlane wrote to Liam Og. "He read out one last night and wrecked the wing. A work of art, though I'll be cutting it to ribbons when I hear it the second time. Daren't let him know I actually appreciate his stuff."[50]

The next day Bobby got his own back. "Do you know that the boys are calling Bik 'Dunlop,' something to do with a Dunlop tyre, he goes on and on." Then Bobby turned the joke on himself, referring to his poem "The Crime of Castlereagh." "He [Bik] said I'd know all about that because I wrote a wee poem with eight thousand words in it. Comrade, I got carried away. You'll have it soon (I hope not, says you)."[51]

A couple of days later, MacFarlane was writing again about Bobby's poetry.

"Charlie just read out another poem—wrecked us all again."

He suggested to Liam Og that Bobby's *Castlereagh Trilogy* should be published. "They tell the whole story," he said.[52]

Soon, Bobby was scribbling all of his poems onto toilet paper and cigarette papers to send out to the movement. Within a week, he had sent out a sheaf of them to Liam Og.

"Did you get the poems?" he asked. "Stinkin!!! I know—well, they weren't that bad. I wrote them quick to get rid of them."[53]

• • •

The Republican leadership still tried to stop the hunger strike. They hunted for Alex Reid to see if he could shift Bobby, saying that he was "bull-headed" and once he got something into his mind he was not for turning. In Reid's absence, Father Faul—"the menace"[54]—tried his hand. On February 15, he spent half an hour in Bobby's cell, trying to convince him to delay the hunger strike. He insisted that they were just following orders from above, so they should tell the movement that they would not do their dirty work for them.

Bobby was especially angry at Faul's suggestion that they were being led around by the noses by the Republican Movement. "We're listening to no one, not even our own movement who are opposed to the hunger strike. We're making our own decisions and we won't give the Brits six days, never mind six months."[55]

Faul was not through, however. Bobby's father phoned Faul, who went to his house to discuss things. Faul seemed ready to exploit his relationship with the Sands family to use as leverage against Bobby. This raised a specter that would haunt Bobby throughout the hunger strike: the families were the weakest link. *He* would hold to his fast until death, but could he be sure that his parents would not order the authorities to feed him after he slipped into unconsciousness? Bobby knew that "the menace" was not beyond using the emotions of the hunger strikers' families against their sons.

Bobby spoke to his parents during their next visit and reassured them that he had taken his decision by himself and that he was not being manipulated. He sought their assurance that they would let him die because it was the only way that the prisoners could win their rights. After the visit, he was still not satisfied that they fully understood him. He wrote them a letter, repeating his points and his plea for their support.

> *My dear father and mother,*
> *By now you will be most disturbed at what is to take place. I do not want to make you anxious or to cause you any more pain. What I told you on the visit I must make sure you understand.*
> *It is no joy to any one of us here to embark upon another hunger-strike. All of us realise and understand too well the consequences involved and torment endured by all the families but we have no alternative—we have tried every conceivable means to avoid this action and to end this protest.*

The Brits are cruel—they are devious and callous. They are trying to cloud the real issue by saying or implying that they are moving to solve the issue and that we are unreasonable. But in fact they have only changed the colour and style of the prison uniform. The whole regime is as rotten as it ever was and we can live here in the H-Blocks for the duration of our sentences and face unparalleled inhumanities, torture and eventual insanity. Or we can fight back with all we have left—our lives. We would prefer to fight even if it means to the death.

Please try to remember I won't be on my own—there will be others—maybe not as many as the first time but that is our decision. It is time for us all to stand up and be brave. I know this may be particularly hard for you and my family but you will have to bear up to it and stand by me all the way. There is nothing I would be afraid of except I should die with my own family opposed to my actions.

Last Christmas was my ninth Christmas here in prison. I've lost a lot because of it, including the wife I love and the son I love. Even so I would go back again tomorrow and fight because I'm not foolish, I'm not wild. I'm intelligent, responsible and hold ideals that generations have died for. I do not enjoy prison. I do not enjoy the thought of death. I have lost many close comrades—all my mates are in gaol or dead.

So please try to understand. I love the two of you very dearly. I am sorry if I caused you worry and anxiety for so long. I am sorry if I am doing so again, but I must.

The Brits will try and move on you and use you to try and break me. Therefore I need you to stand by me. Speak to no one except to say that you back our stand and that you know and have seen England's treatment of Irishmen. See the boys at the Centre—they will keep you right at all times. You should listen to them and help them as best you can.

Please understand that the hunger-strike is our decision—not the IRA or anyone else. Remember that regardless of what may occur the blame for the situation and for what may develop out of it lies roundly on the shoulders of the Brits.

I will write to Bernadette and Marcella and Seán. I'm feeling very bad mainly because I worry that you may break down and

ask me to end the hunger-strike. But I know you can be strong—
I will go on regardless and die with that in mind.
  Remember I love you all very much.
  Your loving son,
  Bobby[56]

A week later, Faul was back in prison. He again asked Sands to postpone the hunger strike. This time he promised Bobby that he would himself organize and participate in a civil disobedience campaign. Once again, Faul claimed that they were being intimidated onto hunger strike. Then he told Bobby that it was a sin to take one's own life. It went against all of the teachings of his church and of the bible.

Bobby was ready for him. He quoted Jesus, from John 15:13, "Greater love hath no man than this, that a man lay down his life for his friends."

Faul knew he was beaten.

"Well, Bobby, I can't argue with you on that," he said and he left the cell. [57]

• • •

An unexpected bombshell hit in the middle of February. On Friday the thirteenth, each woman received a comm from the movement saying that if they began the hunger strike death was the likely outcome. They had to be sure of themselves because if they "backed down at the last minute," they would do irreparable damage to the other hunger strikers. MacFarlane had sent a similar comm to the male volunteers in the H-Blocks.

Mairead Farrell read the comm. She thought about it and agonized over it all day Saturday. On Sunday after mass she sat in her cell and wrote a painful letter to Liam Og,

> *Comrade, After having received and fully considered your comm, I have decided to stand down from the H/S. I don't want to make any excuses for myself. Up until Friday (when I received your comm) I believed that I had given the H/S all the thought possible and was confident that I could carry it through. Until then I thought I was 100% sure but now I have doubt. I don't know what has caused it since I was already aware of everything you pointed out in the comm. All I can say is that I have real fear of letting the Movement down and possibly breaking the H/S at*

*a crucial stage because of this doubt. I don't think I'm good
enough or strong enough to embark on H/S. This has left me
completely shattered . . .*[58]

Mary Doyle wrote a similar note to withdraw her name from the
hunger strike.[59] A few days later, the last woman pulled out. Sile Darragh
briefly considered taking their place, yet she had only a few months left
on her sentence and it made no sense. It was regretfully clear that there
would be no women on the hunger strike.[60]

Bobby was taken aback when he heard that the women had withdrawn.[61] Yet he wrote to Mairead Farrell a few days later to raise her
morale after her difficult decision.

> *Dear Mairead, Just a few lines to hopefully cheer you up and
> let you know I still think you're great. It was not only the right
> thing but a very admirable thing that you and Mary did and for
> that matter the same applies to anyone who does the same. You
> shouldn't feel bad about it or defeated in any manner. What yous
> all have done up there and continue to do will always remain
> unequalled in courage and determination. So you just keep your
> heart and lift your head up. Well, you know I could go on and on
> about every one of you to the point of cryin'. But as long as you
> know we all look up to yous and always stand by yous that's
> what counts.*[62]

● ● ●

Coming up to the hunger strike, Bobby allowed himself the luxury of listening to his radio a bit more. Normally, the radio was only for news
because of its short battery life and security considerations. Bobby's current radio was more precious than most. It had fallen ill and Bobby spent
considerable time getting it back into working order. He told Liam Og,

> *I got Mrs. Dale to talk to me you know after six operations.
> This is the "six million dollar Mrs. Dale," I ask you! I made it
> with old ones and spare parts. It's in four or five bits. We wrap it
> up like a fish supper. Reckon if I'd have worked on it a bit more I
> could have phoned you with it (Big Head).*[63]

After the news he kept the radio on to hear a traditional music program. He took great delight in telling Bik MacFarlane about his secret pleasure. MacFarlane wrote, "Charlie has me wrecked with the traditional music reports Mrs. Dale keeps telling him about. He enjoys tormenting me the sadistic B."[64]

The week before he began the hunger strike Bobby told a new book at bedtime: *Jet II*. He had the men on the edge of their mattresses as he put Jet and his wife Kelly through all sorts of scrapes for several nights running. At the end of one evening, Jet was separated from her and it looked like he was finally dead, but he came bouncing back safe and sound the next night. After a few nights, the prisoners were all speculating about what would happen. Philip Rooney told Tom McElwee that Sands had a morbid craving for sad endings and he was afraid he would kill him off. McElwee replied, cynically, "Well, it's all just a load of Western trash. I hope the pair of them got stiffed!" In the end, there were gasps and sighs of relief when both Jet and Kelly lived happily ever after. Even McElwee was up at the window, raving about the book. Rooney wrote to Sile Darragh in Armagh Jail and instructed her to tell McElwee's fiancée that, "he isn't the big hard man he lets on to be, he's a phony!"

The prisoners regarded telling *Jet*, when he was on the verge of his hunger strike, to be characteristic of Bobby's generosity. This trait was apparent in other ways. Ten days before beginning the hunger strike, he was writing constantly to prisoners in the Armagh and Crumlin Road Jails, giving support and raising their morale. He even wrote a letter to a family in his home area of Twinbrook after he discovered that their child had been one of dozens who were killed on Valentine's night in a tragic fire in the Stardust disco in Dublin.

The prison warders were not so generous. MacFarlane wrote on February twenty-first that "Charlie is getting special humiliation treatment over the mirror after his visits." He worried that Sands would lose his temper and "stick his boot" into a screw and that he would be beaten up or even sent to the punishment cells on the eve of the hunger strike.[65] "He'd get murdered, no problem," MacFarlane wrote. "He came very close to banging one the other night. I'll have to calm him down a bit."

A week before the hunger strike began, the other prisoners noticed that Bobby was going into himself, like an athlete or a performer psyching up for the event. Father Murphy ("Silvertop"), the head prison priest, visited Bobby on Monday. He said he hoped that the British authorities would give them their clothes.

"If they do, we aren't taking them," answered Bobby. "We want the heap."

Maybe they would go a bit further and give them lock-up in their own cells and some privileges, suggested Murphy.

"That might have been alright a few weeks ago, but not now."[66]

During the final week, everyone was remarkably low-key. Before the first hunger strike they all talked about victory. This time, only Bobby's rendition of *Jet II* broke up an otherwise miserable week. Phillip Rooney remarked on the atmosphere the day before the strike began in a letter to Sile Darragh. "I think everybody is of the same opinion that only death awaits the strikers and discussing things like that isn't nice, so nobody bothers." It was not defeatism, he said, just realism.[67]

• • •

On the last night of February, Bobby Sands sat on his filthy wet foam mattress and ate his last-ever meal. It was Saturday, so the meal included a piece of fruit, which the prison administration was legally obliged to provide once a week. Bobby said that it was an irony that this last piece of food he would ever eat was an orange, and it was bitter.[68]

Chapter Twenty-Two

The End

D' éirigh mé ar maidin mar a tháinig an coimheádóir,
Bhuail sé mo dhoras go trom's gan labhairt.
Dhearc mé ar na ballai, 'S shíl mé nach raibh mé beo,
Tchítear nach n-imeoidh an t-iffrean seo go deo.
D'oscail an doras 's níor druideadh é go ciúin,
Ach ba chuma ar bith mar nach raibheamar inár suan.
Chuala mé éan 's ni fhaca mé geal an lae,
Is mian mór liom go raibh me go doimhin foai,
Ca bhfuil mo smaointi ar laethe a chuaigh romhainn,
S cá bhfuil an tsaol a smaoin mé abhí sa domhain,
Ni chluintear mo bhéic, 's ní fheictear mar a rith mo dheor,
Nuair a thigeann ar lá, is feidir ní bheidh mé ann.

(I arose this morning as the screw came,
He thumped my door heavily without speaking,
I stared at the walls, and thought I was dead,
It seems that this hell will never depart.
The door opened and it wasn't closed gently,
But it didn't really matter, we weren't asleep.
I heard a bird and yet didn't see the dawn of day,
Would that I were deep in the earth.
Where are my thoughts of days gone by,
And where is the life I once thought was in the world?

My cry is unheard and my tears flowing unseen,
When our day comes I'll probably not be there.) [1]

—*Bobby Sands, "Nuair a thigeann ar lá"*

The day began quite like any other. The screws left Bobby's breakfast at the door. His portions were much bigger than Malachy's. There was no feeling that something big had just begun. The sense of anticlimax was heightened because it was Sunday and the regular staff was off duty. There was no one of consequence to whom Bobby could announce the fact that he was beginning the biggest protest that ever enveloped an Irish prison. A screw tried to belittle Bobby's refusal of breakfast by muttering, "Fuck, there's another one," then shouting to his fellow screw, "Sands is starting on it this time!" The screws were taking the protest pretty lightly. They did not think it would last very long, especially after the collapse of the first one. They figured the government would come to some sort of settlement with the blanketmen. Certainly, they thought, no one would die.[2]

There were other differences from the first hunger strike. On his doctor's advice, Bobby kept raw salt in his cell and took bits on the tip of a wet finger whereas the previous strikers put salt in their water. Taking raw salt meant that Bobby could easily drink six pints of fresh water every day. The doctor thought salty water made the previous hunger strikers sick to their stomachs.[3]

Bobby was totally focused. Says Jake Jackson, "he knew where he was going and he knew where he would end up; as far as he was concerned his whole life was directed to this point where he was going to die . . . as far as he was concerned, he *had* to die."

This level of intensity and the unwillingness to let himself be distracted came through when Danny Morrison wrote Bobby that his mother had been in a "distressed state" at a public rally just before the hunger strike began. "I don't want to know these things," Bobby told Bik.[4] His concern was reflected in his diary,

My heart is very sore because I know that I have broken my poor mother's heart, and my home is struck with unbearable anxiety.[5]

He explained in the diary why he was on hunger strike.

> *I am a political prisoner. I am a political prisoner because I am
> a casualty of a perennial war that is being fought between the
> oppressed Irish people and an alien, oppressive, unwanted regime
> that refuses to withdraw from our land.*
>
> *I believe and stand by the God-given right of the Irish nation
> to sovereign independence, and the right of any Irishman or
> woman to assert this right in armed revolution. That is why I am
> incarcerated, naked, and tortured.*
>
> *. . . I am dying not just to attempt to end the barbarity of
> H-Block, or to gain the rightful recognition of a political prisoner,
> but primarily because what is lost in here is lost for the Republic
> and those wretched oppressed whom I am deeply proud to know
> as the "risen people."*

In the morning, Bobby went to mass. Some blanketmen treated him
carefully. The conversations were short.

"Right, Bobby?"

"What about ye, Risteard."

That afternoon he wrote letters to the women prisoners in Armagh Jail.
"There is so much I would like to say about them," he wrote in his diary,
"about their courage, determination, and unquenchable spirit of resistance." In the evening, he began writing his last major work, his diary. He
hoped to write a new poem but he kept being distracted by his thoughts.
He was "very annoyed" at the news on his radio that Bishop Daly condemned the hunger strike at mass. Daly was applying double standards,
he thought, condemning them but ignoring the actions of the British government over the years, not least their treatment of prisoners. Bobby
reflected on the differences between Daly and Cardinal Ó Fiaich. He concluded, by now in a cynical mood regarding Catholic clerics, that "it's not
that these people don't want to become involved in politics, it's simply
that their politics are different, that is, British."

Monday, the second day of the hunger strike, was a momentous day.
The prisoners ended the no-wash protest. They looked forward to
washing and shaving. Things, however, did not go according to plan. The
warders were on a go-slow and only five men got to wash, including
Bobby. Then the screws refused to supply hair cutting equipment until

everyone had washed.[6] Some of the men had to wait three hours to go to the toilet while the handful of prisoners washed. It "typifies the eagerness of the screws to have us off the no-wash," Bobby wrote sarcastically, claiming that the go-slow was another example of their petty vindictiveness. On the no-wash protest, the warders could more easily dominate and control the prisoners. Letting them out of their cells again meant an expansion of their arena of conflict.

After the few men washed, they were moved to B-wing, which was "allegedly clean," with new mattresses and blankets. Bobby moved into a cell on his own, which contained a bed as well as a new mattress. For four hours, they had no access to toilets or even pots, so they had to piss out the window.[7] Soon, Bobby realized that his new cell was on the cold side of the wing so he asked to be moved to the opposite side and the request was granted. He also requested an extra blanket, which he draped over the window to stop even the slightest drafts.[8] Bobby's new cell was between the "big cell" at the bottom of the wing and Philip Rooney, the brother of his old comrade Roon. When Bobby asked for a cellmate, the warders told him that they had orders from the governor to keep him alone.

Finally, the governor visited him. He said he had been informed that Bobby was on hunger strike and asked him the reason for his action.

"Political status," replied Bobby.

"Is this for yourself alone?" asked the governor.

"It is for all Republican POWs, both here and in Armagh."

The doctor examined him. He weighed 64 kilograms, blood pressure 116/78, pulse 78.[9] "I've no problems," he wrote in his diary.

His mood picked up when "Silvertop" Murphy, the priest, visited him for a short talk. Murphy told him that his mother was in better spirits. She spoke at a parade the night before. Bobby wrote, "It gave me heart. I'm not worried about the numbers of the crowds." Later, a note from his mother convinced Bobby that "she has regained her fighting spirit—I am happy now." Murphy said Bobby seemed to be in remarkably high spirits. But there was terrible news in another note. Tomboy Loudon's father had died. "I was terribly annoyed," he wrote. "It has upset me."

On Tuesday, the third day of his hunger strike, Bobby Sands awoke feeling "exceptionally well." ("It's only the third day, I know," he wrote in his diary, "but all the same I'm feeling great.") He wasn't even phased when a couple of screws put a table in his cell so that they could place his food directly in front of him instead of on the floor.

"I honestly couldn't give a damn if they placed it on my knee," he claimed.

Nor was he perturbed at their "silly questions" like, "Are you still not eating?" In mid-morning the screw took him to the doctor for his check-up. He weighed sixty-three kilograms. "So what?" he thought.

Back in the cell, he had a newspaper (the *Irish News*) and a book. Bobby had requested Kipling and he got *Maugham's Selection of Kipling's Best*, with an introduction by W. Somerset Maugham. He would read it later. Now he had to get ready for a visit from two journalists, David Beresford of *The Guardian* and Brendan O Cathaoir of the *Irish Times*. Beresford had cultivated a relationship with Danny Morrison but O Cathaoir was more questionable. Bobby remembered a recent article in *Republican News* that called him "a collaborating middle-class Nationalist, or appropriate words to that effect."

When the journalists arrived at the prison they were too well dressed and stuck out like sore thumbs among the prisoners' working-class relatives and girlfriends. As they showed their visiting card and signed in for the visit, a prison officer pulled them aside. He gave them a choice: either sign a document agreeing not to write about anything that was said during the visit, or turn around and go home. They signed the agreement.

Beresford and O Cathaoir were taken to one of the low-walled cubicles in the visitors' room. Soon, they saw coming toward them a "diminutive, Ghandi-like" man, with a long scraggly beard, blue-gray eyes, and "very slight of figure." He was wearing the new "prison-issue civilian-type clothing," double-knit slacks and a bright sweater. They were surprised to find that Bobby was "spotlessly clean." O Cathaoir even noted that, "despite the poor conditions they had endured for so long, he had so prepared for the interview that his nails were well manicured."

Bobby introduced himself first. Then, for thirty minutes he talked and smoked nearly non-stop, taking cigarettes from his two visitors and getting lights from the pipe-smoking screw who was hovering about listening to the conversation.

"We asked no questions and he spent the whole time explaining why he went on hunger strike," recalls Brendan O Cathaoir.[10] Bobby explained that he would probably die, and that he was doing it for his comrades who had endured so much but who had come to the end of what they could do short of a hunger strike. He did not want to die but he expected to die, and he was entirely willing to sacrifice his own life for the principle of political status. Although he was a practicing Catholic, he said, he rejected Bishop Daly's remarks about the hunger strike not being justified.

"If I die, God will understand."

Bobby spoke for a short time in Irish for O Cathaoir's benefit. He said he was motivated by the spirit of freedom and by the examples of Terence MacSwiney, Michael Gaughan, and Frank Stagg. "After four-and-a-half years, the H-Block prisoners were not prepared to endure further torture," he said, adding that after negotiations broke down in January, "we did not want to go back on the no-wash protest. But they moved us from clean to dirty cells." He said a settlement had been possible before Christmas after "unprecedented negotiations" involving the Northern Ireland Office, the Republican Press Center in Belfast, prison authorities, the original seven hunger strikers, a senior clergyman, and himself. He refused to name the men who were involved.

Perhaps the most striking part of the interview was his account of that meeting with Governor Hilditch just before the first hunger strike ended, where the governor told him to call off his game of brinkmanship before Sean McKenna died.

"Thirty will die," Bobby had replied curtly and then walked out of the room.

Bobby told the reporters about the documents from the Northern Ireland Office, saying that they could have been the basis of agreement if the British authorities had translated it liberally into policy. Instead, once the pressure of hunger strike was off it became clear that they had no intention of honoring the spirit of the documents.

Then he impressed on them the degree to which the prison administration had already recognized that they were political prisoners, by dealing with him as their officer commanding. Danny Morrison had been allowed to visit him thirteen times and he was given a room for discussions with the OCs of the other blocks. And, in January, Governor Hilditch had recognized his status when he came into his cell to request a "week's grace" before implementing settlement plans—a request that Bobby "granted willingly." All of this was news to the journalists; until that time it had been kept between Bobby, the prison authorities, and top leaders of the Republican Movement. Then, said Bobby, Humphrey Atkins caved in to Loyalist pressure and introduced a six-point policy that was "aimed at humiliating the prisoners . . . It included requirements which even conforming prisoners do not have to observe."

Finally, Bobby explained the mechanism of the hunger strike, how none of the Armagh women would join, how Bik MacFarlane had replaced him as OC. He ended by trying to impress on the journalists that the protesting prisoners were united and determined to overthrow the criminalization prison regime. Bobby summarized the experience in the following way: "I had a visit this morning with two reporters. Couldn't quite get my flow of thoughts together. I could have said more in a better fashion."

O Cathaoir did not agree. He was impressed with Bobby's "high intelligence, his high motivation, his idealism, and his conscious decision to sacrifice his life as his final commitment to the cause." He felt that Bobby "achieved a rare level of spiritual maturity in the course of this ordeal." In this respect, he was like the spiritual figures who wrote the ancient Irish manuscripts. "They used to argue with God." O Cathaoir came out of the meeting convinced that the prison struggle was "a human rights issue."

As they left the visit, O Cathaoir and Beresford informed a prison officer that Bobby's words were of such vital public interest that they intended to publish, despite the document they signed. O Cathaoir was true to his word. It was a breakthrough for such a sympathetic appraisal to appear in a mainstream newspaper like the *Irish Times*.[11]

Back in his cell, Bobby read the introduction to *Kipling's Best*. He took an instant dislike to Maugham, who justified Kipling's attitude to the Irish by saying that "the Irish were making a nuisance of themselves" when Kipling was in his prime.

"Damned too bad, and bigger the pity it wasn't a bigger nuisance!" he wrote in his diary.

Later that evening Father Toner visited Bobby.

"Feel he's weighing me up psychologically for a later date," Bobby wrote.

Bobby was concentrating on his main concern: to get to the end of his journey without being diverted. Priests were a source of pressure to divert him from his goal.[12]

On Wednesday morning, Bobby took another shower and then he had a shave and hair cut, which made him feel good. Some prisoners joked that it made him look ten years younger, but Bobby wrote in his diary that he felt twenty years older. As usual, he saw the doctor and told him that he had no complaints. He was sleeping well at night although not at all during the day. Bik MacFarlane figured that was because he spent the whole day "yarning" to Philip Rooney. When a governor visited him, he asked for more books and papers and, against expectations, he got every-thing he requested. He was trying to simulate normal cell conditions so that if the authorities tried to move him he could say that there was no reason to do so because he was perfectly comfortable where he was.

In the evening, Bobby noticed that his supper included jam with the bread, a "rarity." "The screws are glaring at the food," he wrote. "They seem more in need of it than my good self."[13] For the first time, he noted his "energy beginning to drain." If his physical energy was beginning to flag, his political energy was not. In his newspapers, he read about the first meeting between Margaret Thatcher and the new U.S. President Ronald Reagan. The two announced plans to counteract "Soviet expan-sionism" in Latin America and the following day Reagan announced an escalation in U.S. troops to support the El Salvadoran government against the FMLN guerrillas. Bobby wrote of the Reaganite expansionism with passion and anger.

> I am abreast with the news and view with utter disgust and anger the Reagan/Thatcher plot. It seems quite clear that they intend to counteract Russian expansionism with imperialist expansionism, to protect their vital interests they say.
>
> What they mean is they covet other nations' resources. They want to steal what they haven't got and to do so (as the future may unfortunately prove) they will murder oppressed people and deny them their sovereignty as nations. No doubt Mr. Haughey will toe the line in Ireland when Thatcher so demands.

The next day, Bobby's physical condition continued to deteriorate. He felt cold, a complaint that would dog him over the next few weeks.[14] He also had a "threatening toothache."

But his main concern was that the authorities would use his family against him. His father had fallen and word of the accident reached the prison welfare office, who informed Bobby that his father had "taken ill." Bobby did not want to know. He wrote in his diary that the welfare people "tried to get me to crawl for a special visit with my family." He asked Bik MacFarlane to tell Liam Og to take action to "completely cut off" the prison administration from his family.[15]

The newspapers carried a statement in the House of Commons by

Secretary of State Humphrey Atkins, stating that the government would not give in to pressure from the hunger strike.

> *It does not annoy me because my mind was prepared for such things and I know I can expect more of such, right to the bitter end.*

His other reading was more productive. He got stuck into some of Kipling's poems and especially liked one that applied to their own situation:

> *The earth gave up her dead that tide,*
> *Into our camp he came,*
> *And said his say, and went his way,*
> *And left our hearts aflame.*
>
> *Keep tally on the gun butt score,*
> *The vengeance we must take,*
> *When God shall bring full reckoning,*
> *For our dead comrade's sake.*

"I hope not," he said to himself. But he quickly added that,

> *I have hope, indeed. All men must have hope and never lose heart. But my hope lies in the ultimate victory for my poor people. Is there any hope greater than that?*

Bobby was slightly embarrassed to admit that he was paying a bit more attention to religion.

> *I'm saying prayers—crawler! (and a last minute one, some would say). But I believe in God, and I'll be presumptuous and say he and I are getting on well this weather.*
> *I can ignore the presence of food staring me straight in the face all the time. But I have this desire for brown wholemeal bread, butter, Dutch cheese and honey. Ha!! It is not damaging me, because, I think, "Well, human food can never keep a man alive forever," and I console myself with the fact that I'll get a great feed up above (if I'm worthy).*

> *But then I'm struck by this awful thought that they don't eat*
> *food up there. But if there's something better than brown whole-*
> *meal bread, cheese and honey, etcetera, then it can't be bad.*

Six days into the hunger strike, Bobby began to feel more isolated. He had no visits from priests for a couple of days and the authorities stopped him seeing his solicitor. It was, he said, "another part of the isolation process, which, as time goes by, they will ruthlessly implement." Soon, he expected, they might move him to the prison hospital and increase his isolation yet further. Although he would be sorry to leave, he was consigned to that fact that "the road is a hard one and everything must be conquered." Bobby was cheered by some news in the papers. His old friend from Twinbrook, Jennifer McCann, told the judge on being sentenced, "I am a Republican prisoner of war and at the moment my comrade Bobby Sands is on hunger strike to defend my rights as a political prisoner." The *Irish News* reported a perceptible rise in public support for the hunger strike.

Apart from reading, his main luxury was the "bog-roll" cigarettes that made their rounds each night. "I'm still getting some smokes," he wrote. "Decadence, well sort of, but who's perfect. Bad for your health." He was feeling slightly weak but he was encouraged that he had not yet experienced any of the headaches that had dogged him throughout his time in the H-Blocks.

On Sunday, the eighth day of his hunger strike, a screw set Bobby's breakfast, on the table while he read. The meals, he thought, just kept getting bigger and better.

In mid-morning he went to the doctor for his daily check-up. Thankfully, "Mengele" (Dr. Emerson) was still off with the flu. The young weekend doctor told him the name of the doctor who had been filling in for Emerson. It was Dr. Ross. Bobby remembered that Ross attended the seven hunger strikers throughout the first strike. He called him "little friendly Doctor Ross" because he liked to talk but as he continued talking and asking questions Bobby began to form the opinion that he was a bit too nosy: not just a physical examiner but "also an examiner of people's minds."

"Which reminds me, they haven't asked me to see a psychiatrist yet. No doubt they will yet, but I won't see him for I am mentally stable, probably more so than he."

Later that morning, Bobby went to mass where the clean-shaven prisoners were all kidding each other about how they looked. An American priest said mass. His uneasiness about what to say was increased by his experiences coming into prison: the "unfriendly soldier" at the gate "in his camouflage uniform and his glaring rifle"; a prison officer who tricked him into posing for a photo. Once in H3, the priest changed into his purple vestments and walked down a corridor, through three prison gates and into the canteen, where the noise was deafening. He saw dozens of men laughing and talking, walking up and down. He described them as "stripped to the waist, their bare feet white on a black floor." It was a natural mistake. These parishioners were not stripped but *dressed to the waist*.

Bobby saw his old cellmate Dixie Elliot speaking to a prisoner he didn't know. He decided to say hello.

"Here, move over," he told Dixie. "Who's this?"

"This is my mate, Bobby, Sy Gallagher."

They sat for a time, Bobby between the two of them, asking about Sy. Where was he from? Did he have a big family? How was he doing? Dixie thought that it was typical of Bobby; the hunger must be gnawing away at him, yet *he* was putting others at ease. It was the last time Dixie ever spoke to Bobby.

Bik called for quiet. Bobby didn't make himself known to the priest and the others respected his privacy. The priest began mass. He was startled when the men responded in the loudest voices he'd ever heard. He told them about when he was in prison for breaking into the local draft board to destroy draft records as a protest against the war in Vietnam. Denis Faul had said that the prisoners love news, so he told them that he'd been at a rally the day before where Ian Paisley had prayed fervently for all the Protestants who were killed by bombs and bullets. He suggested that God was not interested in any sectarian prayer and asked them to pray for all the dead, Protestant and Catholic, IRA, and UDA. They did. He was satisfied. "It was a better prayer than Paisley's."

Then he said, "I want you all to pray for the young man who's on hunger strike." He did not know that Bobby was there. Philip Rooney looked over at Bobby, sitting there as the priest prayed for him. Suddenly he felt very sad.

Back in the cell, the screws delivered dinner. Bobby let it sit as he read a comm from his sister Bernie. Dinner was replaced by another plate of food. Bobby continued to read some wild-life articles in various papers. They brought back memories of his childhood, "the once-upon-a-time budding ornithologist!" Bobby went to the pipes and asked Philip Rooney for a cigarette and they sat and talked. Each day, Rooney expected Bobby to get weaker but he seemed to remain controlled and composed.

"Only for this, I would have liked to have been an ornithologist," Bobby told him.

"Bobby, you don't know, I mean . . . " Philip tried to reassure him that maybe he *would* have a chance at a further life.

"Well, if I *do* get through this, well and good."

Here he was again, thought Rooney, him dying and trying to comfort *me*! They lay there at the pipes, smoking. Nothing they said was profound, but just the act of normal conversation seemed to bring comfort.

Back at his table, Bobby finished his diary.

> *I am awaiting the lark, for spring is all but upon us. How I listened to that lark when I was in H-5, and watched a pair of chaffinches which arrived in February. Now lying on what indeed is my death bed, I still listen even to the black crows.*
>
> *In a few hours time I shall be twenty-seven grand years of age. Paradoxically it will be a happy enough birthday; perhaps that's because I am free in spirit. I can offer no other reason.*

• • •

> *Well, I have gotten by twenty-seven years, so that is something. I may die, but the Republic of 1916 will never die. Onward to the Republic and liberation of our people.*

Bobby got a birthday present when he turned twenty-seven on March ninth: The governor allowed Philip Rooney to come in and brush and mop his cell. It was a welcome distraction, always good to talk to a man straight to his face. He received a lot of birthday cards and was particularly pleased to get a mass bouquet with fifty masses on it from Mrs. Burns from Sevastopol Street, a strong Republican woman who never forgot the prisoners. That night, the lads gave Bobby a birthday concert, the first singsong since the hunger strike began. Although Bik tried to keep life normal, with debates and discussions, there were no jollifications on the wing as there had been during the first hunger strike. Sean Glas called it "the longest wake I was ever at in my life."

Bobby was too tired to sing but before the concert began the men asked him to say a few words. He told the lads that it had been a pleasure to go through this time with them and talked about what was ahead of him. He was glad of the support he had from the comrades around him. He spoke to the young prisoners about the bravery they had already shown and how important it was for them to dedicate their lives to the struggle. He said the hunger strike was not just about the five demands but that it was about their right to resist injustice, to establish that their struggle was political and just. He said that he expected to die but that he was willing to do it for such comrades as them and for the Socialist Republic. The important thing was that they carried the struggle on to victory.[16]

Then everyone did his party piece. Tomboy sang Bobby's song, "The Voyage." Blute McDonnell did "Matthew and Son," starting out at the back of the door, "Ta da da, ta da dum da," and then walking toward his cell door so that the sound got louder for a "fade-in," then into reverse for a fade-out at the end. Tom McElwee's gruff voice came booming out the door. "I can't sing. I want to do a tap dance." McElwee lifted the lids off the two pisspots in his cell, placed them on the floor next to the door, and danced to wild applause.

After the concert, Bobby wrote to Liam Og. He had one last birthday request,

> . . . I was wondering (here it comes, says you), that out of the goodness of all yer hearts you could get me one miserly book and try to leave in the poems of Ethna Carberry—Cissy. That's really all I want. Last request, as they say. Some ask for cigarettes, others for blindfolds, yer man asks for poetry.[17]

• • •

Bobby began to wonder when he would be moved. He thought he noticed "several tactics" by the administration, foremost of which was,

> a deliberate policy of false disinterest, that is, "we couldn't care less" type of thing to make me feel small or insignificant and to try to create the impression in my mind that the H/S is merely confined to my cell.

He noted that, "I was disappointed that I never even got a note from the Dark even if it was just to say good-bye . . . "[18] Nonetheless, Bik Mac-Farlane noted that Bobby was in "pretty cheerful spirits," which he attributed to Bobby's total acceptance of the fact that he would die. Bobby had mentioned it several times during conversation, always "in a quite matter of fact manner."

Liam Og had written to Bobby about the lack of mass protests on the streets, saying that it would be better to try and build a crescendo of protest. Bobby agreed, but in his increasingly detached fashion wrote, "No use in a big flourish at the start and damp down at the end, but to be honest, and if you'll pardon the expression, I just couldn't give a balls!"[19] At the same time, he wrote in his diary that,

> *I always keep thinking of James Connolly . . . I always have tremendous feeling for Liam Mellowes as well; and for the present leadership of the Republican Movement, and a confidence in them that they will always remain undaunted and unchanged.*[20]

If Bobby had come to terms with death, he was still obsessed with a fear that someone would interfere with him achieving it. He felt tremendous support from his parents and Marcella, although his mother was "still a bit inquisitive on 'are you doing this of your own free will, son?'" He reassured her that he was, and even let her keep "a wee bit of hope" that he might not die, even though he was not only consigned to dying but *determined* to die.[21]

It worried him that the clergy might step in to try and end the protest. He wrote in his diary (March 10) that some articles in the newspapers had made him "increasingly worried and wary" that there might be an attempt "to pull the carpet from under our feet and undermine us . . . with the concession bid in the form of 'our own clothes as a right.'" He felt that this was motivated primarily by a common "wish to see the revolutionary struggle of the people brought to an end." A settlement based on "human rights" would still leave them classed as criminals, which would be a major blow against their struggle. Bobby wrote of the priests that,

> *It is the declared wish of these people to see humane and better conditions in these Blocks. But the issue at stake is not "human-*

itarian," nor about better or improved living conditions. It is purely political and only a political solution will solve it. This in no way makes us prisoners elite nor do we (nor have we at any time) purport to be elite.

We wish to be treated "not as ordinary prisoners" for we are not criminals. We admit no crime unless, that is, the love of one's people and country is a crime.

Bobby was especially distrustful of Tom Toner, who was "overtly cordial and like a jackal waiting on prey to physically weaken."[22] He wrote to Liam Og that he did not care to enter into any discussion of "negotiations" or "settlements" but that he was afraid of a rerun of the end of the first hunger strike.

> *. . . what is worrying me is this. I'm afraid that there is a possibility that at a crucial stage (which could be after death) the Brits would move with a settlement and demand [Tom Toner] as guarantor. Now this is feasible, if a man is dying, that they would try to force Bik to accept a settlement to save life which, of course, would be subject to Index's interpretation and we know how far that would get us . . . I've told Bik to let me or anyone else die before submitting to a ploy like that. Well, that's what was bugging me—silly old fool, aren't I!!*[23]

By the twelfth day of his hunger strike, Bobby began to notice his physical decline. "I know I'm getting physically weaker," he wrote. He had poems in his mind, "mediocre no doubt," about the hunger strike and what it had "stirred up in my heart and in my mind." A couple of days earlier, he had written to Liam Og with blacker humor that someone should write a poem about the tribulations of a hunger striker. "I would like to," he wrote, "but how could I finish it?"[24] Now, he wrote, "my heart is willing but my body wants to be lazy, so I have decided to mass all my energy and thoughts into consolidating my resistance." The main threat was intensifying humiliation by some of the screws.

> *Nothing else seems to matter except that lingering constant reminding thought, "Never give up." No matter how bad, how black, how painful, how heart-breaking, "Never give up," "Never*

> despair," "Never lose hope." *Let them bastards laugh at you all*
> *they want, let them grin and jibe, allow them to persist in their*
> *humiliation, brutality, deprivations, vindictiveness, petty*
> *harassments, let them laugh now, because all of that is no longer*
> *important or worth a response.*

Some of the screws teased Bobby incessantly; especially the one they called "Puck" (or the "Goat"), who switched the lights off if Bobby was trying to read and flicked them on and off during the night to bother him when he was sleeping. On March 14, Ricky O'Rawe wrote that he turned Bobby's cell lights on three times the previous night—at 10:00 P.M., 2:00 A.M., and 6:00 A.M.—waking him every time.[25] Bobby wrote of the Goat in his diary (March 16) that,

> *There is a certain Screw here who has taken it upon himself to*
> *harass me to the very end and in a very vindictive childish*
> *manner. It does not worry me, the harassment, but his attitude*
> *aggravates me occasionally. It is one thing to torture, but quite a*
> *different thing to exact enjoyment from it, that's his type.*

Bik MacFarlane wrote, less charitably, that "There's a vindictive little insignificant bastard called B— working on this wing, who goes out of his way to indulge in the pettiest of harassment."[26]

A couple of nights later, Bik wrote that the screws were generally messing about. One night, they refused to let Bobby slop out, even though Philip Rooney rang the bell twice within the hour to tell the warders that Bobby had no water and full pisspot.[27] The screws messed with Bobby's food. The Goat piled it sky high . . . massive plates of beans and chips. "There ye are, son, get them into ye," he teased Bobby. Bobby noticed that the orderlies were stealing the sweet things from his plate. He could not decide whether it was a case of "How low can you get?" or "Well, could you blame them?" One night they left his supper in when Father Murphy was visiting. The plate had a small doughy bun with two bites taken out. "I ask you!" Bobby declared to the priest.[28]

The crisis came to a head one day when the Goat accused Bobby of eating. It was one of the few times that Bobby blew up at a screw. But when the row was over, Bobby was up at the pipe, asking Philip Rooney, "What's the food like?"

Bobby kept his cool on St. Patrick's Day, when a governor came in and saw what he was reading.

"Sands, you're still with us, eh? Ah, I see were doing a bit of reading. What have we got here? Short stories . . . Rudyard Kipling . . . Short stories of Rudyard Kipling, good choice Sands! Short stories are better for you because you won't be around long enough to read novels."[29]

The governor left the cell and Bobby went to tell Rooney what he said. Rooney could hear the anger in his voice and the rage "that he didn't get the opportunity to say something bad enough back to him."[30] But by the time Bobby got to his diary he was more philosophical. "That's the sort of people they are," he wrote. "Curse them! I don't care. It's been a long day."[31] Tom McElwee was not philosophical. When he heard about it he wanted to kill the governor. Bik MacFarlane had to order him not to do anything because he was the key man for smuggling comms with Marie Moore's brigade. Any trouble with screws would hurt Bobby more than it could help him. McElwee had become both fond and protective of Bobby, who was now just two cells away. He wrote to his family of Bobby that,

> He is a really great bloke, just one of those people who never thinks of himself. It nearly broke my heart when I was coming back from slop out the other night and saw him sitting back on the bed with a towel draped around his shoulders and the priest sitting at the side of the bed. He just looked so lonely in the dim light of the cell. It's a long hard struggle for him.[32]

By the time Frank Hughes joined the hunger strike on March 15, Bobby was beginning to noticeably weaken. He found it tiring to comb his hair after a bath. His weight loss had been gradual and only now did the prisoners notice it. The doctor said Bobby was beginning to lose muscle. While he did not have any alarming dizzy spells, he began to feel softness in his calf muscles. Bobby's parents and Marcella visited him on March sixteenth and he told Bik MacFarlane that it was a "very good visit" that had left him "in a more contented frame of mind"[33] His family, however, were "shattered" when they saw him because he could not stand without swaying.[34]

With physical weakness came heightened senses. His sense of smell heightened incredibly and he was bothered by the smell of the warders' aftershave. He could even smell the water in his cell. The cold intensified and he began to experience shortness of breath. Despite the weakness, he kept on smoking the "bog-roll cigarettes" that Philip Rooney passed to him through the pipes. "I smoked some cigarettes today," he wrote in his diary. "We still defeat them in this sphere. If the screws only knew the half of it; the ingenuity of the POW is something amazing. The worse the situation the greater the ingenuity. Someday it may all be revealed."[35]

But he could not defeat them on one thing. He knew that as he weakened he would be moved to the prison hospital. His real trial would begin.

● ● ●

On Sunday, March 22, Bik MacFarlane and Richard O'Rawe were talking before mass. Bobby approached them.

"I think I'll be moved in the next day or so," he said. He gave Richard his radio because he would need it as the new PRO.

O'Rawe did not know what to say. He just looked at Bobby and smiled. Bobby smiled back. They exchanged no words but to O'Rawe, Bobby's eyes were saying, "I'll not see ye again" and, "it was all I could fuckin' do to stop crying."

Then Bobby turned to Bik and asked for a private word. He was concerned about who would replace him when he died.

"Bik, have you got those replacements sorted?" he asked.

"Aye, just leave it with me, it's okay." Bik was distinctly uncomfortable but Bobby pressed him.

"Don't worry about it," Bik insisted. "It's sorted. I've got a list of names here."

Bobby grabbed Bik by the arm and continued, firmly.

"Have you got this sorted out?!"

"Yeah, it's okay. There's no problem."

"No, you're missing the point. *You* need to be on top of this. Who's replacing me? You just need to be certain that you have this, because you need to be of the same mind as me."

Bobby looked straight into Bik's eyes. Bik could see that he was deadly serious. He seemed to think that Bik was not seriously confronting the fact that he *would* die and that his replacement had to be as committed as Bobby. Finally, Bik told him.

"Well, as a matter of fact, I've got Joe McDonnell."

Bobby relaxed his grip immediately.

"Good choice. Joe McDonnell. Great choice. He'll not let you down," he said, adding in the same breath, "Got any fags?"

Bobby went over and talked to some other comrades. Joe Watson remembers Bobby coming over and shaking his hand. All he could come out with was a vague question, "Bob, what do you think?" Bobby just, "turned around and looked at me and I knew by looking at him that he definitely was going to die. It was just a thing in his eyes . . . he looked and he knew." Watson had to move away because it was too emotional.

• • •

The next morning at 9:00 A.M., the screws told Bobby he had an hour to get ready to go to the hospital wing. As they took him to get a shower, Bobby shouted to Tomboy that he was about to be moved. Bik requested to go to the toilet so that he could chat with Bobby before they took him away. "How you feeling?" he asked. Bobby replied that he was "sound." They both expressed surprise that they had kept him there so long. Bobby's last concern was to get the contraband out of his cell. He could not keep things up his anus anymore because he did not have regular bowel movements and it was harder to get them back out again. As Bobby showered, Bik got the screws to let Philip Rooney go into Bobby's cell to clear it out and get his things ready to take with him. Bobby left his best pen for Bik MacFarlane and he gave Jake Jackson his hairbrush.[36] At about ten o'clock, the shout went up the wing, "That's transport for Sands!"

Tomboy requested to go to the toilet. The two old friends met in the corridor and gave each other a final hug.

"Everything okay, Bobby?"

"I'll be all right."

"That's sound."

As he left the wing, Bobby greeted the lads.

"Right lads that's me away, all the best, see youse."

Bik was in the top cell, the last person Bobby passed.

"All the best, Bob."

And he was gone. The prisoners all sat down on their mattresses, shattered. They knew they would never see Bobby Sands again.

• • •

When he got to the hospital, a Professor Love examined Bobby and held a "purely medical conversation" with him. He was satisfied with Bobby's physical state. He had no headaches or "bad signs." On Thursday, Bobby wrote that he was settling in to hospital life. "I'm 54.75 today and everything else is normal," he wrote, apart from a slight burning while urinating. He was mentally alert, walking in the mornings and spending the afternoons sitting up in bed reading. The governor had given clearance for almost everything he needed: a radio, books, a weekly visit. He was getting the *Irish Times* and *Irish Press* every day.

> *If this visitation was meant to damage my resolve it has succeeded only in strengthening it. I have now come to it and I don't feel lonely nor on my own. Maybe it's because I understand and freely accept my situation. So up the Republic!*[37]

• • •

On the fifth day of the hunger strike, the MP for Fermanagh/South Tyrone Frank Maguire had died of a heart attack. Everyone assumed that his brother Noel would succeed him. Additional Nationalist candidates would split the Catholic vote and enable the sole Unionist, Harry West, to win the seat. Bernadette MacAliskey might rerun her anti-H-Block campaign. Sinn Féin was not a threat: the party was very weak in Fermanagh, where their top man was a barely-known twenty-six-year-old schoolteacher named Owen Carron who ran the local H-Block Committee.

Nonetheless, Maguire's death set off light bulbs in Republican heads. They had been awoken by MacAliskey's previous campaign and Bobby's arguments about the advantages of running blanketmen in elections had reached some receptive ears, chiefly Jim Gibney and Gerry Adams. Some accounts credit Gibney as the originator of the idea to run Bobby for the vacant Westminster seat. Others maintain that the idea originated with MacAliskey.[38] Apparently, however, the idea to run Bobby originated in the H-Blocks. Within days after Maguire's death, Bik MacFarlane wrote to the movement suggesting that they run Bobby for the vacant seat. "Do you reckon we might put a H/Ser forward?" he asked Liam Og.

Adams, as vice-president of Sinn Féin, prevailed upon the party's executive to run Bobby for Maguire's vacant seat, *if* they could persuade other Nationalist candidates to give him a clear field. He "never thought

that Bobby getting elected would have moved the British government"
but he did think that it would give new credibility to the prison struggle
and, more importantly, to the overall Republican struggle.

Adams secured undertakings from Noel Maguire and MacAliskey not
to oppose a hunger striker. On March 26, Sinn Féin announced that Bobby
Sands would stand for Maguire's seat. Bobby was excited about the election and told Jim Gibney, "It's a pity I can't go out an canvass with you."
Yet he did not expect personal salvation, telling Gibney,

"Even if I win it doesn't matter. It won't change things. I'll die."

In a comm to Liam Og, Bobby revealed more bemusement than excite-
ment at the idea of being an MP. He even jokingly signed himself as a
British MP.

> When I face the end, comrade, I'll face it fighting and when I
> can't move to fight then I'll just lie down and suffer it to the
> bitter end . . . Fill me in on the by-election and can we get unity
> . . . for all the worry-mongers tell them not to worry. I'm okay
> and comrade, to me these are the last days. Might write you a
> poem. Food's in the cell all the time. Quite decorative actually
> and doesn't bother me at all. Must go you auld ear deafener. Your
> friend and comrade forever.
> —The right honourable Marcella the Woo!![39]

But there were problems. Noel Maguire was having second thoughts
and the SDLP's virulently anti-IRA Austin Currie was threatening to
stand to block Bobby's election. Bik MacFarlane sent his opinion to the
leadership. He argued to run Bobby regardless of who stood against him.

> . . . Looks as though there is plenty of devious activity afloat
> with the election, just as you said—it makes me throw up. One
> thing is very clear—the Brits fear us taking this seat, hence the
> SDLP opposition. If Austin Currie runs against Bob the split
> vote will allow [the Unionist Harry West] to take the seat . . . I
> think we should not allow ourselves to be intimidated or bluffed
> out of this election. I reckon we should tell Maguire that we are
> going to run—just put it to him straight what Currie and that
> shower are up to and ask him to back us . . .[40]

Monday, March 30, was the deadline for nominations for the by-election. Carron and Jim Gibney lodged Bobby's nomination papers early and Maguire also lodged his papers as a ruse to stop Currie running. Maguire intended to withdraw just before the deadline, when it would be too late for Currie to respond. As the 4:00 P.M. deadline neared, Adams and Carron sat in a car around the corner from the electoral offices, just in case Maguire failed to withdraw. In his pocket, Adams had a statement announcing the reasons for Bobby's withdrawal. He explained later that, "We could not afford to have Bobby defeated. The stakes were too high."[41] With less than ten minutes left, Maguire finally arrived. He walked past the reporters who had congregated at the office and went inside. When he emerged, he had his nomination papers back and made a statement to the press.

> *It has now become a question of conscience with me. I have been told the only way of saving Bobby Sands's life is by letting him go forward in the elections. I just cannot have the life of another man on my hands. I am calling my supporters to throw their weight behind Bobby Sands.*[42]

Carron and Adams got out of their car, walked over, and shook Maguire's hand.

As he listened to his radio, Bik MacFarlane was writing a comm to Liam Og about how "sick" he was about the SDLP's participation in the election. Then, in the middle of comm he heard the breaking news that Bobby would have a clear run. For a moment, he forgot his usual grammar-school writing style. "Ya-fuckin-hoo!," he wrote. "Man, I'm nearly in tears . . . we'll murder them, no problem, comrade. It's the people's year, man. I can feel it in my bones."[43] Bobby was pleased with the news, too, but far less ebullient than his old comrades. He still refused to even hope that the election might bring personal salvation. He wrote to Gerry Adams,

> *Seems we've well and truly entered new realms. Hopefully we'll be successful if only for the Movement's sake. I'm just getting the days in, they fly in. Feel myself getting naturally and gradually weaker. I will be very sick in a week or two, but my mind will see me thru. I've no doubt about that. Seen ya on TV,*

*ya big ugly hunk, haven't changed a bit. I'm not at all building
hopes on anything. I'm afraid I'm just resigned to the worse, so
sin sin.*[44] *People find this hard to grasp altho' I'm ensuring I give
my family some hope to hold on to. I've been reading poetry and
Gaelige in the papers and listening to whatever traditional music
there is on the radio and generally carrying on—so for a change
I'm taking it easy (such an excuse, are ye jealous?). Watch your
big self and Beannacht de ort comrade. Marcella XXXXXXX*[45]

Bobby seemed more pleased that he finally got his book of poetry by
Ethna Carberry than with his nomination. The next day, he wrote excitedly to Liam Og,

*Guess what? I got the poetry books! Comrade, I'm in tears. I
never knew that Ethna Carberry was reared under the shadow of
Cavehill. Thanks, comrade. Will ensure the books will go to my
mother where they can be collected by you. I'll write a wee note
to Liam on the inside cover of Alice's book.*[46]

After his initial outburst, even MacFarlane returned to earth. Although
he was "still delighted," he wrote to Adams that unity and "what is good
for the war" were the prime concerns if the hunger strike ended without
gaining the five demands. If a settlement failed, he did not see any option
but to go into the system.[47]

Owen Carron was appointed election agent, which effectively made
him the candidate since the British government refused to even let Bobby
appear on television. Carron had to visit Bobby in prison and have him
sign papers appointing him as his spokesman. Carron expected Bobby to
be the chubby, long-haired man who had become famous overnight from
the hunger strike posters, perhaps with the addition of the scruffy blanketman's beard. Instead, in the prison hospital's dinging room he found a
wirier and frailer Bobby, now with short fair hair and no beard, wearing
pajamas and a dressing gown. After some small talk, Carron told Bobby
not to worry if he decided to come off the hunger strike, that he would
deal with the people outside. "There's no question of that," replied Bobby.
Carron explained the ins and outs of Fermanagh politics. Bobby had a
built-in Nationalist majority but would lose some anti-violence Nationalists through abstentions. With just nine days to the election, it would be a

gruelling campaign. Carron asked Bobby to write an election appeal. It was an indication of Bobby's physical and mental state that he refused. He asked Owen to get the movement to write the appeal themselves.

"A bit taxing on the mind for me, you understand, as after all it is thirty-three days today and I'm concentrating more on staying relaxed in mind, okay, comrade."

He seemed more concerned about getting a copy of the new book the movement was publishing, *Writings of Bobby Sands*. He asked Liam Og to put it in another book's cover and send it in through his lawyer.

Bobby looked forward to extra visits from his election team and he claimed his condition was still "not too bad physically but now and again the water becomes a bit repulsive but I can still drink it . . . I'm well in mind and will remain so, so look after yourselves and regards to one and all, and don't worry your wee selves."[48]

• • •

The campaign was, indeed, grueling. By mobilizing its supporters from across the island, Sinn Féin organized a grassroots campaign that set a pattern for the party's politics into the 1990s and after. They faced hostility from some Catholics and most Protestants. The RUC and the Ulster Defense Regiment harassed canvassers and tore down posters. From the floor of parliament, Labour spokesman Don Concannon said that "a vote for Sands is a vote of approval for the perpetrators of the La Mon massacre, the murder of Lord Mountbatten, and the latest brutal and inhuman killing of Mrs. Mathers."[49] Yet young volunteers from all over Ireland swamped the constituency to raise votes for Bobby Sands. They drove around in convoys, with Irish tricolors flying and Republican music blaring from loudhailers. They held massive campaign meetings. They gave grassroots Nationalists the same sense of agency and possibility of victory that the prisoners had already experienced through their struggles in Long Kesh and Armagh Jail.

The election count took place on Friday, April 10, at the Fermanagh College of Further Education in Enniskillen. A few blanketmen were listening for the result but they were under strict orders not to make any show of celebration if Bobby won because it would show the warders that they had radios. Bik MacFarlane listened as the returning officer announced the result:

"Sands, Bobby, Anti-H-Blocks Political Prisoner, thirty thou . . ."

The voice was interrupted by a huge "yeeeoooohh" from Danny Morrison who stood close to the media's microphones, along with cheers that swept the hall over the stunned silence of the Unionists. Bobby had taken 30,492 votes to West's 29,046.

When the noise died down, the returning officer continued, "I declare that Bobby Sands has been duly elected to serve as a member for the said constituency."

Gerry Adams was driving on the road to Dublin. When he heard the news he began pounding on the steering wheel, shouting, "Fuck it, we've done it, we've done it, we've done it . . ."[50]

In the H-Blocks, the word went through the pipes immediately. In some blocks the men contained themselves to a few quiet "whoops." Others jumped up and down, in an exercise that Raymond MacCartney called "silent screaming." A couple of governors and some NIO officials were in the prison hospital. Old Bobby, the medical orderly, was delighted. "Their faces told the story," he said. "It was a lovely sight." He mentioned to one of the medical officers, within earshot of the officials, that Bobby's cell needed a cleaning because, "after all, we have an MP in the wing now." The officials glared at him.

Old Bobby went into the cell and shook Bobby's hand.

"Well done, son, you deserve it."

"Sure, if you have any problems you can always ask for an MP's visit with me!" replied Bobby.[51]

Later that night, Father Murphy visited Bobby as he was taking a bath. Bobby was "overjoyed" at the victory. The priest felt that the British would have to reach a solution now because they could not let a member of parliament die in a British prison.[52]

In H3, Bik MacFarlane was elated. He was too familiar with the British to entertain thoughts that this would save Bobby. But it was a major victory in their campaign to win popular acknowledgement that the IRA was a political army and they were political prisoners.

> *Comrade, What a day—a real super effort!! Don't know whether to laugh shout or cry. The news was greeted here in silent jubilation (we are very security conscious you see!!). Now I wonder will the opposition be just as quick to declare that the IRA have that popular support they were claiming would be seen*

*if we won this seat. Good old Austin [Currie] was quick to say
we hadn't and it wasn't a vote for the RA [Republican Army].
Up yours too, Austin, my boy. Just looking at the figures; it
would appear that our honourable opponent, farmer West,
received an amount of Nationalist votes—fair play to the dear
sensible bastard. Up theirs, too!! Onward to victory. Hope you
have sobered up sunshine, I'm sitting here picturing the heap of
you swilling down loads of black brew and making right idiots of
yourselves and boy am I jealous?? . . . I'm away here to relax for
a wee while. The strain of this last week has been too much man!!
Congrats to one and all you wonderful people. We really showed
them. Take care and God Bless . . . UP the good old RA and other
such outrageous outbursts. Nite, nite and God Speed. Bik.*[53]

Maggie Thatcher had other ideas. In far-off Riyadh, she emerged from a royal Saudi banquet to insist to the press that the result had changed nothing.

"A crime is a crime is a crime," she said. "It is not political, it is a crime."

• • •

Ironically, the immediate effect of Bobby's election was to shorten his life. Doctor Ross said Bobby was "going downhill very fast" and he blamed his downturn on too many visits and too much talking.

As Bobby weakened, he took visits in his cell rather than the hospital canteen. Marcella and Rosaleen Sands were the usual visitors. Jim Gibney sometimes accompanied them, although he felt increasingly like he was invading their last privacies with their dying son and brother. Priests Toner and Murphy came around to argue (in Toner's case) or just to have a bit of a talk (in Murphy's). A prison dentist came to chat. There were doctors, medical officers, screws, and prison orderlies. Assistant Governor McCartney came most days with his amiable manner. Not a stickler for rules, he allowed Bobby extra visits and letters and kept back the poison pen letters that wished him a slow and painful death. Pat Finucane, Bobby's lawyer, visited to make out his last will and testament.

They all found Bobby sitting on his bed, to the left of the cell as you entered, the head of his bed to the window at the back of the cell, feet to the door. He was dressed in striped pajamas and multicolored bathrobe—

prison-issue, of course. "Just to make the point that you're still wearing our gear," thought Jim Gibney. On the table, to the right along the wall, there was always a meal, even after Bobby was physically unable to eat it. Beside the table was a chair. In one corner by the door was the pisspot, in the other a small locker. There were a few luxuries that Bobby had not known for three and a half years: his books, radio, and bedside kit. The usual fluorescent light was dimmer than most. Bobby's bed was bigger than he'd had in his cell and with a real mattress instead of a cheap foam one.

When Bobby had visitors a warder hovered around, listening and taking notes. Rosaleen found the staff cold and indifferent except one, who she said did everything he could to comfort Bobby. This was a medical officer named Paul, "a caring guy" with "a first-class professional approach."[54] Another sympathetic warder was J—, a Protestant who started his job hating Republicans and ended it hating Loyalists. Although he disagreed with what they had done and he still considered them to be "terrorists," J— admired the IRA prisoners for their dedication. A lot of Loyalist prisoners could not go to bed without sleeping tablets. But he never gave sleeping tablets to Republicans. J— became particularly fond of Bobby. They talked about sport and current events, about anything but politics.[55] But the most sympathetic companion in the hospital was "Old Bobby," the medical orderly who was jailed on a fraud charge. One former blanketman called him "one of the kindest human beings the lads could have wished for in the hospital; he stuck his neck out ten miles to help."[56]

Although Rosaleen Sands found them to be cold, the medical warders took great care of the hunger strikers. As they weakened, the MOs constantly applied cream to their legs, back, and hips and turned them. J—, for one, takes pride in the fact that none of the hunger strikers ever got bedsores.

Not all of the hospital authorities were so thoughtful, however. In mid-April, Jim Gibney was walking with Rosaleen and Marcella toward Bobby's cell when a warder told them that the head doctor wanted to see Rosaleen. The doctor was sitting beside his desk, on which a small tape recorder was running.

"I just want to speak to Mrs. Sands," said the doctor.

She stood listening as he began to explain to her in the finest of detail how Bobby's body would collapse in on itself, how he would slowly die, what would happen to his organs, and what were some possible causes of death.

"The purple marks on his chest and arms are blood vessels that have broken down and collapsed, his eyesight is being permanently damaged, his vital organs are under intense strain. There are a number of ways in which he may die; a brain tumor or a massive coronary attack, his kidneys or liver could collapse."

On he went in a savage psychological assault. And then, the coup de grâce, "Of course, you could stop it all."

Mrs. Sands just stood for moment. She looked at the doctor and said, simply, "Well, now I want to go and see my son."

She told Bobby what happened.

"Look, don't be listening to them," he replied, "because they're trying to break me. They think they can break me through you. Then you stay strong, *because I will stay strong.*"

● ● ●

In the wake of his election victory, Bobby requested a visit from three southern Irish parliamentarians. John O'Connell, an MD, had been minister of health in a previous government. Neil Blaney was minister of agriculture until he was dismissed after being implicated in a plot to smuggle guns to Northern Republicans in 1970. A big, strong imposing man, Blaney remained an independent member of the southern parliament because of his popularity in Donegal. Sile de Valera, from the most famous family in Ireland (granddaughter of Eamon de Valera), had just been elected to the European parliament. O'Connell was awed by the de Valera name, but he could not be awed by Sile because of her self-deprecating nature.

At Long Kesh, they were taken into the entrance hut where, according to O'Connell, they were frisked "as if we were likely to be carrying weapons." Although taken aback at this breach of protocol, none of the three objected. They were locked into the back of a prison van and driven to the hospital wing. Blaney and de Valera sat rigidly on the hard bench along one side of the van, trying not to be thrown off their seats as it sped around the bends. On the opposite side, O'Connell slid back and forth along his bench, thinking clinically about the hazards of being locked into the back of the van with no means of escape should there be an accident. Then they reached the hospital. O'Connell was clearly affected.

"The hospital had an hygienic atmosphere that greatly impressed me, and a silent lack of therapeutic intent that withered me. There were no relatives, no flowers, no suggestion that people were going to get better and get out. No hope."

The MEPs were led to Bobby's cell. Just before the warder opened the door, O'Connell told the two others that he intended to ask him to end his hunger strike.

"You've got visitors, members of the European parliament," the screw told Bobby.

O'Connell led the way into the room, where they found him lying in a hospital gown with a single pillow under his head. He was now in a water bed, which had a pump that emitted a constant and annoying buzz. He lay on a sheepskin rug, with a sheet, a blanket, and a brownish cover "seeming to weigh him down." His face, like the pillow, "lacked all color." Black spots of dried blood were on his dry, cracked lips. To O'Connell, " . . . the reality of how he currently looked was like a physical blow . . . He was skeletal. His eyes were glazed with the inattention of a man already focused away from the routine of daily living . . . I knew immediately that the emaciation was total and that irreversible physical damage had probably already taken place."

O'Connell walked up the left-hand side of the bed. He took Bobby's hand since it was obvious that he could not physically raise his arm. By doctor's reflex he took his pulse. It was "very thready . . . very weak." Worse, he found Bobby's hand to be "ice cold, like touching a dead man. So cold I could not relinquish it, but held it gently in a vain effort to transfer warmth from my hand to his."

Bobby could barely talk, so the three leaned down beside him to hear what he said. They spoke in quiet voices, a natural reaction because Bobby's voice was so low. O'Connell noticed the radio that was sitting on the locker beside Bobby's bed.

"I suppose the radio keeps you up to date?"

"It did with the election results. I was listening to the count."

At this, Bobby became quite animated and even happy. He talked about the hunger strike and why it had happened. He explained the five demands and said that Britain could meet them even then without losing face. As always, he made it quite clear to them that he intended to die if the British would not accede to their demands. As Bobby spoke, his voice grew stronger and his words more fluent. His dry lips cracked with every movement. Despite his physical condition, O'Connell found him "clear in his thinking, resolute in his intention."

Still acting the doctor, O'Connell moved his hand in front of Bobby's face, to find that his wink reflex was going. He felt his weak heartbeat. Bobby had less than a week of life left in him. And then O'Connell did as he had promised. He asked Bobby to quit his hunger strike. Surely it was better to live and fight for what he believed in.

"If you do give up the hunger strike we will fight to get the demands for the prisoners," he said. "Look, you've proved your point. You've proved your point."

There they were, those inevitable words that had angered him so much when spoken by a priest, that he had so feared to hear coming from his mother's lips. But Bobby had crossed this last threshold of fear.

"I knew you would say that," he whispered through a smile. And he told the doctor no, he would not be ending his hunger strike.

De Valera, who held Bobby very gently throughout this exchange, looked at him with tears in her eyes. She and Blaney both told him that he was a hero and they promised him that they would do all that they could to get Margaret Thatcher to respond to the prisoners' demands.

After about forty minutes, O'Connell could see that the visit was becoming a strain on Bobby's remaining strength. They promised him that they would make a statement calling on Thatcher as a matter of urgency to save his life by implementing the five demands. De Valera put her arm behind him, clearly wanting, but unable, to give him a big hug. Blaney bent over to say good-bye and touched Bobby's face "with infinite gentleness" with the back of his giant hand.

As they left the cell, Sile de Valera turned to the warder with a question.

"Why do you keep food at the bottom of his bed?"

"In case he wants to eat."[57]

• • •

The next day, Tuesday, Bobby's parents and Marcella visited him. His speech was slurred, his hearing impaired and his eyes unable to focus. For some time now, he'd had nystagmus, a rhythmic wobbling of the eyes. Once the warders noticed that a hunger striker's eyes were bouncing, they knew that the body was beginning to shut down and that the end was near. He had a severe headache and the fillings had begun to fall out of his teeth. Each movement caused him severe pain. He was practically blind but would not admit it. Marcella watched as he spent twenty minutes trying to screw the cap back onto his bottle of spring water.[58] Nonetheless, he "smiled weakly and made no complaints."[59] According to a family friend, Rosaleen was finally overcome by Bobby's deteriorating condition.

"Son, I'm thinking of taking you off this," she said, suddenly.

"Mammy, just get out of here," replied Bobby, raising his arm with effort and waving toward the door.

She went home and was not there ten minutes before she told John to take her back to see her son in the prison hospital. She wanted to tell him that she was behind him all the way. Later, it haunted her whether she had done the right thing.[60]

Instead, the family asked Charles Haughey to try and resolve the hunger strike. Haughey had been trying to get the European Commission on Human Rights to intervene in the crisis. Perhaps he wanted the strike resolved before the upcoming May elections in the south, where a repeat performance of Fermanagh/Tyrone, this time with blanketmen taking votes from *his* party, could put him out of office. Since the commission's constitution stated that complaints must be signed by a "person, non-governmental organization, or group of individuals claiming to be the victims of the violation," Haughey had to get the Sands family to submit an official complaint before the commission would intervene. He invited them to his Dublin home. There, he told Marcella that if she complained in writing, the commission would visit the H-Blocks immediately and make an "on-the-spot" judgement. Haughey produced the necessary documents and Marcella signed them, hoping that she was saving Bobby's life. Her complaint stated that Britain had violated Bobby's right to life, to protection from inhuman treatment and to freedom of expression (because they had not allowed him access to the media to campaign for the Westminster election).

Two members of the commission, Professors Norgaard and Opsahl, and two commission officials flew to London almost immediately. They held a ninety-minute meeting with British authorities where they agreed that Marcella's complaint was sufficient grounds for the journey but that Bobby would have to confirm the complaint before they could take it any further. They flew on to Belfast.

Bobby was weak; he had been retching for three days. When the commissioners arrived on Saturday, his lawyer, Pat Finucane, told them that he would not see them unless Gerry Adams, Danny Morrison, and Bik

MacFarlane were present. Bobby needed witnesses to "ensure that any settlement arrived at was kept." He remembered the fiasco of December 18 and he would not negotiate independently of movement representatives or his officer in command. The prison authorities called MacFarlane to the prison hospital in hopes that he could change Bobby's mind. The commissioners told MacFarlane that they needed to see Bobby to confirm his complaint.

"If the criteria Bobby laid down have not been met then you're not going to be able to see him," Bik told them.

At this, one official said that the commission had "certain rules of practice" and he did not see how they could ask for Adams and Morrison to be brought into the prison. Opsahl added that talk of "witnesses" had a ring of publicity to it and any consultation with Bobby had to be confidential. Anyway, they were just there to ascertain if Bobby wanted to continue with his application. Bik replied that if the others were allowed in they could find out his position exactly. He asked who was blocking Adams and Morrison. Opsahl replied that it was "the government" but the other official cut in and said that the British *could prevent* advisors from being present. So, said Macfarlane, they were merely *assuming* that the others would be prevented but were now admitting that they had not even asked the British to allow them in. The official said that "they couldn't ask for this."

"Why not?" Bik pressed further. They had already set a precedent by bringing him to see Bobby. Why not contact the British authorities and ask permission to bring in Adams and Morrison, too?

"Well, perhaps I can see him," MacFarlane finally said. He just wanted to see Bobby one last time but he told the commission that he would not even try to get Bobby to change his mind.

As Bik entered the cell, Pat Finucane and Marcella were sitting outside. Old Bobby, the medical orderly, spoke to him in a whisper.

"There's terrible things in this here room, y'know, Bik."

Bobby was propped up in bed, with several big pillows supporting him. He was covered with plain white sheets and blankets. Bik noticed his clean, striped pajamas and his neat and tidy haircut. Bobby's sunken cheeks gave him a "deathly look, almost skeletal." He had lost an incredible amount of weight since Bik last saw him. He looked ghastly, gaunt, and withered and in a lot of pain. He made no audible noises but his face was full of pain. As Bik approached his bed, Bobby knew that someone was there but he couldn't recognize him.

"It's me."

"Oh, yeah, come ahead, Bik."

Bobby's eyesight had deteriorated. His hearing had deteriorated. His speech was slow and labored. Bik sat down by the side of the bed and leaned right up to him, so that they could talk privately. He told Bobby why he was there and they spoke about Charlie Haughey's maneuvering to get the European Commission in.

"You know, that's only a ruse," said Bobby. "It's only a move to get me off the hunger strike."

"Yeah, I know. I've just talked to these people and explained to them that unless they meet the criteria you laid down then I'm not prepared to talk to them."

"Yep, that's right. What about the big lad and Morrison?"

"They're not letting them in."

"Well, then there can't be a meeting."

"I can tell them that on the way back again."

"Now, don't . . ."

MacFarlane knew that Bobby was worried that the commissioners might try to hoodwink him into negotiations in the absence of Adams and Morrison. He cut him off.

"No, that's no problem, I know."

"So you understand what it's all about?"

"Yeah, I've got a full understanding of it. Don't be worrying about it. I'll not be engaging them in negotiations, I'll only explain to them what the situation is."

"Right, that's fine, that's sound, as long as you know."

Bik was shocked at Bobby's physical weakness but impressed by his clarity of mind. "He was sharp, he knew exactly what was happening politically, he knew what that maneuver was about, he understood it fully. He obviously was concerned that his family had been used in such a way by Charlie Haughey. But his chief concern was that nothing was going to happen to knock him off his stride and there was no possibility of me asking him to do anything other than what he wanted to do."

After just ten to fifteen minutes of chat, Bik could see that the strain of talking was too much for Bobby.

"Look, I'm going to leave you because . . ."

"Yeah, that's no problem, no problem."

"I'll go back and tell these people exactly what you said and I'll write to the big lad when I get back."

"Right, no problem, just make sure you're all right."

"Aye, no problem. Everybody was asking and sends their regards and wishing you all the best."

Then Bobby spoke his last words to Bik.

"I'm dying, cara, I'm dying."

It was a bad moment for Bik. It was unbearable to be there but he wanted to stay all day. He couldn't say anything, except, "God Bless, I'll see you again very soon."

Bobby just gave him a quiet laugh.[61]

• • •

The commissioners gave up and went home. In a three-paragraph statement entitled "Marcella Sands v United Kingdom (Application number 9338/81)," they claimed that Bobby did not wish to associate himself with his sister's complaint although he was prepared to see them in the company of three colleagues. "After further consultations the delegation concluded that in the circumstances it was not possible to see and confer with Mr. Sands and accordingly no meeting took place."

That night, Bobby had a crisis. The authorities called his family to the prison, unsure whether he would make it through the night. Before his collapse, Pat Finucane helped him draft a public statement giving his own interpretation of the day's events.

> *The legal submission and request to the European Commission was made in good faith by my sister Marcella who was misled by Charles Haughey into believing that the Commission would deliver on the political prisoners' demands. Mr. Haughey led my family to believe that the British government wanted a way out of the dilemma in which they now find themselves and that the Commission intervention was the vehicle for getting the British off the Armagh/H-Blocks hook . . . because Mr. Haughey has the means to end the H-Block/Armagh crisis and has consistently refused to do so, I view his prompting of my family as cynical and cold-blooded manipulation of people clearly vulnerable to this type of pressure. The Commissioners' intervention has been*

*diversionary and has served to aid the British attempts to con-
fuse the issue.*[62]

Bik MacFarlane was angry about the "Brit mentality" in refusing to
allow a meeting that had the potential to resolve the crisis. He wrote to
Gerry Adams that "their stupidity is unbelievable. I still don't think they
have learned that oppression breeds resistance and further oppression,
further resistance!" They are also arrogant, he said, ". . . they will regret
their stupidity."

Bobby did not get much rest. On Tuesday, the pope's secretary
arrived in Belfast. Forty-five-year-old Father Magee was originally from
County Down and had worked his way to the top of the Vatican bureau-
cracy, as secretary to three popes. When he suggested intervening in the
hunger strike, Cardinal Ó Fiaich was against the idea. A visit at this
stage was unlikely to achieve anything and would probably turn into a
macabre media circus. But papal officials discussed the visit with the
Irish and British governments and decided to come anyway. Things
began badly when the police picked up Magee at the airport in a bul-
letproof car. Ó Fiaich knew this would identify Magee with the authorities but the RUC insisted. They drove Magee around in a convoy, with
police and press cars in tow. Magee saw Bobby three times, asking him
on the pope's behalf to call off his fast. Bobby politely accepted the
pope's gift of a large gold rosary but he refused to end his strike. Magee
met Humphrey Atkins, who was "hostile." Then he left Ireland having
achieved nothing. Bik MacFarlane wrote to Adams that Magee obviously
had an "ulterior motivation" for his visit. It would probably work to the
Brits' advantage and "hardly to our advantage."[63]

By Thursday, Bobby lost all feeling in his mouth and found it even
harder to speak. On Saturday, his eyesight was completely gone and one
side of his body was completely numb.

On Friday, May 1, Jim Gibney visited Ray McCreesh, who was already
quite ill and confined to his cell. Jim had stopped visiting Bobby out of
respect for his family's privacy but he continued to visit the others. This
visit upset Gibney because McCreesh told him that he "thought Francie
Hughes was going to die last night." Hughes was screaming with pain
the whole night.[64] As Gibney walked back down the corridor, he noticed
that Bobby's door was ajar. Curious to see how he was doing but afraid
that the open door meant bad news, Gibney looked in. He could smell

death in the air. Bobby was semi-conscious. He was lying under a cage and his bedclothes were over the cage because even the slightest touch of the blankets on his skin caused severe pain. Rosaleen and Marcella sat by his bedside, his mother holding his right hand, which lay across his body. The pope's rosary beads were around his neck, big and gleaming gold. His eyes were closed.

"Who's that?" asked Bobby, weakly.

"It's Jim," replied Gibney.

"I'm blind. I can't see you."

Bobby lifted up his left hand and Jim took it and softly shook it.

"How are you, cara?"Jim asked.

"I'm okay," replied Bobby. "Tell the lads I'm alright, I'm hanging in here."[65]

Jim did not want to exercise Bobby's remaining strength any further. He just said, "Okay, good-bye." As he spoke these last words, Bobby opened his blind eyes. Jim repressed his shock at the sight. They were bright orange. Bobby's kidneys had failed and the poisons were ravaging his whole body.

This was his state when the British Labour Party's shadow minister for Northern Ireland Don Concannon came to visit. Concannon, who as a Labour minister was directly responsible for withdrawing political status and for building the H-Blocks, flew in from London to inform Bobby that his party opposed political status and backed Thatcher's decision to let him die. He said he did not want Bobby to misunderstand his party's position. John Hume called the visit "a cheap and offensive publicity stunt" and even the chair of the Labour Party of Northern Ireland said Concannon's visit was "totally insensitive . . . like sending a British tank to a Northern Ireland funeral."[66]

Later that afternoon Owen Carron visited Bobby for the last time. He found Bobby "in tremendous pain and obviously close to death." One eye was closed and he could not see from the other. Bobby recognized Carron only by his voice and he spoke "very slowly and with great effort." His mouth was twisted as if he'd had a stroke and Carron noticed his teeth and gums protruding. His body had "a skeleton-like look." Carron thought he could have spanned Bobby's whole chest with his hand. Bobby said "good-bye" to Owen and mentioned all of his friends by name. They should keep their hearts up, he said, Britain needed its pound of flesh. "Tell everyone I'll see them somewhere, sometime."

Carron kissed him good-bye on the cheek. As he arose, he noticed a tear in Bobby's open eye.

Carron left Bobby shortly before 3:00 P.M. He immediately contacted Sean Aylward, assistant to Charles Haughey, in Dublin and "formally lodged" Bobby's dying wish: that Haughey publicly call on Maggie Thatcher to grant the prisoners' five demands. The next day, the head of the Irish Government Information Service informed Carron that there would be no response to the request. Carron sent a telegram asking, "Why not?" but he heard nothing further. Carron was furious. On Monday he released a statement about the Taoiseach's lack of response to Bobby's request.

"I relayed that message on Friday and Saturday but he has not bothered to reply. That shows us that Charlie Haughey is not really interested in the people of Northern Ireland. He forfeits the right to be called leader of any section of the Irish people and he stands condemned at the bar of Irish history."[67]

When Bobby's family arrived at his bedside on Sunday they thought he was already dead. Rosaleen knelt beside him and said an act of contrition in his ear. At this, Bobby nodded and rallied. Through it all, a prison warder stood by, writing down everything.

On Monday, Charles Haughey's secretary phoned Marcella and asked her to go to a hotel in Dundalk to file a new complaint with the European Commission. She refused. The Sands family no longer trusted Haughey. Besides, it was now too late. Bobby only had hours to live. That afternoon at 4:00 P.M. the warder told Rosaleen that she had a phone call. When she left to answer it, a senior prison officer stopped her and told her that she was not allowed to take any calls. Then he said, "Mrs. Sands, I would like you to know that we have done everything for your son."

She looked him straight in the eye and replied, "This place has tortured my son for four and a half years and it has now murdered him."

As she walked away, she could feel the officer's rage.[68]

On Monday evening, Bobby's bowels burst and he was in excruciating pain. The priest administered the Holy Communion and last sacraments and he went into a coma. According to his family, his last words were, "I love you all. You are the best mother in the world. You stood by me."

Now Rosaleen had to face her hardest task. She had promised Bobby that she would not ask the prison doctors to try and revive him after he went into a coma. "He told me not to," she said. "I love my son like any other mother, but I wouldn't, I can't. He asked me not to and I've promised him not to."

Rosaleen could not stand being in the room any longer, watching Bobby die. She left the room. Bobby's father and brother Sean stayed, along with Marcella's husband Sean. The warder J— was sitting at the bottom of the bed and Father Murphy was there.

A little after midnight, Bobby Sands went into Cheyne-Stokes breathing, where he would take a breath and then remain silent for many seconds that seemed like an eternity to those in the room. At one point, he stopped breathing for so long that the warder got up and switched off the pump to the bed, to stop its buzzing and give the family silence in their grief. The change startled Bobby and he took a huge breath.

Seventeen minutes past one in the morning on May 5, 1981.

"He was in a coma and his breathing was labored and it just stopped and that was it."

J—, the warder, went and got Rosaleen.[69] He called the head doctor, who came and pronounced Bobby dead. Finally, the prison officers left the room. The Sands family and Father Murphy were left alone with Bobby.

Chapter Twenty-Three

The Beginning

It's gonna happen, happens all the time
It's gonna happen, till you change your mind!

—*The Undertones*,"It's Gonna Happen"[1]

C olm Scullion had the only radio on the wing. Tomboy Loudon had been keeping a second radio but a few days earlier he lost it down the toilet to a bad case of diarrhea. Scullion swung the precious cargo to Bik MacFarlane a couple of cells away so he could listen to the news. Usually, Bik got the news at midnight and then went to sleep. But that night he waited for the one o'clock news. Nothing.

"Frig it," he told himself. "I'll not even take this down."

At 2:00 A.M. he heard the news again. He only remembered snatches of what was said.

"Bobby Sands died at seventeen minutes past one, MP for Fermanagh-South Tyrone, hunger striker."

MacFarlane woke his cellmate and told him to pass the news down the pipes quietly.

"Look, if you can't waken anybody, don't be battering all over the show because these characters [the screws] will be in to see what's going on."

Then up to the window. Richard O'Rawe and Colm Scullion were together two cells down.

"*Risteard, Scul, suas chuig an fhuinneog* ("Up to the window"). *Fuair Roibeard bás cúpla nóiméad ó shin* ("Bobby died a couple of minutes ago")."

He told them that the Falls Road was already on fire.

Tomboy Loudon was in his cell. When he heard the news he began weeping uncontrollably at the loss of his friend. He heard a voice, "You alright, Tomboy?"

It was Tom McElwee.

"No," Tomboy uttered through sobs.

"Bastards! The bastards!" replied McElwee. "They'll pay for this Tomboy, they'll pay for this."

Bik MacFarlane spoke for a time with Richard O'Rawe. Then he wrote to Gerry Adams at 2:15 A.M.

> *Comrade mor, I just heard the news—I'm shattered—just can't believe it. This is a terrible feeling I have. I don't even know what to say. Comrade, I'm sorry, but I just can't say anything else. May God in his infinite mercy grant eternal rest to his soul. Jesus Christ protect and guide us all.*
> *God bless.*
> *xoxo Bik xoxo*[2]

As Bik MacFarlane was writing to him inside his H-Block cell, Gerry Adams was awoken by a familiar sound. Hundreds of women were clanging their bin lids against the pavement, in the traditional gesture of protest against the British state. Adams had been asleep in a house in the Beechmount area of West Belfast. It was a billet; he could not stay at home for fear of arrest. As soon as he heard the bin lids he knew what it meant. He got dressed and went out the back entry of the house; he never used the front door for fear of being seen. He walked up Oakman Street and Cavendish Street to Harrogate Street, past the old terraced houses. Everywhere, he saw women banging their bin lids, including his wife. And everybody was emotional, including him. Because of Bobby's condition, Sinn Féin's headquarters, a slum building on the Falls Road, was staffed around the clock. Adams walked to the office and met Danny Morrison. Despite their emotions, they got to work. Later, Adams met the Sands family and they started the process of getting Bobby's remains brought home to Twinbrook.

Across the city, in a Protestant area, the hospital warder J— returned home from the end of his shift. He had shed a few tears at Bobby's death and now he lay in bed and listened to the bins rattling on the other side of town. He had never heard such a noise. "What a waste of young life, what a waste of talent," he thought to himself.

In Armagh Jail, Jennifer McCann had the radio. She still hoped against hope that Bobby would survive, right up to the last minute. McCann was in solitary in the cell next to Brenda Murphy and Mairead Halfpenny. She awoke early on Tuesday morning and put the radio on for the five o'clock news. She missed the start of it but the newscaster was still talking about rioting in West Belfast and she knew immediately that Bobby had died. She knocked on the pipes and told the others. When the screws opened the doors for breakfast at 7:30, the women were still crying. When they went out for breakfast, the women stopped crying. They couldn't let the screws see their hurt.

After he finished writing to Gerry Adams, Bik MacFarlane just sat there, numb, for hours. Colm Scullion lay in bed, praying. "Praying and praying and praying. And after all them years of praying, some praying. It was a terrible morning." Eventually, MacFarlane realized they couldn't afford to sit there. The battle was still on. He went to the door.

"Look, lads, Bobby's dead. There's three other lads still on hunger strike. Get down to the comms again. Go back over the addresses. Send out to all of them."

Richard O'Rawe wrote to the movement asking them to put a sympathy insertion in the newspapers from the blanketmen. He said to include the following:

> They have nothing in their whole imperial arsenal that can
> break the spirit of one Irishman who doesn't want to be broke.

"Bobby more or less adopted it as his motto," he told Liam Og. Also, they should insert the words "Legally killed by British intransigence."[3]

Not everyone was in mourning. The screws arrived that morning to a wing of sleepless prisoners. The first thing the blanketmen heard was the screw they called Puck, singing the song from *Oklahoma!*,

"Oh, what a beautiful morning! . . ."

Some other screws were absolutely delighted. They were skipping and hopping around the place. MacFarlane had already warned the men, "Do not under any circumstances fight with any of these screws. Don't say anything because that's exactly what they are looking for. We can do without it, we don't need it. I want this done in a dignified manner. They'll get their comeuppance."

Few British politicians mourned. The NIO released a pathetically terse statement that acknowledged Bobby Sands's death while pointedly ignoring his newfound political status:

> *Mr. Robert Sands, a prisoner in the Maze Prison, died today at 01.17. He took his own life by refusing food and medical intervention for sixty-six days.*

In Westminster, the British parliamentarians ignored their customary tribute to a fallen member, simply announcing the death with a short, terse statement. Thatcher went one better, telling parliament that,

> *This government will never grant political status, no matter how much hunger strike there may be . . . Mr. Sands was a convicted criminal. He chose to take his own life. It was a choice that his organization did not allow to any of their victims.*

The Catholic Church was hardly more sympathetic, despite the efforts that Cardinal Ó Fíach and some individual priests had put into the campaign for prisoners' rights. The Bishop of Down and Connor, which encompasses Belfast, gave a directive that no public masses would be said for "a certain person," which the priests all knew to mean Bobby Sands. The directive caused considerable anger among the clergy, one of whom wrote in his weekly newspaper column that the bishop was practising "junk theology." There was not a chance that the Bishop's directive would succeed. The hierarchy was forced to back down by the clergy, who told them that such an action was unacceptable and it would have unacceptable consequences.[4]

In Republican Belfast, the reaction to Bobby Sands's death was swift and powerful. As soon as the news was announced, thousands of people hit the streets. Hundreds more gathered in front of and inside of the Sands family house in Twinbrook.

• • •

As thousands of visitors came to the Sands house to pay their respects, the first sight they met were the crowds of people who congregated there. Across the road, a group of children built an altar bearing the words "Peace, Justice, Freedom" and the flags of the four provinces of Ireland.[5]

The coffin was placed beside a wall of the living room, shielded from the large crowds outside by venetian blinds. Bobby's body was clothed in a white habit with a Sacred Heart emblem on his chest, the cross from the pope in his hands. For hours on end, Marcella stood by the coffin to greet people as they paid their respects. No one, neither friends nor strangers, could have been prepared for nor have ever forgotten the sight of Bobby Sands's remains. Gerry Adams recalled the wake house. His brother Paddy, who had not even known Sands, kissed him and then he broke down and cried. It was a strange memory that stayed in Adams's head because he hadn't seen his brother cry since he was a child. Danny Morrison and Jim Gibney broke down.[6]

Tens of thousands lined the hundred yards or so between the Sands house and St. Luke's chapel as the body was removed for the funeral mass. There were dozens of camera crews, some from far away countries in Asia and Africa. The Irish tricolor flag, gloves, and black beret were removed from the coffin before it was allowed into the chapel. Had it been a Union Jack and British military paraphernalia, they could have remained. In the mass, the priest spoke about Bobby's "illness." Gerry Adams was "disgusted at this avoidance of the truth."[7]

At 2:00 P.M., the coffin was brought back out from the chapel and the flag, gloves, and beret were placed back on top. A soft rain fell as it began its final journey to Milltown Cemetery, four miles down the Road from Twinbrook in the heart of West Belfast. Sands had thought a lot about where he would be buried and at one point he asked his lawyer to draw up a legal document backing up his request to be buried in County Mayo, next to Michael Gaughan and Frank Stagg, who died on hunger strike in English jails. Sands insisted that he was being neither "naïve" nor "morbidly flamboyant" but that he had serious personal reasons for the request. Earlier, he requested to be buried in Carnmoney Cemetery, just a few hundred yards from his boyhood home.[8]

As the crowd of a hundred thousand made its way out of Twinbrook, a lone piper played the H-Block song. When it got to Andersonstown, in front of the Busy Bee shopping center, the coffin was removed from the hearse and put onto trestles. Four IRA men in full battle dress emerged from the crowd and fired three volleys over the coffin. They bowed their heads, observed a minute's silence, and dispersed back into the crowd.

At Milltown Cemetery, an IRA guard of honor accompanied the coffin to the graveside. The family stood there, all familiar public figures now except young Gerard with his pageboy haircut. Owen Carron delivered the oration. He had known Sands scarcely a month but was now identified with him and would soon succeed him as MP for Fermanagh/South Tyrone, after the British parliament passed the "Bobby Sands law" that excluded convicted IRA men from running for that office. The honor guard presented the tricolor flag, gloves, and beret to Rosaleen. Then, the men of the family, father John, brother Sean and, with some help, son Gerard threw spadefuls of earth into the open grave.

● ● ●

The mass reaction in Ireland to the death of Bobby Sands had a big impact on the public perception of the Republican Movement as a political and, indeed, a *popular* force. While it changed few minds among those who had their minds made up, it made it harder for the British government to maintain the image of Irish Republicanism as a criminal movement. The British portrayal of the Irish conflict is a discourse of "tribalism," where Catholics and Protestants maintain their irrational war against each other despite the best attempts by the British to civilize them. It is a common colonialist discourse. Yet the activities of Bobby Sands illuminated the intensely internationalist side of his political focus. His hunger strike diary insertions, most notably his words against Reagan and Thatcher in Central America, demonstrated how crucial global concerns were to his revolutionary program. He was "thinking globally, acting locally," long before the bumper sticker was invented.

News of his death spurred protests by thousands in major cities of Europe. Motions of sympathy, minutes of silence, and days of mourning were declared in national parliaments of Italy, India, Portugal, Iran, and elsewhere, including several of the United States. The *Hindustan Times* wrote that Margaret Thatcher "allowed a member of the House of Commons, a colleague in fact, to die of starvation. Never had such an incident occurred in a civilized country." And the *New York Times* editorialized that Bobby Sands "bested an implacable British prime minister."

In Tehran, Pedram Moallemian and his teenage friends decided that "there was no way the memory of someone we considered a great revolutionary who had stood up to the British for his people and at the highest cost could be forgotten." They wanted to sneak into the British embassy compound and replace the British flag with an Irish one. Then they decided to change the name of the street on which the embassy was situated. Moallemian made signs in Persian, "Bobby Sands St.," out of white construction paper and blue Magic Markers™ and covered the street signs in front of the embassy. The next evening, when the teenagers returned to see if their signs were still there, they discovered that others had made more signs with the new name. Eventually, the city government renamed the street permanently and the embassy had to move its door around the corner so that its letterhead would avoid bearing the name of Bobby Sands.[9]

In Cuernavaca, Flora Guerrero Goff and hundreds of supporters, behind a banner that read "Bobby Sands, *vivirás para siempre*" ("Bobby Sands, you will live forever"), blockaded a major British exhibit that was to be inaugurated by the British ambassador to Mexico, causing its cancellation. Sixteen organizations and over two hundred individuals from Cuernavaca sent a telegram and letter to Rosaleen Sands, expressing solidarity and citing the parallels between U.S. policies in Mexico and British policies in Ireland. Bobby Sands would have been proudest of their reference to John O'Reilly and St. Patrick's Brigade—Irishmen who were executed after they abandoned the ranks of the invading U.S. Army in 1847 to fight with the Mexicans—as the "greatest bond in appreciation" that the Mexican people owed to the Irish.[10]

In Havana, Fidel Castro put the Irish hunger strikers in rather high company, in a statement that would have galled the Irish clergy who tried to prevent his funeral.

> *The tyrants shake in the presence of men who are able to die for their ideals, after sixty days of hunger strike! Next to this example, what were the three days of Christ on Calvary, as a symbol down the centuries of human sacrifice?*[11]

Given the esteem with which Sands held Che Guevara, Fidel's statement would have been the highest imaginable endorsement for the political legitimacy of his struggle.

On Robben Island, Nelson Mandela joined a group of young prisoners from Umkhonto we Sizwe on a hunger strike that was directly inspired by Bobby Sands. Among other things, they demanded that their young children be able to visit them. After six days, Mandela successfully negotiated an agreement with the prison authorities that enabled children as young as three to visit the island.[12]

In Cerro Hueco prison in Chiapas, Arturo Albores Velasco organized the first hunger strike in that prison's history. After twelve days, from July 20 to August 1, 1981, while the Irish hunger strike continued, the strike won the release of twelve prisoners in Chiapas. It was a key episode in the early history of a movement that would soon emerge on the global scene as the Zapatistas.[13]

And twenty years later in Turkey, when hundreds of political prisoners went on hunger strike, they, too, sent secret messages planning their action and their campaign. The code word in their secret communications for the coming hunger strike was simple and appropriate: Bobby Sands.

• • •

Nine of Bobby Sands's comrades followed him to their deaths. Francis Hughes, the guerrilla fighter who nearly preceded Sands to the grave, died shortly after him, on May 12. Then Ray McCreesh and Patsy O'Hara, the other two from the original four volunteers who began the strike. Joe McDonnell, who was caught in Dunmurry with Sands and who replaced him on the strike died next. Many people thought Margaret Thatcher was softening, that there was hope of a solution before McDonnell's death. Instead, the British army attacked the funeral, hoping to catch the IRA firing party and sending live and plastic bullets flying round the tens of thousands of mourners. After that, the hunger strikers went one by one to their deaths, without any real hope of a solution. Martin Hurson, Kevin Lynch (the man who Sands's comrades in H3 called Barabbas), Kieran Doherty. The last two to die were also comrades from H3. There was big Tom McElwee, who literally carried the fight for his rights into the jail by fighting the screws with his fists, the only weapon he had left. And, finally, "Red Mickey" Devine, who followed Sands's example of using the word as a weapon with his smuggled reports from the H-Blocks.

Gerry Adams still can't think about the hunger strikers without getting really emotional. He feels it is quite strange, since he has known so many people who have died, including some in the most violent circumstances.

"We probably haven't grieved yet," he says. "You see, the thing that you do in Ireland is that when someone close to you dies everyone comes to the wake house and you tell them how they died. A wife will tell the story of how her husband died a hundred times. And, we haven't done that, I think."[14]

Through the summer of 1981, as the ten men died, it became clearer that the Thatcher government would not move. In response, the priest Denis Faul, who had argued with Sands to cancel his hunger strike, decided to do the one thing in his power to end the fast. He put emotional pressure on the families of the hunger strikers to ask that their sons be fed once they went into a coma. He whipped up their emotions and set one family against another in an attempt to turn them against their own sons and the Republican Movement, which he claimed was forcing the men to remain on hunger strike.[15] Eventually, Faul's strategy worked. On September 4, after Matt Devlin went into a coma, his mother intervened to feed him and save his life. Two days later, Laurence McKeown's mother followed suit after her son had been on hunger strike for seventy days. Mercifully, no one died during the following month, although more men went on hunger strike. Finally, on October 3, the prisoners reluctantly called off their fast. They claimed that they had been robbed of the strike as an effective weapon because of the "successful campaign waged against our distressed relatives by the Catholic hierarchy, aided and abetted by the Irish establishment." Under such circumstances, the Thatcher government could sit indefinitely in its intransigence as more prisoners died. Bobby Sands's greatest personal fear had finally come to pass: the hunger strike was broken at its weakest link, the families of the hunger strikers.

• • •

What did Bobby Sands achieve? What was the meaning of his life? In a personal sense, it was a remarkable story of a young boy who approached adulthood with the "normal" concerns of playing soccer, being liked by his peers, perhaps becoming at least a local "star" in one of his sporting pursuits. But he was cursed or blessed by being born into a remarkable place at a remarkable time, in a community where he unwittingly became "the enemy" to the majority of his neighbors and many of his childhood friends. He was forced into a new identity, first to survive and then to recover his dignity. His community struggled in different ways to recover its collective dignity; through a moderate struggle for civil rights that resembled that of the southern United States both in tactics and police reactions; then, through one of the longest-running guerrilla wars in the world. In the process, Sands's community was launched into the international spotlight.

Within this context, Bobby Sands repeatedly reinvented himself. He began as the schoolboy trying to fit in among his peers. As his "peers" changed, he became the enthusiastic but militaristic and not terribly reflexive IRA volunteer. In prison, he became the radical student, using what he learned from his fellow prisoners and from the works of international activists to prepare himself as a grassroots community leader. Then, again in jail, he met new conditions of extreme deprivation as a teacher, writer, organizer and, ultimately, leader of the Irish prison struggle. Everyone adapts to new situations but the remarkable thing about Bobby Sands was *how* he met new circumstances and used new knowledge to raise his awareness and his practice in the subsequent periods of his life. In doing so, he shaped events; he made history.

Sands also reinvented himself culturally, into propagandist, storyteller, and poet. He progressed from listening to stories, to reading them, to recounting them and, finally, to writing his own story. He went from listening to songs as others sang them, to singing others' songs, to writing and singing his own song. Ultimately, others sang his songs. If he became the man with the hat and guitar at the center of attention, he was also more than that, because he changed the role of the man in the hat by creating a new and more profound song to sing.

In the process, he became an international symbol, even an icon of resistance. This, arguably, was not his intention. Yet in the process of leading a relatively small group of protesting prisoners, he built such strong determination and took that determination to such a remarkable end, that the world looked on in amazement and admiration.

Some people, including Gerry Adams, have said that Bobby Sands was just a regular guy in remarkable circumstances. While there is an element of truth to this, it hides the central role that Sands played in creating a culture of resistance within the H-Blocks, by organizing activities that raised morale, from education to nightly entertainments, to the communications structure and propaganda factory that gave the prisoners a sense of agency, a sense that their struggle could be won. In these terms, Bobby Sands was surely *not* "just a regular guy."

But were these remarkable achievements overshadowed by the failure of the prison protest and hunger strike? The British government claimed an outright victory over the hunger strikers and Thatcher continued to repeat her mantra that "a criminal is a criminal is a criminal is . . ."

Yet such would be an extremely shortsighted conclusion. The example of the hunger strikers, concentrated in the image and the name of Bobby Sands, reverberated around the world, giving hope to others who struggled or considered struggling for broadly similar ideals (at the broadest level, for "freedom" or "liberation"). His example inspired thousands to support freedom struggles not just in Ireland but also in other regions including South Africa and Central America. While there is a school of thought that views 1989 as a watershed, an "end of history" after which Bobby Sands's kind of radical politics no longer has a place, there are people throughout the world who refuse to recognize that history has ended. For them, the spirit of Bobby Sands continues decades later. Many Irish people can attest to this: in their travels around the world, strangers greet them with the words, "Ah, Irish . . . Bobby Sands!"

In Ireland, the influence of Bobby Sands and the other hunger strikers has been most profound. The British government may have considered the end of the fast to be its victory, yet the strength of the Republican Movement as a result of the hunger strike, both militarily and electorally, spurred the British and Irish governments into new campaigns to weaken its public image. The British government excluded IRA prisoners from running for major political office. The RUC embarked on campaigns to shut down sources of funding for the IRA and to draw public parallels between the IRA and "Mafia-type" organizations around the world. The British and Irish governments, alarmed at the possibility that Sinn Féin would build on the electoral popularity that began with Bobby Sands, signed an Anglo-Irish agreement in 1985 that aimed primarily to undercut the party's electoral popularity.

In one sense, the British strategy appears to have failed. Although it claimed victory over the hunger strikers, it conceded most of their demands soon after the protest ended. Irish Republican prisoners in the 1990s experienced starkly different conditions from the period of the blanket protest.[16] The Republican Movement and, especially, its political party Sinn Féin gained strength during the 1990s by launching a peace process and parlaying its new political strategy into electoral strength. Sinn Féin became the largest "Nationalist" party in the north of Ireland

and by some counts the third largest party in the south, an electoral position beyond its wildest dreams in 1981. To Gerry Adams,

> *The election of Bobby was just mighty. It was huge in terms of internationalizing the protest, opening up the opportunity to resolve the matters, just a sense of vindication . . . this was the first engagement of that type between the Republican activists and the populous, this was us going to the people and saying "will you support us?" . . . and they did . . . it had huge implications I think for the entire struggle.*

Yet, the nature of the electoral rise of Sinn Féin could also be viewed as a political victory for the British and U.S. governments. Bobby Sands's election to British parliament set some key party leaders to argue for electoral politics as an alternative to armed struggle *and radical community politics*. Arguably, electoral success provoked the moderation of the Republican Movement, a move not just away from militarism but also from *militancy*. Such political moderation was happening world-wide, from the former Soviet Bloc to Central America, by the time Ronald Reagan ended the term of office that he began just as Bobby Sands went on hunger strike. The allure of electoral strength that began with Bobby Sands helped bring Republicans in from the cold.

Undoubtedly, the Republican project two decades after Bobby Sands is different from the project for which he died. A strategy of participating in a Northern Irish parliament to bring about equality and, eventually, a united Ireland is hardly recognizable when set against the project of people's councils and autonomous parallel government that Sands discussed with Gerry Adams in the cages of Long Kesh and then tried to implement in Twinbrook.

Perhaps necessarily so. Che Guevara argued that armed struggle could not succeed in an electoral democracy, where a community has alternative modes of pursuing its objectives. Electoralism was always the alternative discourse to armed struggle in Ireland, ever since Catholics were given the universal franchise in the north and Nationalists began to win elections. In the same way, the transition of Republican politics since the time of "Brownie" and Bobby Sands may demonstrate that autonomous radical politics cannot exist in a social democracy, where citizens can pursue social welfare rights and equality through state channels.

The danger of granting this impossibility, from the radical point of view that Bobby Sands and his comrades held in 1981, is that it allows the electoral road to place limits on a movement's politics. Not only do political parties feel that they must moderate their politics to win more votes, the possibilities of pursuing a radical agenda are even more limited when a movement joins in coalition governments. This has been a problem for many of the liberation movements of Bobby Sands's time, from the Sandinistas and FMLN in Central America, to the ANC in South Africa, to Sinn Féin in Ireland.

Given the Republican Movement's turn away from armed struggle and its apparent political moderation, a debate among his former Republican comrades has been whether Bobby Sands would have gone along with the subsequent trajectory of the movement for which he died. Some of his comrades (including Tommy McKearney from the first hunger strike) left the Republican Movement in 1986, after Sinn Féin decided to send elected representatives to sit in the southern Irish parliament, the *Dail*. The debate escalated after another part of the movement left in 1997 because of the terms of the peace process, in order to form the Thirty-Two County Sovereignty Committee and its associate group, the "Real IRA."[17] The question "who owns Bobby Sands" became public after his sister Bernadette took a leadership role in this movement, while her husband was jailed for allegedly leading the Real IRA. Bernadette Sands-McKevitt stated unequivocally that, "Bobby did not die for cross-border bodies with executive powers. He did not die for Nationalists to be equal British citizens within the Northern Ireland state."[18]

Yet Sands's closest comrades, with just a few notable exceptions like Brendan Hughes, are still among the strongest supporters of Sinn Féin after the Belfast Agreement. It was no accident that when the IRA announced a conclusive end to this phase of armed struggle in July, 2005, it chose Seanna Walsh, Bobby's closest comrade and friend, to read its public statement.

Rather than trying to "claim" Bobby Sands, it would be more productive to ask what we can learn from him.

His strongest principle was his defense of the right of oppressed people to resist. Surely, whether or not he supported the IRA laying down its arms for tactical reasons, he would have continued to defend the right of movements to define their own terms of struggle, including their right to take up arms if necessary. He died to resist the British state's attempts to criminalize his struggle. Would he not equally have opposed efforts to criminalize other struggles, as has been so common post-1989 and especially since September 11, 2001?

The specter of Al Qaeda and the ability of western governments to lump its activities together with those of leftist movements and progressive governments in a supposed "global war against terror," have contributed to reluctance by some Irish Republicans to embrace unarmed militancy as a political strategy. There is severe pressure on the movement to interpret the catchphrase of the Irish peace process, "the development of purely political and democratic programmes through exclusively peaceful means,"[19] to mean that Irish Republicans must pursue their goals by exclusively *electoral* means and adhere to the rule of law in all of their activities. Substantial numbers of Irish Republicans, however, still consider that militancy, protest, and popular resistance are legitimate forms of political expression.

Who can say how Bobby Sands would have developed politically if he had lived through the hunger strike. Yet the Bobby Sands who emerges from these pages would surely have continued to turn his interests and his solidarity southward. He would have been encouraged by the growing resistance to neoliberal globalization in the twenty-first century. Perhaps he would have been intrigued by some of the innovative unarmed strategies of resistance that have emerged in Latin America, possibly drawn to the similarities between his ideas about parallel government in Twinbrook and the recent experiences of indigenous and autonomous movements there. As Ireland and other parts of Europe rush to degenerate their public services in the name of privatization, might he have shown the same enthusiasm to learn lessons from how indigenous people have resisted privatization by popular uprising in Bolivia and Uruguay, as he showed for Che Guevara's or the Tupamaros's attempts to generate guerrilla war among the same people?

One thing is certain: the lesson of Bobby Sands's determination comes through. One image returns over and over again: a naked man locked up twenty-four hours a day in a cell, without even the most rudimentary comforts or reading materials. He turns to his cellmate and chastises him for sleeping all day. "It's a waste of your opportunities, isn't it?"

Just as his consciousness was formed by Che Guevara and Franz Fanon, so too are the consciousnesses of thousands of activists around the world informed by the life and death of Bobby Sands. His determination, surely. And his dignity, even grace.

Jim Gibney grew up around the corner from Bobby Sands. Years later, he lived around the corner from him again in Twinbrook. And he resided near him in several prisons. He visited Bobby Sands throughout the hunger strike and was among the last to see Sands alive. It was Gibney who went into Long Kesh after the first hunger strike ended and tried to convince Bobby Sands not to go on hunger strike, *not* to die. After Sands died, he continued to visit the other hunger strikers, including the nine who followed Sands to their deaths. He recalls watching Bobby, and the other nine, as they persevered on their slow path toward an inevitable and physically painful end.

> *The calibre of this man, there was this electricity around him, but you just knew that here was somebody who had no doubt in his mind, never entertained a doubt in his mind about what was going to happen to him . . . The human instinct is to live and not to die, and these guys almost casually overcame that instinct to live. And they just passed on through it. And the grace with which they did it defies comprehension. Twenty years on, as I get older and think about what they did, it is hard to comprehend that they just walked over that dividing line between life and death. And they did it with such grace.*

Notes

Chapter One

1   Michael Doyle, "Days of Wrath, Nights of Fire," *Today: The Inquirer Magazine* (*Philadelphia Inquirer*), July 12, 1987.
2   Michael Farrell, 1976, pp.90, 136.
3   *Northern Ireland, Planning Advisory Board, Housing in Northern Ireland: Interim Report of the Planning Advisory Board*, Belfast: H.M.S.O., 1944
4   Department of the Environment for Northern Ireland, *Merville Garden Village: Conservation Area*, Belfast: DOENI, n.d. [1995], p.2. The history of the garden villages is found in Alf McCreary, *Making a Difference: The Story of Ulster Garden Villages, Ltd.*,Belfast: Ulster Garden Villages Limited, 1999.
5   This and subsequent quotes from Bernadette Sands are taken from Bernadette Sands, "My Brother Bobby," *An Phoblacht/Republican News*, May 9, 1981, pp. 19-21.
6   Richard Jenkins, *Lads, Citizens, and Ordinary Kids: Working-Class Youth Life-Styles in Belfast*, London: Routledge & Kegan Paul, 1983, p. 34.
7   Bernadette Sands, "My Brother Bobby," *An Phoblacht/Republican News*, May 9, 1981, pp. 19-21.
8   Bernadette Sands, "My Brother Bobby," *An Phoblacht/Republican News*, May 9, 1981, pp. 19-21.
9   *Old Scores*, BBC documentary about the Star of the Sea football club, producer and main reporter, Olenka Frenkiel.
10 This and subsequent quotes or opinions from members of the Star of the Sea football club are taken from the documentary *Old Scores*.
11 Bernadette Sands, "My Brother Bobby," *An Phoblacht/Republican News*, May 9, 1981, pp. 19-21.

12   Apart from his consistent use of the term anti-Christ to describe the pope, Paisley's attitude toward Catholics as a part of Northern Irish society is most famously rendered in a speech to a Loyalist crowd in 1968, after a number of Catholic homes were burned: "Catholic homes caught fire because they were loaded with petrol bombs [Molotov cocktails]; Catholic churches were attacked and burned because they were arsenals and priests handed out sub-machine guns to parishioners." In response to allegations of discrimination in housing, Paisley claimed that Catholics had inferior housing because "they breed like rabbits and multiply like vermin." These quotes are widely repro-duced, for example, at http://en.wikipedia.org/wiki/Ian_Paisley. Also see Ed Moloney and Andy Pollak, *Paisley*, Dublin: Poolbeg Press, 1986.

13   The Ulster Volunteer Force was originally formed in 1913 to fight "home rule," the devolution of some governmental functions to Ireland. It was dis-banded in the early 1920s, although in practice this meant that it was legal-ized as most of its members were incorporated into the Ulster Special Constabulary (B-Specials). There is no direct connection between the two organizations although the Loyalist UVF of the 1960s saw parallels between Home Rule in the 1910s and O'Neillism in the 1960s, viewing both of them as stepping stones toward a united Irish Republic.

14   Peter Taylor, *Loyalists*, London: Bloomsbury, 1999, pp. 42-43; Susan McKay, *Northern Protestants: An Unsettled People*, Belfast: Blackstaff Press, 2000, p.57.

Chapter Two

1   "The Birth of a Republican: From a Nationalist Ghetto to the Battlefield of H-Block," *An Phoblacht*, April 4, 1981, pp.6-7.

2   See *Sunday Times* Insight Team, *Ulster*, London: Cox & Wyman, 1972, pp.106-107.

3   The relationships and interlocking memberships between the IRA and Sinn Féin are ambiguous because of the subversive nature of the IRA and the desire to maintain a public presence in the form of a legal political party. Undoubtedly, there is significant cross-membership although, especially as Sinn Féin grew after the 1994 cease-fire, a large proportion of party members are not army members. Moreover, the power relationship between the two groups has changed over the years. Before 1994, the IRA had unambiguous although not total control over the strategy of "the movement." In recent years, Sinn Féin appears to have become more autonomous of the IRA or, perhaps more precisely, has become a mechanism whereby that part of the IRA that favors a peace strategy has gained public and electoral strength against sections of the IRA that are less convinced of the peace strategy and

who opposed the Belfast Agreement of 1998. I refer to this larger, ambiguous entity, as the Republican Movement (Republicans sometimes call it the "Republican family" and Unionists always call it Sinn Féin/IRA).

4   Community defense was the biggest issue that divided the two groups of Republicans. There were also some political differences. While the Southern-dominated officials explicitly called themselves Marxists, the Northern-dominated Provisionals were a hodgepodge of apolitical Catholics, social Democrats of varied descriptions and some radical Socialists. Many Provisional leaders opposed Marxism because they associated it with the officials' abandonment of armed defense and, in some cases, because they believed it was atheistic and anti-Catholic. Yet their anti-Marxism never extended throughout the Provisional grassroots.

5   These and subsequent quotes of Star of the Sea members come from *Old Scores*, the BBC documentary.

6   Personal conversation. See also, Richard Jenkins, *Hightown Rules: Growing Up in a Belfast Housing Estate*, Leicester: National Youth Bureau, 1982; and Roy Wallace, *Goodbye Ballyhightown*, unpublished, 1995, p.42, quoted in Susan McKay, *Northern Protestants: An Unsettled People*, Belfast: Blackstaff Press, 2000, p.109.

7   Richard Jenkins, *Hightown Rules: Growing Up in a Belfast Housing Estate*, Leicester: National Youth Bureau, 1982, p.12. Susan McKay reports several interviews where older residents describe the new residents with terms like "scum of the earth from the Shankill and the Crumlin." Susan McKay, *Northern Protestants: An Unsettled People*, Belfast: Blackstaff Press, 2000, p.106.

8   Richard Jenkins, *Lads, Citizens, and Ordinary Kids: Working-Class Youth Life-Styles in Belfast*, London: Routledge & Kegan Paul, 1983, pp.36-37.

9   Report by the Ministry of Home Affairs in Accordance with Section 7(2) of the Criminal Justice Act (NI) 1953. As to the Suitability of a Person to Undergo a Sentence of Borstal Training, Signed by J.A. Montgomery for Secretary, March 5, 1973. Antrim County Court R. v. Sands, No.14.

10   "The Birth of a Republican: From a Nationalist Ghetto to the Battlefield of H-Block," *An Phoblacht*, April 4, 1981, pp.6-7.

11   Richard Jenkins, *Hightown Rules: Growing Up in a Belfast Housing Estate*, Leicester: National Youth Bureau, 1982, p.12. The names of "Star of the Sea," Whitehouse, and Rathcoole have been changed back from Jenkins's fictitious names to the actual names.

12   Bernard Fox's recollections are from original notes he contributed to a project that was eventually published as *Nor Meekly Serve My Time*, Belfast: Beyond the Pale, 1994.

13   Bernadette Sands, "My Brother Bobby," *An Phoblacht/Republican News*, May 9, 1981, pp. 19-21. Additional details that were edited out of the original

interview are contained in Silvia Calamati (ed.), *The Trouble We've Seen: Women's Stories from the North of Ireland*, Belfast: Beyond the Pale, 2002, pp.94-101. Another source claims that Bobby was intimidated out of work at gunpoint. *Trade Unions and H-Block*, Belfast: Trade Union Subcommittee of the National H-Blocks Committee, undated.

14   "Willowfield Temperance Harriers," *Belfast Telegraph*, February 19, 1970, p. 22.

15   *Sunday Times* Insight Team, *Ulster*, Harmondsworth: Penguin, 1972, p. 245.

16   Before the IRA killed its first British soldier in February 1971, the British army had already killed eight civilians, mostly Catholics. In July 1970 alone, the British army killed five civilians, including thirty-six-year-old Charles O'Neill, who they deliberately knocked down with an Armored Personnel Carrier. Malcolm Sutton, *An Index of Deaths from the Conflict in Northern Ireland 1969-1993*, Belfast: Beyond the Pale, 1994.

17   *Sunday Times* Insight Team, *Ulster*, Harmondsworth: Penguin, 1972, p.260.

18   This includes the Ulster Defense Regiment (UDR), which replaced the "B-Specials."

19   Eamonn McCann, *The British Press and Northern Ireland*, Belfast: Northern Ireland Socialist Research Center, 1972. Reproduced at http://cain.ulst.ac.uk/othelem/media/mccann72.htm

20   One study recorded 2,069 household moves, 40 percent Protestant families and 60 percent Catholic. John Darby, *Flight: A Report on Population Movement in Belfast during August, 1971*, Belfast: Community Relations Commission Research Unit, 1971; reproduced at http://cain.ulst.ac.uk/issues/housing/docs/flight.htm .

Chapter Three

1   Vigilante quoted in Steve Bruce, *The Red Hand: Protestant Paramilitaries in Northern Ireland*, Oxford: Oxford University Press, 1992, p.46.

2   *The Guardian*, September 27, 1971, quoted in Steve Bruce, *The Red Hand: Protestant Paramilitaries in Northern Ireland*, Oxford: Oxford University Press, 1992, p.48.

3   "Didn't Support Tartan Gangs," *East Antrim Times*, March 10, 1972, p.11.

4   Richard Jenkins, *Lads, Citizens, and Ordinary Kids: Working-Class Youth Life-Styles in Belfast*, London: Routledge & Kegan Paul, 1983, p.35.

5   "Story of Catholics in Fear in Rathcoole," *Irish News*, April 29, 1972, p. 7.

6   "The Birth of a Republican: From a Nationalist Ghetto to the Battlefield of H-Block," *An Phoblacht*, April 4, 1981, pp.6-7.

7   "Squatters Move into Home of Shot Docker," *Irish News*, February 18, 1972, p.2.

8   The following account is taken mainly from interviews with D—.

9   "Support Grows for UDR Fund but RUC Warn about Slogans," *East Antrim Times*, January 21, 1972, p.1.

10   "Thousands in Internment Protests," *Irish News*, February 10, 1972, p.1.

11   *Irish News*, February 11, 1972.

12   "Squatters Move into Home of Shot Docker," *Irish News*, February 18, 1972, p.2.

13   Richard Jenkins, *Lads, Citizens, and Ordinary Kids: Working-Class Youth Life-Styles in Belfast*, London: Routledge & Kegan Paul, 1983, p.82.

14   "Forty Rathcoole RC Families Complain to Police," *East Antrim Times*, April 14, 1972, p.21.

15   "Story of Catholics in Fear in Rathcoole," *Irish News*, April 29, 1972, p. 7.

16   See, for example, "Intimidation Is Two-Way, Say RUC," *Irish News*, May 5,1972, p.12.

17   Bernadette Sands, "My Brother Bobby," *An Phoblacht/Republican News*, May 9, 1981, pp. 19-21.

18   Descriptions of the explosion and funeral are from interviews and from newspaper accounts in the *Belfast Telegraph*, April 7, 1972, p.1; *Irish News*, April 8, 1972, p.1; and *Belfast Telegraph*, April 8, 1972, p.13.

19   *Old Scores.*

20   Richard Jenkins, *Lads, Citizens, and Ordinary Kids: Working-Class Youth Life-Styles in Belfast*, London: Routledge & Kegan Paul, 1983.

21   Susan McKay, *Northern Protestants: An Unsettled People*, Belfast: Blackstaff Press, 2000, p.107.

Chapter Four

1   Most of the following descriptions of early Twinbrook and its social conditions come from Féilim Ó hAdhmaill, *The Function and Dynamics of the Ghetto: A Study of Nationalist West Belfast*, unpublished Ph.D. thesis, University of Ulster, 1990.

2   Bernadette Sands, "My Brother Bobby," *An Phoblacht/Republican News*, May 9, 1981, pp. 19-21.

3   J. Darby and G. Morris, *Intimidation in Housing*, Belfast, N.I.C.R.C., 1974, p.46.

4   Easter is one of the most important commemorative dates in Irish Republicanism. To Irish Republicans, the lily symbolizes those who died in the cause of Irish freedom.

5   "Up the left" is Belfast vernacular for "totally crazy."

6   RUC, "Information as to Previous Convictions," March 5, 1973; Antrim County Court R. v. Sands, No.14.

7   Detective Sergeant Richard Gill, Petty Sessions Dunmurry, Deposition of a Witness, 1 February 1973, Antrim County Court R. v. Sands, No.14.

8   Police notes of Bobby's alleged verbal statements when he was arrested soon after confirm the same point. He allegedly told the RUC that the big military operations were carried out either by the Official IRA or by other, non-local units of the Provisional IRA. Detective Sergeant Richard Gill, Petty Sessions Dunmurry, Deposition of a Witness, February 1, 1973, Antrim County Court R. v. Sands, No.14.

9   Bobby Sands, "From a Nationalist Ghetto to the Battlefield of H-Block," *An Phoblacht/Republican News*, April 4,1981, p.6.

10   The main sources for the descriptions of operations that follow are Sands's signed confessions and depositions of witnesses who were robbed. All such sources must be used with care. In the cases here I have confirmed the events as far as possible by newspaper accounts and interviews with Sands's associates. Furthermore, Sands himself later admitted to his comrades that this period of his life was taken up mainly by robberies, which were "fashionable at the time."

11   "Youths Net £60 in Hold-Up," *Irish News*, September 12, 1972.

12   The story of the Four Square Laundry is reproduced here from several sources, including Jim Cusack, "Much of the Truth likely to Remain Buried," *Irish Times*, May 31, 1999; Gerry Adams, *Before the Dawn*, Dingle: Brandon, 1996, pp.212-213; John McGuffin, *The Guinea Pigs*, London: Penguin, 1974, chapter nine; Raymond Murray, *The SAS in Ireland*, Dublin: Mercier Press, 1990.

13   Additional evidence from Mr. Brian Thompson MIE AMI Prod E, member of staff at Forensic Science Labs, Belfast, March 6, 1973. Antrim County Court, R. v. Sands, No.14. T— insists that the army also found an M-1 Carbine that the unit had taken from the official IRA but this was never mentioned in subsequent army reports.

Chapter Five

1   Undated comm (probably February 1981) from Marcella to "Liam Og."

2   Statement of Robert Gerard Sands D.O.B. 3/9/54. Unemployed. Coachbuilder. 1F Jasmine End Twinbrook. Taken by D/Cont. Walsh in R.U.C. Lisburn on Tuesday, October 17, 1972. [Exhibit 9]

3   Statement of Robert Gerard Sands. D.O.B. 3/9/54. Unemployed. Coachbuilder. 1F Jasmine End Twinbrook.Taken by D/Cont Walsh in R.U.C. Lisburn on Tuesday, October 17, 1972. [Exhibit 10]

4   Statement of Robert Gerard Sands, D.O.B. 3/9//54. Coachbuilder. N.F.A. Taken by D/Const K, Crawford At Lisburn RUC Station on Tuesday, October 17, 1972 [Exhibit 8]

Chapter Six

1   Statement of Complaint, Petty Sessions of Dunmurry, County of Antrim, February 16, 1973.

2   Statement of the Accused, Queen v. Robert Gerard Sands, Petty Sessions District of Dunmurry, February 16, 1973.

3   "Youth Jailed for Armed Robberies," *Irish News*, March 15, 1973, p.8.

4   Quoted in Laurence McKeown, *Out of Time: Irish Republican Prisoners Long Kesh 1972-2000*, Belfast: Beyond the Pale, 2001, p.30.

5   Peter Taylor, *Beating the Terrorists? Interrogation in Omagh, Gough, and Castlereagh*, Harmondsworth: Penguin, 1980, pp.30-31.

6   "Activities," unsigned chapter by Bobby Sands in *Prison Struggle: The Story of Continuing Resistance behind the Wire*, Belfast: Republican Press Center, 1977, p.44.

7   "Out of the ashes of Belfast arose the Provisionals," was the popular phrase of the day. Thus, the Phoenix was the symbol of the IRA's rebirth from the burnt-out neighborhoods that bore the brunt of the attacks by Protestant mobs and the B-Specials.

8   "Screw" is prison vernacular for prison "warders" or guards. The terms are sometimes used interchangeably here, not for derogatory purposes but to capture the atmosphere of prison life.

Chapter Seven

1   Prison officer quoted in Chris Ryder, *Inside the Maze: The Untold Story of the Northern Ireland Prison Service*, London: Methuen, 2000, p.133.

2   Tomboy Loudon interview. "Another Hunger Strike in Long Kesh," *Republican News*, March 30, 1974, p.8.

3   Chris Ryder, *Inside the Maze: The Untold Story of the Northern Ireland Prison Service*, London: Methuen, 2000, pp.134-35. Tomboy Loudon interview.

4   Chris Ryder, *Inside the Maze: The Untold Story of the Northern Ireland Prison Service*, London: Methuen, 2000, pp.137-38.

5   "Society Allowing Long Kesh Shows Moral Depravity," *Irish News*, September 27, 1974, p.5.

6   "Society Allowing Long Kesh Shows Moral Depravity," *Irish News*, September 27, 1974, p.5.

7   "Truesdale Must Go," *Republican News*, September 21, 1974, p.1.

8   Ironically, the prisoners in Portlaoise rioted and the authorities came in and hosed them down with power hoses; all of the books from Cage Seventeen were destroyed in the deluge!

9   Tomboy Loudon interview. According to Kevin Carson, the prisoners knew
     that the authorities were watching and even filming them so the semaphore
     system involved quite a complicated system of code, where the daily key
     was changed among a number of books and magazines.

10   "Detainees Escape Bid Foiled," *Irish News*, September 24, 1974.

11   "We Will Burn Down Long Kesh," *Irish News*, September 26,1974, p.1.

12   "We Will Burn Down Long Kesh," *Irish News*, September 26, 1974, p.1.

13   "'Free Internees'" campaign only way to peace—Dr. Daly," *Irish News*,
     October 2,1974, p.1; "Strikes planned in Support," *Irish News*, October 2,
     1974, p.1; "Churchmen in Maze Prison Talks with Rees," *Irish News*, October
     5, 1974, p.1; "Rees Gets Report on Maze Prison," *Irish News*, October 5, 1974,
     p.1; "Long Kesh Demo Is Called Off," *Irish News*, October 10, 1974, p.1.

14   The following account is taken largely from interviews with various pris-
     oners and published accounts by other prisoners. Where possible, the
     events described herein have been corroborated by other sources. For
     example, a prison officer's account is given in Chris Ryder, *Inside the Maze:
     The Untold Story of the Northern Ireland Prison Service*, London: Methuen,
     2000, p.140.

15   Jim McCann, *The Gates Flew Open*, Belfast: Glandale Publishing, 1998,
     pp.31-32. See also Chris Ryder, *Inside the Maze*, London: Methuen, 2000,
     p.140.

16   Gerry Adams, *Before the Dawn: An Autobiography*, London: Heinemann,
     1996, p.238.

17   CR gas, or Dibenzoxazepine, is a highly toxic and potent sensory irritant
     that is much stronger than CS or other commonly used tear gases. It causes
     eye pain, excessive tearing, and intense skin pain that is long-lasting and
     can return many hours later. Because of its persistent and long-term effect,
     CR is rarely used by "liability conscious agencies." http://www.zarc.com/
     english/tear_gases/crdibenzoxazepine.html

     McCann claims that doctors took blood samples of the prisoners a few
     weeks after the burning of Long Kesh and he sees this as evidence that the
     British ministry of defense used the prisoners as guinea pigs, to test the
     effects of the relatively new and untested gas. Although the British govern-
     ment denies that it has ever used CR gas "operationally," including during
     the burning of Long Kesh, British Minister for the Armed Forces John
     Spellar admitted in parliament in 1998 that "some two hundred hand-held
     spray devices containing 0.05 percent CR were held at HM Prison Maze at
     the time." In 2000, Tus Nua, an ex-prisoner support group, began an inves-
     tigation into the use of CR after the burning of Long Kesh because they dis-
     covered that nearly a fifth of the prisoners who were in Long Kesh
     twenty-six years previously had died of cancer by the age of fifty-five.

http://www.relativesforjustice.com/publications/crgas.html. "MoD" is Ministry of Defense.

18 Jim McCann, *The Gates Flew Open*, Belfast: Glandale Publishing, 1998, p.19.

Chapter Eight

1   Chris Ryder, *Inside the Maze: The Untold Story of the Northern Ireland Prison Service*, London: Methuen, 2000, p.144.
2   Gerry Adams, *Cage Eleven*, Dingle: Brandon, 1990, pp.38-45.
3   "Maze Plea to the Red Cross," *Irish News*, October 21, 1974, pp.1, 8.
4   Chris Ryder, *Inside the Maze: The Untold Story of the Northern Ireland Prison Service*, London: Methuen, 2000, pp.144-45.
5   Details of the escape are from Tomboy Loudon and Seanna Walsh interviews.
6   Hughes has since admitted his leading role in the IRA, although Adams insists he was never a member.
7   Gerry Adams, *Before the Dawn*: An Autbiography, London: Heinemann, 1996, p.243.
8   Joe Barnes interview.
9   Gerry Adams, *Before the Dawn*: An Autbiography, London: Heinemann, 1996, p.246.
10 Merlyn Rees, *Northern Ireland: A Political Perspective*, London: Methuen, 1985, p.224.
11 "British Army Starts Withdrawal," *Republican News*, December 8, 1973.
12 "English Withdrawal Date?" *Republican News*, May 4, 1974, p.1.
13 Two books in Irish with Bobby's inscription from Cage Eleven survive. Bobby repeatedly misspelled the Irish version of his first name as "Riobeard" and later corrected them by writing "oi" over the mistaken "io" in "Roibeard."
14 Brendan Hughes interview.
15 Quoted in Laurence McKeown, *Out of Time: Irish Republican Prisoners Long Kesh 1972-2000*, Belfast: Beyond the Pale, 2001, p.38.
16 Laurence McKeown, *Out of Time: Irish Republican Prisoners Long Kesh 1972-2000*, Belfast: Beyond the Pale, 2001, pp.43-44.
17 The INLA was formed in 1974 as the result of a split with the official IRA, mainly over its unwillingness to fight the British army. While the organization formally maintained the Marxist politics of the official IRA, its members tenaciously pursued what they considered to be an anti-imperialist war.
18 Gerry Adams, *Before the Dawn: An Autbiography*, London: Heinemann, 1996, p.246.

19   Joe Barnes interview.

20   Brownie [Gerry Adams], "Active Republicanism," *Republican News*, May 1, 1976, p.5.

21   Brownie [Gerry Adams], "Active Republicanism," *Republican News*, May 1, 1976, p.5.

22   Jake Jackson interview.

23   Dave Morley, "That Wall," *Republican News*, September 27, 1975, p.2.

24   Sinn Féin's paper in the south of Ireland was called *An Phoblacht*. The two papers finally merged in 1979 under the title *An Phoblacht/Republican News*.

25   Gerry Adams, *Before the Dawn: An Autobiography*, Dingle: Brandon, 1996, p.247.

26   Malcolm Sutton, *An Index of Deaths from the Conflict in Ireland 1969-1993*, Belfast: Beyond the Pale, 1994.

27   Quoted in Gerry Adams, *Before the Dawn: An Autobiography*, Dingle: Brandon, 1996, p.247.

28   Tom Hartley put some of the prison papers in the Northern Ireland Public Records Office, on the understanding that they would remain safe and confidential. Years later, when the British government was trying to crack down on Sinn Féin and particularly *Republican News*, they charged Hartley with treason, a capital offense, on the basis of the content of the papers.

29   These are paraphrased recollections of Mellowes's quotes by Gerry Adams.

30   Brownie [Gerry Adams], "The Republic: A Reality," *Republican News*, November 29, 1975, p.4.

31   Brownie [Gerry Adams], "The Republic: A Reality," *Republican News*, November 29, 1975, p.4.

Chapter Nine

1   Bobby's notes had an important impact on some future prison leaders like Bik MacFarlane. Although Sands was already released when MacFarlane was first sentenced and sent to Cage Eleven, his materials remained behind. MacFarlane was particularly fascinated by the materials on community councils and he asked the Education Officer Denis Donaldson where it came from. "Oh, that's Bobby's stuff." Such early encounters with Bobby Sands were important for several prisoners who would later support him as a leader in the prison struggle in the H-Blocks.

2   Gerry Adams, *Before the Dawn: An Autobiography*, Dingle: Brandon, 1996, p.246.

3   Gerry Adams interview.

4   Gerry Adams, *Cage Eleven*, Dingle: Brandon Books, 1990, p.73.

5   "Activities," unsigned chapter by Bobby Sands in *Prison Struggle: The Story of Continuing Resistance behind the Wire*, Belfast: Republican Press Center, 1977, p.42.

6   "Activities," unsigned chapter by Bobby Sands in *Prison Struggle: The Story of Continuing Resistance behind the Wire*, Belfast: Republican Press Center, 1977, p.44.

7   Gerry Adams, *Before the Dawn: An Autbiography*, London: Heinemann, 1996, p.244.

8   *Radio na Gaeltachta* is the state-sponsored Irish-language radio station.

9   According to Seanna Walsh, although the photograph was a mock-up, they were digging a tunnel at the time the book was written. A couple of months after Bobby and Seanna got out of prison the warders finally discovered it.

10   Seanna Walsh interview.

Chapter Ten

1   Seanna Walsh interview.

2   Eibhlín Glenholmes interview.

3   Seanna Walsh interview.

4   "Twinbrook Becomes Redcap Area: MPs Move into Woodbourne as Two RUC Shot," *Andersonstown News*, May 15, 1976, p.11.

5   According to Ó hAdhmaill, the British army raided a house in 1977 where they found the gestetner machine that they were using to print *Liberty*. They confiscated the machine and arrested the homeowner. Interview with Féilim Ó hAdhmaill.

6   Danny Morrison, "H-Block OC," *An Poblacht/Republican News*, May 9, 1981, p. 23.

7   There is one other point that must be made about Republicans' identification of their broadly working/unemployed-class communities with "the people." Clearly, in the north of Ireland there is a "divided working class" and therefore "the people" from the Republican point of view (i.e., mainly Catholic Nationalists) is only half of *the* people. Similarly, Loyalist working-class parties have referred to their constituencies as "the people," a concept that is equally lacking in this respect. Arguably, the Republican's have greater validity in their conception of "the people" insofar as they would (and do) happily include Protestants in their communities *if* they are Republican. Loyalism, on the other hand, is explicitly racist or sectarian, and has no similar willingness to be inclusive of Catholics (i.e., "the people" is explicitly defined as *Protestant*). See, Peter Shirlow and Mark McGovern (eds.), *Who Are "the People"?: Unionism, Protestantism, and Loyalism in Northern Ireland*, London: Pluto Press, 1997.

8   For an analysis of these fraught relations, see Féilim Ó hAdhmaill, *The Function and Dynamics of the Ghetto: A Study of Nationalist West Belfast*, unpublished Ph.D. thesis, University of Ulster, 1990. Also see numerous articles in the local *Andersonstown News* during this period.

9   A local nursery and primary school taught entirely in Irish, *Bunscoil na Fuiseoige* (School of the Lark), now stands on the spot of the TTA Center. Its founders could not explicitly name it after Bobby Sands because it needed funding and official recognition by the state. Instead, they named it after Bobby's chosen symbol of freedom, the lark, which comes from his best-known prose piece, "The Lark and the Freedom Fighter." The school now flourishes.

10   Quoted from *Old Scores*, BBC documentary.

11   Bernard Fox, manuscript for *Nor Meekly Serve My Time*.

12   Chillingworth also went by the name Sean Greene. Later, in prison, Bobby gave him the nickname Sean Glas, the Irish word for "green" being *glas*.

13   Interview with Eilish Hamil.

14   Jennifer McCann interview.

15   "New Policy Line to Step Up Harassment in Twinbrook," *Andersonstown News*, September 18, 1976, p.12.

Chapter Eleven

1   The following account is compiled from witness statements and other records in court file File 405/77, Antrim County Court, from interviews with participants in the episode and from an interview with an employee of Balmoral Furnishings. Physical descriptions were confirmed by visits to the site.

2   These are the verbatim recollections of J—. It is more likely that the man said, "Lie face down or I'll fuckin' shoot you."

Chapter Twelve

1   The following account is compiled from police interrogation records in court file File 405/77, Antrim County Court, from interviews with participants and from Bobby Sands's smuggled account of his interrogations.

2   Peter Taylor, *Beating the Terrorists? Interrogation in Omagh, Gough, and Castlereagh*, London: Penguin, 1980, p.68.

3   Peter Taylor, *Beating the Terrorists? Interrogation in Omagh, Gough, and Castlereagh*, London: Penguin, 1980, p.155.

4   Peter Taylor, *Beating the Terrorists? Interrogation in Omagh, Gough, and Castlereagh*, London: Penguin, 1980, p.156.

5   The following sequence is reconstructed from an account by Seamus Finucane.

Chapter Thirteen

1   Death certificate, Liam Sands, D76/B1/3937. Pyloric atresia is a rare condition that involves an obstruction at the pylorus, which is the passage linking the stomach and the first portion of the small intestine (duodenum).

2   The Green Cross is an organization that provides aid to the families of Republican prisoners.

3   Gino MacCormaic, manuscript for *Nor Meekly Serve My Time.*

4   A *marley* was Belfast slang for a "marble" and, to the prisoners, this warder's accent made him sound as if he spoke with a mouth full of marbles.

5   "On the boards" is prison slang for being in punishment because one of the main aspects of the punishment regime is removal of beds, forcing the prisoners to sleep on boards rather than a mattress.

6   Bobby Sands unsigned article, "On the Blanket," *An Phoblacht/Republican News*, April 1, 1978, p.2.

7   "They Will Have to Nail Prison Garb on my Back," *Republican News*, March 6, 1976, p.1. Although this quote went down in the history of the H-Blocks, knowledgeable Republicans admit that it was coined by a Republican publicity writer and attributed to Nugent.

8   "Prisoners Not Eating—Claim," *Belfast Telegraph*, January 10, 1977.

9   The Shankill Butchers was a Loyalist gang, associated with the UVF, that killed thirty Catholics during the 1970s and 1980s. The gang got its name because many of the victims were ritually slaughtered. See Martin Dillon, *The Shankill Butchers: A Case Study of Mass Murder*, London: Arrow Books, 1990.

10   "Loyalist Prisoners Renew Demand for Segregation," *Irish Times*, January 8, 1977.

11   "Prisoners Hurt in Rows over Mixing," *Irish News*, January 8, 1977.

12   "Republican Court Protests Continue," *Irish News*, January 12, 1977.

13   "Prisoners Hurt in Rows over Mixing," *Irish News*, January 8,1977.

14   "Loyalist Prisoners Renew Demand for Segregation," *Irish Times*, January 8, 1977.

15   "No Segregation for North's Prisoners," *Irish Times*, January 14, 1977; "The Segregation of Remand Prisoners," *Irish News*, January 18, 1977.

16   Seamus Finucane interview. File 405/77.

17   We should be careful of a prison governor who admits violence while denying that it is official policy. In his work on the "culture of denial," the

criminologist Stanley Cohen shows a series of stages by which states deny human rights abuses. First, they deny them outright. Then, if there is too much evidence to simply deny abuses, high officials argue that they were "not official policy" and blame low officials. This explains, for example, U.S. denial of war crimes from My Lai to Abu Ghraib. Stanley Cohen, *States of Denial: Knowing About Atrocities and Suffering*, London: Polity Press, 2000.

18   Leon Uris, *Trinity*, London: Corgi, 1976, p.517.

19   *Republican News*, September 10, 1977.

Chapter Fourteen

1   "The Early Days," *An Phoblacht/Republican News*.

2   Most of the details of the court hearing are from an interview with Seamus Finucane and from the Court File, Belfast Crown Court, File 405, 1977. Descriptions of the court include additional observations by the author.

3   Belfast Crown Court, File 405.

4   Bobby Sands unsigned article, "Four Forgotten Blanketmen," *Republican News*, January 7, 1978, pp.7-8.

5   Bobby Sands unsigned article, "Four Forgotten Blanketmen," *Republican News*, January 7, 1978, pp.7-8.

6   Captain Black is a brand of pipe tobacco.

Chapter Fifteen

1   Ned Flynn, manuscript for *Nor Meekly Serve My Time*. One prison warder admits that the availability of alcoholic drink heightened the violence in the H-Blocks: "A lot of times some of the things that happened in the prison, that's why they happened. People were coming in under the influence. And some of them get, the drink's in, the wit's out. And they do a bit of chittering and talking and before they know it they fall out with each other." Interview with prison warder.

2   A discussion of the culture of violence in the H-Blocks is in Kieran McEvoy, *Paramilitary Imprisonment in Northern Ireland: Resistance, Management, and Release*, Oxford: Oxford University Press, 2001.

3   Jackie McMullen, manuscript for *Nor Meekly Serve My Time*.

4   Means of communicating are described in Brian Campbell, Laurence McKeown and Felim O'Hagan (eds.), *Nor Meekly Serve My Time*, Belfast: Beyond the Pale, 1994.

5   Tony O'Hara's account of his time with Bobby Sands is related in Tom

Collins, *The Irish Hunger Strike*, Dublin: White Island Book Company, 1986, pp.56-63

6   Tom Collins, *The Irish Hunger Strike*, Dublin: White Island Book Company, 1986, pp.57-58.

7   This explanation of why they dropped Sands's name is given in a later article, "On the Blanket," *Republican News*, January 7, 1978, pp.6-7.

8   "On the Blanket," *Republican News*, November 5, 1977, p.6. Sands was never identified publicly as the author of this article.

9   Gino MacCormaic, manuscript for *Nor Meekly Serve My Time*.

10   The prisoners in B-wing threw out their Christmas dinner because it was "in such a bad state." As a result, the Deputy Governor Albert Miles put every man in B-wing on a "number one diet" for three days. Miles was killed by the IRA the following year.

11   Sands's account of the holidays is in an anonymous article he wrote entitled "Christmas on the Blanket," *Republican News*, January 21, 1978, p.3.

12   "Flu Epidemic," *Republican News*, January 28, 1978, p.5.

13   Statement by P.R.O. of H-Blocks 3, 4, and 5 reprinted in "Flu Epidemic," *Republican News*, January 28, 1978, p.5.

14   "Health on the Blanket," *Republican News*, February 25, 1978, p.5.

15   Gino MacCormaic, manuscript for *Nor Meekly Serve My Time*.

16   Jimmy Burns, manuscript for *Nor Meekly Serve My Time*.

17   Jimmy Burns, manuscript for *Nor Meekly Serve My Time*.

18   Private comm, Gino McCormick to Malachy, 2/19/78.

19   Private comm, Gino McCormick to Malachy, 2/19/78.

Chapter Sixteen

1   Switzerland, of course, is landlocked. Leo Green, *Nor Meekly Serve My Time*, p.37.

2   Jaz McCann, manuscript for *Nor Meekly Serve My Time*.

3   The new IRA structures, including its relationship to a reinvigorated Sinn Féin political party, were summarized in a document that was discovered in the possession of IRA Chief of Staff Seamus Twomey when he was captured in December 1977. See Tim Pat Coogan, *The Troubles: Ireland's Ordeal 1966-1995 and the Search for Peace*, London: Random House, 1995, pp.205-210.

4   "The Agony of It All: A Few Hours Out, Back Four Days Later," unsigned article by Bobby Sands in *Republican News*, June 3, 1978, p.3.

5   Joe McQuillan, manuscript for *Nor Meekly Serve My Time*.

6   PRO, H-Block [Bobby Sands], "H-Block Protest Intensifies," *Republican News*, April 8, 1978, p.6. It is interesting that after just three weeks of

intensified protest Sands (obviously in discussion with Brendan Hughes) was already describing the no-wash as "our long protest."

7   Sean Lennon, manuscript for *Nor Meekly Serve My Time*.

8   Jaz McCann, manuscript for *Nor Meekly Serve My Time*.

9   "The Agony of It All: A Few Hours Out, Back Four Days Later," *Republican News*, June 3, 1978, p.3.

10   It must be added that many blanketmen later contracted illnesses and some died prematurely.

11   Interview with hospital warder.

12   "One of Those Days that Never Ends," unsigned article by Bobby Sands, *Republican News*, June 10, 1978, p.3.

13   Bobby Sands, *One Day in My Life*, Cork: Mercier Press, 1983, p.52.

14   Leon Uris, *Trinity*, London: Corgi, 1976, pp.516-17.

15   "The Agony of It All: A Few Hours Out, Back Four Days Later," unsigned article by Bobby Sands, *Republican News*, June 3, 1978, p.3.

16   Marcella, "Barbed Wire," *An Phoblacht/Republican News*, February 24, 1979, p.2.

17   The "tomb" became a common metaphor for the H-Blocks in the subsequent public campaign for political status. It is not unique. The city jail in New York City, where some other Irish Republicans have spent considerable time, also bears the nickname "the tombs."

18   "One of Those Days that Never Ends," unsigned article by Bobby Sands, *Republican News*, June 10, 1978, p.3.

19   Kevin Campbell, manuscript for *Nor Meekly Serve My Time*, p.34.

20   Thomas Loughlin, manuscript for *Nor Meekly Serve My Time*.

21   Peadar Whelan, manuscript for *Nor Meekly Serve My Time*.

22   Belfast Crown Court, File 405 and interview with Philip Rooney.

23   Laurence McKeown remembers, similarly, how Bobby always seemed to have the screws under his thumb, often getting them to do things for him that they would never do for other prisoners.

24   The report of the talent competition was published under the title "Ole Faces" in *Republican News*, August 12, 1978, p.3.

25   Chris Ryder, *Inside the Maze*, p.181.

26   Tom Holland, manuscript for *Nor Meekly Serve My Time*, p.45-46.

27   Quoted in Chris Ryder, *Inside the Maze*, pp.181-82.

28   "One of Those Days that Never Ends," unsigned article by Bobby Sands, *Republican News*, June 10, 1978, p.3.

29   Joe McQuillan, manuscript for *Nor Meekly Serve My Time*.

30   Joe McQuillan, manuscript for *Nor Meekly Serve My Time*, p.53.

31   Mick O'Dearg, "Older Young Faces," *Republican News*, October 28, 1978, p.4.

32   Sean Lennon, manuscript for *Nor Meekly Serve My Time*.

33   Joe McQuillan, manuscript for *Nor Meekly Serve My Time*.

34   Peter Cunningham, manuscript for *Nor Meekly Serve My Time*.

35   Brendan MacFarlane, manuscript for *Nor Meekly Serve My Time*.

36   Bobby Sands, *One Day in My Life*, Cork: Mercier Press, 1983, p.87.

Chapter Seventeen

1   Bik MacFarlane interview. Interview with Bik MacFarlane, Jackie McMullen, and Gerry McConville, *Feile FM Radio*, February 23, 2001.

2   His "family" now consisted of his sister Marcella, his mother, and his father. His sister Bernadette was on the run in the south of Ireland for her own IRA activities. His marriage with Geraldine was irreconcilably broken. He had not seen his son Gerard for almost nine months but he hoped that his parents might bring the boy up to see him soon, if not "today." "I might see the wee lad today," he writes. "I haven't seen him in almost nine months. It's the health risk. I'm taking a chance seeing him anytime." Bobby Sands, *One Day in My Life*, Cork: Mercier Press, 1983, p.39.

3   This may refer to an attack by the IRA in Crossmaglen, South Armagh, on December 21, when the IRA killed three members of a British army foot patrol. Nineteen seventy-eight had been a very slow year militarily for the IRA, who were clearly on the defensive. As a historian of Sinn Féin wrote of 1978, "The IRA campaign seemed to have settled down to a war of attrition . . . Certainly in 1978 the IRA was no closer to making the British withdraw than it had been when the Provos were formed, perhaps further away." Brian Feeney, *Sinn Féin: A Hundred Turbulent Years*, Dublin: O'Brien Press, 2002, p.284. Under such an extreme military lull, such an attack, coming two days after the sniper killing of another British army soldier, would have been a considerable morale booster for volunteers both inside and outside of jail.

4   "Our day will come."

5   *One Day in the Life of Ivan Denisovich* was first published in the West in 1963.

6   Joe Watson interview.

7   Bobby Sands, *One Day in My Life*, Cork: Mercier Press, 1983, pp.88-91.

8   Years later, after they were released from prison, many of the blanketmen who heard Jet tried to locate the book. They wandered into libraries and second-hand bookshops looking for the novel. They inquired in video shops for the video. Nobody ever found it. Seamus Finucane insists it was one of the dozens of novels that Bobby read when he was on remand in the Crumlin Road Jail or in H-1. Yet, no other prisoner seems to have read the book. This author failed to locate the book through repeated searches of the Internet

and *Books in Print*. The alternative theory is that Bobby made up the story. Tomboy Loudon says that Bobby told him years later that he had made up the story.

I believe the origin of the story is actually quite simple. Bobby loved to memorize songs. One song he memorized was "Jet" by Paul and Linda McCartney. Many of the elements of his story are in the words.

The father: "Jet! Was your father as bold as a sergeant major?"

His impending marriage: "Jet! I can almost remember their funny faces; That time you told me that; You were going to be marrying soon."

The motorbike ride: "Jet! With the wind in your hair of a thousand laces. Climb on the back and we'll; Go for a ride in the sky."

9   Letter from Bobby Sands, H6 to Duirmuid Fox, Cage Ten, May 28, 1979.
10   "The Bold MacKillen" was not published at the time but was included later in the main anthology of Bobby's writings. Bobby Sands, *Skylark Sing Your Lonely Song*, Cork: Mercier Press, 1982.

Chapter Eighteen

1   Quoted in Kevin Kelley, *The Longest War: Northern Ireland and the IRA*, London: Zed Books, 1982. This was quite a document. It also referred to Nationalists who did not support armed struggle as "traitors," "collaborators," and "domestic cockroaches."
2   After prison Governor Albert Miles was killed in late November 1978, in direct retaliation according to the IRA for brutality against the blanketmen, POs were increasingly targeted. The IRA killed prison officers again in December 1978, February 1979, and twice in April 1979. Malcolm Sutton, *An Index of Deaths from the Conflict in Ireland 1969-1993*, Belfast: Beyond the Pale, 1994, pp.112-114.
3   Quoted in Liam Clarke, *Broadening the Battlefield: The H-Blocks and the Rise of Sinn Féin*, Dublin: Gill and Macmillan 1987, p.96.
4   *Irish News*, April 28; *Irish Times*, April 28; *Irish Press*, April 28.
5   *Irish News*, June 16, 1979.
6   Comm from "Marcella" to the Republican leadership, August 4, 1970. Reprinted in Liam Clarke, *Broadening the Battlefield: The H-Blocks and the Rise of Sinn Féin*, Dublin: Gill and Macmillan, 1987, pp. 242-247.
7   Letter from Bobby Sands, H6 to Duirmuid Fox, Cage Ten, May 28, 1979. Cleeky Clarke's departure must have been a big blow to Bobby. Not only had they been close friends in Cage Eleven, constantly sharing music with each other, their relationship developed in H6. They played a game by comm. Cleeky would send a comm through the pipes to Bobby with a clue

from their favorite LP by Loudon Wainwright III. "B-side, third song, second verse, third line. MeXX". Sands would have to work out what the line was and send it back to Clarke in another comm, which he signed "Pinball." Tomboy Loudon interview.

8 Joe McQuillan, manuscript for *Nor Meekly Serve My Time*.

9 Gerry Adams interview.

10 Gerry Adams interview.

11 Hughes and Bobby Sands gave Reid the nickname "behind the scenes" because he kept assuring them that something was happening there. Reid was aware of the nickname and found it amusing.

12 Seanna Walsh, manuscript for *Nor Meekly Serve My Time*.

13 Seanna Walsh, manuscript for *Nor Meekly Serve My Time*.

14 *Irish News*, July 17, 1979.

15 Comm from "Marcella" to the Republican leadership, August 4, 1970. Reprinted in Liam Clarke, *Broadening the Battlefield: The H-Blocks and the Rise of Sinn Féin*, Dublin: Gill and Macmillan, 1987, pp. 242-247. The following extracts are from this comm.

16 Cara, Irish for "friend," is a common form of address between Republicans.

17 This phrase has been used and attributed to Bobby Sands on wall murals and posters and leaflets throughout Ireland since his death. It was not just Bobby's quote. The phrase was commonly used by the blanketmen in their discussions about political activism and the role of community support in their campaign.

18 "Black hack" are the cooperative Black Taxis that provided the major transport system for West Belfast after the public buses were withdrawn after violence broke out. They remain the main means of public transport in West Belfast today.

19 Marie Moore interview.

20 The "girls" included Maggie McCullough, Andrea Lenihan, Theresa Miller, Kate Murray, and Sheila McVeigh.

21 Some prisoners secreted comms underneath their foreskins. They never told the women on the grounds that it would violate their morality and embarrass them more than if they had been inside the prisoners' rectums.

22 Only once was there a serious incident when Mary Hughes was discovered carrying a radio. The warders immediately cleared the visiting areas and the prison car park and claimed that they had found a suspect bomb. Hughes was fined and barred from visiting the prison.

23 Although the name Bobby Sands meant nothing to Moore at the time, Christy Moore meant a lot to Bobby Sands. Some of his songs were among Bobby's standards during singsongs and Moore's former group, Planxty, had been one of his favorites. During his brief period of freedom in 1976, Bobby hitchhiked from Dublin to Galway to see Planxty in concert.

24   Thomas Loughlin, manuscript for *Nor Meekly Serve My Time*. Carberry died in 1902.

25   "A Nation Mourns Its Loss: 'The Troubles' in Ulster Take a Terrible Toll," *Time Europe*, September 10, 1979.

Chapter Nineteen

1   None of the young prisoners in H3 had ever seen Dixie Elliot. From his deep voice, they pictured him as a big tough-looking geezer, "a sort-of Lee Marvin look-alike." It was not until mass on Sunday that they met Elliot. He was just a wee skinny fellow without facial hair. Certainly *not* Lee Marvin.

2   Relations between IRA and INLA prisoners were mostly good. They were strained, however, whenever certain INLA prisoners attempted to push independent policies that the IRA leaders felt were divisive. In H3, Kevin Lynch and Mickey Devine were both very popular with the IRA prisoners.

3   Colm Scullion and Jimmy McMullen interviews.

4   Joan Boyd, "Hunger Strike Threat," *Sunday News*, October 7, 1979, p.1.

5   The following description is taken from Joan Boyd, "The Men on the Blanket," *Sunday News*, October 7, 1979, p.5.

6   "Prison Men in Revolt," *Sunday News*, November 4, 1979, p.1.

7   Dixie Elliot now works as an artist, painting commercial murals on the sides of bars and other public buildings.

8   "Bold Robert" is Robert Emmet, the United Irish leader who was executed in Dublin in 1803, as the *Gull* sailed to Australia.

9   Colm Scullion interview. Also Sile McVeigh and Margaret McCullough interviews.

10   According to one prisoner, Bobby could smell a Parker refill cells away. One time, he slipped a note to Sands, who looked at the handwriting and saw that it was smooth, not shaky like writing from a plastic Bik refill. Bobby was up to the door in no time.

       "Here, have you got a Parker pen over there?"

       "Aye, I have."

       Sands ordered him to send it over to him because he needed it for his work.

11   Gerry Adams, *Before the Dawn: An Autobiography*, Dingle: Brandon, 1978, pp. 271ff.

12   Gerry Adams interview.

13   By general agreement, Alex Reid is an honorable man. He does not generally give interviews but has worked tirelessly behind the scenes in the cause of peace and justice. He made an exception to his policy on interviews to help in the research for this book, despite his feelings about the hunger

strikes: "I didn't want to talk about it, think about it, or go over it ever again," he told me.

14 Cited in Liam Clarke, *Broadening the Battlefield: The H-Blocks and the Rise of Sinn Féin*, Dublin: Gill & Macmillan, 1987, p.115. This was not the only official setback to the prisoners. The U.S. State Department's annual report on human rights, which was published the previous February, also exonerated Britain of any human rights violations.

15 Liam Clarke, *Broadening the Battlefield: The H-Blocks and the Rise of Sinn Féin*, Dublin: Gill & Macmillan, 1987, p.115.

16 "Blirt" was one of Bobby's favorite words; to him, "everyone was a blirt at one time or another." Although widely used throughout Ulster, one source says that *blirt* is a local Antrim word that means a "loudmouth" (Peter Black, "What're ye bargin; about?" *Carrickfergus Advertiser*, October 10, 2001). Another source, says that a *blirt* is "a rainy wind" or a "blow"; in other words, a "loudmouth." P.W. Joyce, *English As We Speak it in Ireland*, Dublin: Wolfhound, 1987, originally published in 1910, chapter thirteen.

17 On the album, Moore credited Bik MacFarlane as co-author of McIlhatton along with Bobby Sands. "Bik shouldn't suffer because Scullion couldn't carry a melody," says Moore.

18 Philip Rooney interview.

19 O'Malley was a Dublin Protestant who became a commander of the IRA during the war of independence. Ernie O'Malley, *On Another Man's Wound*, Dublin: The Sign of the Three Candles, 1936.

20 The background on Ó hEoghus is from Searc's Web Guide to Ernest O'Malley (1898-1957), http://www.searcs-web.com/omall.html.

21 Richard Ellman, *Oscar Wilde*, London: Hamish Hamilton, 1987, p. 500.

22 "Cardinal Has More Talks with Atkins," *Irish News*, September 23, p.1.

23 *Irish News*, September 24, 1980, p.1.

24 The Republican reading of the outcome of the talks between Ó Fiaich and the British was indicated by their headline story in their newspaper of the following week: "Ó Fiaich/Atkins Talks End in Failure: H-Block Hopes Dashed: Blanketmen on the Brink of Total Frustration." *An Phoblacht/Republican News*, September 27, 1980, p.1.

25 Brendan Hughes interview.

Chapter Twenty

1 Bik MacFarlane interview.

2 Bik MacFarlane interview.

3 Memories often conflict. Brendan Hughes says that his argument with

Bobby took place in private, during a discussion "through the pipes." Several other prisoners (including Bik MacFarlane, Jake Jackson, and Richard O'Rawe), on the other hand, say that it took place during mass and recall the argument in some detail. Their detailed accounts give credibility to the version that places the argument in a staff meeting during mass. Yet given the tightness of the Dark's decision making process with Bobby it is surprising that they would have gone into a staff meeting without having such a crucial detail worked out between them. Possibly, the argument began in their cells and continued into the staff meeting.

4   McKenna's father, also called Sean, was one of fourteen "hooded men" who were subjected to sensory deprivation torture following the introduction of internment without trial in 1971. In 1976, in a case involving the "hooded men," the European Commission for Human Rights in Strasbourg found the British government guilty of inhuman and degrading treatment of prisoners in violation of Article Three of the Human Rights Convention. McKenna, Sr. died at the age of forty-two in 1975, allegedly as a result of deterioration of his health that began with his treatment at the hands of the British army in 1971. Sean McKenna, Jr. also alleged that he had been mistreated in police custody. Raymond Murray, *The SAS in Ireland*, Dublin: The Mercier Press, 1990, pp.33-34, 168-69.

5   BS to Liam Og, "4/8/80." The date of this comm is unclear. It appears to read "4/8/80" but that date corresponds neither to the other comms that contain similar discussions nor to the actual chronology of events. August makes no sense because the talks between Cardinal Ó Fíaich and the British government did not break down until September, precipitating the discussions and decisions about a hunger strike. It is also possible that the comm was written on October 8 rather than the October 4, since the latter was a Saturday and the finalized decisions about volunteers were taking place at staff meetings during mass. On the other hand, it is also possible that Brendan Hughes and Sands were making those decisions and then confirming them at the staff meetings.

6   This date is uncertain and might have been a week on either side. I have placed it at October 8 because that date fits best with both Reid's recollection that it was in early October and because it was the last Tuesday before the hunger strike was publicly announced.

7   As an ironic footnote, after some months in Rome Alex Reid realised he had not gone to the Vatican or seen the pope. A week after Bobby Sands died on hunger strike, he made his way to St. Peter's Square to rectify the situation. As he stopped at a shop near the square, he was surprised to see the pope and his retinue coming toward him. As the pope neared, Reid watched in horror while a man stepped toward him and began to fire his pistol into

him. He laughs today, to think that he had been sent to Rome to recover from the stress of gunfire and war in Belfast; now, it had followed him to the seat of his church.

8 Reid has been described by the president of Ireland as "the architect of the [Irish] peace process" (interview with Mary McAleese, *Talkback*, BBC Radio Ulster, December 31, 2003). He is without doubt infinitely more deserving of the Nobel Peace Prize than politicians like John Hume or, especially, David Trimble, who jointly received that award in 1998 for their respective public roles in the Irish peace process.

9 BS to LO, 10/13/80.

10 Joan Boyd, "The Men on the Blanket," *Sunday News*, October 7, 1979, p.5.

11 BS to LO, 10/21/80.

12 According to Adams, from the beginning of the hunger strike "I was in daily contact with Bobby. During this intensely traumatic period, he and I got to know each other thoroughly." Gerry Adams, *Before the Dawn: An Autbiography*, London: Heinemann, 1996, p.287.

13 BS to LO, 8/4/80.

14 BS to LO, 10/13/80.

15 BS to LO, 8/4/80. His concerns were borne out a couple of weeks later, as he wrote out about the increasing levels of harassment, which he tied to the impending hunger strike. "One other thing," Sands wrote, "the screws harassed us on Saturday afternoon with cell searches, wrecking several cells, turning them upside down and one man was taken to the boards. They've also stepped up their night harassment, banging doors with their batons." BS to AP/RN, 8/26/80.

16 "Hunger Strike Declaration," *An Phoblacht/Republican News*, October 18,1980, p.2.

17 BS to LO, 10/13/80. Despite Brendan Hughes's earlier insistence that Bobby could not join the strike because he was also from County Antrim, they were now naming Doherty, who was also from Antrim, among the first seven. This was possible because they had now decided to include a seventh hunger striker to reflect the seven signatories of the Irish Proclamation and, therefore, one of the occupied six counties of Northern Ireland would have two hunger strikers. Given the strength of the IRA in Belfast and the number of Belfast men in the prison leadership, two strikers from Antrim was the most likely outcome.

18 BS to Brownie, 10/15/80.

19 BS to LO, 10/13/80.

20 BS to LO, 10/13/80.

21 BS to Brownie, 10/15/80.

22 BS to LO, 10/13/80.

23   BS to LO, 10/13/80.

24   BS to LO, 10/13/80.

25   BS to LO, 10/13/80.

26   BS to Brownie, 10/15/80.

27   BS to LO, 10/24/80.

28   BS to LO, 10/24/80.

29   BS to LO, 10/24/80.

30   "'On the Blanket' Men to Go on Hunger Strike,"*Irish News*, October 11, 1980, p.1 .

31   "Not Own clothes but 'Civvy-Type State Issue,'" *Irish News*, October 24, 1980, p.1.

32   My emphasis. Quoted in "Lives in Jeopardy," *Irish News* editorial, October 27, 1980.

33   "Church Leaders Urge Both Sides to 'Think Again,'" *Irish News*, October 25, 1980, p.1.

34   "Church Leaders Urge Both Sides to 'Think Again,'" *Irish News*, October 25, 1980, p.1.

35   "Church Leaders Urge Both Sides to 'Think Again,'" *Irish News*, October 25, 1980, p.1.

36   BS to LO, 10/24/80.

37   Colm Scullion comm to his mother, 11/6/80. Colm Scullion interview. The Moy is McKearney's home town.

38   BS to LO, 10/29/80.

39   BS to LO , 10/29/80.

40   BS to LO, 10/27/80.

41   BM to LO, 10/30/80.

42   BS to LO, 9:00 A.M, 10/31/80.

43   There is some confusion of terms here. The prisoners referred to medical warders as "medical officers" or MOs, while such warders refered to themselves as "hospital officers" or HOs. To the warders, MOs were doctors. To retain consistency with the language Bobby Sands and others used in their comms, I will refer to the medical warders as MOs and the doctors as "doctors."

44   BS to LO, 10/31/80.

45   BS to LO, 2:00 P.M., 11/2/80.

46   BS to LO, 11/4/80.

47   BS to LO, 11/4/80.

48   BS to LO, 11/4/80.

49   BS to LO, 11/6/80.

50   BS to LO, 9:00 P.M., 11/6/80.

51   BS to LO, 1:00 P.M., 11/7/80.

52   BS to LO, 1:00 P.M., 11/7/80.

53   BS to LO, 1:00 P.M., 11/8/80.

54   BS to LO, 5:00 P.M., 11/9/80.

55   Liam Clarke, *Broadening the Battlefield:the H-Blocks and the Rise of Sinn Féin*, Dublin: Gill and Macmillan, 1987, p.130.

56   BS to LO, 1:00 P.M., 12/2/80.

57   BS to LO, 12/5/80.

58   Although in comms between Sands and the movement Meagher was simply "the *sagart*" (priest).

59   Alex Reid interview.

60   "The Voice of Reason," *Irish News* editorial, November 1, 1980, p.4.

61   "Hume Offers Services as Mediator," *Irish News*, October 31, 1980, p.1.

62   Colm Scullion interview.

63   House of Commons Debates, December 4, 1980, pp.271-274.

64   "Glimmer of Hope for Solution to the Hunger Strikes," *Irish News*, December 5,1980, p.1.

65   "New Initiative May Result from Dublin Talks," *Irish News*, December 8, 1980, p.1.

66   Although the prisoners thought the medical warders, as part of the system, were in cahoots with the prison authorities and the visitors from the NIO, the warders had a different perspective. They refered to the mysterious visitors, like Blelloch, as "spooks" and felt totally uninformed about what was going on, although they suspected that the Thatcher government was making a deal with the prisoners. Interview with hospital warder.

67   Marcella to Brownie, 12/10/80.

68   Marcella to Brownie, 12/10/80.

69   BS to Brownie, 12/12/80.

70   Marcella to Brownie, 12/15/80.

71   Richard O'Rawe interview.

72   Brendan Hughes interview.

73   The best account so far of these critical hours is contained in David Beresford, *Ten Men Dead*, London: Grafton, 1987. While Beresford does not give footnotes, his account is obviously based on interviews with Brendan Meagher. He also has a crucial eyewitness account, apparently from colleagues at the BBC in London.

74   Marcella to Brownie, 11:00 P.M., 12/20/80.

75   Gerry Adams interview.

76   Meagher's account of his meeting with Michael Oatley (the "mountain climber") and an eye-witness account of Secretary of State Atkins's actions in the BBC television center are taken from David Beresford, *Ten Men Dead*, London: Grafton, 1987, pp.9-12.

77   David Beresford, *Ten Men Dead*, London: Grafton, 1987, p.44.

78   John Feehan, *Bobby Sands and the Tragedy of Northern Ireland*, Dublin: Mercier Press, 1983, p.111.

Chapter Twenty-One

1   Marcella to Brownie, 1:00 P.M., 12/20/80.

2   Marcella to Brownie, 3:00 P.M.,12/19/80.

3   *Parliamentary Debates*, House of Commons, Session 1980-81, December 15, 1980-January 16, 1981, p.674.

4   Gerry Adams, *Before the Dawn: An Autbiography*, London: Heinemann, 1996, p.288.

5   Philip Rooney interview. Another prisoner spoke bluntly about the "carelessness" of the statements by people outside of the prison. He felt the public representatives of the movement put things in such a way that they made it more difficult for the prisoners, even "tying the hands" of Sands and the leaders of the blanketmen. Joe Barnes interview.

6   Gerry Adams interview.

7   Marcella to Brownie, 1:00 p.m., 12/20/80. Even now, at probably the darkest moment of his life, Sands maintained his sense of humor. After having described all of the problems they faced and the awful situations in the H-Blocks, Bobby ended his letter with a desperate joke: "Any chance of the Brits withdrawing?" he asked Adams.

8   Marcella to Brownie, 12/20/80.

9   Marcella to Brownie, 1:00 P.M., 12/20/80.

10   Marcella to Brownie, 8:30 P.M., 12/21/80.

11   These days, Hughes is rather matter-of-fact about what happened. "I really objected to Bobby about another hunger strike," he says, "but Bobby was the OC and it was his decision." Bobby was clearly more agitated. He wrote to Adams, "Dark is being awkward but I told him that I was running things and that I wouldn't budge until I was satisfied it was the right thing to do." Marcella to Brownie, [December 21]

12   Marcella to Brownie, 8:30 P.M., 12/21/80.

13   Marcella to Brownie, 8:30 P.M., 12/21/80. As for Father Toner, Sands was considering some kind of move. "We'll get Index out. We won't move on any phase-out."

14   Magilligan and Maghaberry were the other two major prisons in the north.

15   Marcella to Brownie, 8:30 P.M., 12/21/80.

16   Marcella to Brownie, 12/21/80.

17   Marcella to Brownie, 12/26/80.

18   Marcella to Brownie, 10:00 P.M., 12/24/80.

19   The explicitly political direction, according to some, not only made it harder to attract new supporters but it also alienated some existing supporters like Father Faul, because it threatened their essential conservatism and exposed the differences between their politics and that of the prisoners. From this point in time, Father Faul became less reliable as a supporter of the prisoners and became more and more hostile to the hunger strike.

20   Marcella to Brownie, 12/21/80.

21   Marcella to Brownie, 10:00 P.M.,12/24/80.

22   Marcella to LO, 12/25/80.

23   OC H5 to LO, 12/28/80; Seanna H5 to Liam Og, 12/29/80.

24   An Lamh Dearg [Tommy Gorman] H4 to Liam Og, 12/27/80.

25   Seanna H5 to LO, 12/29/80.

26   Marcella to Brownie, 2/26/80.

27   Marcella to Brownie, 5:00 P.M., 12/29/80.

28   Marcella to LO, 12/31/80.

29   BS to Brownie, 2:00 P.M., 1/1/81.

30   BS to LO, 1/7/81.

31   Brownie from Bik, 1/15/81.

32   BS to LO, 1/21/81.

33   The following account is based on: Interviews: Bik MacFarlane, Jimmy McMullen, Richard O'Rawe, Philip Rooney, and Seanna Walsh; Comms: Seanna Walsh, OC H5, to LO, 1/28/81; Marcella to LO, 1:30 P.M., 1/28/81; Gino MacCormack to his parents, January 28,1981; Manuscripts for *Nor Meekly Serve My Time*: Gerard Clarke, Thomas Loughlin, Laurence McKeown.

34   Bik MacFarlane interview.

35   Marcella to LO, 1:30 P.M., 1/28/81.

36   BS to LO, 8:00 P.M., 1/26/81.

37   Bik, 5:30 P.M., 1/29/81.

38   Bik to Brownie, 8:30 P.M., 2/3/81.

39   Bobby Sands to Army Council, 1/31/81.

40   BS to LO, 1/31/81.

41   Bik to Brownie, 8:30 P.M., 2/3/81.

42   Bik to Pennies, 2/9/81.

43   Sile Darragh, OC Armagh Jail, to LO, 2/9/81.

44   Bik to Pennies, 2/15/81.

45   Tom McElwee, for instance, was a good friend of Bik MacFarlane and he begged him to jump him up the line for the hunger strike. "I've never asked you for a favor but I'm asking you for a favour now. Please bump me up the line. Put me on." McElwee would later die on the hunger strike but MacFarlane did not bump him up into the first four. Brendan MacFarlane interview.

46 Richard O'Rawe interview.

47 According to MacFarlane, Francis Hughes wrote Sands a "fabulous" comm. "Bobby, you don't know me but here's the story," he began. "I wouldn't have had the same kind of politics as you boys, but I've been around the country, I've been through it all and I know I'll not let you down." The comm was optimistic, full of jokes and supportive comments, and, according to MacFarlane, it was a big morale booster for Bobby. Brendan MacFarlane interview.

48 Laurence McKeown, manuscript for *Nor Meekly Serve My Time.*

49 Tom Collins, *The Irish Hunger Strike*, Diblin and Belfast: White Island Book Company, 1986, p.213.

50 Bik to LO, 2.5.81.

51 Marcella to LO, 2/6/81.

52 Bik to LO, 2/8/81.

53 BS to LO, 2/15/81.

54 Faul's first name is Denis and, naturally, given his personality, he got the nickname [Denis] the Menace.

55 Bik to Pennies, 2/15/81.

56 Reproduced in John Feehan, *Bobby Sands and the Tragedy of Northern Ireland*, Dublin: Mercier Press, 1983, p.116.

57 BS to LO, 2/21/81.

58 Mairead Farrell, Armagh Jail to LO, 2/15/81. Almost exactly seven years after she would have begun the hunger strike, March 6, 1988, the British SAS shot dead Mairead Farrell and two IRA comrades, unarmed, in Gibraltar. Because of its cold-blooded manner, as seen by eyewitnesses, and because of a series of horrific events that followed during the funerals of Farrell and her comrades, it became one of the most contentious state killings of the Irish conflict.

59 Mary Doyle to LO, 2/15/81.

60 Sile Darragh, Armagh Prison, to LO, 2/18/81.

61 Bik to Pennies, 2/18/81.

62 BS to Mairead Farrell, 2/21/81.

63 BS to LO, 2/15/81.

64 Bik to Liam Og, 2/19/81.

65 Bik to LO, 2/21/81.

66 Bik to LO, 2/23/81.

67 Philip Rooney to Sile Darragh, 2/28/81.

68 From Bobby Sands's diary (March 1 to March 17), which is reproduced in *Skylark Sing Your Lonely Song: An Anthology of the Writings of Bobby Sands*, Dublin: Mercier Press, 1982, p.153.

Chapter Twenty-Two

1   This is the version of the song that Bobby sang and taught to his fellow prisoners in H3. It is sung to the traditional Irish air *Siun Ní Dhuibir*. Bobby reproduced the song in his diary and he changed the last line to: *"Nuair a thigeann ar lá aithíocfaidh mé iad go mor"* ("When our day comes I will repay them dearly"). Philip Rooney interview.

2   Interview with prison officer.

3   Bik to LO, 3/4/81.

4   Bik to Pennies, 3/1/81.

5   Excerpts are from Bobby's diary, which is reproduced in *Skylark Sing Your Lonely Song: An Anthology of the Writings of Bobby Sands*, Dublin: Mercier, 1982, pp.153-173. The diary covers the first seventeen days of his hunger strike, from March 1 through Saint Patrick's Day.

6   Bik to Pennies, 3/2/81.

7   Bik to LO, 3/3/81.

8   Bik to LO, 3/4/81.

9   Bik to Pennies, 3/2/81.

10 This is not entirely true. An unsigned comm from Bik MacFarlane refers to the visit with the reporters, saying, "Everything went okay except that they were pressuring Bobby for the name of the priest who is acting as mediator." According to MacFarlane, he never gave them the name. Unsigned comm, 3/3/81.

11 Brendan O Cathaoir, "Sands Claims Fast Accord was Broken," *Irish Times*, March 5, 1981, p.5.

12 Bik to LO, 3/4/81.

13 A few days later, he wrote that "there has been a vast improvement in the quality and quantity of food. Stew is the best food here and we've had it three times in seven days." He added, "I have no trouble in resisting the temptation of food because of my frame of mind." BS to LO, 3/9/81.

14 Bik MacFarlane interview. Unsigned comm [Bik MacFarlane] 3/5/81.

15 Bik to LO, 3/5/81.

16 Unsigned, 3/9/81.

17 BS to LO, 3/9/81.

18 BS to LO, 3/9/81.

19 BS to LO, 3/9/81.

20 A couple of days later, Bobby continued to try and theorize what he was protesting for in the deepest sense. He wrote a rather long passage in his diary comparing the poverty of Dublin in 1913 with the present day. Although Irish living standards had improved in that time, he argued, the island was as bad off relative to the rest of the world as it had ever been. He

speculated about how poverty was little better on an average northern Irish wage than on unemployment. Speaking of the capitalists who sleep on others' wounds and toils, he concluded that, "total equality and fraternity cannot and never will be gained whilst these parasites dominate and rule the lives of a nation. There is no equality in a society that stands upon the economic and political bog if only the strongest make it good or survive. Compare the lives, comforts, habits, wealth of all those political conmen (who allegedly are concerned for us, the people) with that of the wretchedly deprived and oppressed. Compare it in any decade in history, compare it tomorrow, in the future, and it will mock you. Yet our perennial blindness continues. There are no luxuries in the H-Blocks. But there is true concern for the Irish people."

21   Marcella to LO, 3/16/81.
22   Diary, March 12.
23   BS to LO, 3/9/81.
24   Bik to LO, 3/10/81.
25   PRO, on behalf of Bik to LO, 3/14/81.
26   Bik to LO, 3/19/81.
27   Bik to LO, 3/16/81.
28   Diary, March 16.
29   Bik MacFarlane interview.
30   Unsigned [Philip Rooney] to LO, 3/25/81.
31   Diary, March 17.
32   Tom McElwee to family (undated but March 1981)
33   Bik to LO, 3/16/81. Bobby's mood on the visit was improved because, for the first time, there were no body searches going to or coming from the visit. A warder told Ricky O'Rawe that Governor Hilditch had informed them that morning that they would be back on normal time and normal wages since the no-wash protest was over. If the NIO was no longer paying them to do the mirror search, said the warder, they would no longer do it.
34   John Feehan, *Bobby Sands and the Tragedy of Northern Ireland*, Dublin: Mercier Press, 1983, pp.120-21.
35   Diary, March 14.
36   LO from Bik 3/23/81.
37   BS to LO, 3/26/81.
38   In one version, a chemist from Coalisland claims that MacAliskey conceived the idea to run Bobby on the couch in his kitchen. Michael Doyle, "Days of Wrath, Nights of Fire," *Today: The Inquirer Magazine (Philadelphia Inquirer)*, July 12, 1987.
39   BS to LO, 3/26/81.
40   LO from Bik 3/29/81.

41   Gerry Adams, *Before the Dawn*, pp.292-93.

42   Quoted in Beresford, *Ten Men Dead*, p.105.

43   Bik to LO, 3/30/81.

44   *Sin sin* is an Irish phrase that roughly translates, "So it goes."

45   Brownie from Marcella 4/2/81.

46   Marcella to LO, 3/31/81.

47   Bik to Brownie, 3/30/81.

48   BS to LO, 4/2/81.

49   Mrs. Mathers was a census enumerator who was killed by the IRA while collecting the census in Derry.

50   David Beresford, *Ten Men Dead*, p.113.

51   Ray McCartney, manuscript for *Nor Meekly Serve My Time*.

52   LO from Tony H5, 4/10/81.

53   LO from Bik, Friday 8:30 P.M., 4/10/81.

54   Correspondence with former blanketman.

55   Interview with hospital warder, J—. "It didn't matter really to me what they'd actually done," says J— of the hunger strikers. "Maybe some of them probably did some horrific things, but at the end of the day it was still young lives that to me were just being wasted . . . A real waste of young life."

56   Correspondence with former blanketman.

57   In fairness, some of the warders were highly annoyed about having to keep food in the cell but they claim they were under strict orders to do so from the Northern Ireland Office. Hospital warder J— hated it because the food smelled good and made him hungry. "We were putting in meals that smelled really tasty," he says. "I can't understand how they didn't eat it." But he also objected for compassionate reasons. "No matter what these guys did, they were still human beings like all the rest of us. To me, taking food in like that, I don't think it was necessary. But apparently the powers that be thought it was."

58   Michael Doyle, "Days of Wrath, Nights of Fire," *Today: The Inquirer Magazine* (*Philadelphia Inquirer*), July 12, 1987.

59   John Feehan, *Bobby Sands and the Tragedy of Northern Ireland*, Dublin: Mercier Press, 1983, p. 126.

60   Interview with family friend.

61   Meeting reconstructed from interview with Bik MacFarlane; Bik to Pennies, 4/27/81; Bik to Brownie, 4/29/81. See also David Beresford, *Ten Men Dead*, chapter three.

62   Quoted in John Feehan, *Bobby Sands and the Tragedy of Northern Ireland*, Dublin: Mercier Press, 1983, p. 128.

63   Bik to Brownie, 4/29/81.

64   Jim Gibney interview. McCreesh wrote to Liam Og that Hughes threw up constantly that night and was having terrible trouble with his eyes. He was so bad that the priests anointed him the previous evening and the doctors were beginning to think that he might die before Bobby. Raymond McCreesh to LO, 4/30/81.

65   Jim Gibney interview. In a previous interview, Gibney gives a slightly different version of Bobby's last words to him: "I'm extremely weak. I'm blind. I can't see. Tell the lads to keep their chins up. I'll see this thing through." Quoted in John Feehan, *Bobby Sands and the Tragedy of Northern Ireland*, Dublin: Mercier Press, 1983, p. 133.

66   John Feehan, *Bobby Sands and the Tragedy of Northern Ireland*, Dublin: Mercier Press, 1983, p. 132.

67   John Feehan, *Bobby Sands and the Tragedy of Northern Ireland*, Dublin: Mercier Press, 1983, p. 134.

68   John Feehan, *Bobby Sands and the Tragedy of Northern Ireland*, Dublin: Mercier Press, 1983, p. 134.

69   Personal communication; prisoner's account of description of Bobby's death by Father John Murphy; John Feehan, *Bobby Sands and the Tragedy of Northern Ireland*, Dublin: Mercier Press, 1983, p. 135.

Chapter Twenty-Three

1   This song, written by Damian O'Neill as a critique of British policy toward the blanketmen and the hunger strikers, was introduced by the Undertones on the BBC's "Top of the Pops" program on May 1, 2001, four days before Bobby Sands died. The record was released on the day of his death.

2   Bik to Brownie, 2:15 A.M., 5/5/81.

3   Richard O'Rawe, PRO to LO, 5/6/81.

4   Desmond Wilson, "Junk Theology," *Andersonstown News*, May 2, 1981, p.2; "Dismay at Bishop's ban," *Andersonstown News*, May 2, 1981, p.1; private communication with Des Wilson.

5   The altar did not last long. Within days, the British army drove a Saracen through it and left the pieces strewn across the field.

6   Gerry Adams interview; Gerry Adams, *Before the Dawn: An Autbiography*, London: Heinemann, 1996, p.296.

7   Gerry Adams, *Before the Dawn: An Autbiography*, London: Heinemann, 1996, p.296.

8   BS to LO, 2/15/81; Seanna Walsh interview. It is a good thing that this thought was abandoned. Years later, Catholic graves and Catholic ceremonies in Carnmoney Cemetery were the target of countless ghoulish

attacks by Loyalists. It is hard to imagine what a Loyalist gang might have done to the grave, or even the interred body, of a Republican icon such as Bobby Sands. Even in Milltown Cemetery, in the densest Republican area of the north and in the view of an army/police watchtower, the graves of the three hunger strikers from Belfast have been repeatedly vandalized, several times by the British army and police themselves.

9   http://www.iranian.com/Times/Subs/Revolution/Aug98/irish.html

10   Press cuttings, telegram, and letter supplied by Charlie Goff.

11   Fidel Castro, "A todos hombres y mujeres que lucharon por la independencia de Irlanda," statement to sixty-eight Conferencia de la Union Interparliamentaria, September 18, 1981.

12   Anthony Sampson, *Mandela: The Authorized Biography*, London: Harper Collins, pp.287-88.

13   Neil Harvey, *The Chiapas Rebellion*, Durham: Duke University Press, 1998, pp.113-14.

14   Gerry Adams interview.

15   McAliskey's account of this long meeting is reproduced in Tom Collins, *The Irish Hunger Strike*, Dublin: White Island Book Company, 1986, pp.592ff.

16   See Laurence McKeown, *Out of Time: Irish Republican Prisoners Long Kesh 1972-2000*, Belfast: Beyond the Pale, 2001.

17   For one inside account of this split within the IRA, see Ed Moloney, *A Secret History of the IRA*, London: Penguin, 2002, pp.476-479.

18   "Sister of Hunger Striker Denounces Peace Process as Deception," *Irish Times*, January 8, 1998.

19   These were the words used by the IRA when it announced an end to its recent phase of armed struggle on July 28, 2005, as read out by Seanna Walsh.

Acknowledgments

I have been blessed by the support of many people while researching and writing this book. Without the help and encouragement of my dear friend Brian, it could never have even started. He was a support throughout, always ready to help unstick me whenever I got stuck. Raymond McCartney's assistance was crucial; he also arranged access to comms by Bobby Sands and other prisoners. Bik MacFarlane and Seanna Walsh spent many hours guiding me through the intricacies of Bobby Sands's life, prison life, and details of prison protest. They also identified others who I needed to interview and cajoled them to talk to me. Laurence McKeown provided the original manuscripts of prisoner testimonies that were eventually incorporated in the book, *Nor Meekly Serve My Time*. Photographs and excerpts from Bobby Sands's writings, unless otherwise stated, are courtesy of *Coiste na n-Iarchimí* and the Bobby Sands Trust. Olenka Frenkiel generously provided a copy of her BBC documentary, *Old Scores*. The Belfast County Court, Public Records Office of Northern Ireland, and the Office of the Chief Justice of Northern Ireland facilitated access to both sets of court records for Bobby Sands. Irish translations were provided by Róise Ní Bhaoill and Sinéad O'Hearn. Just like English, many Irish phrases are colloquial rather than standard, and reflect the actual use of Irish in prison.

Others who helped along the way include David Beresford, Flair Campbell, Ronnie Close, Michael Conlon, Frank Connolly, Kevin Delaney, Charlie Goff, Paddy Hillyard, Jake Jackson, Colm Linden, Agnieszka Martynowicz, Aiden McAteer, Mal McCann, Kieran McEvoy,

Jim McVeigh, Danny Morrison, Féilim Ó hAidhmaill, Siobhan O'Hanlon, Sam Porter, Tommy Ramsay, Clara Reilly, Bill Rolston, John Ross, Caitriona Ruane, Marcella Sands, Phil Scraton, Mark Thompson, Mike Tomlinson, various ex-prisoners and staff at *Coiste na n-Iarchimí,* and Republican activists and others who cannot be named.

I am thankful to the staff at the newspaper collection of the Belfast Public Library, especially the enlightened planners who waited until I finished my research to renovate and close the stacks. I am also grateful for help from staff of the Linenhall Library (although I wish they had waited a bit longer before closing the stacks of their Irish collection) and the *Andersonstown News.*

Many friends and associates of Bobby Sands gave interviews. I thank them all for their generosity, sometimes at great emotional cost. Surprisingly few people refused to talk, even those I doorstepped or telephoned out of the blue. Interviews included Gerry Adams, Joe Barnes, Kevin Carson, Joe Catney, John Chillingworth, Danny Devenney, Denis Donaldson, Dixie Elliott, Seamus Finucane, Diarmuid Fox, Larry Fox, Jim Gibney, Eibhlin Glenholmes, Eilish Hamill, Tom Hartley, Gerard Hodgkins, Brendan Hughes, Jake Jackson, Christy Keenan, Sean Lennon, Tomboy Loudon, Fra McCann, Jennifer McCann, Rab McCollum, Keeler McCullough, Margaret McCullough, Bik MacFarlane, Mary McGinn, Jimmy McMullan, Jackie McMullen, Jim McNeill, Sile McVeigh, Christy Moore, Marie Moore, Danny Morrison, Brendan Ó Cathaoir, Feilim Ó hAidhmaill, Richard O'Rawe, Jimmy Rafferty, Alex Reid, Gerard Rooney, Philip Rooney, Paul Scott, Colm Scullion, Seanna Walsh, Joe Watson, and Des Wilson. I conducted additional radio interviews on *Féile FM* with Tom Hartley, Danny Morrison, Seando Moore, and Gerry McConville. Others, who prefer anonymity, include IRA volunteers, priests, prison warders, and friends of Bobby Sands.

I apologize to those few people I could not interview for one reason or another. I hope you will forgive me for exclusion from the story, in some cases, or for the manner of your inclusion, in others. I have done my best to be fair to those voices that I could not hear firsthand.

To the Sands family I send deepest regards. None of us can begin to know the deep hurt you have experienced. I hope you find peace and that in some way it will help for Bobby's story to finally be told.

Special thanks are due to Frances Goldin and Sam Stoloff, who believed in this project and took it on when other reputable literary agencies found that the subject matter made them too "queasy." Carl Bromley at Nation Books jumped on the manuscript, provided editorial advice, and brought it to print.

Many friends suffered my going on and on about this project. Patrick O'Hearn, Roberto Franzosi, Stephen Bunker, Dena Worzel, and Douglas Hamilton provided encouragement and advice throughout. Annette Comerford put up with my antisocial behavior and still read the manuscript several times over, giving me invaluable advice and emotional support all along. My daughters Sinéad and Caitríona gave up a fair bit of their childhood without too much complaining.

This book is dedicated to all of those who die too young. During the research and writing of this book, the first two blanketmen, Kieran Nugent and Alec Comerford, died from the delayed consequences of the protest. I lost dear friends at too early an age: Stephen Bunker, Sandra Ryan, and my nephew James Padraic O'Hearn. During the same period, millions were, in the words of John Ross, "killed by capitalism," including 2,441,600 girls and women who died needlessly in childbirth, because of poverty. Each of them had a name, and was precious to someone.

Finally, my friends in San Cristóbal and the people of Oventic, especially l@s promoter@s de la Escuela Secundaria Rebelde Autónoma Zapatista "primero de enero," provided hospitality while I did the major edit to the manuscript in 2004. Thanks to them, I am beginning to believe again that another world, a world of solidarity and dignity, the world of which Bobby Sands once dreamed, *is* indeed possible. *¡Sí, se puede!*

Index